APOSTLES OF DENIAL

AN EXAMINATION AND EXPOSÉ OF THE HISTORY, DOCTRINES AND CLAIMS OF THE

JEHOVAH'S WITNESSES

by

EDMOND CHARLES GRUSS

Professor of History and Apologetics
Los Angeles Baptist College
Newhall, California

Distributed by
BAKER BOOK HOUSE
Grand Rapids, Michigan

First printing May 1970
Second printing October 1971
Third printing November 1972
Fourth printing January 1974
Fifth printing June 1975
Sixth printing with revisions, November 1975

Printed in the United States of America

DEDICATED

TO THE CAUSE OF OUR LORD AND SAVIOR

JESUS CHRIST

and

MY FAMILY, Geraldene, Susan and Mark,

constant sources of inspiration to His service

THE AUTHOR

Edmond C. Gruss, Professor of History and Apologetics at Los Angeles Baptist College, in Newhall, California, was born in Los Angeles in 1933. He received his A. B. from Los Angeles Baptist College (1955) and his B. D. from Los Angeles Baptist Theological Seminary (1958). In 1961 he completed the Th. M. in Bible and Theology at Talbot Theological Seminary, La Mirada, California. An M. A. in Modern European History from Drake University was added in 1964.

In addition to his college and seminary teaching Professor Gruss has written articles on the cults and given lectures in area churches. Interest in the cult field stems from his conversion from the Jehovah's Witnesses in 1950. His wife also graduated from Los Angeles Baptist College and is an elementary teacher.

Reflecting his interests, the author is a member of The American Historical Association, Organization of American Historians, Far West Slavic Conference, Society for Early Historic Archeology, and the Creation Research Society.

ABBREVIATIONS OF TRANSLATIONS USED IN THIS BOOK[1]

ASV *American Standard Version* (1901). Unless otherwise stated all quotations from the Bible are from this version.

ED *The Emphatic Diaglott*

KJV *King James Version* (1611).

NWT *New World Translation* (1950-1960). Unless otherwise noted the 1951 revised *New World Translation of the Christian Greek Scriptures* and the five volumes of the *New World Translation of the Hebrew Scriptures* are quoted.

RSV *Revised Standard Version* (1952).

---

[1]Quotation of any of the above translations does not indicate endorsement or agreement with all of its contents.

NOTE:

Quotation marks included in the titles of many of the Witnesses' books have been deleted in most cases.

When pronouns are capitalized in the *New World Translation* it indicates that they are in the plural number.

TABLE OF CONTENTS

TABLE OF CONTENTS—(Continued)

TABLE OF CONTENTS—(Continued)

CHAPTER I

INTRODUCTION

Paul's words in Galatians 1:6-9 mention a "different gospel" (ASV) or "another gospel" (KJV). During these days the world is literally flooded with the writings and representatives of those who are propagating "another gospel" in place of the message "which was once for all delivered unto the saints" (Jude 1:3).

The strange and tragic thing is that so many honest, sincere, good, yet gullible people, are so easily led astray by those who claim some special revelation or place of favor with God. It is because of this situation that it is necessary to take the position of the Bereans of old, of whom the Bible states "that they received the word with all readiness of mind, examining the scriptures daily, whether these things were so" (Acts 17:11). The only way to reveal error is to expose it to the light. That Christians are instructed to reprove and expose that which is false is clearly stated in the words "take no part in the unfruitful works of darkness, but instead expose them" (Eph. 5:11 RSV). Again, in I John 4:1 believers are instructed to "prove the spirits, whether they are of God; because many false prophets are gone out into the world."

The foregoing instructions in the Word of God are especially pertinent when a group makes the claim "that 'THE SOCIETY' is the visible representative of the Lord on earth . . ."[1] and that this "Society," the Watch Tower Bible and Tract Society, is, through its governing body, "under the direct supervision of Christ Jesus at the temple."[2]

[1] *The Watchtower*, 1938, p. 182, quoted in *The Watchtower*, 76:333, June 1, 1955.

[2] *Ibid.*, p. 333.

I. BACKGROUND OF THE TITLE

The title, *Apostles of Denial,* may seem a harsh one to be used to designate any group which claims to be Christian, and for that reason its use requires an explanation. The term "Apostle" is used in its general sense of "a messenger." A messenger is one who is sent forth with a message. That message, if it be for God, must be a message of "sound words" (II Tim. 1:13). That there would be messengers bearing another kind of message, a message of denial, is clearly seen in the Bible. The Word of God sets forth that the "last days" will be marked by such a message. There is to be a denial of Jesus Christ (Jude 1:4), a denial of the atonement (II Pet. 2:1), a denial of sound doctrine (II Tim. 4:3, 4), and a denial of the power of godliness (II Tim. 3:1-5). These verses are just samples of the denials to be expected during the "last days."

The writer has made a thorough study of the history, doctrines and claims of the Jehovah's Witnesses,[3] and cannot fail to conclude that although professedly Christian, this group clearly represents a system adverse to the teachings of the Bible, a system denying God's Word. Thus the title follows quite naturally. Truly the Jehovah's Witnesses have a message and messengers, but this message is, as this book will show, A MESSAGE OF DENIAL, CARRIED BY APOSTLES OF DENIAL!

II. PURPOSE OF THE STUDY

The purpose of this study is to present the history, doctrines and claims of the Jehovah's Witnesses as clearly and as accurately as possible, and to examine these categories in the light of God's Word, in the light of sound exegesis of the original languages in which the Bible was written, and in the light of the best scholarship on the subject. When

[3] The Watchtower Society uses the uncapitalized, "Jehovah's witnesses." The use of the uncapitalized "witnesses" is an attempt to suggest a difference between this group and the other denominations and cults, which are identified by proper names. A further advantage in this idiosyncrasy is the interpretation of every "witness" in the Bible as being a Jehovah's witness—an interpretation which gives an impression of antiquity. In order to avoid confusion, this work will capitalize "Witnesses" in designating the group.

dealing with the history of the Witnesses, an attempt is made to correct many false impressions that the Witnesses have written into their own account of the history of the movement.

A further endeavor is to put into the hands of the pastor, Christian worker, or layman, a tool with which he will be better equipped to meet this growing menace. The hope is that many followers of this group will be willing to find out for themselves whether they are messengers of God or messengers who have been appointed and commissioned by man.

III. IMPORTANCE OF THE STUDY

That the Jehovah's Witnesses have been billed as "the fastest-growing religious movement in the world"[4] would alone make this study an important one. The growth of this group is staggering, from a following of 44,080 ministers reporting in 1928,[5] to 1,880,713 (average) ministers reporting for the year 1974, with a peak of 2,021,432.[6] The Lord's Supper Memorial Service, designated by the Witnesses as the Lord's Evening Meal, is celebrated once a year. It was reported that on April 7, 1974, the world-wide attendance was 4,550,457.[7] From the difference in the foregoing figures it is evident that there are well over two million potential ministers ("publishers")[8] who have not as yet been fully inducted into

---

[4] Marcus Bach, "The Startling Witnesses," *Christian Century*, 74:197, February 13, 1957. See also, William J. Whalen, *Armageddon Around The Corner* (New York: The John Day Company, 1962), p. 15. In the September 1, 1973 issue of the *L. A. Herald-Examiner* Louis Cassels identified the Jehovah's Witnesses as "America's fastest growing religious body . . ." (A-7).

[5] *Jehovah's Witnesses in the Divine Purpose* (Brooklyn: Watchtower Bible and Tract Society of New York, Inc., 1959), chart in rear of book.

[6] *The Watchtower*, 96:27, January 1, 1975.

[7] *Ibid.*, p. 28.

[8] A "publisher" also known as a "Kingdom publisher" or "minister" is equivalent to the position of a church member in a regular church, but active membership in the local Jehovah's Witness congregation is dependent on an active effort of the individual Witness to meet a prescribed quota of hours. A minimum of ten hours a month is typical, but the ideal would be sixty. Other Witnesses, designated "special pioneers" and "pioneers" have monthly goals of 150 hours or more, and 100 hours, spent in the work of distributing the Watchtower propaganda by spoken word and printed page.

the Watchtower program. William J. Schnell estimated that about "10,000,000 persons have been induced to enter it" (Watchtower sphere of influence). These persons are viewed as being in various stages of development in the Watchtower program of indoctrination.[9] The Jehovah's Witnessess' anticipated increase of converts was more that 70,000 per year in 1958,[10] much less than at present.

The Jehovah's Witnesses' two semi-monthly publications, *The Watchtower* and *Awake!*, have reached a huge circulation. As an example, for the month of February, 1969, 22,100,000 copies of these magazines were printed.[11] The tremendous outreach is evident when this figure is multiplied by twelve.

The foregoing figures give an indication of the magnitude of the work and growth of this movement. Other figures could be given to demonstrate the advance of the Witnesses, such as: literature placed, the number of hours put into the work, the calls made in connection with the Witnesses' convert plan, and the countries in which work is being done.[12] The movement is, without question, a great and influential one.[13]

The work of the Witnesses among nominal Christians and new converts has caused the Church of Christ much trouble. With a missionary background, William Kneedler, in his booklet, *Christian Answers to Jehovah's Witnesses*, rightly states that their "work is parasitic on established Christian work and very confusing to new Christians and to those not well-grounded in the reasons for their beliefs."[14]

---

[9] William J. Schnell. *Christians: Awake!* (Grands Rapids: Baker Book House, 1962), pp. 11, 12.

[10] *Jehovah's Witnesses in the Divine Purpose, op. cit.*, pp. 292, 293.

[11] *The Watchtower*, February 1, 1969 (5.6 million); February 15, 1969 (5.6 million). *Awake!* February 8, 1969 (5.45 million); February 22, 1969 (5.45 million). The combined figures for February 1969 indicate an increase of 2.1 million magazines published over the same month in 1968. By February 1975, circulation was 35.1 million.

[12] To give some idea of the world-wide outreach of the Watchtower Society, the January 1, 1975 issue of *The Watchtower* shows this magazine is published in 79 languages, and that the Witnesses are currently operating in 207 countries.

[13] See the charts in the rear of *Jehovah's Witnesses in the Divine Purpose* and the *1975 Yearbook of Jehovah's Witnesses.*

[14] William H. Kneedler, *Christian Answers to Jehovah's Witnesses* (Chicago: Moody Press, 1953), p. 5.

The shame is that most Christians and pastors are not sufficiently aware of the Witnesses' history, their doctrines, and their methods to deal intelligently with them. The following pages set forth some important facts that will better fit any Christian to deal with this definite problem. It is also felt that any honest inquirer after truth will be able to see the human origin of this system.

The present study is important because this movement is one of denial, making converts, but causing them to come under the condemnation of Jesus spoken to the most zealous group of his day:

> Woe unto you, scribes and Pharisees, hypocrites! for ye compass sea and land to make one proselyte; and when he is become so, ye make him twofold more a son of hell than yourselves [Matt. 23:15].

IV. PROCEDURE AND ORGANIZATION

The method of organization is as follows: The background for this movement is set forth, and then some of the recent publications which deal with the history of the Jehovah's Witnesses are evaluated. Next the Witnesses' history is traced through the three major stages of the group: (1) the period under Charles Taze Russell (1870-1916); (2) the period under Joseph F. Rutherford (1917-1942); (3) the period under Nathan Homer Knorr (1942 to present), with an analysis of some modern transitions in the movement.

Then the doctrines of this group are studied both in summary and by direct quotations from the publications of the Watchtower Bible and Tract Society. Their major doctrines are examined in the light of Scripture (with the original languages utilized when needed), Church history, sound Biblical exposition, and the Witnesses' own textbooks.

Next, since the *New World Translation of the Holy Scriptures* is being hailed by the Witnesses as their authority in doctrine, this section examines and evaluates the work from the original languages and from the standpoint of accepted scholarship. Reasons are given why this translation should be rejected. Comments by other reviewers are also included.

Because of the key importance of Biblical interpretation, the study includes an entire chapter which deals with the hermeneutical principles employed by the writers of the Watchtower Society. Examples illustrate each point, and the conclusion drawn is that the interpretive methods used by this group are both arbitrary and invalid.

In order to see the reasons for the success of the Witness movement, some of the main tools of Jehovah's Witness propaganda are examined. To equip the Christian worker to meet this challenge, the art of dealing with this cult both in public and private is discussed.

The concluding chapter reviews the evidence presented, and a summary is made of the conclusions drawn. Testimonies of former Jehovah's Witnesses are included to reinforce the contentions of some points presented.

The Appendices bring together some additional important data which is of profit and help to the reader. The first Appendix contains brief treatments of several smaller Russellite groups. The Olin Moyle letters are included because of their insight into the conditions which existed in Bethel under Judge Rutherford and because of their observations on his leadership. A chronological Bibliography of the major Watchtower publications is included so that the reader can determine where a book or other publication stands in relation to the others. This is important in the study of doctrinal shifts over the years. To equip the Christian worker, an annotated, selective Bibliography of publications useful in dealing with the Witnesses is included. Finally, since the writer was a Jehovah's Witness, his own testimony is given.

The Bibliography is a selective one which includes only texts and material either directly quoted or alluded to in the text.

V. SOURCES OF DATA

This writer, as a young man, was in the Jehovah's Witness movement for almost ten years, and later, though not in direct contact with the organization, followed its work and way of thinking.

Lest anyone claim that the following material and the Jehovah's Witness views presented have not been authenticated by enough Watchtower material, or other sources, the reader is referred to the Bibliography of this work. This writer has in his own personal library more than one hundred bound volumes published by this group, plus hundreds of copies of their periodicals, booklets, tracts, etc., with access to many more. Besides this, the writer has also spoken to many Jehovah's Witnesses both in his home and on the streetcorner. The writer has also corresponded with individual Jehovah's Witnesses, and with the Brooklyn office of the Watchtower Bible and Tract Society. The articles, books and other publications cited by the Society in their publications have in many cases been examined. The writer has also written to and received letters from several of the splinter sects treated in the Appendix, and has several hundred publications of these groups.[15]

Care has been taken to give only representative views and not set up any "straw men," as the Jehovah's Witness have done. Care also has been taken to present the representative doctrines of this group mainly from the latest publications,[16] although there is free use of the older works.

From the standpoint of refutation and of the facts, some of the best conservative scholarship has been used. At times scholars of the more liberal tendency have been used when their views showed impartiality in dealing with the problem under consideration.

To further authenticate the evidence, the writer corresponded with William J. Schnell, author of *Thirty Years a Watch Tower Slave,* and found much information in this and his other works written from firsthand experience.

---

[15] The most helpful publications were the *Back to the Bible Way* magazine published since 1952 by Roy D. Goodrich, and the numerous other publications of this writer, and the many volumes of the *Epiphany Studies in the Scriptures* series, distributed by the Laymen's Home Missionary Movement. Both of these movements are discussed in Appendix A.

[16] This is the only way that one can be sure of presenting a doctrine in the way the Society now teaches it, as it will clearly be shown there have been many doctrinal changes and reverses during the years of this movement's existence. William J. Schnell, on page 13, in his book *Into the Light of Christianity,* writes: ". . . I had observed the Watchtower magazine change our doctrines between 1917 to 1928, no less than 148 times, and had witnessed this chimera take place many times later, and thereafter."

The publication, *The Converted Jehovah's Witness Expositor,* edited by Schnell, was also a valuable source of information. In addition, Ted Dencher, another converted Jehovah's Witness was contacted, and the material in his books, *The Watchtower Heresy versus the Bible* and *Why I Left Jehovah's Witnesses* was of value.[17]

Every effort has been made to present the facts clearly, accurately, and honestly. It is believed that the research for this book has been over a large enough base to warrant the confidence of the reader. It is hoped that the reader will thoughtfully weigh the matters presented.

---

[17] Two additional books by former Witnesses have recently been published and were read by this writer: *Jehovah's Witnesses and What They Believe,* by Stan Thomas; *The Inside Story of Jehovah's Witnesses,* by W. C. Stevenson.

CHAPTER II

JEHOVAH'S WITNESSES: ANCIENT AND MODERN ANCESTORS

What is the background of the Jehovah's Witnesses? Are there actually ancestors of this group which date back before the beginnings in the latter part of the nineteenth century? These questions are quite natural for one to ask in a study of any religious movement.

The Jehovah's Witnesses claim the first of their number was Abel (Gen. 4), and that they are the modern-day representatives of the line of Bible witnesses mentioned in the Old and New Testament. From New Testament times onward the Witnesses outline history as follows: (1) Jesus to Paul, (2) Paul to Arius, (3) Arius to Waldo, (4) Waldo to Wycliff, (5) Wycliff to Luther, and (6) Luther to Russell.[1] The following quotation makes it very clear that Charles Taze Russell was viewed by his early followers as one of the "angels of the church" mentioned in Revelation two and three:

> His explanatory writings on the Bible are far more extensive than the combined writings of St. Paul, St. John, Arius, Waldo, Wycliff and Martin Luther—the six Messengers to the Church who preceeded him.[2]

The period between Arius (died early 4 c.) and Waldo (died early 13 c.) is looked upon as a period of almost no Bible study. Because of the "great apostasy" of the nineteenth century the Jehovah's Witnesses relate:

---

[1] Marley Cole, *Jehovah's Witnesses: The World Society* (New York: Vantage Press, 1955), pp. 26-79.

[2] Charles Taze Russell, *Pastor Russell's Sermons* (Brooklyn: International Bible Students Association, 1917), p. 2.

> . . . It became necessary for Jehovah, in fulfillment of his own prophecy, to raise up his witnesses in these modern times, not as a new religion, but as a climax to the long succession of Witnesses that he has had down through the past millenniums all the way back to Abel.[3]

As one studies the ancestors claimed by the Witnesses, except for Arius, no real relationship can be seen. When looking at the Biblical line, the writer agrees that each worker for God was a witness, but here the similarity ends, as the message of the modern-day Witnesses is not at all congruous with that of the Bible witnesses. A clear exposition of the message preached by the New Testament witnesses will be found in the book of Acts—the Church carrying forth the message received from Christ. Without exception the salvation message of the early church centered around one theme—the Person and work of Christ, His death and resurrection.[4] The Bible witnesses were witnesses of Jesus Christ! Jesus, speaking to His own before His ascension said:

> "But YOU will receive power when the holy spirit arrives upon YOU, and YOU will be witnesses of me both in Jerusalem and in all Judea and Samaria and to the most distant part of the earth" [Acts 1:8 NWT].

Notice, "YOU WILL BE WITNESSES OF ME," not Jehovah's witnesses. The gospel message was the simple message of what Jesus had done. A study of Acts will also show that except for quotations from the Old Testament, the name in which the work of the ministry was carried forth was the name of Jesus Christ.[5] Rackham writes:

> To the Jews the revelation of God was summed up in *the Name*, i.e. the divine name of JHVH which might not be uttered: but in the Acts *the Name* is always that

---

[3] *Jehovah's Witnesses in the Divine Purpose* (Brooklyn: Watchtower Bible and Tract Society of New York, Inc., 1959), p. 10.

[4] For examples of the message of the early church in Acts see: Acts 2:14-40; 3:13-26; 4:2, 10-12, 33; 5:30-32, 42; 8:4-6, 35; 9:20; 10:39-43; 11:20, 26; 13:28-41; 16:30-32; 17:2-4, 18, 31; 18:5; 19:13; 20:21; 24:24; 26:22, 23.

[5] Acts 2:38; 3:6, 16; 4:7, 10, 12, 17, 18, 30; 5:28, 40, 41; 8:12, 16; 9:14-16, 21, 27, 29; 10:43, 48; 15:26; 16:18; 19:5, 13, 17; 21:13; 22:16.

of Jesus Christ; the Christians *call upon his name* (as upon that of JHVH), and his name is borne by them.[6]

That the name Jehovah gave place to the name of the Lord Jesus Christ is clearly seen in Acts. Rackham writes:

> The Israel of old had been separated from the world by the Name of JEHOVAH. They were the people who called upon the Name of the Lord and upon whom his Name was called. But the divine Name which the new sect bears is *the Name* of the Lord Jesus Christ. Into this Name they are baptized; in it they live and speak and work; for it they suffer. Accordingly by "this Name" they are known. They are the people "who call upon the name of the Lord Jesus"; and "upon whom his name is called." And when at last a distinctive name had to be invented for the new body, it was taken from this Name, and they were called the CHRISTIANS. The Jews however could not recognize a name which implied the truth of this faith. . . . So they called his disciples in contempt Nazarenes or Galileans.[7]

Therefore, to follow in the footsteps of the Christian witnesses of the Bible, an individual or a group must be a witness or witnesses of Jesus Christ—witnesses of His sacrificial death, His burial, and His glorious resurrection. Through this message it is proclaimed that "there is no salvation in anyone else, for there is not another name under heaven that has been given among men by which we must get saved" (Acts 4:12 NWT). Those who rejected the testimony of Jesus during His early ministry would not place themselves under *the Name* of salvation in Acts 4:12 and the commission of Acts 1:8 and they "remained Jehovah's Witnesses."[8]

In his booklet, *"Jehovah's Witnesses" in the First and Twentieth Centuries,* Phillip Elliot presents parallels between the Jehovah's witnesses (Israel, Isa. 43:10-11) of Jesus' day and the modern movement of Jehovah's Witnesses. The

---

[6] Richard Belward Rackham, *The Acts of the Apostles* (fourteenth edition; London: Methuen and Co. Ltd., 1901), p. lxxxiii.

[7] *Ibid.*, p. 76.

[8] Philip Elliott, *"Jehovah's Witnesses" in the First and Twentieth Centuries* (second edition revised; Stirling, Scotland: Drummond Tract Depot, [n. d.], p. 15.

Twentieth Century Witnesses in their doctrine are in the same position of unbelief as the rejecting Jew: They deny the deity of Christ, His bodily resurrection, and they oppose the Church of Christ—in so doing they reject the work of the Holy Spirit within the believer. Elliott concludes, "They are just as much in the dark as were the Jehovah's Witnesses of the first century."[9] Walter Stuermann also sees the strong Old Testament Judaistic emphasis of the group and observes:

> Almost everywhere they subordinate Christian and New Testament themes to those of Judaism and the Old Testament. One wonders sometimes whether Jehovah might not just as well dispense with his chief executive officer, Jesus Christ. They will, of course, vigorously deny it; but, in this writer's judgment, the Witnesses are more accurately considered a mutation of a conservative, apocalyptic Judaism rather than a variant of Christianity.[10]

In claiming Arius as an ancestor, the Witnesses write of him as one "who had wielded the 'sword of the spirit' to prove that the trinity was not Scriptural or Christian. . . ."[11] In claiming Arius, they must also claim his condemnation on just grounds. To set the matter straight, Arius' doctrine of Christ, not his view of the Trinity, was condemned in the Council of Nicea in A. D. 325.[12]

---

[9] *Ibid.*, pp. 16-22.

[10] Walter E. Stuermann, "The Bible and Modern Religions: III. Jehovah's Witnesses," *Interpretation*, 10:345, July, 1956.

A former Jehovah's Witness wrote the following in a letter to *Christianity Today*: "I was raised a Baptist, but in my teen years became associated with Jehovah's Witnesses. While I maintain great respect for their fundamental knowledge of Bible *texts* and morality, my six years with them left me in spiritual dearth. Why? No Christ! How wonderful it is to read and hear about Christ again! One learns a lot about ancient Israelitish history from them [Jehovah's Witnesses], but so little about Christ." *Christianity Today*, 9:305, December 18, 1964. It is evident from the foregoing that actual experience in the Jehovah's Witnesses confirmed Stuermann's contention.

[11] *What Has Religion Done for Mankind?* (Brooklyn: Watchtower Bible and Tract Society, Inc., 1951), p. 271.

[12] Kelly explains: "In the Arian struggle, as we have seen, the question agitating men's minds was the full deity of the Son, and although this was an essential constituent in the doctrine of the Trinity the latter was at first kept in the background." J.N.D. Kelly, *Early Christian Doctrines* (New York: Harper and Brothers, Publishers,

A study of Jehovah's Witness doctrine reveals a clear line of descent from Arius, but the writer wonders why the Witnesses do not include the Socinians in their history, as their views of the Trinity and other doctrines are identical to the Socinian position.[13]

In Waldo, Wycliff, and Luther, about the only similarity that can be observed is that these men and their groups worked outside the church of their time. With Russell and the Bible Students, light dawns according to the Witnesses. Cole writes:

> Jehovah's witnesses feel that when their immediate predecessors, the Bible Students, plunged into an "objective examination of Christendom's doctrines," they were taking the biggest single step since the days of Jesus toward restoring "doctrinal teachings originating in the Bible," teachings that had been buried under "more than fifteen centuries of Pagan sludge."[14]

1958), p. 252. Speaking of the Nicean Council, Kelly writes: "At its outbreak the problem of the Trinity as such might not seem to have been directly involved. The theological issue at stake was, or seemed to be, a much narrower one, viz. the status of the Word and His relation to the Godhead" (*ibid.*, p. 223). The reader is referred to *Early Christian Doctrines*, pp. 226-31, 225, 281, 282, for the teaching of Arius and the Arians on Christ and the Trinity. It is interesting to note that Arius and his followers (in contrast to the Jehovah's Witnesses) did not deny the personality of the Holy Spirit, although the later Arians "regard Him merely as the noblest of the creatures produced by the Son at the Father's bidding..." (*ibid.*, pp. 255, 256). Other contrasts between the Arians and the Witnesses on the Person of Christ could be mentioned here— the comparison indicates that the Jehovah's Witnesses are more heretical than the Arians.

[13] "In the sixteenth century the Socinians declared the doctrine of three Persons possessing a common essence, to be contrary to reason, and attempted to refute it on the basis of the passages quoted by the Arians. . . . But they even went beyond the Arians in denying the pre-existence of the Son and holding that Christ, as to His essential nature, was simply a man, though He possessed a peculiar fulness of the Spirit, had special knowledge of God, and since His ascension received dominion over all things. They defined the Holy Spirit as 'a virtue or energy flowing from God to men.' In their conception of God they were the forerunners of the present day Unitarians and Modernists." L. Berkhof, *The History of Christian Doctrines* (Grand Rapids: Wm. B. Eerdmans Publishing Company, 1937), p. 100.

[14] Cole, *op. cit.*, p. 48.

William J. Schnell, a member of the Jehovah's Witnesses for more than thirty years, views the background of Russellite theology as a background of heresies, the Watchtower Society having "succeeded in weaving the threads of all former heresies and cults into the make-up for a New World Society."[15] That this statement is true, and is even an understatement, can be seen in a careful study of the history of Christian doctrine; an understatement, in that Russell and his successors not only accepted old heresies but created new heresy which had never appeared before. Russell, directly or indirectly, picked up such errors as Universalism (later modified), Unitarianism, second probationism, restorationism, and a peculiar method of Biblical interpretation—a mixture of Swedenborgian or Pietist[16] and Socinian[17] methods.

A study of the nineteenth century history of the movement reveals several groups which form a foundation for Russellism. The Adventist movement is acknowledged as an "early voice" in the background of the movement, but little credit is given to the Adventists. Concerning an early Adventist publication Russell acquired, the statement is made

[15] William J. Schnell, *Into the Light of Christianity* (Grand Rapids: Baker Book House, 1959), p. 207.

[16] Emanuel Swedenborg (1688-1772) would be classified as a mystical interpreter. He is typical in that he sought for a threefold sense in Scripture. Akin to this method is the Pietistic mode of Biblical exposition. ". . . Pietism concedes the sanctity of the Scriptures, and seeks in them the lessons of eternal life; but as to principles and rules of exegesis it is more lawless and irrational. . . . He sets himself up as a new oracle, and while assumming to follow the written word of God, puts forth his own *dictum* as a further revelation." Milton S. Terry, *Biblical Hermeneutics* (second edition; Grand Rapids: Zondervan Publishing House, [n. d.], p. 166.

[17] United with the Swedenborgian-Pietist is the Socinian method of interpretation. Of this method Berkhof writes: ". . . Their exposition proceeded on the assumption *that the Bible must be interpreted in a rational way, or—perhaps better—in harmony with reason.* As the Word of God it would not contain anything that was in contradistinction to reason, that is, according to them, *nothing that could not be rationally apprehended.* Thus the doctrines of the Trinity, of Providence, and of the two natures in Christ, went by the board. They constructed a theological system that consisted of a mixture of Rationalism and Supernaturalism. And while they gloried in their freedom from the Confessional yoke, their exegesis was, after all, dominated by their dogmatic system." Louis Berkhof, *Principles of Biblical Interpretation* (second edition; Grand Rapids: Baker Book House, 1950), p. 29.

that "he had had little regard for their doctrines."[18] Although he did not acknowledge his borrowing from Adventism, van Baalen writes: "One wonders why Charles Taze Russell was so unwilling to acknowledge his sources when his system of errors reveals so plainly the traces of Mrs. Ellen G. White."[19] This connection is further seen by Lehman Strauss:

> Though the followers of Russell and Rutherford deny today that their leaders continued the movement of Miller, there is sufficient testimony in their own books to prove that Mr. Russell believed that he had discovered the errors of Mr. Miller, and then proceeded to set new dates for the coming of the Lord. But the new dates of Russell failed, as did those later inserted by Rutherford.[20]

It is difficult to understand why the Jehovah's Witnesses do not claim or even mention in their history the Christadelphian movement, a "small cult founded by John Thomas in 1848 and characteristically devoted to millennialism and soul-sleep, but holding the distinguishing doctrine that the Holy Spirit is merely a power."[21] A Christadelphian, Benjamin Wilson, is mentioned in connection with *The Emphatic Diaglott* which he published and from which the "light" on the invisible "second presence" of Christ came. How much else was borrowed from the Christadelphians only Russell knows, but it is certain that this group is a definite source of Russellite theology.[22] Except for minor differences, there

---

[18] *Jehovah's Witnesses in the Divine Purpose, op. cit.*, p. 18.

[19] Jan Karel van Baalen, *The Chaos of Cults* (fourteenth edition; Wm. B. Eerdmans Publishing Company, 1951), p. 220.

[20] Lehman Strauss, *An Examination of the Doctrine of "Jehovah's Witnesses"* (New York: Loizeaux Brothers, 1942), p. 8.

[21] John H. Gerstner, *The Theology of the Major Sects* (Grand Rapids: Baker Book House, 1960), p. 179.

[22] Years after this conclusion had been drawn it was with interest that this writer read the following from the pen of one who became a follower of the Watchtower in 1913 and who to this day is a student of the movement: "Dr. Thomas' work may have helped young Russell to catch a glimpse of the 'TWO SALVATIONS,' of the 'high calling age' and of the 'Millennial age,' which was the key to the mystery." And from the same page in the next column: "It could well be that Dr. Thomas' voluminous citation of earthly-blessing Scriptures was the Spirit's key which unlocked the divine mystery to young Russell's astute mind." Roy D. Goodrich, "Freedom from Confusion," *Back to the Bible Way*, 15:397, 399, January--February, 1966.

is almost a word-for-word agreement between the Christadelphian and the Russellite theology in several areas.[23]

The facts which have been brought out serve to show that the theological basis for Russellite theology was not as Biblical or unique as Russell would have one believe.

Another strong factor in the background and formation of the doctrines of Russellism was the strong aversion of Russell to the teachings of predestination and eternal punishment. From the position of a skeptic he built a system, with the points of theology developed from his contacts and the imaginations of his mind. He then sought to make the Word of God support and prove his preconceived theory. Such can be easily seen in this "proof-text" theology which tears verses and parts of verses out of context to justify a previously determined view. This reverse reading of the Bible is mentioned in Volume I of *Studies in the Scriptures*, where, speaking of the Bible, Russell writes: ". . . Let us

---

[23] See the article, "Christadelphians," *Dictionary of Sects, Heresies, Ecclesiastical Parties, and Schools of Religious Thought*, p. 106. On pages 473-78 *The Watchtower*, August 1, 1962 issue, contains an article on the Christadelphians entitled, "Christadelphianism of God or of Man?" Although the group is criticised and it is concluded that it is of man, basic agreement on many issues is evident. Several of the criticisms made of the group would not have been items of difference between Russell's position and the group—for example, the criticism of the Christadelphians not vindicating Jehovah's name and the Christadelphian emphasis on a more limited outreach. When the article criticizes the lack of unity in the sect, there is no hint of the many splits within the Witnesses over the years (See Appendix A). The article states: "Why so much splitting? Why so many divisions? Does it not indicate a lack of love? a form of pride? May 'opinionated' not be a word for it? . . . Surely this love is lacking among Christadelphians and therefore stamps their work as being, not of God, but of men" (p. 475). This same statement would seem to condemn the Witnesses just as legitimately!

An interesting and competent study of the Christadelphians is included in the book *Sects and Society*, pp. 219-314. The author of the text, Bryan Wilson, makes the following statement which confirms the point made above: "Russellism, as Christadelphians referred to the earliest demonstrations of the faith of Jehovah's Witnesses, came in for special attack, since this creed bore certain resemblance to Christadelphianism itself, and beguiled some brethern." Bryan R. Wilson, *Sects and Society: A Sociological Study of the Elim Tabernacle, Christian Science, and Christadelphians* (Los Angeles: University of California Press. 1961), pp. 294, 295.

examine the character of the writings claimed as inspired, to see whether their teachings correspond with the character we have *reasonably* imputed to God. . . ." [24]

A study of the background of the early Russellite movement has revealed a direct or indirect connection with the doctrines of religious movements of the past which have been condemned or rejected by the church. This study has also connected Russell's theology with the contemporary Christadelphian and Adventist movements. Much of Russell's theology grew out of his own personal feelings and his strong tendency toward rationalism. The basis of the theology of Russell as well as the present Jehovah's Witnesses has served equally well as the foundation of the Unitarians and Modernists of this day. In final analysis, the Witnesses, the Unitarians, and the Modernists stand for the denial of Biblical historic Christianity.[25] With this ancient and modern ancestor relationship established, the next consideration will be to examine some recent publications which deal with the history of the movement.

---

[24] Charles Taze Russell, *The Plan of the Ages* (Vol. I of *Studies in the Scriptures.* 7 vols.; Brooklyn: International Bible Students Association, 1886), p. 41.

[25] In the 1962 edition of J. K. van Baalen's, *The Chaos of Cults*, this writer's thesis, *Apostles of Denial*, is cited: "Gruss mentions in addition to Adventism the following sources of Russellism: Arius, Socinus, Swedenborg, Unitarianism, Christadelphianism. . . . The present writer, however, questions whether the early leaders of either Mormonism or Jehovah's Witnesses possessed a sufficient theological background for such plagiarism" (p. 257).

In explanation of the position taken in the thesis and in this book, it might be stated that the above named individuals or groups were not necessarily followed directly in each case, but the same general errors of interpretation and doctrine were included in the new cult. It is this writer's contention that if Russell and the Witnesses claim such as Jesus, Paul, Waldo and Wycliff as their predecessors, it is even more legitimate, because of similarities, to see Socinus, Swedenborg and the Unitarians, etc. as part of their heritage. The Witnesses and Russell identified themselves with Arius, and sufficient evidence has been cited to make it probable that Christadelphian ideas were followed by him.

CHAPTER III

THE HISTORY OF JEHOVAH'S WITNESSES: SOME RECENT PUBLICATIONS

For a movement as large as the Jehovah's Witnesses, very little written history proceeded from the organization until the publishing of the series: "Modern History of Jehovah's Witnesses," commencing with the January 1, 1955 issue of *The Watchtower*.[1]

Much exposé type of writing has been produced by opponents of the Witnesses. Much of this has been good but brief, while some writers have dealt with the movement either from an out-of-date contact or from second-hand information.

In 1953, Walter R. Martin and Norman H. Klann published their book, *Jehovah of the Watchtower,* which devoted a portion of its contents to the truth of the history of the Jehovah's Witnesses. The history and the evidence presented is well-documented and well-written and there are indications that the Watchtower Society felt the weight of the publication. With the first *Watchtower* issue of the Witnesses' history, the statement was made:

> Many have wondered how the Jehovah's witnesses came into existence. Multitudes have gone to accusers and attackers, thinking to get unprejudiced, undistorted

---

[1] The chapter "Jehovah's Witnesses of Modern Times" in *Religion in the Twentieth Century* by Nathan Homer Knorr, the president of the Society, seems to have been the nearest approach to a Witness-written history to appear before the 1955 series. Nathan Homer Knorr, "Jehovah's Witnesses of Modern Times," *Religion in the Twentieth Century*, Vergilius Ferm, editor (New York: The Philosophical Library, 1948), pp. 381-92. A brief treatment of the history of the movement also is included in *Qualified to Be Ministers* (1955), pp. 297-345.

> information about the modern witnesses of the Most High God. That authentic information may be made available to all for general enlightenment and for the correcting of many who have been misled by antagonistic would-be informers we begin here a series of articles on a "Modern History of Jehovah's Witnesses."[2]

Then in 1959, the Watchtower Bible and Tract Society published its first volume-sized history of the movement. The book, *Jehovah's Witnesses in the Divine Purpose,* is actually based on the series which appeared in 1955. The history is put into a popular and interesting form, with many illustrations and pictures. The book rewrites the history and the facts in many places, and authority for almost every statement is from Watchtower sources. Many views held in the early years of the movement are either reinterpreted or not mentioned. Since the series in *The Watchtower* is the basis for the book, the following review of the book is equally true of the series. Space permits citing a limited number of examples which should adequately demonstrate the intent of the publishers of *Jehovah's Witnesses in the Divine Purpose.*

1. After a lengthy discussion to establish everyone from Abel to the Apostle John as a Jehovah's witness (i.e., a person witnessing for Jehovah, and therefore the modern Jehovah's Witnesses are part of that line), the statement is made: "That means that all Christians in the first-century congregation were witnesses of Jehovah. . . ."[3]

This ignores Christ's declaration in Acts 1:8 which makes the early Church "witnesses of me," i.e., witnesses of Jesus Christ.[4]

2. The Witnesses look upon their growth and expansion as signs of God's presence. The blessing of the work also indicates to the Witnesses that God chose Russell and his publications as His instruments.[5]

That this is no proof of God's favor can be seen in the growth of other movements, some of which are directly

---

[2] *The Watchtower*, 76:4, January 1, 1955.

[3] *Jehovah's Witnesses in the Divine Purpose* (Brooklyn: Watchtower Bible and Tract Society of New York, Inc., 1959), p. 9.

[4] See the discussion in chapter two.

[5] *Jehovah's Witnesses in the Divine Purpose, op. cit.*, p. 16.

opposed to God's plan. Communism, for example, has grown according to the work and propaganda put forth; the Seventh-day Adventists and the Latter-Day Saints are also examples of groups which have experienced great growth. Growth is certainly no measure of God's presence with a group.

3. In a quotation taken from the first volume of *Studies in the Scriptures,* the following claims are made for C. T. Russell: "He was not the founder of a new religion . . . He revived the great truths taught by Jesus and the apostles . . . He made no claim of a special revelation from God. . . ."[6]

The foregoing statements are but a sampling of that which is found in just one paragraph. It has already been stated that Russell's religion was new in that he gathered together, reworked and created heretical ideas and brought them into his system. The evidence has shown and will further show that he did not revive the truths of Jesus and the apostles. His message was one of denial of almost every doctrine of the Bible! It is strikingly strange, if he never claimed special revelation from God, that he claimed to be the ONLY channel of revelation. Acceptance of Russell as "that servant" of Matthew 24:45, 46 was made a test of fellowship. Ellis, quoting from a "souvenir" of Russell's famous convention trips, which was endorsed by a facsimile of his signature, cited the following:

> "If any oppose the Lord by opposing the Channel (i.e., The Watch Tower Bible and Tract Society) and the Servant (i.e., Russell) the Lord has delegated to do his work, to that extent he loses the favor, the Spirit of the Lord; light becomes darkness, and he is soon outside."[7]

This sounds much like his statement that it would be better to leave the Bible unread than to leave off reading *Studies in the Scriptures,* for reading the Bible alone after having studied his books would leave a person in darkness after two years. So that none can question this statement, the following is documented from *The Watch Tower,* September 15, 1910:

---

[6] *Ibid.,* p. 17.

[7] William T. Ellis, "Investigating An Investigator," *The Continent,* (microfilm): 1344, September 26, 1912.

> If the six volumes of SCRIPTURE STUDIES are practically the Bible topically arranged, with Bible proof-texts given, we might not improperly name the volumes—the Bible in an arranged form. That is to say, they are not merely comments on the Bible, but they are practically the Bible itself . . . Furthermore, not only do we find that people cannot see the divine plan in studying the Bible by itself, but we can see, also, that if anyone lays the SCRIPTURE STUDIES aside, even after he has used them, after he has become familiar with them, after he has read them for ten years—if he then lays them aside and ignores them and goes to the Bible alone, though he has understood his Bible for ten years, our experience shows that within two years he goes into darkness. On the other hand, if he had merely read the SCRIPTURE STUDIES with their references, and had not read a page of the Bible, as such, he would be in the light at the end of two years, because he would have the light of the Scriptures.[8]

The Finished Mystery ends all doubt about the "Pastor" making "no claim of a special revelation from God":

> He listened to the word direct from the mouth of God, spoken by holy men of old as moved by the Holy Spirit. . . . Pastor Russell's warning to Christendom, coming direct from God. . . . He said that he could never have written his books himself. It all came from God, through the enlightenment of the Holy Spirit.[9]

Russell's claim to special light or inspiration in the writing of his doctrinal works sounds typical of the claims made by many of the cult founders. The Watchtower organization is still viewed as God's channel for truth today and claims that God speaks only through that one channel.

4. Concerning the Russell-White debate of 1908 the Witnesses report that "thousands were on hand to observe the easy victory for Russell . . ." and it is also stated that "other debate challenges were made by others and accepted, but at the last moment the challengers would withdraw."[10]

---

[8] *Watch Tower Reprints*, p. 4685.

[9] C. J. Woodworth and George H. Fisher (comp. and ed.), *The Finished Mystery* (Vol. VII of *Studies in the Scriptures*, 7 vols; 1918 edition; Brooklyn: International Bible Students Association, 1917), p. 387.

[10] *Jehovah's Witnesses in the Divine Purpose*, *op. cit.*, p. 44.

Here is another example of biased reporting in this quotation based on a 1908 *Watch Tower*. The background of this statement discredits White's motive for the debate as a desire to capitalize on Russell's popularity.

Was the debate an "easy victory for Russell"? The following quotation (from the Publisher's Announcement of the book recording the Russell-White debate) is in direct contrast to the Witnesses' statement as it says of White:

> While only forty years of age, and in appearance on the platform young enough to be Mr. Russell's own son, he nevertheless handled his part of the program in a manner that proved him to be a master of the occasion.[11]

The publishers back up this statement with the entire text of the debate. After reading the account, it is quite clear that time after time Russell violated the rules of the debate. One practice Russell employed throughout was not to answer the arguments of his opponent at all, but to use the time in airing his doctrines in order to gain converts. It is also reported that Russell many times had his rebuttal prepared beforehand, so that he could not actually answer any of his opponent's arguments. This method caused White to state:

> . . . I have never heard any man undertake to reply unto an argument that had been made without in some way attempting to take up the argument and show that it did not teach what the man that made it says that it did.[12]

Although this writer does not agree with White's defense of baptismal regeneration, a study of the text of the debate will surely refute the Witnesses' report of "easy victory for Russell." For victory in a debate, the victor must meet and defeat the opponent, not propagandize to receive applause from his followers and the uninformed. The latter part of the statement ("the challengers would withdraw") which implies that opponents were afraid to debate with Russell is also false. Cook remarks that Russell "oft-repeated challenges to ministers to debate with him, when the fact is

---

[11] John Allen Hudson (ed.), *Russell-White Debate* (second edition; Cincinnati, Ohio: F. L. Rowe, 1912), "Publishers Announcement."

[12] *Ibid.*, p. 17.

that when he himself is challenged he avoids the contest with specious excuses."[13]

5. In the same category of debates, the Rutherford-Troy debate of 1915, held in the Trinity Auditorium in Los Angeles, is reported by the Witnesses in this fashion: "The entire series of debates proved to be a signal victory for Rutherford. . . ."[14]

The text of the debate can be found in the *Los Angeles Tribune,* April 22-26, 1915. The April 25th issue of that paper clearly shows the biased view of the Watchtower statement as it reports: "As the audience was the only judge, each person carried away with him his own opinion as to which contestant won the majority of points." Thus the report given of a "signal victory for Rutherford" is just an opinion of the Watchtower Society.

6. The important matter of Russell being recognized as "that faithful and wise servant" of Matthew 24:45-47 is played down and the account seems to place the "error"

---

[13] Charles C. Cook, *All About One Russell* (Philadelphia: Philadelphia School of the Bible, [n. d.]), p. 37. Another way a debate could be avoided was to impose impossible restrictions so that the proposed meeting could not possibly be held. For example, in 1926 arrangements were underway for Dr. B. H. Shadduck to debate a representative of the Watch Tower. One of the propositions governing the debate included the following:" 'That B. H. Shadduck, D. D. furnish a bond of $500 as a guarantee that he will not . . . refer to any quotation contained in any periodical or book published by the International Bible Students Association, and if the Rev. B. H. Shadduck shall . . . refer to any quotation or book published by the International Bible Students Association he shall at once pay the sum of $500 to his opponent in this debate.' " B. H. Shadduck, *The Seven Thunders of Millennial Dawn* (third edition; Ashtabula, Ohio: Homo Publishing Co., 1928), p. 5. (The quotation is taken directly from one of the handwritten propositions governing the debate.) The demand not to cite any publication was necessary as statements included in later editions of texts had been changed and Shadduck had various editions of these publications. A public exposure of these changes would clearly brand Russell a false prophet (Deut. 18:20-22). See page 31 of Shadduck's book for his other experiences in attempts to engage in a debate.

[14] *Jehovah's Witnesses in the Divine Purpose, op. cit.,* pp. 56, 57. Rutherford (J. F. Rutherford) was C. T. Russell's successor as leader of the Society. Troy (J. H. Troy) was a Baptist minister.

not on Russell's own claims but the mistake of his followers, because Russell had supposedly repudiated that position.[15]

As has already been shown from the literature of the convention trips, Russell's being the "faithful and wise servant" was a test of fellowship. In the preface of *The Finished Mystery* Pastor Russell's position is clearly stated as "the messenger to the Laodicean Church . . . To give the Household of Faith meat in due season. . . ."[16] On the very next page, one reads: ". . . 'that wise and faithful servant' of the Lord—CHARLES TAZE RUSSELL."[17] In the book's commentary on Revelation 3:14 the claim is related:

> The special messenger to the last Age of the Church was Charles T. Russell, born February 16, 1852. He has privately admitted his belief that he was chosen for his great work from before his birth.[18]

Of this book (*The Finished Mystery*), the book *Jehovah's Witnesses in the Divine Purpose,* states: "This seventh volume, therefore, contained largely the thinking and comments of Pastor Russell during his lifetime."[19]

7. Rutherford is said to have worked "to root out any remnants of creature worship that might be left in the organization."[20]

This sounds commendable, but the fact is that Rutherford tried to do away with the popularity of Russell in order to take the place he occupied in the hearts and minds of the people. At first he adopted and propagated Russell's doctrines almost unchanged, but after a short time he repudiated and changed them in many places. That Rutherford "rooted out" all creature worship but his own is clearly seen.

---

[15] *Ibid.,* pp. 68, 69. In the September 15, 1909 issue of the *Watch Tower* Russell set forth the view that he was "that servant" referred to in Matthew 24:45-47, etc.

[16] *The Finished Mystery, op. cit.,* p. 4.

[17] *Ibid.,* p. 5.

[18] *Ibid.,* p. 53.

[19] *Jehovah's Witnesses in the Divine Purpose, op. cit.,* p. 70.

[20] *Ibid.,* p. 69. In "Olin Moyle's Original Letters" (Appendix B), Rutherford's absolute control of the Society is confirmed. In the last letter, Moyle writing to Judge Rutherford stated: "This is further evidence that in your unrighteous course you have exalted and placed yourself and your commands above the laws of God."

Davidson writes:

> Everything was done in the name of Judge Rutherford, the tracts were all his personal messages, the Watchtower became filled with his personal opinions and the newly acquired radio station WBBR spent 90 per cent of its broadcasting time propelling his booming voice into the metropolitan New York ether.[21]

Another indication of Rutherford's one-man control is found in the study by Stroup:

> If a Witness voiced an opinion at variance with that of the central organization he was "Satan-inspired" and was subsequently cut off from the fellowship of "true believers." This procedure applied even to duly elected chairmen of local groups. More and more the leadership gravitated into the hands of one person, Mr. Rutherford, so that by the time of his death the entire organization, including the Board of Directors, was controlled by this one man.[22]

After Rutherford was almost forced off the air, phonographs and records appeared to perpetuate his voice and message. Then in 1931, when Rutherford changed the name to "Jehovah's Witnesses," it almost completely cut the movement off from the past.

8. Another typical rewriting of the facts is found in the following statement concerning the year 1925: "The view had been somewhat general among the anointed that the remaining members of the body of Christ would be changed to heavenly glory that year."[23]

This statement implies that the error was on behalf of the "anointed" and didn't have any encouragement or foundation. The fact is that Rutherford himself had seeded and nurtured this hope for years previous to 1925, two concrete examples being the book *The Harp of God* and the booklet *Millions Now Living Will Never Die!* The prediction was that Abraham, Isaac and Jacob were to return to earth in 1925 and the "new order of things," under their earthly

---

[21] Bill Davidson, "Jehovah's Traveling Salesmen," *Colliers*, 118:77, November 2, 1946.

[22] Herbert Hewitt Stroup, *The Jehovah's Witnesses* (New York: Columbia University Press, 1945), p. 24.

[23] *Jehovah's Witnesses in the Divine Purpose, op. cit.*, p. 107.

rulership would take place in that year. Rutherford wrote with assurance: "Therefore we may confidently expect that 1925 will mark the return of Abraham, Isaac, Jacob and the faithful prophets of old. . . ."[24] An extended quotation from the same source, by Rutherford, clearly shows what was to be expected.

> When does this world end? If we can definitely fix this period, then it is an easy matter to determine when the divine promises with reference to life everlasting will be opened to the world in general. We therefore propose to prove in this argument that the social order of things, the second world, legally ended in 1914, and since that time has been and is passing away; that the new order of things is coming in to take its place; that within a definite period of time the old order will be completely eradicated and the new order in full sway; and that these things shall take place within the time of the present generation and that therefore there are millions of people now living on earth who will see them take place, to whom everlasting life will be offered and who, if they accept it upon the terms offered and obey these terms, will never die.[25]

Notice that Rutherford says, "WITHIN A DEFINITE PERIOD OF TIME THE OLD ORDER WILL BE COMPLETELY ERADICATED AND THE NEW ORDER IN FULL SWAY." This he predicted for 1925! Schnell writes that in the convention of that year in Germany, Rutherford gathered the German Bethel family around him and said, " 'Boys you don't want to go to heaven now, when there is so much work to be done on earth. It seems the Lord wants US to do the work that we thought the princes would do.' "[26] Schnell continues, "He talked for three hours to us that night, and when he got through, he had talked us out of going to heaven."[27]

There was nothing new in this type of thing, for Russell did the same concerning 1914. Macmillan, who had been in the movement some time, writes of the 1914 period, "I believed it myself sincerely—that the church was 'going

---

[24] Joseph F. Rutherford, *Millions Now Living Will Never Die!* (Brooklyn: International Bible Students Association, 1920), pp. 89, 90.

[25] *Ibid.*, p. 12.

[26] *The Converted Jehovah's Witness Expositor*, 2:1, Issue 3, 1958.

[27] *Ibid.*

home' in October."[28] Russell began hedging in the early part of 1914 in *The Watch Tower* and wrote: "'If later it should be demonstrated that the church is not glorified by October, 1914, we shall try to feel content with whatever the Lord's will may be. . . .'"[29] Then on the same page he prepared for the fall of his prophecy: "'If in the Lord's providence the time should come *twenty-five years* later, then that would be our will.'"[30]

9. Russell's separation from his wife is reported in typical Witness manner. Supposedly the separation came about because Mrs. Russell wanted too strong a voice in the publication of *The Watch Tower*.[31]

The reason given in the text does not at all agree with the statement of the judge or the court record. The evidence given for divorce cited that his "conceit," "egotism" and "domination" were such as to make life intolerable for his wife. Further his conduct toward other women was termed "improper." With these facts on record, J. J. Ross printed a tract, *Some Facts About the Self-Styled "Pastor" Charles T. Russell,* which appeared in June, 1912. In this tract he writes: "In 1879, he married Miss Marie F. Ackley, who divorced him a few years ago on the ground of cruelty and of having wrong relations with other women."[32] This charge and many others caused Russell to bring suit against Ross for defamatory libel. These statements against Russell were found true and Russell lost the case with the jury handing down the verdict "No Bill."

10. The following statement from all outward appearances would seem true from the figures given by the Watchtower: ". . . The Society has always been primarily a Bible society."[33] This refers to its dissemination of Bible truths and Bibles.

---

[28] A. H. Macmillan, *Faith on the March* (Englewood Cliffs, N. J.: Prentice-Hall, 1957), p. 47.

[29] *The Watch Tower,* 1914, p. 4, quoted in *Jehovah's Witnesses in the Divine Purpose, op. cit.,* p. 59.

[30] *Ibid.,* p. 59.

[31] *Ibid.,* p. 45.

[32] J. J. Ross, *Some Facts and More Facts About the Self-Styled "Pastor" Charles T. Russell* (Philadelphia: Philadelphia School of the Bible, [n. d.]), p. 4.

[33] *Jehovah's Witnesses in the Divine Purpose, op. cit.,* p. 255.

That comparatively little in the way of Bible distribution has been done by the Witnesses is easy to establish. In June of 1960 less than 3,000,000 copies of the entire Bible or almost 6,000,000 Bibles and portions of it had been printed by the Watchtower.[34] This number of Bibles published in relation to the other materials such as books, booklets and magazines published makes the odds at least two hundred to one for a Bible to be distributed instead of the Watchtower literature.[35] Of those 6,000,000 Bibles and portions published, over 1,400,000 have been the *New World Translation of the Christian Greek Scriptures* and over 2,100,000 volumes of *New World Translation of the Hebrew Scriptures.* These are propaganda devices, not the pure Word of God. The *King James Version* and the *American Standard Version* printed by the Watchtower Society have Witnesses' concordances and other Jehovah's Witness material in the rear which also dilute the truth. A more correct claim would be that the Society has always been primarily a propaganda machine!

The book *Jehovah's Witnesses in the Divine Purpose* is also to be criticized not only on what it says but also on grounds of what it does not say.

11. Why is there no mention of the court case with J. J. Ross? This is the case which Russell lost when he was unable to show that Ross' charges in the tract *Some Facts about the Self-Styled "Pastor" Charles T. Russell,* were false. Russell was charged with very grave actions. The trial record was in the files of the High Court of Ontario—Russell vs. Ross—"defamatory libel," March 17, 1913. (This writer was informed by a reputable authority that the court record of this trial had mysteriously disappeared.)

12. Why is there no mention of the evidence brought into court in Russell's divorce case? The Witnesses' account makes it clear that Russell was not guilty or accused of adultery, which is true according to Mrs. Russell's testimony.[36] What Russell was charged with however, is just as morally degrading for one who claimed to be a special

---

[34] *The Watchtower,* 81:599, 601, October 1, 1960.

[35] See the charts in the rear of *Jehovah's Witnesses in the Divine Purpose* from which this estimate was made.

[36] *Ibid.,* p. 45.

servant of God. This writer hesitates to introduce the following record into the text, but it is necessary in the face of the Watchtower's incomplete account. The following is an example of the testimony given by Mrs. Russell under oath, under direct examination by her attorney, Mr. Porter:

> "Q. State to the court and the Jury what talk, if any you had with this girl Rose, in regard to her relations with your husband, which you communicated to your husband.
>
> A. . . . 'Rose has told me that you have been very intimate with her, and that you have been in the habit of hugging and kissing her and having her sit on your knee and fondling each other, and she tells me you bid her on no account tell me, but she couldn't keep it any longer.' "[37]

Concerning this and other facts found in Ross's booklet, he writes: "What I now tell the reader is firsthand knowledge and I will be prepared to defend it in the Court of Law."[38]

13. Why is there no mention of the "Miracle Wheat" scandal in which Russell sued the *Brooklyn Daily Eagle* for $100,000—but lost?[39]

14. Why is there no mention that the "extensive journey" of December, 1911, to March, 1912, which supposedly was a missionary journey to show the failure of Christian missions, was actually an advertising stunt and a fraud?[40] Large sums of money were spent to advertise the meeting in the New York Hippodrome where the results of the trip were given.

An evaluation of the enterprise is given by *The Missionary Review of the World:*

> We do not believe in advertising what we have reason to consider a fraud, but at times attention should be

---

[37] Ross, *op. cit.*, pp. 28, 29.

[38] *Ibid.*, p. 17.

[39] The Watchtower advertised wheat seed for sale at $1.00 a pound which was called "Miracle Wheat," and it was asserted that it would yield five times as much as conventional wheat. The *Brooklyn Daily Eagle* published a cartoon exposing this venture, which caused Russell to sue for $100,000 damages. The wheat was investigated by government departments, and it was tested by governmental tests in which it was rated low. Therefore the *Eagle* won the suit.

[40] *Jehovah's Witnesses in the Divine Purpose, op. cit.*, p. 51.

> called to frauds already widely advertised . . . advertising is an art, and the financial success of many a "fake" business enterprise is due to expensive and skillful use of printer's ink. Pastor Russell is a great advertiser, and has deceived many good people into thinking him a great teacher.[41]

Mr. W. T. Ellis, Editor-a-field of *The Continent,* after interviewing Russell personally and reading Russell's report, concluded: ". . . I declare that his alleged 'investigation' of missions was no investigation at all. . . . Russell simply made a short, quick, sight-seeing journey around the world."[42] The missionary tour covered 116 days, nearly all of which was on ships or trains.

15. The point is made that the "Pastor's" sermons were carried by 3,000 newspapers in the United States, Canada and Europe, with the implication that all the papers carried the messages because of popular appeal with the space given free. The question is asked: "Did the Society have to pay for this space like advertising, or did the newspapers pay Russell?" The answer is given: "The newspaper space was given free and the telegraphic expense was borne by the Society."[43] What is not mentioned is that much of the space was paid for at regular advertising rates. The following documentation is direct from the statement of the International Bible Students themselves. From the April, 1915, *Los Angeles Tribune,* issues of the 12th, 19th, 24th, and 26th, heading the two column full length messages of Russell in a box are these instructive words: ". . . We are permitted to publish these instructive sermons in the leading newspapers, paying therefor at advertising rates. INTERNATIONAL BIBLE STUDENTS ASSOCIATION."[44] Again the

---

[41] "A Peculiar Investigation of Missions," *The Missionary Review of the World,* 25 New series: 538, July, 1912.

[42] William T. Ellis, "Investigating An Investigator," *The Continent,* (Microfilm): 1414, October 10, 1912.

[43] *Jehovah's Witnesses in the Divine Purpose, op. cit.,* p. 50.

[44] Heading Russell's sermon in the October 12, 1914 issue of the *New York Times,* (p. 5) is the following: "Pastor Russell's Syndicated Sermons appear weekly in aproximately fifteen hundred newspapers in the United States, Canada, Great Britain South Africa, Australia and Scandinavia, in four languages. As New York is not controlled by the Syndicate we have contracted for the publication of these instructive sermons in the leading newspapers of this metropolis, paying there-

Watchtower account omits the facts which are easily found by anyone interested in getting the truth.

A further interesting note is recorded by Brown, as he writes of Russell's advertising:

> Even the papers, however, are beginning to rebel, and only recently, the Chicago Tribune and the Chicago Herald, each in turn, cancelled its Russell contract, and followed these cancellations with a public apology for running the Russell copy, even for pay.
>
> The Tribune, which claims to be America's greatest daily, in cancelling the Russell contract, offered as a reason, not that "Pastor" Russell advanced new theories in the religious world, but the cancellation was decided upon because of his questionable reputation in the world of morals and business.[45]

16. It is interesting that in order to cover doctrinal changes, the Witnesses omitted from their historical account the 358-page book, *Life*. This book, in keeping with the theology of Russell, sets forth in unmistakable language the future hope of the Jew in realizing the promises made to

---

for advertising rates — INTERNATIONAL BIBLE STUDENTS ASSOCIATION." See also the *New York Times* issues of September 21, 28; October 12, 19, 26; November 2, 9, 29; and December 7, 14. (All issues are for the year 1914.) The appearance of Russell's sermons in the *New York Times* seemed to be an attempt to capitalize on the events of that year in the light of the predictions he had made. It is interesting that the sermons in the Times appeared in September, 1914, not having been published in the paper before, nor appearing after the month of December of the same year. Could this be explained by the failure of the great expectations predicted for that year?

The following statement by a Bible Student helps to explain the "popularity" of the Russell sermons: "If we were asked how it happened that the Pastor Russell Sermons gained such remarkable acceptance, we would of necessity say, it did not 'happen,' but was unquestionably of the Lord's blessing and direction. If it were then asked what were the main agencies used by the Lord to secure such remarkable results, we would say voluntary and unstinted efforts by consecrated brethren. Nothing influences a newspaper editor more than letters from his readers and we venture to say that tens of thousands wrote letters of appreciation of the sermons." Robert Hollister, *Meet Our British Brethren* (no imprint), p. 6.

[45] John Elward Brown, *"In the Cult Kingdom" Mormonism, Eddyism and Russellism* (Siloam Springs, Arkansas: International Federation Publishing Company, [n. d.]), pp. 51, 52.

Abraham. The following is a typical statement from *Life*: "First we shall consider the certainty of the promises that Israel shall be returned to Palestine."[46] This literal interpretation of Old Testament prophecy cramped the Watchtower Society in its teaching of the Bible, so after a short time the literal was allegorized. Schnell remarks, "As the book's red cover had augured, it was but a red herring and its premises were soon discarded by the Society."[47]

17. A strange request was made by the New World Translation Committee: "the one request of the translation committee was that its members remain anonymous even after their death."[48]

Why? This omission of information is needed, as evidence has been presented that N. H. Knorr and F. W. Franz headed the committee of seven. Knorr and Franz are presently the president and vice-president of the Watch Tower Society. The following quotation which summarizes and comments on testimony given in 1954 by Franz, is enlightening:

> According to the SCOTTISH DAILY EXPRESS, Nov. 24, 1954, Franz testified:—
>
> (1) That he and N. H. Knorr head the secret Translation Committee of seven.
> (2) That Franz and Knorr,—not the Committee have the last word.
> (3) That he, Franz, is the head of the Society's Publicity Department.
> (4) That translations and interpretations Emanate From God in this way:
>   (a) They are INVISIBLY COMMUNICATED to the Publicity Department.
>   (b) This is accomplished by "ANGELS OF DIFFERENT RANKS WHO CONTROL WITNESSES."
>
> From its beginning The Watch Tower Society has fulminated against all such as this, as DEMONISM, WARNING AGAINST IT CONSTANTLY FOR DECADES.

---

[46] Joseph F. Rutherford, *Life* (Brooklyn: International Bible Students Association, 1929), p. 120.

[47] William J. Schnell, *Thirty Years a Watch Tower Slave* (Grand Rapids: Baker Book House, 1956), p. 90.

[48] *Jehovah's Witnesses in the Divine Purpose, op. cit.*, p. 258.

ACCORDING TO THE WATCH TOWER, THEN, THE WATCHTOWER HAS SUCCUMBED TO *DEMONISM*![49]

As has been shown by just the few examples brought forth, this history of the Jehovah's Witnesses, first in serial form and finally in book form, is full of inaccuracies and rewritten history. This account is certainly not unbiased, and much cannot be received as trustworthy. A full study of this book would occasion a book of equal or even greater length. After this brief review the reader is left to weigh the facts presented to determine the credence that should be given to this book—*Jehovah's Witnesses in the Divine Purpose.*[50]

Shortly following *The Watchtower* series, from a secular publishing house, Vantage Press, came Marley Cole's book, *Jehovah's Witnesses: The New World Society* (1955). This

---

[49] The quotation is found beneath the article in the *Scottish Daily Express*, November 24, 1954. The duplicated *Express* article and the comment is found in publication 321 of Back to The Bible Way publications. "Back to the Bible Way" are publications which have been written and distributed by Roy D. Goodrich, 517 N. E. Second Street, Fort Lauderdale, Florida. Although Mr. Goodrich has much informative material dealing with the Watchtower Society and can be considered authoritative in much of what he says in this area, his theology is still basically that of C. T. Russell with some important changes. The abbreviation BTTBW will be used to designate these publications. Most of these numbered materials are mimeographed. Some of the names which appeared on this literature over the years are: Back to the Bible, Jehovah's Witnesses—with Florida address, The Bible Way Publications, Back to the Bible Publications, The Bible Students, and the author's name, Roy D. Goodrich. The address has never changed.

This writer has checked the comments against Franz' recorded testimony in the *Scottish Daily Express* article and found that they are accurate.

[50] W. J. Schnell writes as follows: "My story—my 'open and-above-board' attack and expose of the NEW WORLD SOCIETY OF JEHOVAH'S WITNESSES—has obviously forced a total change in the Society's tactics. For the first time in its 85 years of checkered existence, it has had to go on record and into print—black and white—to produce its history. . . . This book is a colossal whitewash! Nevertheless, it is a concrete basis for me upon which to operate in debunking the Watchtower heresy. Thus, my coming back, *Is the New World Society of Jehovah's Witnesses Christian?* must prove one thing; namely, that the NEW WORLD SOCIETY is not Christian." *The Converted Jehovah's Witness Expositor*, 5:3, Issue 2, 1961.

book is all that the Jehovah's Witnesses could wish for as a propaganda weapon. The Jehovah's Witnesses were urged both to buy and distribute it. Cole's study was advertised in *The Watchtower,* and the following is a typical claim: ". . . It presents for the first time in book form authentic information on the history, activities and doctrinal views of Jehovah's witnesses."[51] Although Cole wrote the book reputedly as a non-Jehovah's Witness, the results are the same.[52] The Society's advertisement in *The Watchtower* actually terms non-authentic[53] much of its own history and doctrine. This statement sweeps aside court records, newspaper reports, and other documented evidence as untrustworthy.

After reading the book, this writer was forced to the conclusion that the book was very biased and not objective in the least.[54] Cole let the statements made by The Watchtower Society on history and doctrine stand as fact. Although the book is well presented and interesting, Cole does not

---

[51] *The Watchtower,* 76:511, August 15, 1955.

[52] Cole's book was reviewed briefly in the August 8, 1955 issue of *Awake!* (p. 16). Neither the advertisement nor the review gives any hint that Cole was a Jehovah's Witness—a fact the Society seemed determined to hide. That Cole was a Witness can be proven beyond question. The following is quoted from a letter dated April 1, 1954, addressed to W. J. Schnell Co.: "I have completed a book about Jehovah's witnesses, having done the work under the Society's direction and with their approval on the work. . . . When published the Witnesses themselves will of course buy a lot of copies because the Society approves the work. The Society is not sponsoring the project. They would simply like to see an authoritative work on Jehovah's witnesses published by commercial publishers and sold like regular published material, so it may reach people who will not read the Society's own works. As for the financial accruements, whatever there are will come to the author, me, and if I wish to contribute part or all of its earnings I may do so. But the Society will have no connections in this respect to the project. . . ." The letter is signed, "Yours in publishing the Good News, Marley Cole." From the foregoing information one can easily see why Cole's book became a best seller. That Cole was a Witness is also established in his article in *The Nation,* June 9, 1951, pp. 539-41.

[53] Authentic: "Implies accordance with fact or actuality, thereby implying full trustworthiness." *Webster's New Collegiate Dictionary.*

[54] See the following text which devotes considerable space to a refutation of much "fiction" and biased reporting in the book. Walter R. Martin and Norman H. Klann, *Jehovah of the Watchtower* (sixth revised edition, 1963; Grand Rapids: Zondervan Publishing House, 1953), pp. 175-89.

possess the qualifications for the job, for he certainly is not a theologian, nor does he demonstrate that he has any first-hand knowledge concerning the history of the movement outside the biased Jehovah's Witness information which is presented throughout. This writer agrees with the statements of the reviewers in *Jehovah of the Watchtower* that "misrepresentation is exactly what a great deal of his book is, owing principally, however, to the Watchtower sources utilized."[55] And in concluding the review:

> The authors feel that this book by Mr. Cole is on the whole untrustworthy, and does not accurately present the full picture of the Watchtower, and that what it does present is a heavily biased, pro-Russellite interpretation of the whole movement.[56]

As to objectivity, Martin and Klann conclude that the book is "an almost complete loss."[57]

Following his *Jehovah's Witnesses: The New World Society,* Cole wrote *Triumphant Kingdom.*[58] The review of his first book would also be in order for the second.

In 1957, A. H. Macmillan came out with *Faith on the March,* printed not by the Society, but by Prentice-Hall. Macmillan had been associated with the movement for almost sixty years when he wrote the book. He was a member of the Brooklyn headquarters staff. The foreword was written by N. H. Knorr, president of the Watch Tower Bible and Tract Society. The book was reviewed in *The Watchtower* issue of May 15, 1957. This book also proved to be a successful propaganda weapon. Woven into the narrative is the Watchtower system of doctrine. Macmillan justifies and reinterprets doctrinal and date changes.

Macmillan's book seems almost an answer or parallel to the anti-Watchtower book by William J. Schnell, *Thirty Years a Watch Tower Slave,*[59] which appeared a year before. The

---

[55] *Ibid.*, p. 176.

[56] *Ibid.*, p. 189.

[57] *Ibid.*

[58] *Triumphant Kingdom,* published by Criterion Books, 1957, 256 pages. This book did not achieve the success of Cole's first.

[59] Mr. Schnell confirmed this writer's view and stated that Macmillan's book did undercut the effectiveness of *Thirty Years a Watch Tower Slave. The Converted Jehovah's Witness Expositor,* 5:1 Issue 2, 1961.

volume lays open for the first time the inner workings of the Watchtower Society, and for this reason it should be read by all who wish to see the real Watchtower organization. This book by Schnell was followed by another, *Into the Light of Christianity,* which deals more with answering the doctrines of the Jehovah's Witnesses.[60]

The Watchtower Society-inspired publications are seen to be biased, non-objective propaganda tools—tools to pull in the uninformed and unthinking. Doubtless their effect has been telling and will continue to be so. The books written to show the Jehovah's Witnesses' organization in its true light are also having a telling effect. The books, *Thirty Years a Watch Tower Slave,* and *Into the Light of Christianity,* have already been instrumental in freeing thousands of Jehovah's Witnesses from the Society.[61] The book *Jehovah of the Watchtower* after its appearance in 1953 went through several printings and was enlarged to double its original size. A revised edition was published in 1974.

---

[60] In a letter received during the latter part of 1962, Schnell reported that "*Into the Light of Christianity* has been so effective that the Watchtower prohibits Jehovah's Witnesses to possess it under any circumstances. Already 714 JW's have been disfellowshiped for the mere possession of this book." The Witnesses' publication, *Preaching Together in Unity* (Brooklyn: Watch Tower Bible and Tract Society, 1955), reveals the seriousness of the action against the person disfellowshiped: "Disfellowshiping is a serious matter and means that the wrongdoer is put out of Jehovah's New World society" (p. 38). "Disfellowshiped persons will not be recognized by anyone in the congregation and the right hand of fellowship will not be extended to them" (p. 39).

[61] In *The Converted Jehovah's Witness Expositor* (6:1, Issue 4, 1963) Schnell reported "8, 491 Jehovah's Witnesses free." In a letter dated May 12, 1966 to this author, Schnell reported: ". . . I do not have a conclusive report to give other than testimonies and letters received over the past nine years, and our tabulation shows these [Witnesses having come free through the efforts of Schnell] to be 12,106, but that is very conservative. In Germany alone, our collaboraters indicate a loss of 9,500 persons to the Watchtower system since my book FALSCHE ZEUGEN STEHEN WIDER MICH appeared."

Other tracts, booklets, articles and books[62] have appeared in the last few years dealing briefly with the history of the Watchtower movement, but because of space, mention has been made only of the books which have exerted the greatest influence in the understanding and debunking of the Witnesses' history.

With this background in mind, the next chapter deals with the study of the movement in its early beginnings, the period under Charles Taze Russell (1870-1916).

---

[62] There have been some excellent book-sized treatments on the Witnesses, all of which are quite objective. Listed chronologically they are (full entries in the Bibliography); Milton Stacey Czatt, *The International Bible Students* (1933). The book is an abbreviated Ph. D. thesis and it is now dated in its treatment. Herbert H. Stroup, *The Jehovah's Witness* (1945). Stroup's work is a pioneer effort and a published Ph. D. thesis. Edgar Roysten Pike, *Jehovah's Witnesses* (1954). Pike's work divides its coverage of the Witnesses into three sections: (1) Who They Are (2) What They Teach (3) What They Do. William H. Cumberland produced, "A History of Jehovah's Witnesses" (Unpublished Ph. D. thesis, The State University of Iowa, 1958). A good study with much primary source documentation. William J. Whalen, *Armageddon Around the Corner* (1962). This is an informative work, written by a Roman Catholic layman.

Author's Note

After the publication of this book another significant treatment of the history of the movement was discovered. This 418-page study by Timothy White is titled, *A People for His Name: A History of Jehovah's Witnesses and An Evaluation* (Vantage Press, 1968). Timothy White is a pseudonym.

In 1969, English writer Alan Rogerson published *Millions Now Living Will Never Die* (London: Constable), 216 pp.

Chapter IV

THE HISTORY OF JEHOVAH'S WITNESSES: THE PERIOD UNDER CHARLES TAZE RUSSELL (1870-1916)

With these words written in 1912, W. T. Ellis characterized Charles Taze Russell as he found him in personal interview:

> I sought a prophet and found a business man! Instead of a humble seeker after truth, I found the cleverest propagandist of the age—a man before whom John Alexander Dowie, Mary Baker Eddy, Madame Blavatsky, Abbas Effendi, "Elijah" Sanford and Joseph Smith pale into puerile ineffectiveness.[1]

Is this estimate of Russell just? To find the answer, this chapter will retrace the life of this man who was one of the most controversial religious leaders of his time. Actually, the first segment of Watch Tower Bible and Tract Society history is largely the history of Charles Taze Russell—he was the Society.

I. Background and Formative Years

Charles Taze Russell was born on February 16, 1852, in Old Allegheny (now a part of Pittsburgh), Pennsylvania. He was one of three children born to Joseph and Eliza Birney Russell. His parents were Presbyterians of Scotch-Irish descent. Russell's father ran a clothing store business, and did well in this endeavor. Russell's mother died when

---

[1] W. T. Ellis, "Investigating an Investigator," *The Continent*, (microfilm): 1342, September 26, 1912.

he was but nine years of age. At fifteen he joined his father in the growing chain of clothing stores.

One E. D. Stewart, a follower of Russell, reflects the typical attitude of the Bible Students as he writes that Charles' parents "were of the 'orthodox' faith, and up to the age of fifteen he believed all and only such doctrines as his sectarian minister took the trouble to teach him." [2]

All went well for Russell until at the age of sixteen he tried to win an infidel friend to Christianity but "the infidel completely routed young Russell, and he became a skeptic. He saw, for instance, that with the doctrine of eternal torment in it he could not believe the Bible. . . ."[3] This account explains why Russell, in order to accept the Bible, had to eliminate the doctrine of eternal punishment. Thus at an early age he rejected most of his early training as a member of the Allegheny City, Pennsylvania, Congregational Church and the local Y. M. C. A. He made a study of the oriental religions, but they did not satisfy him. During this period of a shaken faith, a struggle began—he could not believe the teaching he had received as a child, the creeds of the orthodox churches, but he could not throw Christianity away altogether.

At the age of eighteen the ray of light which caused a return to some form of faith was found in a dingy basement near one of Russell's clothing stores. His experience is recorded in these words:

> Seemingly by accident, one evening I dropped into a dusty, dingy hall, where I had heard religious services were held, to see if the handful who met there had anything more sensible to offer than the creeds of the great churches. There, for the first time, I heard something of the views of Second Adventists, the preacher being Mr. Jonas Wendell. . . . [4]

There is good evidence to believe that from the Adventists, a remnant of the old Millerite movement, Russell received his "light" on the non-existence of eternal punishment, the second coming of Christ, and Biblical chronology. After this experience with the Adventists, he joined them.

---

[2] E. D. Stewart, "Life of Pastor Russell," *Overland Monthly*, 69:129, February, 1917.

[3] *Ibid.*, pp. 129, 130.

[4] *Watch Tower Reprints*, p. 3821.

A short time later Russell and some of his business and social friends got together to study the Bible. It is interesting to note that one of the study group members was Russell's father, who died in 1897 after having been a close associate in the work. This group, according to Russell's report systematically studied the Bible, and as would be expected, the first finding was on the subject of hell and soul-sleep after death. Macmillan writes concerning their new find: "This was certainly a departure from the spiritual fare they had been receiving through the creeds based on tradition."[5] It is strikingly strange for one to study the Bible starting from this point. Actually, according to his own position as cited by Stewart, Russell had to eliminate the doctrine of eternal punishment to believe the Bible, a method of study seen throughout the system. The Bible was studied in the light of a previously conceived theory.

After a time Russell began to differ with Adventism on Biblical interpretation, especially on the manner and object of the Lord's return, although the chronology was left intact. Russell crystallized his views in the pamphlet *The Object and Manner of the Lord's Return.*

From his study group Russell went forth with a no-hell doctrine. Ferguson in his characteristic style writes:

> . . . After a careful and painstaking study of Holy Writ he came to the comforting conclusion that the Bible did not teach the doctrine of hell. With this good news, he began at the age of twenty a ministry which lasted forty-two years and cheered the hearts of hill-billies in every nook and cranny of the democracy.[6]

---

[5] A. H. Macmillan, *Faith on the March* (Englewood Cliffs, New Jersey: Prentice-Hall, 1957), p. 21. The heart of Russell's theology is the denial of immortality and eternal punishment. But this doctrine will not bring satisfaction, so man's efforts are viewed as qualifying him for life and future bliss. "Thus Russell taught that man must obtain everything by merit. In the interest of his theory he divided the history of the world into three great dispensations. In each of these man is given an opportunity to merit for himself the right to live in this world forever by obedience to God's laws. . . . Russell's 'divine plan' is the coarsest kind of work-righteousness." F. E. Mayer, *Jehovah's Witnesses* (revised 1957; St. Louis, Mo.: Concordia Publishing House, 1942), p. 14.

[6] Charles W. Ferguson, *The Confusion of Tongues* (Garden City, New York: Doubleday, Doran and Co., 1929), p. 67.

The Pittsburgh study group, Russell's first congregation, elected him "Pastor." During this period Russell began the forming of what Schnell terms a "Layman's revolt." In this revolt all former work of Christians was set aside and ridiculed. As Schnell writes: "He spoke of them as grievous errors and departures from the faith."[7] After all orthodoxy was derided, Russell slowly became the sole source of truth.

In 1876, while Russell and his congregation were studying the Bible, another Adventist, N. H. Barbour of Rochester, New York, was editing a magazine, *The Herald of the Morning*. Russell was on a business trip in Philadelphia, when he came upon a copy and noticed that Barbour agreed with his view concerning the invisible return of Christ. The two men later united in the publication of the Adventist *Herald of the Morning,* which had suspended publication because of lack of support. Russell supplied most of the funds and acted as coeditor, while Barbour, a printer, did the printing. Barbour's Rochester group and Russell's Pittsburgh group were also united. Fired with the desire to propagate the new found "truths," Russell curtailed his clothing business activities, which brought him more than a quarter of a million dollars when finally liquidated. In 1877 Russell and Barbour collaborated on their first book, *Three Worlds or Plan of Redemption.* In the same year Russell called all the ministers of the Allegheny and Pittsburgh areas together and set before them the "proofs" of the Lord's presence, but all rejected his message. Having given up his business interests—at least his clothing stores—he embarked upon speaking engagements.

II. Years of Organization and Growth

Russell and Barbour came to disagree on the atonement, and in 1878 the two parted. This resulted in Russell's founding, in 1879, the new publication, *Zion's Watch Tower and Herald of Christ's Presence,* with a first printing of 6,000 copies. From 6,000 copies monthly in 1879, *The Watch Tower* (*The Watchtower* after October 15, 1931) has prospered

[7] William J. Schnell, *Another Gospel* (second edition: Seattle: The Life Messengers, [n. d.]), p. 2.

beyond Russell's fondest dreams, with 17,650,000 copies currently coming off the press (February 1975). It was also during 1879 that Russell married Maria F. Ackley. Russell's wife became quite active in her husband's work. She answered many letters to *Zion's Watch Tower* and also wrote articles. During this period other congregations were organized. Russell and some of his associates would visit those who had subscribed to his magazine, and these were united into study groups using *Zion's Watch Tower* for study and later the *Millennial Dawn* series books (later titled *Studies in the Scriptures*).

In 1881 Russell wrote *Tabernacle Shadows of the "Better Sacrifices"* and also *Food For Thinking Christians*. As has been the case with any religion holding to progressive revelation, Russell later discouraged his followers from studying these early works because they were immature.[8] Being a self-educated theologian, Russell put down his "truths" for others before his own theology was fully developed, and theology is still in flux in the Jehovah's Witness movement today. With Russell's theology changing and developing over the years, he switched the attention from his early works to the *Studies in the Scriptures,* which began to appear in 1886.

In 1881 Russell called for co-laborers to gather subscriptions for *Zion's Watch Tower*. In 1884 Zion's Watch Tower and Tract Society was organized into a corporation.[9] During this period since Russell's founding of the *Zion's Watch Tower,* difficulties with some of his followers began to arise.

---

[8] According to the Witnesses, God gives light so as to give a new, never-before revealed understanding of the Scripture—not new as an addition to the Bible but new light on the understanding. Most of such revelation is very subjective.

In the *Watch Tower,* July 15, 1906 issue, Russell stated his attitude toward some of his earlier efforts: "Some would perhaps like to know my present opionion of them—whether I think them profitable books to loan to truth-seekers. To this I reply, Certainly not; because the very immature views of God's truth therein presented fall far short of what we now see to be God's wonderful plan." *Watch Tower Reprints,* p. 3825.

[9] The organization which Russell founded has since appeared under many names and addresses.

Many early converts seemed to come from fundamentalist groups who for some reason were dissatisfied with their churches. Russell claimed that most of his followers were from Methodist, Presbyterian and Baptist backgrounds. Possibly the acceptance of evolution by many ministers, along with the findings of higher criticism, caused some laymen to join forces with a new movement which opposed both, not realizing the position of the Russellite group on other doctrines. Although only a few ministers came into the fold, those that did so were gladly welcomed.

With the appearance in 1886 of the first volume of the *Millennial Dawn* series, *The Plan of the Ages,* Russell provided the first real foundation and basis upon which all his subsequent theology would be based. This book is still advertised by The Laymen's Home Missionary Movement and The Dawn Bible Students Association as the key text to the *Studies in the Scriptures.* It has a claimed circulation of over 10,000,000 copies.[10] The book teaches that God has one harmonious plan, a plan which gradually was being revealed to man. Besides attacking evolution and the creeds of orthodoxy, it also denies eternal punishment, the Trinity, man's possession of a soul, and the physical return of Christ. Faith in secular governments is discouraged. The second probation theory is also advanced in this book. All men would receive a second chance to be saved on the millennial earth. The other volumes of *Studies in the Scriptures* appeared progressively in 1889, 1891, 1897, 1899, 1904, and 1917.

With more literature being printed and increasing sales, in 1889 the Society moved into a new and larger building in Pittsburgh. This property was held by another firm originated and owned by Russell, the Tower Publishing Company. In 1909 the headquarters was moved to Brooklyn, New York. For this purpose, Russell purchased the old Henry Ward Beecher home and a church known as Plymouth Bethel which was renamed the Brooklyn Tabernacle.

Russell felt that God had revealed His plan to him alone, and that orthodoxy was to be attacked, for it presented not God's plan but Satan's. The "truth" of Russell was then disseminated to "the household of faith."

---

[10] *The Bible Standard and Herald of Christ's Kingdom,* 47:40, May 1966.

For several years Russell's work went almost unnoticed, either because his movement was so small or the threat of his new doctrine was not regarded seriously. Some felt that to bring his teachings into the open would create favorable publicity. Then after 1910 many booklets, tracts, and articles began to appear exposing Russell's doctrine and life. Russell's true character and scholarship were shown for all to see.

The period from 1893 until Russell's death in 1916 was a period of trials and scandals. Stanley High writes: "The doctrine he preached was millennial. But there was very little millennial about his own earthly interlude. He was frequently involved in lawsuits and controversy."[11]

The year 1893 marked arrangements for the first national convention, which was held in Chicago with an attendance of 360. The practice of conventions in key cities continued with both local and national conventions being held. The success and growth of the convention idea can be seen in the conventions of the Jehovah's Witnesses in recent years.

With growth came internal troubles. In 1893, several prominent members of the Society tried to wrest control from Russell, although the conventions tended to hold together the work against attacks both from without and within. Russell's charm and personal magnetism seemed sufficient to convince most of his followers that the attacks against his person were not true.

In 1903 Russell entered into his first public debate, a debate with Dr. E. L. Eaton, a Methodist minister. The book *Jehovah's Witnesses in the Divine Purpose* says, "On the whole, Russell came off victorious for each of the six debates. . . ."[12] Eaton wrote that the report of the *Pittsburgh Gazette* "did not fairly represent my side of the issue."[13] This might well be true. Eaton later wrote an entire book entitled *The Millennial Dawn Heresy* in which he refuted Russell's doctrine.

---

[11] Stanley High, "Armageddon, Inc.," *Saturday Evening Post*, 213:19, September 14, 1940.

[12] *Jehovah's Witnesses in the Divine Purpose* (Brooklyn: Watchtower Bible and Tract Society of New York, Inc., 1959), p. 42.

[13] E. L. Eaton, *The Millennial Dawn Heresy* (Cincinnati: Jennings and Graham, 1911), pp. iii, iv.

In 1908 Russell had another series of debates, this time with L. S. White of the Disciples of Christ. It has been shown in a previous chapter that the victory was claimed for Russell. In reality, Russell did not carry the debate at all. After this debate Russell did not appear on the debate platform again. Some have suggested that the scandals surrounding his life may have been the cause.

After difficulties with his wife, she finally left him in 1897, at which time he supported her and provided her a house in Pittsburgh. In 1903 Russell withdrew his support and three years later Mrs. Russell sued him for separation; the case was won by Mrs. Russell after giving what has been described as "sensational testimony." The decree for separation was explained by the Judge as the same as divorce.

To save the "Pastor" from court action, J. F. Rutherford and four other Bible students raised $10,000 to pay back-alimony.

Concerning Russell's character, as revealed by the court proceedings, Cook seems fair as he writes:

> As to Russell's private character we are disposed to take the charitable view, for after reading the main points of evidence in the suit brought by his wife for divorce, our conclusion is that while he undoubtedly treated her cruelly and un-Christianlike, and acted improperly toward other women, he was not proven guilty of sexual immorality.[14]

Russell was accused of many fraudulent schemes. His famous missionary journey of 1911 and 1912 has been discussed in the previous chapter. The "Miracle Wheat" episode of 1913 probably was the most famous. Russell sued the *Brooklyn Daily Eagle* for $100,000 when the *Eagle* made public facts concerning the sale of the "Miracle Wheat" and also published a cartoon. Russell lost the case. The *Brooklyn Daily Eagle's* interest went far beyond "Miracle Wheat." An interesting point of the testimony concerned the shady financial activities of the Society.

At times some of the things which Russell endorsed would be almost humorous, were it not for the premature death of some who believed in his cures. Russell advertised

[14] Charles C. Cook, *All About One Russell* (Philadelphia: Philadelphia School of the Bible, [n. d.]), p. 5.

cancer cures, and cures for grippe and typhoid, which of course were fraudulent.

Another question often asked deals with Russell's scholarship. Did Charles T. Russell possess the qualifications to discredit all previous scholarship and contradict all other Bible teachers? Did he possess the ability to establish a new theology?

Professor S. A. Ellis, termed a "neutral observer"[15] by Cole, writes of Russell:

> ". . . One of the noblest, grandest characters of all history . . . . As a logician and theologian he is doubtless without a peer today. In his research for Biblical Truth and harmony he is without a parallel in this age. Without a blemish in his character, with the loftiest ideals of God, and the possibilities of man, he towers like a giant, unmatched."[16]

The following quote from *Pastor Russell's Sermons* is typical of the view held by Russell's followers: "But when the history of the Church of Christ is fully written, it will be found that the place next to St. Paul . . . will be occupied by CHARLES TAZE RUSSELL."[17] Rutherford speaks of Russell as "the greatest Bible student of modern times. . .."[18]

From these appellations bestowed upon him (along with Russell's own claims) the investigator would expect to find in Russell a real scholar, a theologian, a tower of morality and honesty—a man unjustly persecuted.

What are the facts? Concerning his early training in school, J. J. Ross relates:

> . . . Under the examination, he admitted that, at the most, he had attended school only seven years of his life, that the public school, and that he had left school when he was about fourteen years of age. . . .[19]

---

[15] Marley Cole, *Jehovah's Witnesses: The New World Society* (New York: Vantage Press, 1955), p. 55.

[16] *The Finished Mystery, op. cit.*, p. 125.

[17] Charles Taze Russell, *Pastor Russell's Sermons* (Brooklyn: International Bible Students Association, 1917), p. 3.

[18] Joseph F. Rutherford, *Millions Now Living Will Never Die!* (Brooklyn: International Bible Students Association, 1920), p. 20.

[19] J. J. Ross, *Some Facts and More Facts About the Self-Styled "Pastor" Charles T. Russell* (Philadelphia: School of the Bible, [n. d.]), p. 18.

While it is certainly true that God has used the uneducated to do great works for Him in fields of evangelism and the teaching of morals, etc., it will be seen from history that when God brought about a reformation or a new movement, He usually used a scholarly Luther or Wesley. The cults today show the consequences of men who have entered into the religious realm without the proper equipment. The "unlearned" fishermen in the day of Christ knew the Hebrew and Greek, which are absolutely essential for one to be taken as an authority on doctrine. That Russell knew neither is court evidence. In order to cover his ignorance in court, he lied and claimed he knew the Greek. When confronted by the Greek alphabet, he was unable to read it. Brown, speaking of several cult leaders, including Russell, writes:

> Each of these religious founders was as ignorant of the dead languages as a woodpecker, and yet each has the effrontery to ask the public to believe that they have gone back to the Scriptures, in their original languages, Greek and Hebrew, and have given to the world the "correct" interpretation of these essential passages.[20]

Although Russell was a prolific writer and certainly an ingenious man, with gifts in business, he was not equipped to undertake the role he claimed.

Van Baalen wisely comments:

> It is true that a child may find the way of salvation in an emphasized gospel of John; it is just as true that there are difficult portions in the Bible the interpretation of which a man should no more tackle without a solid theological education than one should begin to practice medicine or law without studying what medical science or jurisprudence have found in former generations.[21]

Russell's followers however, credited him with being a scholar and a theologian, as well as an historian; his literary efforts were distributed only second to the Bible. None of this impressed W. T. Ellis as he wrote:

---

[20] John Elward Brown, *"In the Cult Kingdom" Mormonism, Eddyism and Russellism* (Siloam Springs, Arkansas: International Federation Publishing Company, [n. d.]), p. 65.

[21] Jan Karel van Baalen, *The Chaos of Cults* (fourteenth edition revised and enlarged; Grand Rapids: Wm. B. Eerdmans Publishing Co., 1951), pp. 193, 194.

> I found not a blazing zealot and a fearless proponent of a peculiar school of biblical interpretation, but a shrewd old man, who probably could not hold a job for a week on the average newspaper. . . .
>
> His knowledge of human nature not only saves him, . . . but also conceals his limitations—theological, historical, literary, geographical, social and economic.[22]

Russell was known for inserting phrases and whole sentences into the heart of Scripture passages. By this method he taught his doctrines. It was in 1913 that the "Great Paraphraser" C. T. Russell, had no words to paraphrase! It all came about when the Rev. J. J. Ross, pastor of James Street Baptist Church, Hamilton, Ontario, published a tract in June, 1912. The tract, *Some Facts About the Self-Styled "Pastor" Charles T. Russell,* brought action against Ross by Russell.[23] On December 2, 1912, Russell issued a summons charging Ross with criminal, defamatory libel. Russell had silenced others this way, but Ross would not back down, for he stood on evidence which could not be refuted.

The following are samples of the charges made in Ross's tract: Rev. Russell was "known as the crank preacher" (p. 3) and that "he never attended the higher schools of learning, knows comparatively nothing of philosophy, systematic or historical theology, and is totally ignorant of the dead languages" (pp. 3, 4). As far as his title was concerned " 'Pastor' Russell was never ordained and has no church affiliation" (p. 4). Concerning Russell's divorce: "In 1887, he married Miss Marie F. Ackley, who divorced him a few years ago on the ground of cruelty and of having wrong relations with other women" (p. 4). Ross then writes: "By 'The Brooklyn Eagle,' he stands charged with defrauding his wife of her dower interest" (p. 6) and of "influencing the sick and dying to make wills in his favor, with engineering the sale of a property worth $35,000 for $50 for the purpose of defrauding another" (p. 6) and "judging from his advertisements of himself, many do not think him normal, and so are persuaded that he is self-deceived" (p. 6). Ross

[22] Ellis, *op. cit.,* p. 1342.

[23] The Tract was combined with other evidence and the results of the trial in a booklet, *Some Facts and More Facts About the Self-Styled "Pastor" Charles T. Russell,* from which the following quotations are taken.

designated Russell's *Studies in the Scriptures* teachings as "the destructive doctrines of one man, who is neither a scholar nor a theologian" (p. 7) and "the whole system of Russellism is anti-rational, anti-scientific, anti-Biblical, anti-Christian and a deplorable perversion of the Gospel of God's dear Son" (p. 7).

Russell's suit, in order to win, needed to prove the charges made were not true, whereas Ross had to prove his charges were true or stand guilty as a "defamer of character."

Ross writes:

> Under oath, he [Russell] positively and most emphatically denied every charge made against him. The leaflet was read part by part to him and he was asked by the Crown Attorney, "Is this true?" His answers throughout were "No, no, no," "Absolutely untrue." . . .[24]

The case came before the Grand Jury of the High Court of Ontario on March 17,1913. The only evidence presented was Russell's own testimony under cross-examination by Ross's lawyer. It is clear from the transcript of evidence that Russell actually perjured himself. Thus, after the jury compared the charges made with the evidence presented by Russell himself, it found no ground for the libel charge against Ross, and handed down the verdict "No Bill."[25]

"The Photo-Drama of Creation," a film presentation with the synchronization of sound on records, produced by Russell at great expense, was first shown in 1914. This seemingly innocent project was just another propaganda weapon. Russell printed a scenario of the entire "Photo-Drama."[26] The frontispiece of the scenario claims that "The Photo-Drama" is "unsectarian and Inter-Denominational." Actually the film is a clever presentation of Russell's theology. The commentary or narrative together with the pictures were successful in winning converts. The creeds of the orthodox churches were misrepresented.

---

[24] Ross, *op. cit.*, p. 17.

[25] Walter R. Martin and Norman H. Klann, *Jehovah of the Watchtower* (sixth revised edition, 1963: Grand Rapids: Zondervan Publishing House, 1953), p. 22.

[26] Published in 1914 under the title: *Scenario of The Photo-Drama of Creation.*

For example, on Russell's favorite denunciation, the doctrine of hell, the following is found depicting orthodoxy: On one page a picture of the frozen section of Dante's Inferno is made a representative view of orthodoxy. The slide immediately under this one is a horrible one, showing the unbelievers' popular concept of Satan with a pitchfork, tail, horns, and a hideously deformed face. Under Satan's feet are seen the skulls of the departed; men are also pictured writhing in fire. In the background there are demons in the likeness of Satan. Under this slide there is the caption: "ADAM AND EVE NOW—CREEDAL THEOLOGY."[27]

On another page a slide is shown which depicts the heathen idol Molech. The statement is found on the page across from the picture that the orthodox creed idols are worse than the idol Molech.[28] It is no wonder that orthodox ministers objected to the showing of "The Photo-Drama." It was rarely presented after Russell's death.

During the last forty years of Russell's life, it is reported that:

> he traveled a million miles, delivered 30,000 sermons and table talks—many of them 2½ hours long—wrote over 50,000 pages . . . of advanced Biblical exposition, often dictated 1,000 letters per month, managed every department of a world-wide evangelistic campaign employing 700 speakers. . . .[29]

Russell maintained his busy schedule up until the time of his death. His last public discourse was given on October 29, 1916, at a convention in Los Angeles. Russell died on October 31, 1916, on a train enroute to Bethel headquarters in Brooklyn. Menta Sturgeon, who accompanied Russell on this journey, called the conductor and porter of the train into the room to watch Russell die. Wrapped in a "toga" made at his own request, Russell passed from this earthly scene in silence.

---

[27] *Ibid.*, p. 11.

[28] *Ibid.*, p. 63.

[29] C. J. Woodworth and George H. Fisher (comp. and ed.), *The Finished Mystery* (Vol. VII of *Studies in the Scriptures,* 7 vols.; Brooklyn: International Bible Students Association, 1917), p. 57.

III. Reasons For Success

How can the success of this man be explained? He lacked education; he was no theologian although he developed his own theology; he was not a scholar; he was plainly a man that at times could not be trusted; he was clearly a perjurer before the courts; he was left by his wife because of his conduct; his teachings denied almost every cardinal doctrine of the Bible. From his claims and those of his followers he certainly was the greatest egotist of his age. The unsound foundation of Russell has formed the cornerstone for the Jehovah's Witness movement and the numerous Russellite sects which are orbiting around the Watchtower Society. Although Russell is dead, the revolt that he founded is still very much alive.

Again the question, why was Russell so successful? The following reasons are suggested: (1) Russell knew human nature and how to control it. His famous "Free-No Collection" attracted many persons. (2) There is no doubt that Russell had a personal magnetism. Some have recounted that with a Bible in his hand he could hold a large audience at attention for several hours. (3) His theology, although not Scriptural, was rational. The rational approach drew many. With such a doctrinal basis even the non-Christian found a ground for agreement. (4) Russell's appeal to Scripture drew many who did not see the wrong usage of the Bible. Davies comments: "It has been established that there are over 5,000 different Scriptural citations in the books of Russell."[30] (5) Russell's key propaganda subject was hell. This subject packed the meetings in many places and drew many who wished to get rid of eternal punishment. (6) His teachings were spread far and wide through the printed page (through newspaper advertisements and the colportage work), by the speaking engagements of Russell and other Watch Tower representatives, through the popular "Photo-Drama," and through both local and national conventions. (7) The mastery of making economical books must also be recognized as a reason for growth. (8) The teachings of Russell offered the down-trodden and the afflicted

---

[30] Horton Davies, *The Challenge of the Sects* (Philadelphia: The Westminster Press, 1961), p. 109.

a time of triumph in the end. He offered a spiritual means to a material end. (9) As it has been brought out before, evolution and higher criticism have been accepted by many ministers, which caused many church members to search for something which opposed such a trend. (10) Russell was convinced of both his claims and his message, and the repetition of his doctrines and claims brought results.

Russell's death left a large void in the Watch Tower organization. Russell had been the Society, and his successor had to be a man of unusual abilities and ideas to salvage a one-man organization which had made all prophecy apply to events in his lifetime. The man to whom the mantle of this self-styled Elijah fell was Joseph Franklin Rutherford, affectionately known as "Judge."

Author's Note

In a reprint edition of Millerite George Storrs' (1796-1879) *Six Sermons* and two other articles, Roy Goodrich concludes that all the major points of "Present Reformation Truth" proclaimed by Pastor Russell were first published by George Storrs in his *Six Sermons* and in the *Bible Examiner*.

For more information on George Storrs see: LeRoy Edwin Froom, *The Prophetic Faith of Our Fathers* (Washington, D. C.: Review and Herald, 1954), IV, pp. 804-09.

Chapter V

THE HISTORY OF THE JEHOVAH'S WITNESSES: THE PERIOD UNDER JOSEPH FRANKLIN RUTHERFORD (1917-1942)

I. Background and Early Years of Administration

Joseph Franklin Rutherford was born in Morgan County, Missouri, on November 8, 1869. There were five girls and three boys in the Rutherford family, Joseph's parents were Baptists. He worked his way through college, studying law. After completing his law education, he was tutored by Judge E. L. Edwards for two years. At twenty he became a court reporter and at twenty-two was admitted to the bar and began to practice law. He acted as public prosecutor and special judge.

In 1894 Rutherford's path was crossed by some Watch Tower pioneers. After purchasing three volumes of *Studies in the Scriptures,* he became interested in the message of the movement. Both Rutherford and his wife[1] immediately started a further study of the new-found doctrines. In 1906 he gave himself wholeheartedly to the movement and by the next year he became legal counselor to the Watch Tower. During this time he also gave public talks as a representative of the

[1] Almost nothing is found concerning Rutherford's wife or his son or their part in the work. In a letter from The Watchtower Bible and Tract Society dated November 30, 1960, the following information is given: "Brother Rutherford did have a wife. She was an invalid, however, and lived on the west coast. This may be partly the reason why she is not mentioned in biographical material as Brother Rutherford spent his time generally on the eastern coast in New York City. His wife did believe in the truth although his son did not."

Watch Tower. He was admitted to the New York bar in 1909 the year the Society moved its headquarters to that state. When Russell died, Rutherford gave the funeral address.

Rutherford's personality in most ways was in direct contrast to Russell's. Russell was always in public view and a popular idol, whereas Rutherford avoided public appearances as much as possible and was seldom photographed. Russell was kind, tactful and warm in his contacts with those about him. The Judge was more direct and sharp, and seemed quite cold, distant and reserved. After his popularity grew, it was almost like challenging Jehovah God Himself to oppose him. At conventions he would appear briefly and then disappear. This mystery which surrounded Rutherford's life accounts somewhat for his success as the leader of the Watch Tower. Like Russell, he had the ability to hold large audiences. Rutherford's senatorial appearance and loud booming voice were added assets which gave the movement the personality it needed. Both Russell and Rutherford were utterly confident of their Scriptural expositions. Rutherford's expositions were built upon the foundation Russell had laid, with Rutherford supplying some deviations as he progressed.

The two years following Russell's death were critical ones for the Watch Tower Bible and Tract Society; there was dissention within and persecution without. During these years thousands of followers left the movement.

The chief task, then, was to select a new president to carry on the work of Russell. Rutherford, the new president, was elected in the corporation meeting held in January, 1917. After a short time in office, he found a loophole in the Watch Tower charter and deposed four Board members who were causing trouble. Rutherford's real reason for enforcing the charter was to determine who should run the Society, because the four directors were attempting to make the entire Board the directing body. Paul S. L. Johnson, who later founded the Laymen's Home Missionary Movement, was another source of trouble.[2]

---

[2] For Johnson's account of the controversy see: Paul S. L. Johnson, *Merariism* (Vol. VI of *Epiphany Studies in the Scriptures*. 17 vols.; Philadelphia: Paul S. L. Johnson, 1938), pp. 7-96.

The book, *The Finished Mystery,* published under Rutherford's direction, was another source of trouble in the Board. The book broadened the gap in the Bethel headquarters, caused much dissension in the local congregations, and paved the way for governmental action against the Witnesses. Before dissenting Board members could act against Rutherford, they were dismissed from office. The Judge was working for absolute conformity on matters of doctrine and organization. The four directors and Johnson were asked to leave Bethel. Many of the ousted directors and other dissenters expelled at this time later formed the Dawn Bible Students Association and others organized the Layman's Home Missionary Movement. Rutherford's purges of opposition continued through his entire administration. This fight for power is very important, for if the Society had been ruled by the Board of Directors, the movement probably would have remained closer to the teachings of Russell. The Dawn group believes that revelation ceased shortly before Russell's death, while the Jehovah's Witnesses stress a progressive revelation which has repudiated in many cases previous doctrines and interpretations of Scripture. The dissenting members were branded the "evil slave class" and they were attacked in *The Watch Tower,* a practice that was followed under Rutherford's entire administration.

In 1918, the government came in and not only seized the publications (later returned) of the Society in Bethel, but in May, 1918, took eight prominent officials into custody. The trials and persecutions of the Bible Students probably were a result of war hysteria. The literature disseminated by the Bible Students revealed they were little concerned with which side won the war.

In 1918, with Bethel closed, the Society members who remained endeavored to continue the work in Pittsburgh. Rutherford and staff remained in jail for nine months. In the spring of 1919 they were released, and in 1920 the indictments were dropped. This period in jail only served to harden the core of the organization and to make more bitter the later attacks on government and religion. The action of the government was looked upon as religiously instigated. During his stay in prison, Rutherford contracted a lung condition which remained with him the rest of his life.

II. Years of Doctrinal Change and Expansion

When Rutherford was released from prison in March, 1919, he found only a skeleton of the organization which was flourishing before the prison term and the closing of Bethel.

In January of 1919 Rutherford had been re-elected president and shortly thereafter he started a reorganization of the work. In October of 1919 *The Golden Age* began to be published. This magazine dealt mostly with social matters, and current events from the Bible Students' viewpoint. Meanwhile, *The Watch Tower* magazine continued its uninterrupted publication. At first Rutherford hewed closely to the Russellite line, but after a few years "new light" came and slowly Russell's writings, person and books were forgotten. No longer was Russell behind the veil "managing every feature of the Harvest work."[3] His position had been usurped!

Rutherford dealt heavily in his brand of progressive revelation, that is, that God had a definite time to reveal certain Biblical facts. Therefore, each of Rutherford's new books revealed some of God's new truth. Rutherford and the Watch Tower organization became God's sole dispenser of truth, for God spoke only in revelation to Rutherford and a choice few who just happened to be in the editorial departmen of *The Watch Tower* magazine.

In early attempts at "new revelation," Rutherford was bound somewhat to definite time predictions in his expositions and books. As he gained experience, time prediction became more vague and he dealt more with light on past fulfillments. Progressive revelation revealed that the Witnesses and their enemies were found in the pages of the Bible, especially in the Old Testament prophets and the book of Revelation. Rutherford also shifted the emphasis of Russell from the atonement and restitution of all things to the vindication of Jehovah's name, which is still the primary emphasis of the Witness movement today. This explains why its message is centered in the Jehovah of the Old Testament and not the Christ of the New Testament. This shift

---

[3] George H. Fisher and Clayton J. Woodworth (comp. and ed.), *The Finished Mystery* (Vol. VII of *Studies in the Scriptures*, 7 vols., Brooklyn: International Bible Students Association, 1917), p. 144.

occasioned the new name, "Jehovah's Witnesses," which also was needed to give the movement distinction from the approximately 40,000 Bible Students that over the years left the movement for one cause or another. The doctrine of vindication of Jehovah came to crystallization in the three-volume set *Vindication,* which is an "exposition" of the entire book of Ezekiel. In line with the doctrine of progressive revelation, Rutherford writes in the Preface of Volume I of *Vindication:*

> Jehovah caused to be written, more than 2500 years ago, what in the Bible is called Ezekiel's Prophecy. During the centuries that prophecy has been a mystery sealed to all who have sought to unlock it. God's due time has come for the prophecy to be understood.[4]

This is the typical approach. The book *Life* begins with a statement in the foreword: "Job is an outstanding character of the Bible. The book bearing his name has long been a mystery, to be understood only in God's time."[5] The signals to the Watch Tower as God's channel must have become garbled, for the message of *Life,* as the previous chapter has revealed, was sent to the scrap heap of discarded expositions a short time after it appeared. The new revelations came so fast that the books could not keep up with them. An advertisement for *The Watchtower* in the rear of the book *Riches* states:

---

[4] J. F. Rutherford, *Vindication* (Brooklyn: Watch Tower Bible and Tract Society, 1931), I, 5. It should be remembered that Rutherford's interpretation of Ezekiel was not the first of the Society's commentaries on the book. *The Finished Mystery* (1917) devoted more than 220 pages to the exposition of Ezekiel. Obviously, a new interpretation was needed as many of the statements in *The Finished Mystery* were out-of-date and did not fit the new positions of the Society. The most prominent figure in the exposition is C. T. Russell and on page 483 the reader is told that Russell was a sign. It is further claimed that Russell was "Christ's representative in the world, the sole steward of the 'meat in due season'. . . ." Rutherford's statement would seem to repudiate the expositions in *The Finished Mystery,* the Preface of which claims that the "book may properly be said to be a posthumous publication of Pastor Russell" (p. 5). Supposedly this book was the subject of Biblical prophecy (pp. 167, 168). Rutherford's statement therefore rejects a text which was prophesied in the Bible!

[5] J. F. Rutherford, *Life* (Brooklyn: Watch Tower Bible and Tract Society, 1929), p. 7.

> Too many and too rapid now are those unfoldings of Bible prophecy and truths, so that books cannot be written and published fast enough by the Watch Tower Society to present them all. But YOU CAN GET THEM in the only magazine of its kind: The Watchtower.[6]

The main purpose of shifting the Watch Tower message from more of a message of Christ, to that of the vindication of Jehovah's name, was to cause the group to grow in spite of rejection. Because, according to the Society, those Bible Students of Jehovah's Witnesses were serving Jehovah directly; they were vindicating His name regardless of whether their presentation met with acceptance or rejection. The Witnesses' book, *Let God Be True,* in commenting on John 1:29, 36, makes clear the secondary importance of Christ's death:

> Thus John showed the secondary purpose for which the Son of God came to earth, namely, to die as a holy sacrifice to Jehovah God in order to cancel the sins of believing men and to free them from death's condemnation. . . .[7]

Vindication of the Father's name first and salvation second is the Watchtower message. This emphasis seems to ignore the fact that the Father's name is vindicated by the salvation of man—if God's name even requires vindication in the eyes of men.[8]

At the convention in Cedar Point, Ohio, in 1922, which 20,000 Witnesses attended, the slogan for advance, "Advertise the King and Kingdom," marked an emphasis which has carried through even to this day. This slogan actually meant to advertise the Rutherford literature, and especially the message of "Millions Now Living Will Never Die"; this message was propagated from one end of the earth to the other.

---

[6]J. F. Rutherford, *Riches* (Brooklyn: Watch Tower Bible and Tract Society, 1936), advertising in rear of text.

[7]*Let God Be True* (second edition; Brooklyn: Watchtower Bible and Tract Society, Inc., 1946), p. 38.

[8]"And if Jehovah must be vindicated, To whom then shall he prove himself supreme? And whose regard does God so highly value that He must vindicate himself before them?" Roger D. Quidam, *The Doctrine of Jehovah's Witnesses, A Criticism* (New York: Philosophical Library, 1959), p. 104.

With the book *Prophecy* in 1929, Rutherford set forth a two-era division of church history pictured by the two prophets Elijah and Elisha. Rutherford writes, "The work of Elijah foretold the work of restoring the fundamental truths to the true Christians. . . ."[9] This first era was the work of Russell and his followers which ended in 1918, whereas the Elisha work began in 1919. Rutherford writes, "Elisha was anointed in the place of Elijah, to carry on and complete the work that Elijah had begun."[10] Those who realize and see this division of time and work will with Elisha "have a double portion of the spirit. . . ."[11] The "double portion" of the spirit was attested by the increase in the Witness work. Rutherford's attempt was to smooth over the disagreements of the old Bible Students so as to enable him to give "new light" and a new mission to the organization.

Opposition to the Judge's new doctrines lacked unity and strength. The Judge kept all opposition off balance by presenting his new doctrines after first laying a careful groundwork in previous volumes and writings. With his "light in due time" and with the Watch Tower as God's channel, none could question his new doctrines. Did not the Judge base it all on Scripture? If some would continue to disagree, they automatically became the "evil slave class," without any hope of eternal life. Because of this threat, many gave up their reactionary thinking and fell into line.

It should be remembered that Russell's prophetic program occupied the period between 1874 and 1914, which put prophecy in a stalemate, for it had run its course. When the Judge reapplied Matthew 24 to the period after 1914, this handicap was removed. Many things could not be understood until *after* 1918 according to the Judge because of the new Elisha period which started then.

---

[9] J. F. Rutherford, *Prophecy* (Brooklyn: Watch Tower Bible and Tract Society, 1929), p. 201.

[10] *Ibid.*

[11] *Ibid.*, p. 202.

With the beginning of the Elisha work all in the group were members of the heavenly class, two divisions being made.[12] There were no heavenly-earthly class distinctions.

The development into various classes[13] within the group was a progressive thing. These classes are recorded by Schnell as he writes: "First to be recognized was the Mordecai-Naomi class, followed from 1922 to 1929 by the Ruth-Esther class, and after 1931 by the unlimited Jonadab class or the people of good will."[14]

These classes, as they evolved, always did so at a lower level. A super class was growing at the same time to overshadow all the other classes. This super class was the Watch Tower Bible and Tract Society, which eventually put all other classes in total dependence upon its doctrinal provender.

The Mordecai-Naomi class was the remnant of the 144,000 on earth which with Christ made up the Watch Tower body of Christ. Because of the large numbers of this class that became unfaithful and became part of the "evil slave class," the Ruth-Esther class came into existence to fill the vacancies left by the defectors.[15] The new class, which evolved after 1931, was known as the "Jonadabs" or the "Great Multitude." This class, formerly a heavenly one, became an earthly class which did not seek after the spirit-begotten or "born again" experience. This doctrinal move was absolutely necessary, for under the old doctrine there was no room for expansion after the 144,000 member figure was filled, and emphasis on a new group was demanded as many new converts were joining the organization.

---

[12] The book, *The Finished Mystery*, identifies the "Great Multitude" as a heavenly group. Commenting on Revelation 7: 4: ". . . Reference is made to another company, also spirit-begotton" (p. 130). See the classes on page 134. The two heavenly groups were the "Little Flock" and the "Great Company." The latter group became an earthly unregenerate class in Rutherford's new interpretation.

[13] The "Mordecai-Naomi" class and the "Ruth-Esther" class are set forth in the book *Preservation* (1932). The "Great Multitude" or "Jonadab" class is discussed in *Preparation* (1933), and *Salvation* (1939).

[14] William J. Schnell, *Thirty Years a Watch Tower Slave* (Grand Rapids: Baker Book House, 1956), p. 43.

[15] *Ibid.*, p. 44.

With the ascendancy of the Society, which started early after Rutherford's administration began, the independent congregations were gradually drawn into the Society's orbit. Slowly the "elective elders" of each congregation were purged and the congregations surrendered their independence. The purging of the "elective elders" and the loss of democratic rule in the individual congregations was looked on by Watch Tower publications as a "cleansing." A gradual process of total "Theocratic" organization was realized in 1938, as the various congregations by resolution signed away their independence.[16]

Other doctrinal developments had been occurring since Rutherford's administration began. Russell's position as "that servant" or "the servant of the Laodicean period of the church" was completely set aside by 1928. The Laodicean period (formerly in Russell's era) became the period from 1919 on and the Watch Tower Society took Russell's position. This latter shift can be seen in the following statement from the book *Theocratic Aid to Kingdom Publishers:*

> His spirit or active force was at work in its production. It is passed to his people through the "faithful and wise servant" as "meat in due season" to strengthen them in the work of gospel-preaching.[17]

In 1928, the Great Pyramid of Gizeh was rejected as a valid Biblical interpretive device, a position which Russell had diligently held.[18] A good reason for Rutherford's rejection might well have been that the Pyramid had been discredited anyway, and the dimensions had been changed in Witness books to keep pace with the altered dates of prophecy.[19] Another reason which forced the rejection was the shift of emphasis from the Elijah to the Elisha period. The great Pyramid had been interpreted by Russell as placing

---

[16] *Jehovah's Witnesses in the Divine Purpose* (Brooklyn: Watchtower Bible and Tract Society of New York, Inc., 1959), pp. 148, 149.

[17] *Theocratic Aid to Kingdom Publishers* (Brooklyn: Watchtower Bible and Tract Society, 1945), p. 9.

[18] See the discussion of the Great Pyramid of Gizeh in *Thy Kingdom Come,* Volume III of *Studies in the Scriptures,* pp. 313-76.

[19] See the discussion and reproductions of the pages from *Studies in the Scriptures* which show these changes in *The Seven Thunders of Millennial Dawn* by B. H. Shadduck, pp. 17-20.

emphasis on 1874 as the beginning of a period of trouble; this did not fit in the emphasis being placed on the period after 1914. Later editions of *Studies in the Scriptures,* volume III, actually did shift the 1874 date to 1915. Rutherford's rejection of the Pyramid "provoked violent criticism from older members of the movement who had grown up under Russell's teaching and many withdrew from it."[20]

Another major switch was seen in the interpretation of prophecy in regard to the Jews. The promises to Israel were interpreted literally by Russell and Rutherford as late as 1929. Literal interpretation was set aside and spiritual interpretation took its place. The new doctrine transferred the promises of the Jews to the "spiritual Israelites," the Jehovah's Witnesses.[21]

The transition from a Christological center of interest to a Jehovah-centered emphasis is evident not only in the name and teachings of the Witnesses, but also in the renaming of *The Watchtower.* In March of 1939, *The Watchtower and Herald of Christ's Presence* became *The Watchtower Announcing Jehovah's Kingdom.*

Along with the more important doctrinal shifts came the refusal to salute the flag, an issue which became important in the United States in 1935. The foregoing doctrinal shifts are some of the main ones made during Rutherford's administration.[22]

---

[20] Charles S. Braden, *These Also Believe* (New York: The Macmillan Company, 1949), p. 362.

[21] This shift is clearly seen in Rutherford's book *Vindication,* in discussing Ezekiel 36: "Therefore this prophecy must have its chief fulfilment upon the true people of God's kingdom which are now on the earth" (II, p. 258). Again, in discussion on Ezekiel 36:8-10: "This prophecy could not be applied properly to natural Israel, but does apply to God's faithful people now on earth" (II, p. 260).

[22] The flag salute controversy is discussed in chapter 8.

Although the present writer does not agree with the doctrinal aberrations of either Russell, Rutherford, or Johnson, Johnson (*op cit.,* pp. 189-730) gives numerous additional examples of changes in doctrine and interpretation. He lists 140 contradictions where Rutherford violates Russell's teaching on pp. 373-76, and then comments: "If we would point out the details coming under point (62) above—'Misrepresenting thousands of verses properly interpreted by "that Servant"'—our list would swell into thousands of details; for almost never does he allude to or quote a passage in an article on his pet views but he corrupts its sense" (p. 377).

Under Rutherford's administration open war was declared on religion, politics and commerce. Schnell writes concerning this attack that it "assailed every concept ever taught in Christianity and attacked practically every practice civilized men of the past 2,000 years have painstakingly evolved."[23] The strongest of vindictive language was hurled at all except the Watch Tower and its followers. The following quotes and summaries are representative:

The book *Prophecy* contains a chapter titled "Satan's Organization" which represents all of Christendom, both Catholic and Protestant, liberal and conservative.[24]

The book *Religion* states that "all religion originated with and is forced upon the people by the Devil and his associate demons. . . ."[25] All forms of worship are included in this statement. (The Witnesses had held until a few years ago that there could not be any true religion.) This book remarks: "Again let the people be reminded that religion is a snare and a racket, originating with the Devil. . . ."[26] On another page one reads: "Like the people of Athens, 'Christendom's' religion is demonism, resulting from the fear of men and the influence of demons."[27]

The book *Enemies* sets forth the adversaries of God. The third chapter, entitled "Religion," lists this as one of the enemies of God. This book radiates Rutherford's hatred as he writes: "All liars and murderers are religionists."[28] "Religion has ever been the chief instrument employed by the Devil to reproach the name of Almighty God and turn the people away from the Most High."[29] The enemies of God are classified as invisible and visible. The visible enemies of both God and man are:

---

[23] Schnell, *op. cit.*, p. 99.

[24] Rutherford, *op. cit.*, pp. 124-72.

[25] J. F. Rutherford, *Religion* (Brooklyn: Watchtower Bible and Tract Society, 1940), p. 104.

[26] *Ibid.*

[27] *Ibid.*, p. 83.

[28] J. F. Rutherford, *Enemies* (Brooklyn: Watch Tower Bible and Tract Society, 1937), p. 118.

[29] *Ibid.*, p. 67.

> Religion, religious organizations, and practioners of religion (in these religious organizations are included thieves, robbers, liars, whoremongers, murderers, man-stealers or kidnappers, frauds, cheats); and all suchlike religion and religious practices being the means of blinding the people to the truth, and using a great mountain of lies behind which the racketeers hide themselves.[30]

The foregoing statements can be considered typical. This attitude of hate caused one writer in 1940 to caption his article on the Jehovah's Witnesses: "Jehovah's Witnesses Make Hate a Religion."[31] Although more tact is now used and the words somewhat softened, the modern-day Witnesses maintain the same attitude.

Nevertheless, during Rutherford's administration the sect grew and prospered. The losses in membership were more than recompensed by the strength of those remaining in the organization. Absolute submission to the demands and doctrines of the "Theocracy" with visible headquarters in Brooklyn, New York, was gained. Literature was pouring from the headquarters at a tremendous volume. Rutherford himself produced more than one hundred books and booklets.

It is interesting to note that the claim of the Society has been that the literature produced was either sold at cost or at a loss. That this was not the case is easy to establish. The literature sales were boosted in order that the work could expand. Each piece of literature sold yielded a nice profit if the following information is reasonably correct. Stanley High relates:

> A writer for the New York Evening Post recently took samples of the Rutherford books and pamphlets to a New York publisher. The publisher reported he could sell the twenty-five-cent books for eleven cents, the pamphlets for two cents, and make a normal profit on both.[32]

If the reporter's information is correct, a rapid check of volumes and publishing figures in the books alone on this writer's shelf—produced on the above margins—would yield

---

[30] *Ibid.*, p. 306.

[31] Stanley High, "Armageddon, Inc.," *Saturday Evening Post*, 213:18, September 14, 1940.

[32] *Ibid.*, p. 53.

a profit of several million dollars. It must also be remembered that the individual book price could be cut down considerably by a cut in labor cost, as the Bethel employees receive almost nothing for their services. Another factor to consider is that some of the earlier books were sold for forty-five cents each, postpaid. The booklets also were printed by the millions.

The literature sales coupled with voluntary gifts were surely more than sufficient to expand the work. This may be one reason why the Society has always been reluctant to open its books, even to its own officers!

When Rutherford died, he left behind him not only a tight-knit, organized "Theocracy," but also a self-propagating and self-indoctrinating organization which has complete control over its members.

III. Reasons for Rutherford's Success

What are some of the main reasons for success under Rutherford? (1) He had the ability to unite the loose congregations under the one "Theocratic" dictatorship. (2) Rutherford's administration thrived on expectancy: the "Millions Now Living Will Never Die" campaign, the expectancy which was built around the soon-returning princes who were due to arrive in 1925 (and who were still due when Rutherford died), and the expectancy stirred up by the book *Children* which placed the end just around the corner. (3) Rutherford's legal training helped him hold control of the organization over would-be usurpers of power. His legal training helped him to hold the ignorant who were coming into the organization. (4) The principle of stating something often enough until people believe it was certainly proven under Rutherford's reign. "Two years before his death, which occurred in 1942, he claimed that over three hundred million copies of his writings had been circulated."[33] (5) Every member was a minister and many gave generously of their time. (6) Jerome Beatty, in 1940, after observing the Witnesses in meetings and reading their literature, wrote:

---

[33] J. Paul Williams, *What Americans Believe and How They Worship* (revised edition; New York: Harper & Row, Publishers, 1962), p. p. 440.

> The rank-and-file members, I am convinced, sincerely believe that Judge Rutherford is leading them toward a delightful and exclusive, heaven-on-earth. The practices which have stirred public demonstrations against them spring from a blind faith in their leader rather than from any subversive conspiracy. . . . The judge trumpets forth his individual interpretations of the Bible, and none of his followers ever questions them.[34]

Beatty also observed:

> Most of the witnesses I saw were obviously longing for contentment, rest, and security. . . . Hating all political leaders, they find in Judge Rutherford a lift that helps them through their misery.[35]

These are some of the reasons for success under the administration of Judge Rutherford, who died at the age of seventy-two, after twenty-five years as president of the Watch Tower Bible and Tract Society.

---

[34] Jerome Beatty, "Peddlers of Paradise," *American Magazine*, 130:53, 54, November, 1940.

[35] *Ibid.*, p. 71.

CHAPTER VI

THE HISTORY OF THE JEHOVAH'S WITNESSES:

THE PERIOD UNDER NATHAN HOMER KNORR

(1942 to present)

With Rutherford's death in 1942, there seemed to be no halt in activities in the headquarters of the Watchtower Bible and Tract Society. The work of Rutherford's administration had united the loosely knit organization, and there was nothing to do but to elect a successor.

The choice of the directors was Nathan H. Knorr, who actually ran the Brooklyn Office the last few years of Rutherford's life. Knorr was born on April 23, 1905, in Bethlehem, Pennsylvania. At the age of sixteen he associated himself with the Allentown, Pennsylvania, Bible Students, and after graduating from high school in 1923 he took a job in Bethel.

After a short time at Bethel, in which he rapidly advanced in Biblical training, he acted as a representative of the Society, giving lectures in and around Brooklyn. He quickly advanced in Bethel and in 1932 served as factory production manager, after having acted as co-ordinator of printing activities. In 1934 he became a director of the New York corporation; he also was a member of the editorial staff. The next year he was elected vice-president. In 1940 he became vice-president of the Pennsylvania corporation. After Rutherford's death he was elected president of both American corporations as well as of the International Bible Students Association of England. Each of these positions are lifetime.

Less conspicuous than Russell and Rutherford, he is both a writer and speaker. Under his leadership the Witness movement has forged forward with youthful enthusiasm and a vigorous program of expansion. Knorr regards his distinctive position as having an educational emphasis. It seems from the results that Knorr is also a brilliant administrator. President Knorr has done a thorough job of remodeling the Watchtower Society.[1] When Knorr took the movement in hand in 1942 there were just over 115,000 Witnesses; by 1975 there were over 2,000,000.[2]

Under the new administration the average Witness has been trained in general Bible knowledge.[3] Under Rutherford the average publisher did not know much about the Bible, because all he needed to do was to play the phonograph or present Rutherford's book or booklets. Under Knorr the Witnesses have been trained in their doctrine and in better methods of presentation.

The Theocratic Ministry School was established in 1943 to train the men of each congregation in public speaking and in the use of Bible aids. A portion of this training was devoted to argumentation.[4] In 1958 women were also able to register in the school, and in place of delivering talks they were permitted to demonstrate door-to-door witnessing procedure.

In 1943 the Watchtower Bible School of Gilead was founded in South Lansing, New York. This school ran two classes each year, with five months training for each class. A prerequisite for application was that the candidate had spent at least two years in full-time witnessing work. Of the many applications, the hundred best candidates were selected for each class. Upon graduation these students were sent at the Society's designation to fields foreign or home. Gilead was moved in 1961 and

---

[1] William J. Whalen, *Armageddon Around the Corner* (New York: The John Day Company, 1962), p. 70. Whalen entitles his chapter (pp. 68-80), "President Knorr Remodels the Watchtower."

[2] *The Watchtower*, 96:27, January 1, 1975.

[3] Two examples of the emphasis on general knowledge of the Bible are the books *Equipped For Every Good Work* (1946) and *All Scripture Is Inspired of God and Beneficial* (1963). Both volumes are essentially simplified Bibical introductions with some added treatments on various Biblically related subjects.

[4] See for example, *Theocratic Aid to Kingdom Publishers* (1945), pp. 201-19 and *Qualified to be Ministers* (1955), pp. 197-207.

> the Gilead School in Brooklyn now has a ten-month course through which it is training mature ministers to care for this large organization of preachers that has been built up in other lands.[5]

Along with the training program, the Society had also been pushing *The Watchtower* and *Awake!* The Watchtower Society has followed in the footsteps of its founders in the printing of new books.[6] In 1957, to keep pace with the huge publication increase, a new thirteen-story printing plant was completed. A ten-story addition to the printing establishment was completed in 1967.

The year 1950 marked the appearance of the first volume *(New World Translation of the Christian Greek Scriptures)* of the new Bible translation, the *New World Translation of the Holy Scriptures.* The last volume of the Old Testament appeared in June of 1960 and the entire Bible was brought together in one volume in 1961. As Russell and Rutherford had crystallized their thought and doctrine in their books, just so the Watchtower Society has made its translation reflect the Witnesses' doctrinal views.[7]

Since 1950, "The New World Society" has become a title in common usage. The title describes the body of the Jehovah's Witnesses since they form the future earthly society in the new world.

The Society has come into closer contact with each congregation. Watchtower representatives take more time to individually train each minister in his preaching activity. Another method which came into use was the development of sermons to be used in house-to-house and "back-call"[8]

---

[5] *The Watchtower,* 83:636-37, October 15, 1962.

[6] See Appendix C for texts published during the Knorr administration.

[7] See chapter 10 for further information on the *New World Translation.*

[8] A "back-call" is a return visit to the home or other place where a previous contact has been made by the Witness. "Back-calls" are made as follow-ups to literature placements, or if any interest is shown. A total of 89,903,578 back-calls were recorded for the 1968 service year. *The Watchtower,* 90:25, January 1, 1969. This figure grew to 151,171,555 in 1974.

work. This sermon by each individual minister takes the place of the record ministry under Rutherford.[9]

"The New World Society" is growing because of its tremendous advertising. Missionary work in foreign lands is also expanding rapidly. This is shown by the increase in the workers reporting, as well as the expansion and construction of buildings in many of the foreign branches. Another move for growth and expansion was the construction of a new eleven-story headquarters building in Brooklyn, dedicated in October, 1960. This also included the new Gilead school. All evidence points to a program of world-wide work and expansion.

Hayden C. Covington, the legal council of the Watchtower until several years ago, cannot be overlooked as a key figure in the rise and growth of the Jehovah's Witnesses. Covington joined the legal staff in Brooklyn in 1939. He waged numerous court cases for the Witnesses, with many fought before the Supreme Court. His record was one of almost complete success. Schnell reports the story of Covington's severance from his post:

> Our pipeline into the inner sanctum of the Society began appraising us of increasing differences between Knorr and Covington—by 1963 there were open quarrels, sometimes so loud they could be heard four floors below. In fact, this continuing quarrel became the spice of every meal in the Bethel family. Covington wanted the Society to cease opposing the State and desired a moral cleanup in the Bethel home. Knorr was for the

[9] In 1953 the Watchtower Society published *Make Sure of All Things* (revised, 1957). This 415-page book is a topical Bible handbook which helps the Witness in his presentation of the Watchtower Society's doctrine. (See Chapter 12 for more details on this book.) More recently, a smaller (32 pp.) booklet, *Sermon Outlines* was published. This booklet contains 60 subjects. Each subject is broken down into one or more sections, each section being a sermon. Some 244 different sermons are in this small booklet which easily slips into a Bible. With this preplanned message or argument at his disposal the Witness can easily defend his doctrine and cite the quotations for his position which gives the impression that he is well-versed in the Bible. This writer has noticed that in correspondence with Witnesses the above mentioned publications have been a source for verbatim copied comments on doctrine. In 1965 an expanded handbook much like *Make Sure of All Things* was published. The work is entitled: *Make Sure of All Things; Hold Fast to What Is Fine.*

> *status quo*, so our informers alleged. Finally, Covington was forced to resign and assume a private practice.[10]

Covington's name has appeared recently (1967) as the attorney for Cassius Clay (Muhammad Ali) in his fight against the military draft. The *New York Times* reported that Covington filed a suit against Clay for legal fees of $284,615.[11]

To better understand the drawing power and the appeal of the Jehovah's Witnesses this analogy made by Roger Baldwin, head of the American Civil Liberties Union, a defender of the Witnesses in Court, is cited:

> . . . "The Jehovah's Witnesses are a gauge of the world's despair and disgust with civilization. The Communists promise despairing people immediate reform and privileges here on earth. The Witnesses promise them immediate reform and privileges in a Next World which is just around the corner. That's what draws in the converts."[12]

In 1955, Werner Cohn published an article in *The American Scholar* entitled "Jehovah's Witnesses as a Proletarian Movement." This article, which is based on his master's thesis, characterizes the Witnesses as a proletarian sect. He uses proletarian "to describe a movement which lives in, but is not of, a given society."[13] If one accepts Cohn's thesis, then much of the success of the Witnesses should be found

---

[10] Mass-distribution letter from the Christian Mission To Jehovah's Witnesses (March, 1967), headed "Operation Liberation: A Confidential Report."

[11] *New York Times*, October 17, 1967, p. 51.

[12] Bill Davidson, "Jehovah's Traveling Salesmen," *Colliers*, 118:72, November 2, 1946. Catholic Albert Muller, a recognized expert on the Jehovah's Witnesses, further analyzes the appeal of the group and mentions the following: (1) "Some persons will be attracted by the glitter of a sect that makes a little man feel important." (2) Some are discontented with their religion. (3) Many find comfort in a no eternal hell doctrine. (4) Some are drawn to the prospects of an everlasting utopia on earth. (5) Others are inclined toward pacifism. (6) Some are disgruntled "with the world and seeking an early end of it. . . ." (7) "Others, tending toward radicalism, find an outlet for their emotion. . . ." (8) "The intensive study of the Bible and the warmth to be enjoyed in the brotherly community of this sect appeals to many others." Albert Muller, "Jehovah's Witnesses Call," *Homiletic and Pastoral Review*, (reprint): 681, May, 1963.

[13] Werner Cohn, "Jehovah's Witnesses as a Proletarian Movement," *The American Scholar*, 24:282, Summer, 1955.

among individuals or groups that consider or find themselves outside the mainstream of society. One such group is the American Negro. In another article by Cohn in *The Crisis* he stated that "Witness doctrines find a particularly fertile soil in the Negro community."[14] In the same article, he explains his estimate of the typical Witness and the reason for the appeal of the group to the Negro:

> Jehovah's Witnesses constitute a protest organization of the spiritually disinherited. People belong to it who have a vague and general feeling that the world is no good for one reason or another, they think of themselves as having been left out of things. Witness doctrines make a powerful appeal to this feeling of being excluded. And given a world in which negroes actually are excluded from many of the benefits of society, it is indeed not surprising to find many of them in this kind of protest organization.[15]

As a final observation on the reasons for the growth of the Witnesses at the present time, Catholic scholar John A. O'Brian is cited. O'Brian was conducted on a tour of the Bethel printing plant and upon completion he wrote his article "Jehovah's Witnesses: A Visit to Headquarters," in which he concludes:

> What is the explanation of their astonishing increase? It is the missionary zeal that prompts them to call at every home in their respective communities once or twice a year. It is their publication of unprecedented quantities of propaganda and their willingness to stand on street corners to sell it. It is their willingness to instruct families in their own homes and stay until they become active members.[16]

Subsequent chapters of this text further develop this period of history of the Jehovah's Witnesses.

---

[14] Werner Cohn, "Jehovah's Witnesses and Racial Prejudice," *The Crisis,* 63:6, January 1956. In this article Cohn estimated that of the Witnesses in America "about half are Negro" (p. 5). Whalen recorded that "estimates of the percentage of Witnesses in the United States who are Negroes range from 20 per cent to 30 per cent. At any rate, the proportion is considerably higher than among the general population." Whalen, *op. cit.,* p. 203.

[15] *Ibid.,* p. 9. For a further analysis dealing with those who join the New World Society and why, see: Whalen, *op. cit.,* pp. 191-206.

[16] John A. O'Brian, "Jehovah's Witnesses: A Visit to Headquarters," *Catholic Digest,* 27:63, December, 1962.

CHAPTER VII

THE HISTORY OF JEHOVAH'S WITNESSES:

A PERIOD OF TRANSITION

Many points of transition found in the Watchtower Society have been discussed and touched upon thus far. This chapter brings together the various transitions mentioned with some additional information.

1. In this latest administration a shift has been seen in personality emphasis. Although Knorr probably enjoys the same powers as his predecessors, Russell and Rutherford, he is not always in the forefront as they were. The writings of the group are now anonymous.[1] There are no prominent names of men on the lips of the Witnesses as previously. The names of men have given way to such names as "The New World Society."

2. There is also an evident transition in some of the terminology used by the Witnesses, for example, the term "religion." Rutherford wrote in his book *Enemies* (1937):

---

[1] Only a few in the leadership of the Society know who writes the books and other publications. Correspondence from the Society is not signed, but rubber stamped "Watchtower Bible and Tract Society." Occasional by-lines are given to Bethel workers or pioneers giving their testimony of happiness as a Jehovah's Witness. (For examples see *The Watchtower* April 1, 1963; March 15, 1963; January 15, 1966; March 1, 1966.) These testimonies are important to the Watchtower Society since there are many thousands who have left the movement that have just the opposite to recount. Many former Jehovah's Witnesses have directed scathing attacks upon the Society which expose the Society as an organization of fear and domination. See the testimonies included in chapter 14.

> There is no such thing in existence as "the Christian religion," because all religion proceeds from God's enemy, the Devil. "Christian religion" is a misnomer, fraudulent and deceptive. . . . Religion is entirely out of place in the church of God.[2]

The book *Theocratic Aid to Kingdom Publishers,* one of the training manuals used in the Theocratic Ministry School, says of religion: " 'Religion' is the doing of anything that is contrary to Jehovah's will."[3] Another chapter relates: "The practice of religion or demon-worship . . . has for its purpose the turning of mankind away from worship of the true God, Jehovah."[4]

In the book *What Has Religion Done for Mankind?,* the transition is seen. The twenty-sixth chapter is titled "Pure Religion Alone Survives the World's End." Another page states: "Jehovah's King who now reigns A. D. 1914 is highly interested in religion."[5]

In the Jehovah's Witness vocabulary the term "religion" is now quite respectable.[6]

Other shifts in terminology are seen. Local assemblies were termed "companies," which name was changed to "congregation." The leader of each company was "a company servant," this being changed to "congregation servant." The designation "minister" is also a sign of transition of terminology. The former designation for all regular workers was exclusively "publisher." "Publisher" is still used, but there is a new emphasis on "minister."

3. There is a definite transition seen in the building program of the Witnesses. This is seen both locally and in

---

[2] J. F. Rutherford, *Enemies* (Brooklyn: Watch Tower Bible and Tract Society, 1937), p. 130.

[3] *Theocratic Aid to Kingdom Publishers* (Brooklyn: Watchtower Bible and Tract Society, 1945), p. 284.

[4] *Ibid.,* p. 288.

[5] *What Has Religion Done for Mankind?* (Brooklyn: Watchtower Bible and Tract Society, Inc., 1951), p. 324.

[6] According to the *Edinburgh Evening News,* January 7, 1955 issue, the Jehovah's Witnesses would be "legally recognized as members of a religious denomination. . . ." This judgment was given after a nine-day test case which cost the Witnesses $14,000. The Witnesses were now a *religious* denomination! In the testimony, Vice-President F. W. Franz even referred to the organization as "our sect." BTTBW publication 306, pp. 1-4.

the Society headquarters and branches. The local congregations of Jehovah's Witnesses a few years ago met mostly in homes and rented halls. More and more communities are witnessing the establishment of a modern Kingdom Hall. Among the latest buildings built in Brooklyn was the new headquarters, with the latest and most elaborate appointments. The Witnesses are thus planning to indoctrinate the world.

4. A transition from an untrained to a trained ministry is seen. The standards of training are not the same as orthodox churches would require, but are sufficient to equip the Witness in presenting the Watchtower message. The educational program makes the Witness more efficient in working with Watchtower materials. The Theocratic Ministry School, The Watch Tower Bible School of Gilead, and the new Gilead training for administrators all point to an educational program. Since 1959 the presiding ministers of the congregations known as "congregational servants" or "overseers" and other special representatives of the Watchtower Society have received a special one-month training course. New presentation aids have also been produced.

5. The last few years have witnessed a transition from a despised religious group to one which yet has its enemies, but is now socially acceptable, and even acceptable to certain representatives of Christianity.[7]

---

[7] The article by Pete Martin, "Pete Martin Visits a Family of Jehovah's Witnesses," (*Christian Herald*, 89:23-25, 42-49, 76-79, April, 1966) is an example of the kind of treatment the Witnesses now receive from the Christian press. The article was valuable propaganda for the group. In a recent letter from W. J. Schnell (5/66) he stated that an article which was written by another author and submitted to the *Christian Herald* which would have balanced the favorable treatment of the Martin article was rejected with the statement: "'This would never do to appear together with the interview we had Mr. Martin write about Jehovah's Witnesses.'" In concluding the article Mr. Martin said: "While I accept almost none of their doctrines, I am sure of this much: they are Dedicated, and you have to spell that with a capital D. They believe. I mean, *really believe!*" (p. 79). To this statement Schnell commented: "All I can say to this is that here is more eloquent proof just how far the spirit of ecumenicism will drive our moderns and liberals in Christendom to embrace even its worst enemies. . . ."

In the last paragraph of Schnell's letter an amazing example of the current trend is given: ". . . In the face of a Jehovah's Witness

6. A transition is being seen in the social classes being reached by the movement. More of the middle class members of society are going into the movement. The Witnesses are even reaching some college graduates, a group formerly little influenced. But the outreach to this group is still exceedingly limited. Whalen comments:

> But the caliber of membership in the Society seems to be rising. Some recruits have been baptized from the ranks of white-collar workers, craftsmen, physicians, although most Witnesses continue to engage in factory work, farming and unskilled labor. Hardly any hold college degrees. . . .[8]

7. A further transition is seen in the doctrines of the group. This must be the case because of the belief in progressive revelation. Many passages of Scripture have been reinterpreted. For example, new light came in 1950 concerning the "princes." These were originally such men of old as Abraham, Isaac and Jacob, etc. They were expected for many years, but they never did come. The outstanding members of the group today can also become "princes" because of their work.[9] Another significant change relates to the interpretation of who the "superior authorities" (NWT) of Romans 13:1-7 are. The accepted interpretation until November 1, 1962 was that "The Superior Authorities are the Most High God Jehovah and his exalted Son Jesus Christ." The new interpretation makes the "superior authorities" human governors and governments, a complete reversal of the former position.[10]

---

circuit convention, the churches of this area courageously organized mass meetings, inviting the undersigned to fly there and speak. But this pastor and his church disassociated themselves from sponsoring this rally. And he did even more: he visited the company servant of Jehovah's Witnesses and *apologized* for the action of his fellow-ministers!"

[8] William J. Whalen, *Armageddon Around the Corner* (New York: The John Day Company, 1962), p. 204.

[9] Compare *Let God Be True* (first edition) pp. 258-261, with the 1952 revision pp. 263-65. See also *Jehovah's Witnesses in the Divine Purpose* (Brooklyn: Watchtower Bible and Tract Society of New York, Inc., 1959), p. 252.

[10] For the former interpretation see *This Means Everlasting Life* pp. 196-99. For the new interpretation see *The Watchtower*, November 1, 15 and December 1, 1962.

8. The Watchtower Society and the average Witness now seek worldly recognition in the realm of scholarship. This shows a definite reaction to contemporary influences. Accepted scholars are eclectically appealed to and quoted.

9. There is also a transition in the publication of the cult's history, a subject which formerly was little dealt with. The last fifteen years have produced more written history of the group than all the other years combined.

10. The Witnesses' "message" approach is more developed and tactful. The individual ministers now have a previously prepared door-to-door and back-call sermon.

11. A further transition may be found in the way the Watchtower Society treats its members who leave the Society. In the days under Rutherford, a person of any consequence who differed from the stand of the Society was attacked in *The Watchtower*. The new way of handling such individuals is total silence—an ignoring of the individual. This is illustrated by the silence concerning the work of William Schnell, a former prominent member of the Society headquarters. This does not mean, however, that former Witnesses who were disfellowshiped or who defected are not attacked among the Witnesses in private.

12. During Rutherford's administration, Negroes attended their own segregated assemblies. In the summer of 1958, Everett C. Parker covered the Witnesses' "Divine Will International Assembly" in New York City. He reported some of his impressions as follows:

> An outside observer was mightily impressed by two things: the unfailing good humor of the delegates and the complete racial and national equality evidenced everywhere. Negroes, whites, Orientals mingled freely, talked, traveled and ate together.[11]

In the September 17, 1958 issue of *The Christian Century* Werner Cohn wrote a letter of rejoinder to Mr. Parker's impression of the racial situation. His interesting letter is quoted almost in full:

> SIR: Your New York city correspondent (Aug. 20) was understandably but nevertheless unfortunately

---

[11] Everett C. Parker, "News of the Christian World," *The Christian Century*, 75:954, August 20, 1958.

mislead when he wrote of the "complete racial and national equality evidenced" among Jehovah Witnesses. It is true that nowadays Witnesses of various races intermingle at international conventions. But this is an innovation of recent years. Before that, separate conventions were held for Negroes and whites. Witness publications have repeatedly defended South Africa's official *apartheid*. Furthermore, when I did research on the Witnesses in 1953 and 1954 I found that all southern and most border states had separate local congregations for Negroes and whites. This held as far north as Asbury Park, N. J. I also found that although the American membership of the organization was approximately 50 per cent Negro, the top leadership was completely white. . . .

I do not say that the Witnesses constitute a very aggressive force for prejudice or segregation. But neither is it true, as Witness leaders try to make it appear in the north, that the sect stands in the forefront of racial brotherhood. Despite their eccentric and cantankerous theology, Witnesses tend toward quite commonplace and pedestrian attitudes on race.[12]

It can be concluded then that the policies of the Witnesses toward the racial question have changed.

In summary, then, transitions are seen in: personality emphasis, terminology, the increased educational program, the educational and social classes being reached, social acceptability, doctrines, the seeking of world recognition, historical enlightenment, the presentation of the message, the treatment of the Jehovah's Witnesses that leave the movement, and segregation policies.

---

[12] Werner Cohn, "Letters to the Editor," *The Christian Century*, 75:1055, September 17, 1958.

CHAPTER VIII

A SUMMARY OF WHAT THE JEHOVAH'S WITNESSES BELIEVE

In the following summary of the essential doctrines of the Jehovah's Witnesses, the attempt has been to present their doctrines as they have stated them. The treatment is not intended to be comprehensive, but rather selective.[1] Documentation for each point is taken from Witness sources.[2]

I. SOURCE OF AUTHORITY: THE BIBLE

The Bible is the Word of God and is truth.[3] The Bible was recorded through men of God by verbal, plenary inspira-

[1] For a comprehensive study of the doctrines of the Jehovah's Witnesses the reader is referred to the following: *The Four Major Cults*, by Anthony Hoekema, pp. 237-371. This book, by an able theologian, gives one of the best studies on the theology of the Witnesses. In his treatment he refutes many of the contentions of the group. The present writer is indebted to Dr. Hoekema for some ideas in the handling of the material included in this chapter. This chapter is also published in a separate volume: *Jehovah's Witnesses* (Eerdmans, 1972).

A brief outline presentation is found in *Jehovah of the Watchtower* (sixth revised edition, 1963), by Martin and Klann, pp. 30-43. *Jehovah's Witnesses; Who They Are, What They Teach, What They Do*, by Royston Pike, has an excellent section on doctrine under "What They Teach," pp. 30-87.

[2] All entries, unless otherwise noted, will refer to Watchtower publications. The footnote entries will also be abbreviated.

[3] For comprehensive studies of the Witnesses' view of the Bible and Bible books see: *Equipped for Every Good Work* (1946). This book is the equivalent of a Biblical introduction. The book *All Scripture Is Inspired of God and Beneficial* (1963) is the most recent and complete treatment, updating and expanding the areas of the foregoing text. *From Paradise Lost to Paradise Regained* (chapter 7) and *Let God Be True* (Chapter 4, revised ed.) have briefer treatments.

tion. The apocryphal books are not part of the Canon and should be rejected. The correct designation of the Old Testament is "Hebrew Scriptures," and of the New Testament, "Christian Greek Scriptures." God's distinctive Biblical name is "Jehovah."

Concerning the Bible, it is declared:

> It is true. It is never proved to be false and thrown aside as not worth anything. So we can depend on what God's Word, the Holy Bible, tells us. By inspiration He wrote it for us. We should study it and believe it and obey it.[4]

The Bible is viewed as the final source of authority: "There can be no question about it: The Holy Scriptures of the Bible are the standard by which to judge all religions."[5] The foregoing quotations clearly lead one to believe that the Bible is given a high place by the Witnesses and that it is accepted by the group as the ultimate standard in religious beliefs.[6]

Although the Watchtower Society uses many versions of the Scriptures, the *New World Translation of the Holy Scriptures* has come to occupy a position of authority in the writings of the group.[7]

II. Doctrine of God

Definition and attributes. The book *Make Sure of All Things* gives this definition of God, whose distinctive name is Jehovah:

---

[4] *From Paradise Lost to Paradise Regained,* p. 68.

[5] *What Has Religion Done for Mankind?* p. 32.

[6] Although the stated position is sound, the interpretations of the Bible by the Watchtower Society supplant the clear teachings of the Scriptures. Hoekema's comment is to the point: "Instead of listening to Scripture and subjecting themselves wholly to its teachings, as they claim to do, they actually impose their own theological system upon Scripture and force it to comply with their beliefs." Anthony Hoekema, *The Four Major Cults* (Grand Rapids: Wm. B. Eerdmans Publishing Company, 1963), p. 238. See chapter 11 for a discussion of the methods of interpretation employed by the Witnesses.

[7] A full treatment of this important Watchtower translation is given in chapter 10.

> Greatest Personality in the universe, distinguished by that exclusive name. The Great Theocrat, the Unfailing Purposer, the True and Living God, Creator and Supreme Sovereign of the universe.[8]

God is a spirit, invisible, personal, eternal. He is holy, a God of goodness and mercy, grace and truth. His principal attributes are love, wisdom, justice and power.[9] God is omniscient, omnipotent, immutable, but he is not omnipresent.[10]

Jehovah's vindication is the major theme and primary purpose of history according to the Jehovah's Witnesses. This becomes evident from their statements: "His vindication is more important than the salvation of men."[11] Again, "Since vindication of Jehovah's name and sovereignty is the foremost doctrine of the Bible, his name and kingdom find first place in the model prayer."[12]

How was God's universal sovereignty transgressed and how will God's vindication be accomplished?

> Adam and Eve lost their relationship as God's children in his universal organization when they joined in the rebellion against Jehovah's universal sovereignty.
>
> . . . Yet today the great issue before all heaven and earth is, Who is supreme? Who in fact and in right exercises the sovereignty over all the universe? Jehovah's primary purpose is to settle this issue. To do so means the vindication of his universal sovereignty or dominion.
>
> . . . When Jehovah thus vindicates his universal sovereignty by destroying all his foes in heaven and in earth, then he will be again the great Theocrat or theocratic Ruler over all creatures that live.
>
> . . . God's name must eventually be sanctified by Jehovah's own stupendous act of vindicating himself at the universal war of Armageddon.[13]

The foregoing quotations indicate that although love is viewed as one of the principal attributes of God, love is subordinated to God's vindication which places stress on His power and justice.[14]

---

[8] *Make Sure of All Things*, p. 188.

[9] *Ibid.*

[10] *Ibid.*, p. 191.

[11] *Let God Be True*, (revised ed.), p. 29. All subsequent quotations will be from the revised edition.

[12] *Ibid.*, p. 163.

[13] *Ibid.*, pp. 27-29.

[14] For a fuller development of this point see: Hoekema, *op. cit.*, p. 260.

Denial of the Trinity. The unity of God is strongly held, but by unity the Witnesses mean "there was, therefore, a time when Jehovah was all alone in universal space."[15] God was not the Father until His first creation: "Until his first creation Jehovah God was sonless; by it he became a father."[16]

The Trinity is viewed as *"a false, unbiblical doctrine."*[17] As to its origin, the Trinity is "ancient Babylonish paganism c. 2200 B. C. Brought into the deflected 'Christian church' about the second century, being especially established in the Nicene Creed, A. D. 325."[18]

As to the authorship of the doctrine of the Trinity, the Witnesses claim "that God was not the author of this doctrine. . . . The obvious conclusion is therefore, that Satan is the originator of the trinity doctrine."[19]

On Christ's relation to the Godhead in John 1:1-3 the Witnesses argue:

> Does this mean that Jehovah God (*Elohim*) and the only begotten Son are two persons but at the same time one God and members of a so-called "trinity" or "triune god"? When religion so teaches it violates the Word of God, wrests the Scriptures to the destruction of those who are misled, and insults God-given intelligence and reason.[20]

Denial of the personality of the Holy Spirit. The Holy Spirit is not a person but is an impersonal force: "So the holy spirit is the invisible active force of Almighty God which moves his servants to do his will."[21] In the Subject Index of *Make Sure of All Things* there are no entries under "Holy spirit," but a note says: "See Active force." This conception has been incorporated into the *New World Translation* where the word "spirit," when applied to the Holy Spirit, is never capitalized.

---

[15] *Let God Be True, p.* 25.
[16] *New Heavens and a New Earth,* p. 24.
[17] *Make Sure of All Things,* p. 386.
[18] *Ibid.*
[19] *Let God Be True,* p. 101.
[20] *The Truth Shall Make You Free,* p. 45.
[21] *Let God Be True,* p. 108.

God's works, creation. Jehovah created all that exists.[22] His first creation was Jesus Christ through whom He created all other things:

> He is not the author of the creation of God; but, after God had created him as his firstborn Son, then God used him as his working Partner in the creating of all the rest of creation.[23]

The spirit realm was created before the material universe.[24] The creation of the universe took place billions of years ago.[25] The creative days in Genesis 1:2 ff. transpired less than 48,000 years ago. Each day is 7,000 years in length. The days of creation are explained:

> In fact, they were great periods of time thousands of years long. Measured by the length of the "seventh day," on which God desists from work and is refreshed, each of those days was 7,000 years long. Man being created toward the close of the sixth day, he was put on the earth toward the end of 42,000 years of earth's preparation. So in the course of time the grand cycle of seven "days" will add up to 49,000 years. The Bible time-schedule indicates that slightly more than a thousand years of this cycle remains yet to be run.[26]

Evolution as God's method of creation is rejected.[27]

---

[22] *Make Sure of All Things,* p. 78.

[23] *Let God Be True,* p. 33.

[24] *Make Sure of All Things,* p. 79.

[25] *Your Will Be Done on Earth,* p. 43. The booklet, ***What Do the Scriptures Say About "Survival After Death"?*** is specific on the age of the universe: "Unknown time before he created our 4½-billion-year-old visible universe Jehovah made his first creation" (p. 58).

[26] *Let God Be True,* p. 168. Until the publication of the book *The Truth Shall Make You Free* (1943) it had been taught that 6,000 years had ended in the 1870's (notice above: "slightly more than a thousand years of this cycle remains yet to be run."). *Studies in the Scriptures,* II, p. 33. Russell wrote the following in 1904: "How long is it since Jehovah ceased, or rested in, his creative work? We reply, that it is now a little more than six thousand years." *Studies in the Scriptures,* VI, p. 49.

[27] *Let God Be True,* chapter 7, "Why Evolution Cannot Be True"; *Did Man Get Here By Evolution or By Creation?*

III. SATAN AND THE ANGELS

Under the Father's direction the Son created other spirit creatures. The three classes are cherubim, seraphim and angels. These are all spirit sons of God. "They were all sons of God because of receiving life from Jehovah and by his only begotten Son, the Word."[28] By the agency of the Son, God created Lucifer* as another glorious spirit son. Each spirit son of God had a definite duty. Christ also was an angel, the archangel Michael.[29] "From his superiority over the other angels the prehuman first-born Son of God could be called an 'archangel'."[30] Lucifer, having rebelled against God, became Satan. Satan then turned to his angelic charge, corrupted them, and caused them to fall and become demons. Satan directed the demons who followed him into an organization. The most aggressive and capable were given a superior position and became demon princes, invisible rulers over the political powers which would rise in the earth. The remainder of the fallen spirits were placed under the demon princes as intermediaries between them and man. In 1914 Satan and his demons were cast out of heaven and restricted to the vicinity of the earth.[31] Satan's task is to persecute the earthly "seed of the woman," the Jehovah's Witnesses, and to cause mankind to remain outside the "New World Society" and perish. Satan and his demons are all doomed to annihilation. After the millennium they will be cast into the lake of fire: "That spells absolute and endless destruction for them."[32] "The ultimate end of Satan is complete annihilation."[33]

IV. DOCTRINE OF MAN

Man's original state and nature. Man was created in the image of Jehovah God, and became God's earthly son: "So man was made in God's image by being given some of

---

* The Witnesses no longer believe "Lucifer" to be a personal name for Satan. *The Watchtower,* 86:406, 407, July 1, 1965.

[28] *The Truth Shall Make You Free,* p. 52.

[29] *The New World,* p. 284.

[30] *New Heavens and a New Earth,* p. 28.

[31] *Ibid.,* p. 284.

[32] *Ibid.,* p. 355.

[33] *Let God Be True,* p. 64.

the qualities God has, qualities that were not given to animals."[34] Man was created perfect.

Contrary to the teachings of orthodoxy, man does not possess a soul:

> . . . Man is a combination of two things, namely, the "dust of the ground" and "the breath of life." The combining of these two things (or factors) produced a living soul or creature called *man*.[35]

The doctrine of the immortality of the soul finds its origin with Satan: "Thus it is seen that the serpent (the Devil) is the one that originated the doctrine of the inherent immortality of human souls."[36]

Man's fall and the consequences. The disobedience of Adam to God's command recorded in Genesis 3 was an historical event. Jehovah's instruction to man is recorded in Genesis 2:16, 17:

> And Jehovah God also laid this command upon the man: "From every tree of the garden you may eat to satisfaction. But as for the tree of the knowledge of good and bad you must not eat from it, for in the day you eat from it you will positively die" [NWT].

If Adam, who was created perfect, had not disobeyed God, he would not have died:

> Adam disobeyed this command of God and brought upon himself and his posterity the condemnation of death. Had perfect Adam not sinned, it would have been possible for him, though mortal, to live on earth forever and to bequeath life to his children.[37]

In addition to death for man as a penalty for sin there were other results: "That which was lost was perfect human life, with its rights and earthly prospects."[38] The earth was cursed and Adam and Eve were expelled from Eden.[39] A further result to Adam's posterity was inherited sin, imperfection, and disease.[40] Man was placed in a state of disability

[34] *From Paradise Lost to Paradise Regained*, p. 19.
[35] *Let God Be True*, p. 68.
[36] *Ibid.*, pp. 74, 75.
[37] *Ibid.*, p. 74.
[38] *Ibid.*, p. 114.
[39] *Let Your Name Be Sanctified*, pp. 42, 43.
[40] *What Has Religion Done For Mankind?*, p. 63.

which had not existed before.[41] The final penalty for man's disobedience was to be annihilation.[42]

How disabled was man as the result of the fall? It is evident after reading numerous Watchtower publications which deal with Adam's disobedience, and its consequences, that the Witnesses hold a very weak view of sin. This is concluded because unregenerate man (the Great Multitude does not seek the "born again" experience) is capable of pleasing God with his works.[43]

V. Doctrine of Christ: His Person

Anthony Hoekema points out that "in order to understand Jehovah-Witness teaching on the person of Christ, we shall have to distinguish between a prehuman, a human, and a posthuman state."[44] The following presentation uses these three categories.

The prehuman state. "Jesus, the Christ, a created individual, is the second greatest Personage of the universe."[45] The coequality with the Father is denied:

> Prior to coming to earth, this only-begotten Son of God did not think himself to be co-equal with Jehovah God; he did not view himself as "equal in power and glory" with Almighty God. . . .[46]

Christ, as the archangel Michael, was "a god," a mighty one, but not God.[47]

---

[41] *Let God Be True*, p. 119.

[42] *New Heavens and a New Earth*, p. 84.

[43] A weak view of sin naturally stems from a rejection of eternal punishment and a denial of the deity of Christ. It should be remembered that under Russell's theology, as under the present Watchtower regime, eternal life is gained by the merit of the individual. Hoekema also questions the reality of the Witnesses' claimed "disability" as the result of the fall and states: "I conclude that, though Jehovah's Witnesses appear to teach an inherited disability on account of Adam's sin, their theology belies this assertion. For a 'disability' which enables unregenerate man to have true faith, to dedicate his life to God, and to remain faithful to Jehovah is no disability at all!" Hoekema, *op. cit.*, p. 269.

[44] Hoekema, *op. cit.*, p. 270.

[45] *Make Sure of All Things*, p. 207.

[46] *Let God Be True*, p. 34.

[47] *Ibid.*, pp. 32, 33, 106.

Christ did not possess immortality:

> Did this firstborn Son possess immortality, that is deathlessness? That he did not have this quality and was not immortal at that time is proved by later facts as well as plainly stated in the Bible. . . . The time came, however that Jehovah God opened up to his Son the opportunity to gain immortality.[48]

The human state. From the standpoint of orthodoxy, one commendable doctrine concerning Christ, accepted by the Witnesses, is His virgin birth: ". . . God miraculously transferred his life from heaven to the womb of a Jewish virgin, Mary of Bethlehem."[49] Yet, the incarnation and the two natures of Christ are denied and it is taught that Jesus (while on earth) was a perfect man, nothing more, nothing less.

> A divine miracle occurred when Jesus was "made flesh". He was not an incarnation in flesh, but *was* flesh, a human Son of God, a perfect man, no longer a spirit, although having a spiritual or heavenly past and background.[50]

"Incarnation" is defined and applied in *Make Sure of All Things:*

> . . . A clothing, or state of being clothed, with flesh; taking on, or being manifested in, a body of flesh. Scripturally, it describes the condition of angels appearing to mankind on earth. *False religion* claims it is the "union of Christ's divinity with his humanity."[51]

At his birth the Son of God became a man, Jesus, and he became "the Christ" or Messiah, only at his baptism. "By pouring out his holy spirit upon the baptized Jesus, God anointed him with the spirit to be the long-promised King . . . Jesus became the Messiah. . . ."[52] It was at his baptism that Jesus was "born again."[53]

The posthuman state. The bodily resurrection of Christ is rejected. Christ Jesus "was resurrected as a spirit crea-

---

[48] *The Truth Shall Make You Free,* p. 44.
[49] *New Heavens and a New Earth,* p. 150.
[50] *The Kingdom Is at Hand,* p. 49.
[51] *Make Sure of All Things,* p. 179.
[52] *Let God Be True,* p. 38.
[53] *The Watchtower,* 75:681, November 15, 1954.

ture."[54] Concerning what happened to the body of Christ, there is mostly silence in the latest books. Russell wrote: "Whether it was dissolved into gases or whether it is still preserved somewhere as the grand memorial of God's love, of Christ's obedience, and of our redemption, no one knows. . . ."[55]

The writer of the *Awake!* article, "In What Body Did Jesus Appear?" explains:

> His human body, the one in which he was impaled, was removed from the tomb by the power of God. Had it remained there it would have been an obstacle in the way of faith of his disciples, who were not instructed in spiritual things until the giving of the holy spirit later at Pentecost.[56]

Several reasons for the resurrection of Christ were:

> One reason was to reward Jesus for his faithfulness. . . . Jesus Christ was also raised from the dead so that he could turn over to God the right to human life that he had kept by dying faithful. . . . Jesus was also raised from the dead that he might restore Paradise. . . . And above all, Jesus was raised from the dead that he might uphold God's rulership by destroying all the wicked in God's due time.[57]

Since the "resurrection"[58] of Christ was a spiritual one, his post-resurrection appearances were accomplished by materializing bodies for the occasion:

> Usually they could not at first tell it was Jesus, for he appeared in different bodies. He appeared and disappeared just as angels had done, because he was resurrected as a spirit creature. Only because Thomas

---

[54] *From Paradise Lost to Paradise Regained*, p. 144.

[55] *Studies in the Scriptures*, II, p. 129. See also, *The Watchtower*, 74:518, September 1, 1953, where it is stated: "What happened to the perfect fleshly body of Jesus after his death? . . . The Scriptures answer: It was disposed of by Jehovah God, dissolved into its constituent elements or atoms."

[56] *Awake!*, 36:26, June 8, 1955.

[57] *From Paradise Lost to Paradise Regained*, pp. 144, 145.

[58] This writer agrees with Hoekema and others that the Witness view of the resurrection of Christ is no real resurrection at all and should be placed in quotation marks. Their view would more correctly designate a new creation.

would not believe did Jesus appear in a body like that in which he had died.[59]

Since none but God had immortality, it was given to Christ at his resurrection: "Christ Jesus was first to receive immortality as a reward for his faithful course on earth. . . ."[60] His ascension is viewed as that of a spirit creature. As he ascended in the presence of his disciples he disappeared from sight.[61]

In his exaltation "God exalted his son Jesus to be higher than he was before he lived and died as a man."[62] In this new state of exaltation "Jesus is made the Head under Jehovah of God's capital organization over the entire Universe."[63]

VI. Doctrine of Christ: His Work

The ransom. The doctrine of the atonement, more commonly termed "ransom" of Christ is accepted as *"a true Bible doctrine."*[64] It is defined as

> that which buys back, loosens or releases, providing deliverance from trouble, distress and calamity, or more especially, releasing from inherited sin and from prospects of eternal death as a result of sin.[65]

The ransom for man's sin was provided by Jehovah God in sending his Son Christ Jesus to earth to provide "through

---

[59] *From Paradise Lost to Paradise Regained,* p. 144.

[60] *Let God Be True,* p. 74.

[61] *Ibid.,* pp. 34, 40.

[62] *Ibid.,* p. 40.

[63] *Ibid.* Hoekema's conclusion to the study of the Person of Christ as viewed by the Witnesses is helpful: "I conclude that what the three states of Christ's existence in Watchtower theology really amount to is this: angel—man—angel, with no real continuity between the three. A little reflection will reveal how devastating this view is of the Christology of the Scriptures. The individual who laid down his life at Calvary was not the individual who existed previously in heaven and was God's agent in creation: the individual who is now ruling over his heavenly Kingdom is not the individual who died on the cross for us. Really, Jehovah's Witnesses have three Christs, none of whom is equal to Jehovah and none of whom is the Christ of the Scriptures." Hoekema, *op. cit.,* pp. 275, 276.

[64] *Make Sure of All Things,* p. 294.

[65] *Ibid.,* pp. 293, 294.

him and his death a redemptive price."[66] The work of Christ is that of a perfect man who gave his life on the torture stake (they do not use the word "cross") as a sacrifice for sin:

> God made his beloved Son a perfect man, and Jesus was faithful, went into death, and was afterward resurrected by God's power and exalted to heaven, there presenting to God the merit or value of his perfect human life.[67]

The death of Christ provided an exact payment ("corresponding ransom") for that which was lost:

> Yet we know that Jesus came to earth to provide a corresponding ransom by his perfect human life. The ransom, therefore, must be equal to the thing lost, namely, perfect human life as Adam had it in Eden. . . . God's justice would not let Jesus, as a ransom, be more than a perfect man.[68]

This perfect human life once sacrificed could not be taken back again without nullifying its redemptive power.[69]

Who is ransomed? Adam is not included in the number ransomed because he sinned willfully: "He had perfect life, and this he deliberately forfeited. There is no provision in God's ransom for Adam."[70] Cain is also outside the ransom.[71] Each individual determines whether the benefits of the ransom will be received. "Those willfully wicked and hardhearted toward Jehovah's provision do not have ransom merit and life forced upon them . . . ."[72] Those who do not experience one of the resurrections are outside the ransom.[73]

In conclusion, the Witnesses' view of the atonement is very different from that held by orthodoxy and in essence is a rejection of that Biblical doctrine.

---

[66] *Let God Be True*, p. 113.

[67] *Ibid.*, p. 117.

[68] *Ibid.*, pp. 105, 106.

[69] *Ibid.*, p. 116.

[70] *Ibid.*, p. 119. This is a departure from the teaching of C. T. Russell and the earlier position taken by J. F. Rutherford in *Reconciliation* (pp. 323, 329), etc.

[71] *The Watchtower*, 86:174, March 15, 1965.

[72] *Let God Be True*, p. 120.

[73] *Make Sure of All Things*, p. 296.

VII. Doctrine of Salvation

In a discussion of soteriology as understood by the Witnesses one must distinguish between two classes: (1) "The Congregation of God," with a heavenly calling and whose hope is to live and reign with Christ,[74] and (2) the "Great Crowd," with an earthly hope. They will live on a restored paradise earth. Since the vast majority of Jehovah's Witnesses are in this class,[75] primary consideration is given to how the members of this calling gain eternal life.

Salvation for the Great Crowd. Salvation is not completed by faith, although faith in Jehovah God and Jesus Christ are required: "God's will is that, to make good his salvation to everlasting life, the believer must be a preacher in this world."[76] Actually, salvation is realized by works:

> Accepting the message of salvation and devoting ourselves to God through Christ and being baptized in water is only the beginning of our exercise of faith. . . It sets us on the way to everlasting life, but it does not mean our final salvation.[77]

---

[74] This class is also designated: "Body of Christ," "Bride of Christ," "Chosen Ones," "Elect," "Holy Nation," "Israel of God," "Kingdom Class," "Anointed," "Little Flock," "New Creation," "144,000," "Remnant," "Royal House," "Royal Priesthood," "Sanctuary Class," "Sons of Levi," "Spirit Begotten," "Spiritual Israel," and "Spiritual Sons."

The selection for the anointed class is according to God's choice. The heavenly calling was first extended in A. D. 29 and is viewed as rapidly nearing its end. Salvation for this class differs from that of the Great Crowd in the following respects: (1) They sacrifice "all human life right and hopes, even as Jesus did." (2) They are presently justified by faith in the ransom. (3) They are born as spiritual sons of God by God's holy spirit and are baptized into Christ's body and receive of his anointing. (4) They are sanctified by God, but sanctification must be maintained by their works. *Let God Be True,* pp. 298-303.

[75] This class is also commonly designated as "Great Multitude" and "Other Sheep." The ones partaking in the annual Lord's Evening Meal on April 12, 1968 amounted to only 10,619 out of an attendance of 2,493,519. The smaller number would represent the living members of the Congregation of God which remains. *The Watchtower,* 90:26, January 1. 1969.

[76] *This Means Everlasting Life,* p. 137.

[77] *Ibid.,* p. 181.

As would be expected, the Witnesses attack the security of the believer: "The popular religious expression, 'Once saved, always saved!' is false and dangerous."[78]

Willful sin of a Jehovah's Witness brings destruction:

> God will destroy all who willfully entangle themselves again in sin for the selfish pleasure it gives the depraved flesh. Their being associated with the Theocratic organization which is in the way of salvation will not save them or excuse them, but it means their greater responsibility.[79]

In the popular text, *From Paradise Lost to Paradise Regained,* the following steps are listed in order to gain paradise and life: (1) "If you want to receive God's blessings you must study his Bible."[80] (2) Association with the Witnesses is essential to salvation:

> What is the second of the things that you must do to get ready for life in the new paradise? You must meet with other people who have this same knowledge and faith, for these today make up a New World society.[81]

This point is summarized: "Remember that meeting with the people who really study such good things of God's Word is a thing that you must do to gain God's favor and life in the new paradise"[82] (3) In this point men's cooperation with God for salvation is taught:

> The third thing that you must do in order to receive God's favor is to change your living from the former way to God's way. You must repent of the things that you have done that were wrong. You must ask Jehovah to forgive these wrong things. You must accept Christ's ransom through which this forgiveness is possible. And you must dedicate your life to Jehovah, deciding to belong to him and to serve him and to do things his way.[83]

As one that is dedicated to God, the convert must also be a preacher and a witness to survive Armageddon: "Only the preachers of God's kingdom can expect to be protected dur-

---

[78] *Ibid.*

[79] *Ibid.*, p. 187.

[80] *From Paradise Lost to Paradise Regained,* p. 242.

[81] *Ibid.*, p. 244.

[82] *Ibid.*, p. 246.

[83] *Ibid.* Dedication requires baptism.

ing the end of this world and to live through Armageddon into the new world."[84]

The new birth. When Jehovah's Witnesses are asked if they believe in the new birth, they can truthfully say, "Yes." But the inquirer must go deeper and ask who receives this new birth. In John 3:3 Jesus spoke of being "born again." Witnesses state that "it is a gross twisting of the Scriptures to throw open Jesus' words at John 3:3 to make them embrace all mankind."[85] The ones that must be "born again" are the members of the 144,000 or Congregation of God because these have the heavenly hope: "The only ones who are 'born again' are the 144,000, together with their Head, Christ Jesus, who make up the Kingdom."[86]

The Great crowd does not need the new birth: "This 'great crowd' of people are not 'born again,' nor do they need to be 'born again,' because they gain everlasting life on the earth."[87]

VIII. Doctrine of the Ordinances

Two ordinances are viewed as enjoined by the Word of God. These are baptism and the Lord's Evening Meal.

Baptism. Water baptism is required as a necessary step of obedience for all followers and it is defined and explained as:

> Complete submergence, immersion, dipping. . . . Christian water baptism is an outward symbol, as a testimony before witnesses, of the baptized one's complete, unreserved and unconditional dedication and agreement to do the will of Jehovah God, the Universal Sovereign, through Christ Jesus his King. It means his own will is buried (as by the immersion in water) and he comes up from the water to do only God's will and walk in newness of life thereafter.[88]

---

[84] *Ibid.*, p. 249.

[85] *The Watchtower*, 75:681, November 15, 1954.

[86] *Ibid.*, p. 683.

[87] *Ibid.*, p. 682. The twofold division of the Witnesses into an earthly and a heavenly class makes much of the Bible of little or no meaning to the majority of the Witnesses. This is true because much of the New Testament only has application to the anointed class. The Witness doctrine on this point robs its followers of the only means for peace, joy and entrance into the Kingdom of God.

[88] *Make Sure of All Things*, p. 27.

Three reasons are given for baptism by total immersion: (1) The meaning of the word baptism. (2) Baptism is likened to burial. (3) The early Christians employed only immersion.[89]

The Lord's Evening Meal. The Lord's Supper is a memorial of the death of Christ replacing the passover celebration. The only ones to partake of the Supper are the anointed class. "Those who comprise the great crowd of other sheep, not being members of Christ's body, do not partake of the Lord's evening meal."[90] Unleavened bread and fermented wine are used in the observance of this memorial.[91] Although only a small number partake of the elements all Jehovah's Witnesses and "persons of good will" are urged to attend.

IX. Doctrine of the Last Things

The "return" or "second presence" of Christ. The first official presence of Christ began with his baptism in Jordan and continued until his death three and one-half years later. Before the ascension he promised to "return." The purpose of the promised "return" was "to establish his kingdom,[92] to rule amidst his enemies, to judge the nations and to bring

---

[89] *Awake!*, 38:5, 8, February 22, 1957. For the anointed there is also "a baptism into 'Christ's body'." *Let God Be True*, p. 300.

[90] *The Watchtower*, 78:199, April 1, 1957.

[91] *Ibid.*, p. 198.

[92] It is important to understand specifically what the Witnesses mean by the "Kingdom of God." The best brief definition is found in *Make Sure of All Things*, p. 226: "The Kingdom of God is a Sovereign-empowered theocratic government under an administration of divinely appointed Kings. Jehovah himself is the great Everlasting King. (1 Tim. 1:17; Rev. 15:3; Jer 10:10) He has taken into association as coregent his Son Christ Jesus. God has purposed the Kingdom as the capital or ruling part of his universal organization. It is comprised of the King Christ Jesus and 144,000 associate kings taken from among men. It is entirely heavenly, having no earthly part. All becoming members must be resurrected and given spirit bodies. At times the term 'kingdom' is applied to the one (in the Scriptures, Christ) who has the rank, quality, attributes and authority of a king. The term also is used to refer to the realm over which the Kingdom government exercises control. This Kingdom began operation in full power with the enthronement of Christ in the heavens, A. D. 1914." For a further discussion of the subject see *Let God Be True*, pp. 134-44.

salvation and deliverance to faithful mankind."[93] The nature and time of this event is further explained:

> This second presence (*par-ou-si'a*) of Christ the Messiah was to be invisible and the unmistakable sign he gave shows conclusively that this return of Christ began in the year 1914. Since that time Christ has turned his attention toward earth's affairs and is dividing the people and educating the true Christians in preparation for their survival during the great storm of Armageddon. . . .[94]

Since the "return" was an invisible one, it can only be "recognized by the eyes of one's understanding. . . ."[95] "Today the evidence of Christ's presence is all about us, and yet so-called 'Christendom' does not see it."[96] The year 1914 also marked that time when Satan was cast out of heaven to the earth, and the end of the Gentile times.[97] The period which began in 1914 and is continuing at the present time is the "end of the world." What is meant by this expression?

> So the "end of the world" does not mean the end of this world in destruction. If it did there would be no need to raise up witnesses for the "end of the world."
>
> The Bible term "end of the world" means, here, a new time period, the "time of the end" of this old world. This time period had its beginning in 1914; it will close when this world ends in destruction. So 1914 marked the beginning of the "time of the end" for this world.[98]

Before the "accomplished end" (the close of the "time of the end") Matthew 24:14 must be carried out: " 'And this good news of the kingdom will be preached in all the inhabited earth for the purpose of a witness [for a witness, 1961 ed.] to all the nations, and then the accomplished end will come [the end will come, 1961 ed.]' " (NWT).

---

[93] *Make Sure of All Things*, p. 319. "Return" is enclosed in quotation marks because Christ's coming was neither visible, physical or actual.

[94] *Ibid.*

[95] *Let God Be True*, p. 198.

[96] *Ibid.*, p. 199.

[97] *Ibid.*, pp. 201, 202. Specifically how the 1914 date and the beginning and end of the Gentile times were determined is discussed in chapter 9.

[98] *From Paradise Lost to Paradise Regained*, p. 174.

Christ's coming to the spiritual temple. The year 1918 marked the appearance of Christ at the spiritual temple:

> . . . He came to the spiritual temple as Jehovah's Messenger and began to cleanse it. . . . That marked the beginning of the period of judgment and inspection of his spirit-begotten followers.[99]

At this time the "spirit-begotten" members of Christ's body that had already died, were raised and joined him. The rest of the body members will join him as they die.[100]

The Resurrections. The Witnesses' definition of resurrection reflects their view of death being a cessation of existence:

> Resurrection is a restoration to life of the non-existent dead. . . . It is an act of God dependent entirely upon God's marvelous power through Christ and upon His memory of the dead. It is the reactivating of the life pattern of the creature, a transcription of which is on record with God, and is referred to as being in His memory. . . . Hence, according to God's will for the creature, in a resurrection one is restored or re-created in either a human or a spirit body and yet retains his personal identity by the setting in motion of the distinctive life pattern of that individual.[101]

In addition to the resurrection of Christ which made the other resurrections possible the Witnesses distinguish additional resurrections which are distinct as to who are raised, the manner of resurrection and the time.

1. The "first resurrection" (or "earlier resurrection") is spiritual and applies to Christ and the 144,000. None of these members were raised until 1918, after the second "return" of Christ. Being a spiritual "resurrection" indicates that it was invisible to human eyes and that those raised were raised with "spirit bodies." Since all the members of Christ's body had not died before 1918, those of the "remnant" "receive an immediate change to spirit life" when they die.[102] Some of the "remnant" will not experience death and this change until during the millennium.[103]

---

[99] *Let God Be True,* p. 202.

[100] *Ibid.,* p. 203.

[101] *Make Sure of All Things,* p. 311.

[102] *Let God Be True,* pp. 203, 278.

[103] *Babylon the Great Has Fallen! God's Kingdom Rules!,* p. 637.

2. The next resurrection in time sequence is an earthly one (i.e., to earthly life), and is designated the "resurrection of life." These individuals will be raised with physical bodies and will include: (1) those faithful witnesses before the death and resurrection of Christ, and (2) the "other sheep" who have died before Armageddon. This resurrection will occur early during the millennium.[104]

3. The last earthly resurrection, which occurs later during the millennium, is the "resurrection of judgment" which includes

> those persons whose hearts may have been wanting to do right, but who died without ever having had an opportunity to hear of God's purposes or to learn what he expects of men. Many of these have been decent people. They may have been sincere in their belief. But still they "practiced vile things."[105]

More on these last two resurrections is included in the discussion of events during the millennium.

The separation of the "sheep" and the "goats." Since Christ's coming to the temple in 1918 the judgment of the nations began. The people of the nations are being separated into two classes which are called the "sheep" and the "goats" (based on Matt. 25:31-33.). The "goats" are destined to destruction. The "sheep" or "other sheep" are in line for eternal life. How is one's status determined? "One's attitude toward the remnant of Jehovah's annointed witnesses and the message of his theocratic government reveals one's attitude toward Jehovah's installed King."[106] A short time yet remains until the separation will be finished, and then follows the Battle of Armageddon.[107]

The Battle of Armageddon. This battle is the "most terrific war of all time,"[108] in which Jehovah will remove all wickedness from the universe:

---

[104] *Let God Be True*, pp. 279, 280; *From Paradise Lost to Paradise Regained*, pp. 228, 229.

[105] *From Paradise Lost to Paradise Regained*, p. 229.

[106] *Let God Be True*, p. 204.

[107] *Ibid.*, p. 205.

[108] *You May Survive Armageddon into God's New World*, p. 30.

> It will completely destroy the invisible and visible parts of Satan's world and thus it will spell the accomplished end of this wicked old world. It will be the climax of the tribulation which Jesus predicted. . . .[109]

Fighting against God will be the Devil and his demons along with all the nations of the earth. "Fighting on the side of Jehovah will be Christ Jesus and all the armies in heaven. Christ will lead heavenly armies of powerful angels."[110] The Jehovah's Witnesses will have no part in fighting the battle.[111]

Armageddon will begin just after the Devil attacks the New World society which he hates because of its growth, happiness and peaceful condition. "Gog the Devil uses the nations and rulers of the earth to attack the New World society."[112] The attack really is an attack on God's kingdom which calls for a showdown fight and "the settling of the question, Who rules heaven and earth?"[113] All those outside the New World society will perish along with Satan and his demons. More than two billion will die.[114] "Not a human on the side against Jehovah's theocratic organization will survive. None of their dead will be given a decent burial in memorial tombs."[115] Dead bodies will be found from one end of the earth to the other and will be eaten by the worms, birds and beasts until nothing is left except the bones. These bones will be gathered by the Armageddon survivors who will bury them to cleanse the earth.[116] Satan and his demons will be placed in the abyss. What is this abyss? "For Satan and his demons a thousand years in the abyss will mean a millennial deathlike powerlessness and inactivity."[117] The abyssing of the Devil and his demons marks the end of Armageddon.[118] "Armageddon is over. Gone now are the invisible troublemakers! Gone are all the nations! Gone are all

---

[109] *Let God Be True*, p. 259.

[110] *From Paradise Lost to Paradise Regained*, pp. 204, 205.

[111] *Ibid.*

[112] *Ibid.*, p. 206.

[113] *Ibid.*, p. 207.

[114] *You May Survive Armageddon into God's New World*, p. 341.

[115] *Ibid.*, pp. 342, 343.

[116] *Ibid.*, pp. 343, 344. * The burial of bones by Armageddon survivors is no longer taught, Jehovah will accomplish the disposal. *The Nations Shall Know that I am Jehovah—How?* (1971), p. 377.

[117] *Ibid.*, p. 346.

[118] *Ibid.*

the goatlike people! Gone is the old world—gone forever! A new world begins."[119]

The millennium, Messiah's thousand-year reign. During the thousand-year reign the 144,000 will reign and rule with Christ from heaven.[120] The earth will be cleansed and become a paradise under the direction of Jehovah. Conditions for growth will be perfect, and the people on the earth will be taught how to plant and tend the garden.[121] Conditions on earth will be perfect with all that had harmed man or that made him sad removed. Violence and wickedness will not exist and men "will be at peace with themselves, with their neighbors and with their God. They will be at peace even with the animals."[122]

Further happiness will be brought to the dwellers upon the earth by the birth of children to the Armageddon survivors who were married, or who marry, during the millennium.[123] Although these children will be born free of birth defects they will not be perfect, and they must be taught in the ways of Jehovah. When the earth reaches a point where it is filled, "people will stop having children, and no more children will be born."[124] The earth will have been filled by three groups:

> There will be (1) the people who will have lived through Armageddon, (2) the children who will have been born to them and (3) other people . . . who will have been brought back from their graves to live in the paradise earth.[125]

The earthly "resurrection of life" and "resurrection of judgment" have already been discussed, but there are several details of these events which should be included here. First to be raised will be the "princes" who will be theocratic rulers (these are faithful men of old such as Abraham, David, Moses, etc.). They will be joined early by the "other sheep."[126]

---

[119] *From Paradise Lost to Paradise Regained,* p. 211.

[120] *Ibid.,* p. 218.

[121] *Ibid.,* pp. 220, 221.

[122] *Ibid.,* p. 222.

[123] *Ibid.,* p. 223; *Let God Be True,* p. 269.

[124] *From Paradise Lost to Paradise Regained,* p. 225.

[125] *Ibid.,* p. 226.

[126] *Ibid.,* p. 232. Some of the "other sheep" who survive Armageddon, along with some who are resurrected will also be "princes."

"Later, in God's own time, the people who receive the 'resurrection of judgment' will return from the memorial tombs."[127] With the raising of billions of "unrighteous dead" a tremendous educational effort will be necessary to teach them God's law. Those who obey receive life, those who disobey are annihilated.[128] The Jehovah's Witnesses are even now preparing for the educational work during the millennium. In his address to the graduating class of Watchtower Bible School of Gilead on November 23, 1964, president Knorr pointed out that

> not only would the missionaries help the people to whom they preached, but at the same time they would be receiving training for the expanded work during Christ's 1,000-year reign, when the billions of dead will be resurrected and will need instruction and training.[129]

The willfully wicked have no resurrection. These would include such as Adam and Cain, those who perished in the flood, those of the "evil slave" class (former Jehovah's Witnesses), and those who fight against God in Armageddon.[130]

The judgment day. The "judgment day" is a one thousand-year day of judgment which is directed toward the inhabitants of the millennial earth. The subjects of this judgment and the result of disobedience are explained:

> Those who come forth to a "resurrection of judgment" will be judged during the thousand years of Christ's reign. . . some of the people who are resurrected for judgment, or some who are born as children to the people who live through Armageddon, still may refuse to serve God. Anyone who refuses to obey God's kingdom after a long-enough trial will be put to death.[131]

The final judgment. The final judgment or test comes at the end of the thousand-year reign of Christ. By this time paradise and man will have been fully restored to per-

---

[127] *Ibid.*, p. 233.

[128] *Ibid.*, p. 229.

[129] *1966 Yearbook*, p. 52.

[130] *The Watchtower*, 86:174-76, March 15, 1965; *From Paradise Lost to Paradise Regained*, p. 236.

[131] *From Paradise Lost to Paradise Regained*, p. 237. This judgment then relates to what a person does during the millennium and not what he has been doing during his lifetime.

fection. All dwellers upon the earth will be subjected to the test.[132]

The last test will occur as Satan and his demons, who were abyssed at the beginning of the millennium, are loosed for a little while. Satan's nature will have remained the same and his attempt will be to lead the men upon the earth away from God. These that follow after Satan's rebellion will be destroyed by fire from heaven and Satan and his demons will also suffer the same fate.[133]

In conclusion:

> By the execution of judgment after this one last test the perfect earth will be cleansed. Everyone who would ever disobey Jehovah will be gone. Everyone who remains will have proved that he will really obey God forever. . . . Never again will there be even a single case of rebellion or disobedience against him anywhere on earth![134]

Jehovah's sovereignty over all his creation will have been vindicated![135]

The final state. The Witnesses strongly deny the doctrine of eternal punishment. Commenting on the origin of the doctrine of hell they write:

> The false conception of eternal torment after death was introduced into apostate Christianity, and by the fourth century after Christ was firmly entrenched in false religion. It is based on Satan's original lie in Eden.[136]

It is argued that the doctrine of eternal punishment cannot be true for four reasons: "(1) It is wholly unscriptural; (2) it is unreasonable; (3) it is contrary to God's love, and (4) it is repugnant to justice."[137]

The Greek word Gehenna is viewed as the "symbol of annihilation or everlasting death in unconsciousness from which there was to be no awakening." Not only Gehenna, but also "the second death" and the "lake burning with fire

---

[132] *Ibid.*, p. 238.
[133] *Ibid.*, p. 239.
[134] *Ibid.*, pp. 239, 240.
[135] *New Heavens and a New Earth*, pp. 355, 356.
[136] *Make Sure of All Things*, p. 155.
[137] *Let God Be True*, p. 99.

and sulphur" are also symbols of everlasting destruction or annihilation.[138] All from Adam to those who followed the Devil in his final rebellion, who have been judged unworthy of life, will have been annihilated along with Satan and his demons.

Having passed the final test in the Devil's last rebellion those upon the earth who remain will look forward to endless existence and blessing upon the paradise earth. Their names will be "written in the book of life." They will serve Jehovah through the endless time to come.[139]

The 144,000 will spend eternity reigning with Christ in heaven "as his joint heirs and co-rulers in Jehovah's glorious Theocracy."[140]

X. Other Distinctive Doctrines

Blood transfusion. The giving or the taking of blood transfusions is a violation of God's covenant of the sanctity of life. The position of a Jehovah's Witness parent is explained:

> Jehovah's witnesses do not reject blood for their children due to any lack of parental love. . . . They know that if they violate God's law on blood and the child dies in the process, they have endangered that child's opportunity for everlasting life in God's new world.[141]

The further implications of a blood transfusion are presented:

---

[138] *New World Translation of the Christian Greek Scriptures* (second ed., 1951), p. 767. In addition to annihilation as expressed by the above as a condition for the dead, there are some words that express temporary conditions for humans and rebellious spirit creatures: The Hebrew word *Sheol* and the Greek word *Hades* means "gravedom or the common grave of mankind." *Make Sure of All Things*, p. 155. "*Tartaros* speaks of a degraded or debased condition only for rebellious spirit creatures during their conscious lifetime with the certainty of annihilation awaiting them at the time of their execution." *Ibid.*

[139] *From Paradise Lost to Paradise Regained*, p. 240.

[140] *Let God Be True*, p. 132.

[141] *Blood, Medicine and the Law of God*, p. 54. This entire booklet of 62 pages gives a comprehensive explanation of the doctrine.

> It may result in the immediate and very temporary prolongation of life, but that at the cost of eternal life for a dedicated Christian. Then again, it may bring sudden death, and that forever.[142]

The flag salute. The Witnesses are not unique in their refusal to salute the flag, but they were the ones that conducted the legal battle in the courts. The flag salute became an issue late in 1935 and the compulsory salute was declared legal by the Supreme Court on June 3, 1940. A reversal of this decision came on June 14, 1943.[143]

The Witnesses refuse to salute the flag of any country, declaring it idolatry, and that to salute "ascribes salvation to the national emblem and to the nation for which it stands."[144] Such a saluting is a violation of his covenant which will bring certain destruction.[145]

Commenting on the contents of Hayden Covington's (the Society's lawyer) brief to the Supreme Court in the *Barnette* case, David Manwaring stated:

> Finally, Covington pointed to the Witness doctrine of the "covenant"; while a non-Witness might salute and later repent, a Witness who thus broke his agreement with God would be doomed irrevocably. Thus, Witness children were forced to choose between persecution and absolute damnation.[146]

Military service. The Witnesses claim that they are neutrals because they are ambassadors of God's kingdom.[147] They also claim exemption from military training as ministers. "The preaching activity of Jehovah's ministers entitles them to claim exemption from performing military training and service in the armed forces of the nations in which they dwell."[148] Joining the military effort of the country in

---

[142] *Ibid.*, p. 55.

[143] *Let God Be True,* p. 241.

[144] *Ibid.*, p. 242.

[145] *Salvation,* p. 266.

[146] David R. Manwaring, *Render Unto Caesar* (Chicago: The University of Chicago Press, 1962), p. 218.

[147] The Witness view of neutrality carries over to the relationship of the individual to his government. They stand apart from all political envolvement such as voting and running for office. For a brief presentation on this position see: *Make Sure of All Things; Hold Fast to What Is Fine,* pp. 351-59.

[148] *Let God Be True,* p. 237.

which Witnesses live would result in the Witness "being guilty of desertion and suffering the punishment meted out by Almighty God to deserters."[149]

The Jehovah's Witnesses and Israel. The gathering of the Jews to Palestine is not a fulfillment of prophecy. Israel has been set aside, and now the promises of God to the Jews are being realized in spiritual Israel, the Jehovah's Witnesses.[150]

XI. Summary

Most of the major doctrines and denials of the Witnesses have been surveyed in this chapter. One can clearly see that from the standpoint of orthodoxy their doctrinal system is one chiefly of denials. These include a denial of (1) the Trinity, (2) the deity of Christ, (3) the personality of the Holy Spirit, (4) the inherent immortality of the soul, (5) the total depravity of man, (6) the bodily resurrection of Christ, (7) the atonement (8) the finished work of Christ and the need of the new birth for all, (9) the second coming of Christ, (10) eternal punishment, etc. Many other doctrinal denials and perversions could be mentioned.

If space would permit, a further examination would demonstrate that there is an almost perfect agreement on the foregoing denials by both Russell and Rutherford.[151] Russell, Rutherford, and the Watchtower Society of today form an unbroken "apostolic succession"—APOSTLES OF DENIAL!

---

[149] *Ibid.*, p. 238.

[150] *Ibid.*, p. 218. As has been previously indicated, the position is in direct contradiction to that taken earlier.

[151] Russell, Rutherford, and the Society today are in close agreement on the "fundamentals" of denial, but thousands of reinterpretations of Scripture and many new doctrinal points have evolved since Russell's death which would place them in strong disagreement.

For a quick comparison of teachings see: *Jehovah of the Watchtower* (sixth revised edition, 1963), pp. 37-41, which compares five doctrines of Russell with those of the present movement. *Russellism Exposed,* by P. E. Hewitt, is an excellent checklist for the teachings of Rutherford and Russell.

CHAPTER IX

A REFUTATION OF SOME OF THE MAJOR DOCTRINES OF THE JEHOVAH'S WITNESSES

It is impossible within the space of one chapter to deal with every argument advanced by the Jehovah's Witnesses in the thousands of publications distributed over the years. The major doctrines and the typical arguments which characterize the Jehovah's Witness doctrinal position can be examined and the answers in refutation presented to satisfy the unbiased reader that the Witnesses' theological system is contrary to fact and to God's Word.

I. THE TRINITY AND THE DEITY OF CHRIST

It is especially in this central doctrine of Christianity which concerns the nature of God that the Witnesses have completely misrepresented orthodoxy and perverted the teachings of the Bible. The following material is an examination and refutation of the supposedly unanswerable, *Let God Be True* chapter, "Is There a Trinity?," pages 100-111.[1] This book and the chapter have been selected for four reasons: (1) To show the fallacious content and argument. (2) The book was one of the most popular ever published by the Jehovah's Witnesses. (3) The chapter is typical of the logic and evidence presented in the entire book. (4) It is also typical of the Witnesses' arguments concerning their rejection of the Trinity.

On page 100, the book presents tritheism as orthodoxy as it defines the Trinity: "The doctrine in brief is that there are three gods in one. . . ." After this erroneous

---

[1] The 1952 revised edition has been used.

definition the book cites the *Catholic Encyclopedia* which gives a brief portion of the Athanasian Creed as part of its definition. This portion of the creed in itself shows the misrepresentation of the Witnesses' "three god's in one" as it says: ". . . there are not three Gods"!

From the incomplete quotations and faulty definition the book then concludes that the explanation of such a doctrine "is very confusing." From this word "confusing" the Witnesses feel justified in bringing in a part of I Corinthians 14:33 which reads: "God is not the author of confusion." Then the conclusion is drawn: ". . . It is at once seen that such a doctrine is not of God."

An examination of I Corinthians 14:33 quickly reveals that the subject under discussion is that of keeping order in the churches in the exercise of the gifts of tongues and prophecy. Verse 40 concludes: "But let all things be done decently and in order." So the context of the verse rules out the Witness use. A study of the word "confusion" (*akatastasia*) clearly shows that it is used in reference to a state of disorder, disturbance, or unruliness.[2] From the Witnesses' own *New World Translation,* the wrong use of the verse is seen: "For God is a God, not of disorder, but of peace." The Witnesses then have concluded concerning the Trinity—after offering no evidence, after misrepresenting orthodoxy, after using a verse out of context and not understanding the meaning of a word, "that such a doctrine is not of God."

On page 101 the supposed origin of the Trinity doctrine is given. "The origin of the trinity doctrine is traced back to the ancient Babylonians and Egyptians and other ancient mythologists." On whose authority? The book *Make Sure of All Things* gives the Witnesses' answer. After reaffirming the position set forth by *Let God Be True,* the text instructs the reader to see two sources.[3] The first source indicated is McClintock and Strong's *Cyclopaedia* under "Trinity."

[2] Walter Bauer, *A Greek-English Lexicon of the New Testament and Other Early Christian Literature,* ed. and trans. William F. Arndt and F. Wilbur Gingrich (Chicago: The University of Chicago Press, 1957), p. 29. Hereafter this work will be designated Arndt-Gingrich.

[3] *Make Sure of All Things* (Brooklyn: Watchtower Bible and Tract Society, Inc., 1953), p. 386.

This writer would strongly urge the reader to read the "Trinity" article which completely refutes the position set forth in both *Let God Be True* and *Make Sure of All Things*.[4] Possibly the compilers of *Make Sure of All Things* actually wished to refer the reader to the article "Trinity, Heathen Notions of," which follows the "Trinity" article. If this is true the compilers again have their position refuted as the article begins:

> In examining the various heathen philosophies and mythologies, we find clear evidence of a belief in a certain sort of trinity, and yet something very different from the Trinity of the Bible.[5]

The next instruction is to see "*The Two Babylons*, pp. 16, 17."[6] After reading the entire section it can be clearly seen that the purpose of the author of *The Two Babylons* is not to show the origin of the doctrine from the ancient pagans, but to show the corruption of the Trinity by the Catholic Church, as Mary is inserted into the Trinity. Hislop shows that paganism *corrupted* the Trinity and did not originate it. On the very page the reader is instructed to see, the footnote states:

> Some have said that the *plural* form of the name of God, in the Hebrew of Genesis, affords no argument for the doctrine of plurality of persons in the Godhead, because the same word in the plural is applied to heathen divinities. But if the supreme divinity in almost all ancient heathen nations was triune, the futility of this objection must be manifest.[7]

On the next page Hislop completely exposes the Witnesses' appeal to his book as he writes concerning the pagan's trinity:

> All these have existed from ancient times. While overlaid with idolatry, the recognition of a Trinity was universal in all the ancient nations of the world proving how deep-rooted in the human race was the primeval

---

[4] John McClintock and James Strong, "Trinity" *Cyclopaedia of Biblical, Theological, and Ecclesiastical Literature* (New York: Harper & Brothers, Publishers, 1881), X, 551-56.

[5] *Ibid.*, p. 556.

[6] *Make Sure of All Things, loc. cit.*

[7] Alexander Hislop, *The Two Babylons* (first American edition; New York: Loizeaux Brothers, 1916), p. 17.

> doctrine on this subject, which comes out so distinctly in Genesis.[8]

In the concluding remarks of the chapter, Hislop shows the point of the chapter and the distinction between the Roman and pagan trinities and the true Trinity:

> Will anyone after this say that the Roman Catholic Church must still be called Christian, because it holds the doctrine of the Trinity? So did the Pagan Babylonians, so did the Egyptians, so do the Hindoos at this hour, in the very same sense in which Rome does. They all admitted A trinity, but did they worship THE Triune Jehovah, the King Eternal, Immortal, and Invisible?[9]

To miss completely the point of Hislop's argument is either very poor scholarship, or deliberate misrepresentation!

On page 101 of *Let God Be True,* the next point that is made is that Tertullian introduced the term *trinitas* (Latin) into ecclesiastical writings, and Theophilus introduced the triad into Greek ecclesiastical writings, although neither was Scriptural. That this proves nothing is easily demonstrated. The Witnesses themselves use terms that are not Scriptural, but which are descriptive of what they feel the Bible teaches; for example, "Theocracy," or the designation "New World Society."

Next, the book states that Constantine called a Council in 325 which confirmed the doctrine of the Trinity. Concerning this doctrine it is claimed: "It thus came to be declared the doctrine of the religious organization of Christendom, and the clergy have ever held to this complicated doctrine" (p. 101). This statement by the Witnesses is contrary to all authoritative church history written on the subject. Any church history book will show the real purpose of the Council of Nicea was to set forth the doctrine concerning the deity of Christ. Martin and Klann state: "At least eighty-six sources, all of them soundly documented, prove beyond doubt that at the Council of Nicea in 325 A. D., the main issue was the Arian heresy. . . ."[10] That the latter part of the

---

[8] *Ibid.,* p. 18.

[9] *Ibid.,* p. 90.

[10] Walter R. Martin and Norman H. Klann, *Jehovah of the Watchtower* (sixth revised edition, 1963; Grand Rapids: Zondervan Publishing House, 1953), p. 178.

Witnesses' statement is also false is shown by Berkhof as he writes concerning the decision at Nicea:

> The decision of the Council did not terminate the controversy, but was rather only the beginning of it. A settlement forced upon the Church by the strong hand of the emperor could not satisfy and was also of uncertain duration.[11]

James Orr writes:

> It would be a shallow reading of history to attribute the defeat of Arianism in the early Church to the anathemas of councils, the influence of court favor, or any other accidental circumstances. It perished through its own inherent weakness.[12]

Finally, the writer in the Witnesses' book *Babylon the Great Has Fallen!* shows the contention in *Let God Be True* is false:

> However, the trinitarian decision of this Council did not bring tranquility to the eastern religious organization, and the Arian controversy continued to be carried on very warmly. . . .
>
> Toward the close of his life Emperor Constantine favored the side of antitrinitarian Arius, Constantine being helped in this direction by Eusebius of Nicomedia. So Arius was recalled from exile, and many of the trinitarian bishops were banished.[13]

It was Eusebius of Nicomedia, mentioned above, an Arian Bishop, who baptized Constantine. Again the Witnesses show their inadequate scholarship and dishonesty, this time in church history.

After starting with no evidence, misrepresenting orthodoxy, using Scripture out of context, not understanding the meaning of a word, misrepresenting the source of the Trinity doctrine, bringing in irrelevant material and changing the events of church history, the Witnesses make this "authori-

---

[11] L. Berkhof, *The History of Christian Doctrines* (Grand Rapids: Wm. B. Eerdmans Publishing Company, 1937), p. 91.

[12] James Orr, *The Christian View of God and the World* (Wm. B. Eerdmans Publishing Company, 1954), p. 44.

[13] *Babylon the Great Has Fallen! God's Kingdom Rules!* (Brooklyn: Watchtower Bible and Tract Society of New York, Inc., 1963), pp. 478, 479.

tative" statement: "The obvious conclusion is, therefore, that Satan is the originator of the trinity doctrine" (p. 101).

Next, the book purports to give "the main scriptures used to support the trinity doctrine" (p. 102). These verses are I John 5:7; John 10:30; I Timothy 3:16; and John 1:1 (p. 102). It would be surprising to any well-informed Christian to find that these verses are the "main scriptures used to support the trinity doctrine." The doctrine of the Trinity is not based on a few isolated proof texts. Warfield writes:

> It is not in a text here and there that the New Testament bears its testimony to the doctrine of the Trinity. The whole book is Trinitarian to the core; all its teaching is built on the assumption of the Trinity; and its allusions to the Trinity are frequent, cursory, easy and confident.[14]

The verses cited by the Witnesses will be dealt with as found in *Let God Be True*.

Again, on page 102, another obvious misrepresentation of the Biblical doctrine concerning the Trinity is given. Orthodox ministers are represented as explaining the Trinity by saying, "That is a mystery" and illustrating the Trinity "by using triangles, trefoils, or images with three heads on one neck. . . . it [is] a bit difficult to love and worship a complicated, freakish-looking, three-headed God." This writer agrees with Tanis as he comments concerning this statement: "This is a vile caricature and deliberate misrepresentation of the biblical doctrine concerning the triune God."[15] As usual, the Witnesses have given a distorted view of orthodoxy. While *Let God Be True* did not document the allusion to a "three-headed God," the background for the statement is taken from *The Two Babylons*. Hislop does not deal with the orthodox presentation of the Trinity at all, but the corruption of the doctrine by some Papal churches.[16]

On the same page of *Let God Be True,* the Witnesses state another deliberate misrepresentation concerning the "three-headed God":

---

[14] Benjamin B. Warfield, *Biblical and Theological Studies* (Philadelphia: The Presbyterian and Reformed Publishing Company, 1952), p. 32.

[15] Edward J. Tanis, *What the Sects Teach* (Grand Rapids: Baker Book House, 1958), p. 9.

[16] Hislop, *op. cit.*, p. 17 ff.

> The clergy who inject such ideas will contradict themselves in the very next breath by stating that God made man in his own image; for certainly no one has ever seen a three-headed human creature" [p. 102].

First, no Christian of any intelligence believes in a "three-headed God." Next, the text deliberately misrepresents what orthodoxy believes about man's creation in the image of God. The writers of this Jehovah's Witness text know this, but the insertion of such an unrepresentative view is to sway the uneducated and unthinking. What is here represented as orthodoxy is actually Mormon theology, inasmuch as it makes man's image of God a physical image. Orthodoxy as well as the Jehovah's Witnesses believe that "God is a Spirit" (John 4:24 ASV, NWT). In *Let God Be True,* page 145, the Witnesses teach that man's being made in the image of God was not a physical image: "Not that man had the same form and substance as his Creator, but that he had God's attributes."

The first "proof text" of orthodoxy is dealt with, the verse in I John 5:7 (p. 103). The Witnesses wax eloquent on this verse as being a glaring example of adding to the Bible. Wilson's *Emphatic Diaglott* is cited as authority that the text

> ". . . is not contained in any Greek manuscript which was written earlier than the fifteenth century. It is not cited by any of the Greek ecclesiastical writers; nor by any of the early Latin fathers . . . evidently spurious."[17]

While the present writer is not trying to defend the insertion of the verse in the text, it should be pointed out that the quotation from *The Diaglott* is not accurate, as a check of the critical apparatus in *The Greek New Testament*

---

[17] Benjamin Wilson, *The Emphatic Diaglott* (1942 edition; Brooklyn: International Bible Students Association, [n. d.]), p. 803.

On this quotation various printings of the 1942 edition of *The Diaglott* read "fifth century" and "15th century."

There have been some efforts to defend the appearance of I John 5:7 in the Received Text. For those interested, one such effort, "Notes on the Vindication of I John 5:7," is distributed by the Trinitarian Bible Society, 217 Kingston Road, London, S.W. 19 3NN England.

reveals. Two fourth century writers, Priscillian and Varimadum, quote the verse as though genuine.[18]

Conservative scholars feel that this verse is justly left out of the text, not because it is false in its teaching, but because there is some doubt of its appearance at this place. Most Bibles which have notes concerning the text will point out this insertion. For example, *The Scofield Reference Bible* has the note: "It is generally agreed that v. 7 has no real authority, and has been inserted."[19] It can be seen that in the Witnesses bringing forth this text as a "main support" for the Trinity, an attempt has been made to set up a "straw man" so that they can knock it down and claim an easy victory.

The next text treated is John 10:30: "I and my Father are one." This verse is explained by reference to John 17:20-22; I Corinthians 12:12; Ephesians 5:23; and I Corinthians 11:3. The conclusion is then stated: ". . . Just as Christ and his body members are regarded as one, so are Jehovah and Christ regarded as one. They are all one in agreement, purpose and organization" (p. 104). Because of space, just one of the references from which this conclusion is drawn will be examined. John 17:20-22 is used in most Witness writings as the explanation of John 10:30. It is informative, as J. B. Rowell points out, to realize that the Jehovah's Witnesses' explanation of this text is the same argument that the famous infidel Thomas Paine used.[20] Rowell also shows that the well-known skeptic Earnest Renan associated these two verses to deny Christ's deity. As an examination of the two contexts will show, there is a vast difference in the oneness in the two passages.[21] John 10:30 sets forth the oneness of essence, equality and Godhead. John 17:20-22 sets forth oneness because of redemption and union with Christ. That the Jews understood Christ's claim is plain from their response in verses 31 and 33. The blasphemy

---

[18] *The Greek New Testament,* ed. by Kurt Aland, Matthew Black, *et al.* (New York: American Bible Society, 1966), p. 824.

[19] C. I. Scofield (ed.), *The Scofield Reference Bible* (new and improved edition; New York: Oxford University Press, 1945), p. 1325.

[20] J. B. Rowell, *The Deity of Jesus Christ Our Lord* (Canada: Hebden Printing Co. Ltd., [n. d.]), pp. 6, 7.

[21] *Ibid.*, pp. 7-10.

that the Jews charged Christ with was that of claiming the attributes of God; accordingly, He put Himself under Jewish law as punishable by stoning.

After the conclusion on John 10:30, that the Father and the Son are one only "in agreement, purpose and organization," the Witnesses argue: "If this were not the logical conclusion Jesus would never have said: 'My Father is greater than I. . .' " (p. 104). The latter part of this quotation, John 14:28, has been a leading text for the Arians of every age. First it should be pointed out that only God can compare Himself with God. The meaning of the passage is seen by comparing it with Hebrews 1:4. The term used in John 14:28 for "greater" is *meizon*. The Hebrews passage uses *kreitton*, as it describes Christ as being "better" than the angels. The words show the contrasts intended in each context. In John 14:28, Christ the God-man who had emptied Himself of the prerogatives of deity can say: "My Father is greater than I"; He is greater in a quantitative sense. This is a description of His position as a servant and not a comparison of nature or quality. In Hebrews 1:4 the word is found that does express a qualitative distinction. The word which would have been used to prove the contention of the Witnesses would be the word *kreitton*, used in Hebrews 1:4.[22]

The next passage cited is I Timothy 3:16. Again the Witnesses cite a passage which has a textual difficulty. The *King James Version* reads: "God was manifest in the flesh"; the *American Standard Version* reads: "He who was manifested in the flesh." Actually, this much should be sufficient to show that orthodoxy understands that the *King James* reading needed correction to fit better the evidence on hand. Next the Witnesses write: "Had this been God Almighty incarnated, which it would have to be if the trinity were true, then these words of John would be false" (quoting John 1:18 that "no man hath seen God at any time. . ."). Again the Jehovah's Witnesses' textbook misrepresents the position of orthodoxy. Orthodoxy holds to the incarnation of God the Son and not of God the Father, a fact that is very clear throughout the Bible and is actually seen in the passage in John 1:18 which the textbook cites. "No man hath seen

---

[22] Martin and Klann, *op. cit.*, pp. 196-99.

God at any time; the only begotten Son [God only begotten], who is in the bosom of the Father, he hath declared *him.*" It was God the Son that became incarnate.

On page 105 the Witnesses argue (after quoting Hebrews 2:9 which speaks of Christ being "made 'a little lower than the angels' ") that "if the trinity doctrine is true, then God was lower than the angels while on earth; which is contrary to his supremacy." Again God and the Son of God are not distinguished. John 1:14 states: "And the Word became flesh, and dwelt among us (and we beheld his glory, glory as of the only begotten from the Father), full of grace and truth." As to His humanity, Christ was a little lower than the angels; as to His deity, the Scriptures testify: "For in him dwelleth all the fulness of the Godhead bodily" (Col. 2:9). The word here translated "Godhead" means "the state of being God."

On page 106 the text quotes the *New World Translation* rendering of Philippians 2:6-8:

> Who, although he was existing in God's form, gave no consideration to a seizure, namely, that he should be equal to God. No, but he emptied himself and took a slave's form and came to be in the likeness of men. More than that, when he found himself in fashion as a man, he humbled himself. . . .

From this verse, and preceding this quotation, the erroneous view concerning the atonement held by the Witnesses is introduced. In essence, Christ must be a perfect corresponding sacrifice for what Adam lost, which makes it mandatory that Jesus be nothing more than a perfect man. Supposedly this Philippians passage teaches that Christ was merely a perfect man while upon earth and not equal with God while in heaven.

Bishop Lightfoot's thorough examination and explanation of the passage demonstrates that the Witnesses' understanding and translation of this passage is not correct. In his conclusion to the study of the words *morphe* ("form") and *schema* ("fashion") he writes:

> Thus in the passage under consideration the *morphe* is contrasted with the *schema,* as that which is intrinsic and essential with that which is accidental and outward. And the three clauses imply, respectively the true divine nature of our Lord, *morphe theou,* the true human na-

ture *morphe doulou,* and the externals of the human nature *schemati hos anthropos.*[23]

In the selection of the proper translation for the word *harpagmos* (translated "seizure" NWT "usurpation" ED, "a thing to be grasped" ASV, "robbery" KJV) the context and Paul's thought in general must determine the meaning. After a careful weighing of the possibilities, Lightfoot concludes with the following:

> "*Though* He pre-existed in the form of God, *yet* He did not look upon equality with God as a prize which must not slip from His grasp, *but* He emptied Himself, divested Himself, taking upon Him the form of a slave."[24]

The passage is explained by Grimm-Thayer:

> . . . *Who, although* (formerly when he was *logos asarkos*) *he bore the form* (in which he appeared to the inhabitants of heaven) *of God* (the sovereign, opp. to *morph. doulou*), *yet did not think that this equality with God was to be eagerly clung to or retained. . .*[25]

That Christ was more than perfect man while on earth is shown from such passages as John 10:30 and Colossians 2:9.

The last text considered is John 1:1. The verse as commonly translated reads: "In the beginning was the Word, and the Word was with God, and the Word was God" (KJV, ASV, RSV). The Greek in John 1:1 is as follows:

> *En arche en ho logos, kai ho logos en pros ton theon, kai theos en ho logos.*

The Emphatic Diaglott, a work published by the Witnesses, is cited as an authority for a revision of the reading, so that the last clause reads, "and a god was the Word." *The Diaglott* rendering is used as justification for the equally

---

[23] J. B. Lightfoot, *Saint Paul's Epistle to the Philippians* (revised text; London: Macmillan and Company, 1913), p. 133.

[24] *Ibid.,* p. 111. See the detached note, pp. 133-37. See similar excellent translations by Arthur Way, *The Letters of St. Paul,* J. B. Phillips, *Letters to Young Churches,* Gerrit Verkuyl (ed.), *The Berkeley Version in Modern English,* and Richard Weymouth, *The New Testament in Modern Speech.*

[25] Joseph Henry Thayer (ed. and trans.), *A Greek-English Lexicon of the New Testament Being Grimm's Wilke's Clavis Novi Testamenti* (fourth edition, Edinburgh: T & T. Clark, 1901), p. 418. Hereafter this work will be designated Grimm-Thayer.

incorrect translation of the Witnesses' *New World Translation,* which reads: "Originally the Word was, and the Word was with God, and the Word was a god."[26]

The following arguments, among others, are advanced by the Witnesses in defense of the reading of the last clause in the *New World Translation.*

First, the translation is justified because of the absence of the definite article before "God" in the last clause. Second, the *New World Translation* (in the Appendix on pages 773-77) gives additional evidence: *An American Translation* renders "The Word was divine," and *A New Translation* by James Moffatt renders "the Logos was divine." Several Greek grammars are also quoted. The conclusion is drawn that "every honest person will have to admit that John's saying that the Word or Logos 'was divine' is not saying that he was the God. . ." (pp. 773-74). A footnote on page 776 gives a long list of texts to prove the translation of the predicate nominative in the *New World Translation* is justified.

With the readings from *An American Translation* and *A New Translation* bolstering the *New World Translation's* rendering of John 1:1, the tendency to call in liberals for support is manifest. It must also be pointed out that the translation "divine" may not say that Christ was "the God" to the Witnesses—but one must go further and say that the Greek does not give any justification for such a reading! The word for "divine" is interpretation, not translation. Metzger writes:

> As regards Jn. 1,[1] Colwell's research casts the most serious doubts on the correctness of such translations as "and the Logos was divine" (Moffatt, Strachan), "and the Word was divine" (Goodspeed), and (worst of all) "and the Word was a god" (so the recently published Jehovah's Witnesses' *New World Translation of the Christian Greek Scriptures* [1950]).[27]

Concerning the omission of the article, A. T. Robertson states:

---

[26] The 1961 revision, *New World Translation of the Holy Scriptures,* reads: "In [the] beginning the Word was, and the Word was with God, and the Word was a god."

[27] Bruce M. Metzger, "On the Translation of John 1:1," *The Expository Times,* 63:125, January, 1952.

> As a rule the article is not used with the predicate noun even if the subject is definite. The article with one and not with the other means that the articular noun is the subject.[28]

Colwell's conclusions on the translation of the predicate nominative are as follows: "A definite predicate nominative has the article when it follows the verb; it does not have the article when it precedes the verb."[29]

> . . . A predicate nominative which precedes the verb cannot be translated as an indefinite or a "qualitative" noun solely because of the absence of the article; if the context suggests that the predicate is definite, it should be translated as a definite noun in spite of the absence of the article.[30]

On John 1:1 Colwell states: "The opening verse of John's Gospel contains one of the many passages where this rule suggests the translation of a predicate as a definite noun."[31] Colwell's rule cannot find an exception in John 1:1 as the context makes no such demand. This is further supported

---

[28] A. T. Robertson and W. Hersey Davis, *A New Short Grammar of the Greek Testament* (New York: Harper and Brothers Publishers, 1933), p. 279.

[29] E. C. Colwell, "A Definite Rule for the Use of the Article in the Greek New Testament," *Journal of Biblical Literature*, 52:13, January, 1933.

[30] *Ibid.*, p. 20.

[31] *Ibid.*, p. 21.

Robert H. Countess made a study entitled "The Translation of *Theos* in the New World Translation." In the conclusion to the study Countess stated that the NWT rendering of John 1:1 was unfortunate "for several reasons: (1) It shows ignorance of a particular nuance of the Greek language; (2) The translators have established a principle regarding the article to which they themselves have been unfaithful 94% of the time; and (3) The 'preferred religious view' of an Arian-type cult has influenced the rendering of a very important passage. The 'Foreword' of the NWT disclaims any prejudice or bias for its translation." Robert H. Countess, "The Translation of *Theos* in the New World Translation." *Bulletin of the Evangelical Theological Society*, 10:160, Summer, 1967.

While Countess does not view Colwell's rule as absolute, he does say, "In view of the available data, however, one must concur with Colwell when he says that 'And the Word was God' may not be regarded strange in a Gospel that concludes with Thomas' exclamation in 20:28, *ho kurios mou kai ho theos mou*" *(ibid.)* See also the article by Philip B. Harner in the March 1973 issue of the *Journal of Biblical Literature*, pp. 75-87.

by the end of the Gospel of John in Thomas' declaration in John 20:28. None of the Witnesses' examples cited in the Appendix of the *New World Translation* to support the "a god" translation are parallel. In every case but three (John 1:21, 6:51, and 15:1, and these are special cases), the predicate noun stands *after* the verb. Actually then, the "proofs" of the *New World Translation* are confirmations that Colwell's rule is sound and that the *New World Translation* and *Diaglott* renderings are to be rejected. Thus on the Greek usage, "and the Word was God" is the correct rendering.

It is also interesting to note that John 1:1 is not the only verse in the first chapter of John where the article in the Greek is omitted before *theos*. There are four examples of this in verses 6, 12, 13 and 18. To translate any of these as the Witnesses have John 1:1, "a god," is indefensible, as the *New World Translation* itself demonstrates on these verses.

On page 776 of the Appendix the *New World Translation* translators quote from the recognized authority, A. T. Robertson, in support of their "a god" rendering: "Among the ancient writers *ho theos* was used of the god of absolute religion in distinction from the mythological gods."[32] (Supposedly proving that God with the definite article is to be distinguished from God without the article.) What the translators failed to include was Robertson's further statement: "In the N. T. however, while we have *pros ton theon* (John 1:1, 2), it is far more common to find simply *theos*, especially in the Epistles."[33]

On pages 774 and 775 the translators quote Dana and Mantey who they misuse, as a check of these citations demonstrate.[34]

To this evidence also may be added the weight of the great majority of the translations and versions now in exis-

---

[32] A. T. Robertson, *A Grammar of the Greek New Testament in the Light of Historical Research* (fourth edition; New York: George H. Doran Company, 1923), p. 761. Arndt-Gingrich state that *theos* is used of "the true God, sometimes with, sometimes without the article." Arndt-Gingrich, *op. cit.*, *p.* 357.

[33] Robertson, *loc. cit.*

[34] Cf. H. E. Dana and Julius R. Mantey, *A Manual Grammar of the Greek New Testament* (New York: The Macmillian Company, 1955), pp. 140, 148, 149. See Dr. Mantey's own reaction in M. Van Buskirk's *The Scholastic Dishonesty of The Watchtower* (Caris, P.O. Box 1783, Santa Ana, Calif. 92702).

tence, as well as almost every recognized Greek scholar. The writer has checked over twenty translations as well as many commentaries based on the Greek, and in every case (except for Moffatt's and Goodspeed's readings) the translation "the Word was God" or its equivalent was found.[35]

One of the strongest arguments against the *New World Translation* reading is the fact that such a reading would be absolutely abominable to the Jewish ear. The Jews were strict monotheists and to accept the Witnesses' translation would make John guilty of polytheism. The New Testament makes it clear that the believers were worshipping Christ (Matt. 14:33; 28:9, 17; John 20:28).[36]

On page 107, the Jehovah's Witnesses introduce four more verses, three of which are wrongly understood. The argument is as follows: (1) "Psalm 90:2 declares that God is 'from everlasting to everlasting'." (2) If this is true Jesus could not be God for He had a beginning. (3) Proof that Jesus Christ did have a beginning is found in Revelation 3:14; John 1:14; and Colossians 1:15.

Revelation 3:14 is quoted according to the *New World Translation* rendering which makes Christ "the beginning of the creation by God." On the surface this verse seems to say that Christ was God's first creation, but an examination of the scripture shows this understanding is not acceptable. The first thing which is erroneous is the translation of the verse. The translation "by God" cannot be justified, for the genetive *tou theou,* means "of God" and not "by God." For the translation given by the Witnesses the genitive would require the proposition *hupo,* which is not found in the passage.[37] The second word which is wrongly understood is the Greek word *arche,* translated "beginning." Concerning

---

[35] An interesting and informative presentation on the deity of Christ with special reference to John 1:1 and the Witnesses' official reply is found in the article by Victor Perry, "Jehovah's Witnesses and the Deity of Christ," *The Evangelical Quarterly,* 35:15-22, January-March, 1963.

[36] For an excellent presentation on worship given to Christ see: Anthony A. Hoekema, *The Four Major Cults* (Grand Rapids: Wm. B. Eerdmans Publishing Company, 1963), pp. 339-44.

[37] Dana and Mantey, *op. cit.,* p. 112: "In fact, agency is expressed with the aid of *hupo* more frequently than it is by all the other methods combined."

the word in this context Grimm-Thayer define: *"That by which anything begins to be, the origin,* active *cause. . . ."*[38] A. T. Robertson commenting on Revelation 3:14 specifically rejects the Witnesses' position:

> Not the first of creatures as the Arians held and the Unitarians do now, but the originating source of creation through whom God works (Col. 1:15, 18, a passage probably known to the Laodiceans, John 1:3; Heb. 1:2, as is made clear by 1:18; 2:8; 3:21; 5:13).[39]

So Christ is termed the "originating source of creation" through whom God the Father works and not a creature created by God. John 1:3 is an exposition of this verse.

John 1:14, which speaks of Jesus Christ being the "only begotten of the Father," is construed by the Witnesses to mean that Christ was created. The Greek word for "only begotten" is *monogenes.* The meaning of the word as found in the most scholarly of works is "only one of its kind, unique." As Arndt-Gingrich point out, the word *monogenes* is used only of Jesus in the Johannine literature, and the meanings *"only, unique* may be quite adequate for all its occurrences here."[40] Grimm-Thayer render the word,*"single of its kind, only. . . ."*[41]

In Colossians 1:15 the Witnesses understand that "the firstborn of every creature" applied to Christ means that Christ was created. That this is not the intent of the word can be easily seen by examination. The word for "firstborn" is *prototokos.* Metzger sets aside the Witness' claim as he writes: "Actually the verb 'to create' in reference to the relation of the Son of God to the Father appears neither here nor anywhere else in the New Testament."[42] Had Paul

---

[38] Grimm-Thayer, *op. cit.*, p. 77.

[39] A. T. Robertson, *Word Pictures in the New Testament* (New York: Harper and Brothers, 1933), VI 321. Cremer states that *arche* in Revelation 3:14 "signifies the causal relation of Christ to the creation of God. . . ." *Hermann Cremer, Biblio-Theological Lexicon of New Testament Greek,* trans. William Urwick (fourth English edition; Edinburgh: T. & T. Clark, 1895), p. 115.

[40] Arndt-Gingrich, *op. cit.*, p. 529. For an extended discussion on *monogenes* see Martin and Klann, *op. cit.*, pp. 190-96.

[41] Grimm-Thayer, *op. cit.*, p. 417.

[42] B. M. Metzger, "The Jehovah's Witnesses and Jesus Christ," *Theology Today,* 10:76, 77, April, 1953.

intended to speak of Christ being created, he had a word available, *protoktistos*. The idea conveyed by the word in Colossians 1:15 is priority to all creation and sovereignty over all creation. Lightfoot makes this clear as he writes:

> . . . It declares the absolute pre-existence of the Son. At first sight it might seem that Christ is here regarded as one, though the earliest, of created beings. This interpretation however is not required by the expression itself. . . .
> God's "first-born" is the natural ruler, the acknowledged head, of God's household.[43]

On page 107, *Let God Be True* deals with the Holy Spirit. With I John 5:7 discounted, no place is given to the Scriptural proof of the personality of the Holy Spirit. Again orthodoxy is misrepresented, as the text states: "The general thought about the 'Holy Ghost' is that it is a spirit person. . . ." Notice how the text speaks of the Spirit as "it." After a series of deductions, without any Scripture cited, *Let God Be True* concludes: "So the holy spirit is the invisible active force of Almighty God which moves his servants to do his will" (p. 108).

What do the Scriptures say concerning the personality of the Holy Spirit?[44] Can it be demonstrated from the Scripture that the Holy Spirit is a person? Entire volumes have been written to present Scripturally the Person and work of the Holy Spirit. Limited space permits only a brief presentation.

1. The Holy Spirit acts as a person and possesses the attributes of personality. (a) He teaches and brings to remembrance (John 14:26). "But the helper, the holy spirit which the Father will send in my name, that one will teach YOU all things and bring back to YOUR minds all the things I told YOU" (NWT). Notice even the New World Translation must say "the helper" and "that one." (b) He guides, speaks and hears (John 16:13):

---

[43] J. B. Lightfoot, *Saint Paul's Epistles to the Colossians and to Philemon* (revised text; Grand Rapids: Zondervan Publishing House, [n. d.]), pp. 146, 147. For a further discussion on *prototokos*, see Cremer, *op. cit.*, pp. 555-6; Arndt-Gingrich, *op. cit.*, p. 734.

[44] Personality is demonstrated by the application of personal terms to the Holy Spirit which convey the idea of intellect, sensibility and will.

> However, when that one arrives, the spirit of the truth, he will guide YOU into all the truth, for he will not speak of his own impulse, but what things he hears he will speak, and he will declare to YOU the things coming [NWT].

Notice: the Holy Spirit "he will guide you," "he will not speak of his own impulse," "he hears," and "he will declare." Acts 10:19: ". . . The spirit said. . ." (NWT). (c) He intercedes (Rom. 8:26). ". . . But the spirit itself pleads for us with groanings unuttered" (NWT). The next verse clearly shows the distinction of personalities: "Yet he [Jehovah] who searches the hearts knows what the meaning of the spirit is, because it [the Spirit] is pleading in accord with God for holy ones" (NWT). The word translated "pleading" is *entugchano* which means to intercede, or plead for someone.[45] The same word is found in Hebrews 7:25 used of Christ: "Consequently he is able also to save completely those who are approaching God through him, because he is always to plead for them" (NWT). Romans 8:34 speaks of Christ "who is on the right hand of God, who also pleads for us." To this writer's mind it is ridiculous to say that the "invisible active force of God" intercedes in man's behalf before God, unless the Spirit is a person! (d) He forbids certain actions (Acts 16:6, 7). ". . . They were forbidden by the holy spirit to speak . . . but the spirit of Jesus did not permit them" (NWT). (e) He sends into service (Acts 13:4). "Accordingly these men, sent out by the holy spirit. . . " (NWT). (f) He searches (I Cor. 2:10). ". . . For the spirit searches into all things, even the deep things of God" (NWT). (g) He appoints and decrees (I Cor. 12:11). "But all these operations the one and the same spirit performs, making a distribution to each one respectively just as it wills" (NWT). This verse makes it clear that the Holy Spirit wills. This word is used of a person, of God, and of Christ.[46] (h) The Holy Spirit is "another helper," "comforter," or "advocate" (John 14:16, 26; 15:26; 16:7). With the word "another" (*allos*) "another of like kind," Christ also identified himself as an "advocate" or "comforter." (See also I John 2:1.) (i) The Holy Spirit

---

[45] Arndt-Gingrich, *op. cit.*, p. 269.

[46] *Ibid.*, pp. 145, 146.

is classed along with persons as though He were a person (Acts 15:28). "For the holy spirit and we ourselves have favored adding no further burden to YOU. . . " (NWT). (j) The Holy Spirit is identified as a person in the baptismal formula (Matt. 28:19). "Go therefore and make disciples of all the nations, baptizing them in the name of the Father and of the Son and of the holy spirit. . ." (NWT). The verse becomes ridiculous if it is read "baptizing them in the name of the Father and of the Son and of the 'invisible active force of God'."

2. The Holy Spirit can be treated like a person. (a) He can be grieved (Eph. 4:30). "Also do not be grieving God's holy spirit. . ." (NWT). (b) The Holy Spirit may be blasphemed (Matt. 12:31). ". . . The blasphemy against the spirit will not be forgiven" (NWT). (c) The Holy Spirit may be lied to (Acts 5:3). (d) The Holy Spirit can be insulted or outraged (Heb. 10:29). (e) The Spirit can be resisted (Acts 7:51). ". . . YOU are always resisting the holy spirit. . ." (NWT).

3. The Holy Spirit is sometimes identified by the use of the masculine demonstrative pronoun as in John 14:26, 15;26, 16:7, 8 and 13, 14. Although the *New World Translation* attempts to explain away the appearance of the masculine pronoun in these passages, A. T. Robertson shows that its use is evidence for the personality of the Holy Spirit:

> Two passages in John call for a remark, inasmuch as they bear on the personality of the Holy Spirit. In 14:26 . . . the relative *ho* follows the grammatical gender of *pneuma*. *Ekeinos,* however, skips over *pneuma* and reverts to the gender of *parakletos.* In 16:13 a more striking example occurs . . . Here one has to go back six lines to *ekeinos* again and seven to *parakletos.* It is more evident therefore in this passage that John is insisting on the personality of the Holy Spirit, when the grammatical gender so easily called for *ekeino.* Cf. *ho* in Jo. 14:17, 26 and *auto* in 14:17.[47]

The personality of the Spirit is clearly evident for any who take the Word of God for what it says. It is only as the Bible is questioned and its testimony set aside that the personality of the Spirit is not seen. It may also be added

---

[47] Robertson, *Grammar, op. cit.*, pp. 708, 709.

that the verses which have been quoted concerning the personality of the Spirit appear in a weakened form in the *New World Translation,* but still the teaching is clear.

The deity of the Spirit also is adequately shown by the foregoing material which demonstrates His personality. The Bible further shows: (a) The Holy Spirit is called God and bears names which belong to God (Acts 5:3, 4, 9; II Cor. 3:17, 18). (b) Divine attributes are ascribed to the Spirit (I Cor. 2:11; 12:11). (c) Divine works are attributed to the Holy Spirit (Gen. 1:2; John 3:3, 8).

The remaining three and one-half pages of *Let God Be True* are devoted to questions and misrepresentations almost too painful to record, such as: "If Jesus was God, then during Jesus' death God was dead and in the grave" (p. 109). Death is here presented as cessation of existence and again the Witnesses give a misrepresentation of orthodoxy.

The following has been found in the Witnesses' presentation of the Trinity in *Let God Be True.* The book misrepresents and perverts orthodoxy; it tears verses out of context and gives meanings to words which were never intended; it often misrepresents the authorities it cites; it reaches conclusions after offering not one scintilla of evidence; it presents a faulty understanding of church history; it evades the scriptural opposition of its opponents; it introduces Mormonism as orthodoxy; it calls on infidels and skeptics as allies in holding common beliefs; it demonstrates an almost complete ignorance of Greek grammar and vocabulary. This chapter is typical of that which is offered in the entire book!

A Further Presentation of the Trinity

Volumes have been written on the Scriptural doctrine of the Trinity. The following is not intended to be a full exposition of the doctrine, but only a brief presentation to answer some of the common questions and problems raised by the Witnesses.

The difficulty of setting forth the doctrine (its lack of simplicity). C. S. Lewis shows the position of orthodoxy as he writes:

> If Christianity was something we were making up, of course we could make it easier. But it isn't. We

can't compete, in simplicity, with people who are *inventing* religions. How can we? We're dealing with Fact. *Of course* anyone can be simple if he has no facts to bother about![48]

The Trinity a mystery. In what sense does the minister and theologian use the term "mystery" when he speaks of the Trinity? The Trinity is a mystery in that it is a fact about which man has a certain knowledge, but along with the knowledge he also is to a considerable extent ignorant; man has knowledge, but not complete knowledge. It is not contradictory, but beyond human powers of understanding. A view of God which is fully understood by man's reason could not be a view of a God Who is infinite. A God Who is fully understood is a God set forth in the image of man. When theology speaks of mystery, as it speaks of the Trinity, it does not set forth something which is peculiar to theology alone. The entire universe is filled with mysteries—things known in part, but not fully understood. The doctrine of the Trinity as set forth at times seems contradictory. The fault lies not in the doctrine but in the inadequacy of language to express that which is infinite. To quote at length from Leonard Hodgson as he discusses the mystery of the Trinity:

> There is all the difference in the world between a mystery which is alleged to exist in spite of admitted irrationality, and a mystery which is acknowledged because it is believed to embody a rationality which we are not yet sufficiently experienced and educated to comprehend.
>
> . . . One often meets people who seem to think that the doctrine of the Trinity is an encumbrance to the simple faith of the Christian believer, thinking this because they assume that the unities of our experience are of the simple type and the complex unity of the Trinity a figment of the ecclestiastical imagination . . . we have no actual experience of any existing unity in this world of space and time which is not of the organic type. . . . If either of the two types of unity is to be called a figment of human imagination, the absolutely simple and undifferentiated unity of the mathematician has the greater claim to that status.[49]

---

[48] C. S. Lewis, *Beyond Personality* (New York: The Macmillan Co., 1945), p. 13.

[49] Leonard Hodgson, *The Doctrine of the Trinity—Croall Lectures 1942-1943* (London: Nisbet and Co., Ltd., 1943), pp. 93, 94.

Some interesting quotes and references found in the Watchtower publications. A point made by the Watchtower publications concerning Isaiah 9:6, John 1:1 and 20: 28 etc., is that Jesus Christ is a "mighty God" but not "the Almighty God."[50] The verse in Revelation 1:8 reads in the *New World Translation:* " 'I am the Alpha and the Omega,' says Jehovah God, 'the One who is and who was and who is coming, the Almighty'." This is one case in which the Witnesses' translation has inserted "Jehovah" for "Lord." This verse was applied to Jesus Christ by Charles Taze Russell who wrote:

> It is since His resurrection that the message has gone forth—"All power in Heaven and in earth *is given* unto Me." (Matt. 28:18.) Consequently it is only since then that He could be called the Almighty.[51]

So even Russell attributed the title "Almighty" to Christ, and to be consistent with the best of texts, according to Russell's position, Christ would here be designated "Lord God Almighty."[52] One marginal reference on this verse in the *New World Translation* cites Matthew 24:30 which speaks of Jesus Christ. Another marginal reference on this verse cites Revelation 21:6, ". . . I am the Alpha and the Omega, the beginning and the end." Russell understands this title to be used of Christ.[53] Revelation 22:13, which reads, "I am the Alpha and the Omega, the first and the last, the beginning and the end," is also understood by Russell as speaking of

---

[50] *Let God Be True, op. cit.*, pp. 32, 33.

[51] *Zion's Watch Tower*, April 15, 1893, p. 115, quoted in C. J. Woodworth and George H. Fisher (comp. and ed.), *The Finished Mystery* (Vol. VII of *Studies in the Scriptures.* 7 vols; Brooklyn: International Bible Students Association, 1917), p. 15.

The Dawn Bible Students still accept Russell's interpretation of Revelation 1:8: "The speaker in this text seems clearly to be the resurrected Jesus. (See vss. 10, 11)" *The Dawn*, 34:56, May, 1966.

[52] Realizing the implications of these titles when applied to Christ, the Witnesses presently deny that Christ is addressed as "Alpha and the Omega" in Revelation 1:8; 21:6 and 22:13. The title "the First and the Last," when applied to Christ in Revelation 1:17 and 2:8, is viewed by the Witnesses as "limited in its meaning by being associated with the resurrection." In Revelation 22:13, which they apply to Jehovah, the meaning of the same title is viewed as without limitations. *Awake!* 47: 27, 28, June 8, 1966.

[53] *The Finished Mystery, op. cit.*, p. 318.

Christ.[54] The threefold title found in this verse is the title that only Jehovah God could bear, yet the title is here applied to Christ. The marginal references in the NWT cite Revelation 1:8 and Isaiah 48:12. The Revelation passage has already been examined and the latter reference associates "I am the first and the last" with Jehovah of the Old Testament.

That Revelation 22:12 refers to Jesus Christ (and therefore v. 13 must also) is seen when this verse is compared with Revelation 2:18-23, 22:20, and 22:7. *The Finished Mystery,* commenting on Revelation 22:7, records: "See Rev. 16:15; 22:10, 12, 20. Jesus is the speaker."[55]

In Revelation 2:18-23 (NWT) the speaker is plainly identified as "the Son of God . . ." (2:18). In verse 23 the Son of God says: " '. . . I am he who searches the innermost thoughts and hearts, and I will give to YOU individually according to YOUR deeds'." The marginal references in the NWT cite several passages. Every Old Testament verse listed refers to Jehovah God!

When Christ is called "Alpha and Omega," "First and the Last," "Beginning and End," etc., one can do nothing else than conclude that Jesus Christ is God!

Some Old Testament indications of the Trinity. 1. The Unity of God (Deuteronomy 6:4): " 'Listen, O Israel: Jehovah our God is one Jehovah' " (NWT). An alternate reading given is " 'Jehovah is our God; Jehovah is one'." Yet even this word for "one" (*echod*) expresses a compound unity. That this word expresses not absolute one, but unity, can be seen in the use of the word in such passages as Genesis 1:5 and 2:24. In the first passage day and night are united into a compound unity by *echod,* literally into "day one." The second passage, speaks of man and wife, who unite and "become one flesh" (NWT). The passage views two individuals constituting a real oneness. Ezra 2:64 clearly shows the use of *echod* as it could be literally translated: "And the whole assembly was as one."[55a] The word for absolute oneness *(yachid),* although appearing twelve times

---

[54] *Ibid.,* p. 336.

[55] *Ibid.,* p. 334.

[55a] For a discussion of the root meaning of *echod* and its translation see: David L. Cooper, *The Eternal God Revealing Himself* (Harrisburg, Pa.: The Evangelical Press, 1928), pp. 50-60.

in the Old Testament, is never used of the unity of Jehovah God.

2. The plural noun *Elohim* is used with the plural verb. The plural noun and verb are significant, for the Witnesses contend: ". . . The trinitarians argue that the use of *Elohim* with a singular verb means there are three coeternal, coequal Persons in one God. . . ."[56] The Witnesses, among others, have tried to make the plural form a plural of majesty: "The form of the title *Elohim* is plural, the plural of excellence or majesty and not to denote a multiple personality."[57] That this is not the case is pointed out by Knight as he writes:

> Some have suggested, for example, that the word is a plural of majesty. But surely that is to read into Hebrew speech a modern way of thinking. The Kings of Israel and Judah are always addressed in the singular in our Bible records.[58]

The use of the plural noun is seen in such verses as Genesis 35:7 and 20:13. The use of the plural verb and noun is a clear indication of the Trinity in the light of the New Testament.

3. Plural pronouns are used in passages referring to God: "'. . . Let us make man in our image, according to our likeness. . .'" (Gen. 1:26 NWT). "'. . . The man has become like one of us. . .'" (Gen. 3:22 NWT). Genesis 11:7, 8 is also significant: "'. . . Let us go down and there confuse their language. . . . Accordingly Jehovah scattered them. . .'" (NWT). These verses clearly show the plurality in the Godhead.

4. The Holy Spirit is distinguished from Jehovah God. The person of the Holy Spirit is hidden in the *New World Translation* rendering of Genesis 1:2, where the Witnesses translate "God's active force." The Spirit of God is dis-

[56] *New Heavens and a New Earth* (Brooklyn: Watchtower Bible and Tract Society, Inc., 1953), p. 36.

[57] *New World Translation of the Hebrew Scriptures* (Brooklyn: Watchtower Bible and Tract Society, 1953), I, p. 29.

[58] G. A. F. Knight, *A Biblical Approach to the Doctrine of the Trinity* (Scottish Journal of Theology Occasional Papers No. 1. Edinburgh: Oliver and Boyd Ltd., 1953), p. 20.

tinguished from God in such passages as: Genesis 1:2; Psalm 51:11; Isaiah 11:1, 2 and 48:16.

5. Old Testament passages unite the three Persons. The Son of God says: "Come ye near unto me, hear ye this; from the beginning I have not spoken in secret; from the time that it was, there am I; and now the Lord Jehovah hath sent me, and his Spirit" (Isa. 48:16 ASV). Isaiah 63:8-10 is also very clear; God is seen as the "Saviour," the Son of God is seen as "the angel of his presence," and in verse 10 the Holy Spirit is named.

The Angel of Jehovah is identified as Jehovah. To the Witnesses, "The Angel of Jehovah" ("Jehovah's angel") is Jesus Christ in his prehuman form.[59] By taking this position, the Witnesses themselves set forth unanswerable evidence that Jesus Christ is Jehovah! In the following presentation, the *New World Translation of the Hebrew Scriptures* is used. The theophanies or Christophanies which are presented are listed in the order in which they appear.

1. Genesis 16:7-14. In verses 10-12 "Jehovah's angel" speaks. Verse 13 reads: "Then she [Sarah] began to call the name of Jehovah, who was speaking to her. . . ."

2. Genesis 21:17-19. The Angel of God is identified with God.

3. Genesis 22:11-18. The Angel of Jehovah is the mouthpiece of God, and He uses the first person as if it were Jehovah speaking. Abraham receives and accepts the appearance as a theophany of Jehovah Himself (v. 14).

4. Genesis 31:11-13. The Angel of God speaks to Jacob and says: " 'I am the God of Bethel . . .' " (v. 13). "The God of Bethel," (Gen. 28) could be no less than Jehovah!

5. Genesis 32:24-30. Jacob wrestles with "a man" (v. 24), but proclaims in verse 30 " 'I have seen God face to face. . . .' " Hosea 12:4, 5 identifies the man as the Angel of Jehovah—Jehovah Himself.

6. Genesis 48:15, 16. Jacob associates the "angel" (Angel of Jehovah) with God as an instrument of redemption. The only *goel* of man is Jehovah God (Isa. 44:6).

7. Exodus 3:2-6. In verse 2 the Angel of Jehovah appears to Moses, but it is as Jehovah and as God that the divine visitor speaks (v. 4).

---

[59] *New Heavens and a New Earth, op. cit.*, p. 27.

8. Exodus 14:19-24. In verse 19 the account makes it clear that it was "the angel of God who was going ahead of the camp of Israel. . . ." In Exodus 13:21 "Jehovah was going ahead of them. . . ." See also 14:24, which places Jehovah in the same position as the Angel of Jehovah (14:19).

9. Judges 2:1-5. The Angel of Jehovah speaks as Jehovah.

10. Judges 6:11-24. In verses 11 and 12 "Jehovah's angel" is distinct from Jehovah. In verse 14 "Jehovah's Angel" becomes Jehovah Himself. In verse 22 "Jehovah's angel" and "Lord Jehovah" are both brought into the account. Verse 23 goes back to Jehovah alone, and the next verse records that "Gideon built an altar there to Jehovah. . . ."

11. Judges 13:2-23. In verse 3 "Jehovah's angel" appears to Manoah, and he is called a "man of God" by Manoah. The angel is termed many times "Jehovah's angel" and in verse 22 Manoah says: " 'We shall positively die, because it is God that we have seen'."

Proceeding from the Witnesses' own position that the Angel of Jehovah was Jesus Christ, no conclusion is possible but that the Jehovah of the Old Testament is the Lord Jesus Christ of the New Testament.

The identification of Christ with Jehovah in the New Testament. The New Testament writers often apply Old Testament passages which refer to Jehovah to Christ in the New Testament.[60] (1) Matthew 3:3, Mark 1:2, 3, Luke 3:4 and John 1:23 all quote Isaiah 40:3: "Listen! Someone is calling out in the wilderness: 'Clear up the way of Jehovah, YOU people! Make the highway for our God through the desert plain straight!' " (NWT). (2) Malachi 3:1 (applied to John in Matt. 11:10) and 4:5, 6 is quoted in Luke 1:17:

> Also he will go before him with Elijah's spirit and power, to turn back the hearts of fathers to children and the disobedient ones to practical wisdom of righteous ones, to get ready for Jehovah a prepared people [NWT].

When the phrase, "he will go before him," is connected with Malachi 3:1 (where Jehovah says, "and he must clear up a

[60] For an extended study and an index of verses beyond those presented here see: Edward W. Eckman, "The Identification of Christ with *Yahweh* by New Testament Writers," *The Gordon Review*, 6:145-53. Summer, 1964.

way before me") it is seen that Christ is no mere representative, but He is identified with Jehovah. (3) Hebrews 1:10-12 addressed to Christ, is a quotation of Psalm 102:25-27. Psalm 102 is addressed to Jehovah (v. 1, "O Jehovah" NWT) and the name "Jehovah" is mentioned elsewhere in the Psalm. What the writer of the Psalm declared of Jehovah is declared of Christ in Hebrews (1:8 ff.). (4) The quotation in I Peter 2:3 of Psalm 34:8 is unmistakable. The marginal reference in the NWT makes the connection. Psalm 34:8 says in part: "O TASTE and see that Jehovah is good. . ." (NWT). The context of I Peter 2 clearly identifies the "Lord" there as Jesus Christ. The Witnesses also understand the context in the same way, applying I Peter 2:4-6 to Christ.[61] Why is "Lord" in I Peter 2:3 not translated "Jehovah"? (5) Isaiah 6:1, 3, 10, which tells of Isaiah's vision of the glory of Jehovah, is explained by John (John 12:37-41) as the glory of Jesus Christ. Note especially verse 41. (6) Other examples of Christ's identification with Jehovah are: Isaiah 45:23 quoted in Philippians 2:10 ff.; Joel 2:32 quoted in Romans 10:13, and Isaiah 45:23 quoted in Romans 14:11.[62]

The foregoing verses are just a sample of the many which are found in the New Testament.

Jesus Christ addressed as God. The testimony to the deity of Christ is so great that if it could be proven that Jesus Christ was never addressed as "God" it would not affect the conclusion that He was God manifest in the flesh—but it can be definitely established that Christ was so addressed.

Christ is addressed as "God" *(theos)* without question in John 1:1; John 1:18 (the best manuscripts and the older fathers read "the only begotten God"); John 20:28; Titus 2:13; Hebrews 1:8; II Peter 1:1 and I John 5:20. Romans 9:5 is taken by many as a direct reference to Christ as God; the interpretation depends on the punctuation. A full stop after "flesh" would make the words "who is over all God

[61] *The Watchtower*, 86:749, December 15, 1965. It is interesting that the *Watch Tower Publications Index* listings show no entries under I Peter 2:3. The same is true for Russell's *Studies in the Scriptures*.

[62] In Romans 10:13 and 14:11 the NWT obscures the truth by inserting "Jehovah" in place of "Lord." Both verses should be understood of Christ. C. T. Russell was honest enough to acknowledge this. See *Studies in the Scriptures*, I, pp. 100, 101; III, p. 369.

blessed for ever" a benediction. No stop or a comma would apply the words to Christ. Cullmann concludes that the benediction ending "is hardly the one suggested by a philological and material consideration of the context."[63]

In the Appendix note in the *New World Translation of the Christian Greek Scriptures* (pp. 781-83) on Titus 2:13, no real evidence is given for the translators' rendering of the verse: "While we wait for the happy hope and glorious manifestation of the great God and of our Savior Christ Jesus." Several translations are mentioned which translate the verse generally as the Witnesses have, but, there is no grammatical explanation. Metzger points out:

> This rendering, by separating "the great God" from "our Savior Christ Jesus," overlooks a principle of Greek grammar, which was detected and formulated in a rule by Granville Sharp in 1798. . . . This verse in Titus, therefore, must be translated . . . "Awaiting our blessed hope, the appearing of the glory of our great God and Savior Jesus Christ."[64]

The rendering of II Peter 1:1 follows the same rule and should be translated: " '. . . Our God and Savior Jesus Christ'."[65]

One Old Testament reference should be mentioned: in Isaiah 9:6 the Messiah is designated the "Mighty God," even in the *New World Translation.* The Hebrew words translated "Mighty God" *(el gibbor)* in Isaiah 9:6 also appear in Isaiah 10:21. This reference uses the identical expression to identify Jehovah. Hoekema points out that this designation "is, in Old Testament literature, a traditional designation of Jehovah—see Deuteronomy 10:17, Jeremiah 32:18, and Nehemiah 9:32."[66] When Witnesses attempt to make a dis-

---

[63] Oscar Cullmann, *The Christology of the New Testament,* trans. S. C. Guthrie and C. A. M. Hall (Philadelphia: The Westminster Press, 1959), p. 312.

See the discussion which presents evidence that the last clause should be applied to Jesus Christ in William Sanday and Arthur C. Headlam, *A Critical and Exegetical Commentary on the Epistle to the Romans* (New York: Charles Scribner's Sons, 1915), pp. 232-38.

[64] Metzger, "The Jehovah's Witnesses and Jesus Christ," *op. cit.,* p. 79.

[65] *Ibid.*

[66] Hoekema, *op. cit.,* p. 332.

tinction and say that Christ is a "Mighty God" and Jehovah alone is the "Almighty God," they must violate the Scriptures and teach polytheism. The *New World Translation* rendering of Isaiah 44:6-9 shows that the Witnesses are wrong: "'. . . Besides me there is no God. . . . Does there exist a God besides me? No, there is no Rock'."

True, others are designated "gods" (angels, idols, false gods, magistrates), but these are never made objects of true worship. Paul makes the situation clear in I Corinthians 8:4-6:

> . . . There is no God but one. For even though there are those who are called "gods," whether in heaven or on earth, just as there are many "gods" and many "lords," there is actually to us one God the Father, out of whom all things are, and we for him, and there is one Lord, Jesus Christ, through whom all things are, and we through him [NWT].

B. B. Warfield remarks cogently: "You cannot prove that only one God exists by pointing out that you yourself have two."[67] When the Witnesses admit that there is a "Mighty God" and an "Almighty God" they are doing just this and they make the admission that they are polytheists!

Arndt-Gingrich point out that Ignatius (died c. 110) calls Christ "God" in many passages.[68] He is an important witness to the Christological thought of the early Church because he was born shortly before or after the ascension and his life spanned the writing of the New Testament. In his Epistles to the Ephesians and to the Romans he used such expressions as: "Jesus Christ our God," "in the blood of God," and "our God Jesus Christ." Ignatius also wrote: "For our God, Jesus Christ, was conceived in the womb of Mary. . . . God appeared in the likeness of man." At another place he stated: "Permit me to be an imitator of the passion of my God."[69] It is evident that the Christological statements of John and Paul were preserved by Ignatius.

Titles of Jehovah applied to Christ. An entire volume could be written on this line of proof for the deity of Christ:

---

[67] Warfield, *op. cit.*, pp. 75, 76.

[68] Arndt-Gingrich, *op. cit.*, p. 357.

[69] J. B. Lightfoot, *The Apostolic Fathers*, ed. J. R. Harmer (1891 edition; Grand Rapids: Baker Book House, 1962), pp. 63-68, 75-79.

> One of the most remarkable things in our Lord's ministry is the quiet assurance with which he unhesitatingly applies to Himself titles from the Old Testament which are there indisputably used of Jehovah. Moreover, the writers in the New Testament often ascribe such titles to Christ.[70]

Those listed by Bruce and Martin are: "First and Last" (cf. Rev. 2:8; 22:13 with Isa. 41:4; 44:6; 48:12); "I Am" (cf. John 8:58 with Exod. 3:14); "Author of Eternal Words" (cf. Matt. 24:35 with Isa. 40:8); "Light" (cf. John 1:4-9; 8:12 with Ps. 27:1 and I John 1:5); "Rock" (cf. Isa. 8:14 with I Pet. 2:6-8); "Bridegroom" (cf. Isa. 62:5 with Mark 2:19); "Shepherd" (cf. Ps. 23:1 with John 10:11 and Heb. 13:20); "Forgiver of Sins" (cf. Acts 5:31 with Jer. 31:34); "Redeemer" (cf. Hos. 13:14 and Ps. 130:7 with Tit. 2:13, 14); "Saviour" (cf. Isa. 43:3 with II Pet. 1:1, 11); "Co-Partner of Divine Glory" (cf. Isa. 42:8 with John 17:1-5 and I Cor. 2:8), and "Judge" (cf. Joel 3:12 with Matt. 25:31-46).[71]

Two classes of Trinitarian texts. There are two classes of texts which support the Trinity doctrine: (1) Those which associate the three Persons, and (2) those which attribute deity to the three Persons individually, a category which has already been adequately discussed.

The association of the three Persons is seen in: (1) the baptism of Jesus (Matt. 3:16, 17); (2) the baptismal formula (Matt. 28:19); (3) the apostolic benediction (II Cor. 13:14); (4) Ephesians 4:4-6; (5) Ephesians 2:18; (6) Ephesians 3:1-5, 14-17; (7) Ephesians 5:18-20; (8) I Corinthians 12:4-6; (9) I Peter 1:2; (10) John 15:26; (11) John 14:26, and (12) Jude 1:20, 21. The foregoing passages are a few of many found in the Scriptures.[72]

The foregoing evidence on the Trinity, the deity of Christ and the personality of the Holy Spirit is fragmentary in comparison to the vast amount of Scriptural material available. The honest student of the Word of God will reject the denials of the Jehovah's Witnesses. It is important to

---

[70] F. F. Bruce and W. J. Martin, *The Deity of Christ* (Manchester: North of England Evangelical Truth, 1964), p. 6.

[71] *Ibid.*, pp. 6-14.

[72] A more extensive list is included in J. N. D. Kelly, *Early Christian Creeds* (New York: Longmans, Green and Co., Inc., 1950), p. 23.

remember that the unscriptural rejection of the Trinity affects every other cardinal doctrine of the Bible.

II. The Bodily Resurrection of Christ

It has been seen in the statements of the Witnesses dealing with the resurrection of Christ, that there is an outright denial of His bodily resurrection. This view was forced on the Russellite theology by Russell's ideas on the second coming of Christ, for to him, Christ's "second presence" was an invisible one, and therefore His resurrection also must be a spiritual resurrection. In the article, "How Does Christ Come the Second Time?,"[73] the inseparable linking of the resurrection and the second invisible presence is seen.

Under the subheading, "How Will Christ Come Again," the question is asked: "Should we expect Christ to come again in a human body?" The answer is, "No."[74] The Witnesses arguments in rejection of the bodily resurrection of Christ and the examination and refutation of these points follow.

1. The favorite text quoted by the Watchtower publications in the rejection of the bodily resurrection, and in proof of Christ's being raised a spirit creature, is I Peter 3:18:

> Why, even Christ died once for all time concerning sins, a righteous person for unrighteous ones, that he might lead YOU to God, he being put to death in the flesh, but being made alive in the spirit [NWT].

"In the spirit" is interpreted by the Witnesses to mean that Christ rose a spirit creature. It should be noticed that the verse does not say that Christ was raised a spirit, but "in the spirit." The last clause is, as J. A. Schep says, "a most outstanding *crux interpretum*."[75] After considering a number of interpretations, including the idea of a spiritual resurrection, Schep advances the understanding of the passage which seems best to meet the demands of the context and the analogy of Scripture:

---

[73] *The Watchtower*, 76:101-04, February 15, 1955.

[74] *Ibid.*, p. 101.

[75] J. A. Schep, *The Nature of the Resurrection Body* (Grand Rapids: Wm. B. Eerdmans Publishing Company, 1964), p. 74.

> This, then, is what the clause seems to declare: Jesus was (violently) put to death as one who in body and soul was "flesh," i.e., in a state of humiliation because of our sins; but in the resurrection he was made alive as one who in body (flesh) and soul was and is "Spirit," i.e. full of the Holy Spirit's power, life, and glory.
>
> This interpretation fits naturally into the context and is in conformity with the teachings of I Corinthians 15:45, 46. . . .[76]

The view that Christ rose as a spirit creature is also unacceptable as an understanding of I Peter 3:18 because such an interpretation is clearly contradicted in the Gospels, by Paul and in Peter's messages "recorded in Acts, which imply the empty tomb and the preservation of Jesus' flesh."[77]

2. In further support of the spiritual resurrection of Christ, I Corinthians 15:45 is quoted: "It is even so written: 'The first man Adam became a living soul.' The last Adam became a life-giving spirit" (NWT). In I Corinthians 15:36-50 Paul is answering the twofold question: " 'How are the dead to be raised up? Yes, with what kind of body are they coming?' " (I Cor. 15:35 NWT). The contrast in verse 45 is not referring to the bodily form of Christ or Adam, but to the kind of life within them. One might well understand, the first Adam had soul life (life of the natural man); Christ had spiritual life (life fitted for heaven).[78]

3. Another favorite argument to demonstrate that Christ experienced a spiritual resurrection is the expression "flesh and blood cannot inherit God's kingdom" (I Cor. 15:50 NWT). The Witnesses reason that to lay aside "flesh and blood" one must become a spirit creature. The expression appears in four other places in the New Testament (Matt. 16:17; Gal. 1:16; Eph. 6:12; Heb. 2:14. The words in the last two verses are inverted.).

"In all the passages just mentioned, it is obvious from the context that 'flesh and blood' does not denote the substance of the human body." What then is the meaning? It is an expression which "belongs to the Rabbinic vocabulary" which placed "particular emphasis on man's earthly

---

[76] *Ibid.*, p. 77. See J. F. Rutherford's *Salvation*, p. 40.

[77] *Ibid.*, p. 76. See Peter's message in Acts 2:26-32.

[78] Schep gives an extended examination and explanation of this passage, *ibid.*, pp. 72-79.

condition as a frail and perishable creature, in contrast to the eternal and almighty God."[79] What then is the meaning of "flesh and blood cannot inherit God's kingdom"? Just what Paul says is the meaning, namely, that a change is necessary (15:51, 52): "For this which is corruptible . . . must put on immortality" (15:53 NWT). The passage does not teach that one must be deprived of a body of flesh, but that the body must be changed to fit it for the new realm where it will spend eternity. The Witnesses fail to consider that according to orthodoxy Christ's body was changed to fit it for heaven. Christ's body was a glorified body of "flesh and bones" (Luke 24:39).

4. The appearances of Christ in which He was not recognized demonstrate to the Witnesses that Christ's body did not rise from the dead, but he merely materialized bodies for the occasions of His appearances. In support, the follow-points are made: (a) When Mary saw Christ she did not recognize Him but took Him to be the gardener. (b) The two disciples on the road to Emmaus thought Him to be a stranger. (c) Christ was not recognized by the disciples that were fishing except for the miraculous draught of fishes. (d) Only to satisfy doubting Thomas, did Jesus materialize a body of similar form to the old.

A. The first reference to Mary is found in John 20:11-16. There are several good reasons why Mary did not recognize Jesus. (1) John 20:1 says that it was still dark when Mary reached the tomb: ". . . While there was still darkness. . ." (NWT). Her failure to recognize Christ could have been because of darkness. (2) Mary's thoughts are shown to be occupied completely with grief when she looked into the tomb and saw the angels. What she saw did not seem to register in her mind at all. Mary was neither startled nor afraid nor did she address the angels. The word used for Mary's weeping is *klaio,* which means loud and unrestrained weeping. Her eyes were blurred with tears as she saw Jesus. Just as she saw but did not see the angels, she saw Christ. The seeking of the dead sometimes keeps people from seeing the living. (3) Verse 14 says that Mary turned toward Christ, and again in verse 16 she turned toward Him. The second use of "turn" seems to imply that she had not

[79] *Ibid.*, pp. 201, 202.

looked fully at Him before. The NWT apparently makes this same distinction, as in verse 14 it translates "she turned back" and in verse 16, "upon turning around." (4) One must not overlook the possibility that Christ's clothing may have been different. (5) Mary was not looking for the risen Christ. Her mind was far from the fact of an accomplished resurrection. (6) Orthodoxy does not believe that Christ looked exactly the same as before His death. Christ was no longer the man of sorrows; His face reflected the glory and triumph of His resurrection. (7) It is only natural that Mary would turn and recognize Christ when He spoke her name. She was a stranger there, and hearing her name opened her eyes to recognize Him.

B. The reference to the two disciples on the road to Emmaus is found in Luke 24: 13-35. There are several good reasons for their not recognizing the risen Christ. (1) The scripture states in verse 16 that "their eyes were kept from recognizing him" (NWT). In this verse there is the use of the passive verb which denotes an agent external to them. The passive verb with the same force is used also in verse 31: "At that their eyes were fully opened. . ." (NWT). (2) It should be noticed in verse 16 that the article *tou* is used with the infinitive. This could either indicate purpose or result. Result seems the best, and therefore the verse would read: "But their eyes were held so that they did not recognize him." Christ had a definite purpose for keeping his identity secret. The passage seems to bear out the fact that Christ was so easily recognizable that it required a hiding of his features to keep from being recognized. (3) Other factors could be brought in: they were absorbed in conversation; they were all walking side by side, and Jesus' face could have been covered by the hood on His clothing; they may not have recognized Him because His clothing was different. Actually, none of these reasons are required, considering the Scripture's statement, indicated by points one and two.

C. The account of the disciples who did not recognize Christ until the miraculous catch of fish is recorded in John 21:1-14. There is no difficulty in this passage whatever for nonrecognition of Christ, for verse 8 shows that the disciples were "only about three hundred feet away. . ." (NWT). Realizing also that it was early morning and that there was such a distance between them, little wonder they did not recognize Him!

D. The reference to doubting Thomas is found in John 20:24-29. Although the Witness article states, "Only to satisfy doubting Thomas did Jesus appear in a form similar to that which he had before he died,"[80] this is not the only case in which Christ appeared in similar form. In Luke 24:36-43 and John 20:19-26 Christ appeared to the eleven in like form. Christ says in Luke 24:39, 40:

> "See my hands and my feet, that it is I myself; feel me and see, because a spirit does not have flesh and bones just as YOU behold that I have." And as he said this he showed them his hands and his feet [NWT].

All one must do with the passage is to take Christ at His word. The only way to reject this testimony is to deny the Bible willfully. If the long ending of Mark is accepted, Christ rebuked even the unbelief of the disciples concerning His bodily resurrection (Mark 16:14).

5. The ability of Jesus to go through closed doors seems to be a problem to the Witnesses. They point out that this would be impossible if He had a real body. There are three considerations that should be brought out at this point: First, the Jesus that was resurrected was the same Jesus that died. Second, in some ways He was different. He had a glorified body which fitted Him for heavenly life. He was not a spirit, but He had a spiritual body (I Cor. 15:42-46). Third, "nowhere in the Gospels is it said that Jesus' body passed through closed doors."[81] The Witnesses do not consider that Christ did the impossible when He walked on the water before the crucifixion. Is it any more of a miracle to pass through material, a conclusion which is not required by Scripture?

6. The Witnesses' view of the atonement also results in the rejection of the bodily resurrection. The Witnesses reason: ". . . Having sacrified his human life as a ransom, to take it back would be to cancel the ransoming of the human race."[82] This is an interesting view, and it also should

---

[80] *The Watchtower*, 76:102, February 15, 1955.

[81] Schep, *op. cit.*, p. 141.

[82] *The Watchtower*, *loc. cit.*

be noticed that it is not accompanied by any Scriptural proof. A comparison of Matthew 20:28 and John 10:17, 18 shows the fallacy of such a view. "'Just as the Son of man came, not to be ministered to, but to minister and to give his soul [margin, 'life'] a ransom in exchange for many'" (Matt. 20:28 NWT). John records Jesus' words:

> This is why the Father loves me, because I surrender my soul [Margin, "life"] in order that I may receive it again. No man has taken it away from me, but I surrendered it of my own initiative [John 10:17, 18, NWT].

Nothing can be clearer than these words of Christ; the life which He surrendered would be the same life which He would take again.

The following additional evidence is offered to show why orthodoxy believes in the bodily resurrection of Christ. Psalm 16:9 ff. which speaks prophetically of the resurrection of the Messiah, is so clear in its reference to the resurrection and the preservation of the body that it was quoted by Peter on the day of Pentecost. Psalm 16:9, 10 reads:

> Therefore my heart does rejoice and my glory is inclined to be joyful. Also, my own flesh will reside in security. For you will not leave my soul in Sheol. You will not allow your man of loving-kindness to see the pit [NWT].

Peter's quotation in Acts 2:26, 27 reads:

> On this account my heart became cheerful and my tongue rejoiced greatly. Moreover, even my flesh will dwell in hope: because you will not forsake my soul in Hades, neither will you grant your man of loving-kindness to see corruption [NWT].

The fact of the resurrection is attested by the raising of the body, not by the raising of a spirit. "Corruption" *(diaphthora)* is used only in reference to the body. Grimm-Thayer comment: ". . . *Corruption, destruction;* in the N. T. that destruction which is effected by the decay of the body after death. . . ."[83]

The Scriptures also make it clear that Christ in the heavenlies now dwells in a glorified body. Philippians 3:21

---

[83] Grimm-Thayer, *op. cit.*, p. 143; Arndt-Gingrich, *op. cit.*, p. 189.

contrasts man's present body with the glorification in store: "Who will refashion our humiliated body to be conformed to his glorious body. . ." (NWT). This verse shows that the *body* of redeemed man will be transformed into the likeness of the glorified *body* of Christ.

The Scripture in several places (I Cor. 15) speaks of a spiritual body *but never* that Christ became a spirit. The phrase "spiritual body" would be a contradiction of terms if it signified only a spirit. Rather, it implies a body adapted to the realm of the spirit, that is, the presence of God.

Romans 8:11 as quoted in the *New World Translation* makes it very clear that it is the body that shall be raised and that Christ's body was raised:

> If, now, the spirit of him that raised up Jesus from the dead dwells in YOU, he that raised up Christ Jesus from the dead will also make YOUR mortal bodies alive through his spirit that resides in YOU [NWT].

The mortal body is the subject of this verse. Verse 10 has already established that man's spirit has life, and just so the body will also be given life. The mortal body will be given life, or as I Corinthians 15:54 shows, the corruptible will put on incorruption and the mortal will put on immortality.

The passage in John 2:19-22 is subjected to the usual imaginative interpretation by the Witnesses, but the testimony of Scripture is very clear as it records Jesus' words, and the understanding of the disciples and Jews. What did Jesus mean by "the temple of his body" (v. 21)? The temple of God in I Corinthians 3:16 is plainly the body of the believer. The same thing is found in I Corinthians 6:19:

> What? Do YOU not know that the body of YOU people is the temple of the holy spirit within YOU which YOU have from God? Also, YOU do not belong to yourselves, for YOU were bought with a price. By all means, glorify God in the body of YOU people. [NWT].

In Mark 16:6 the angel presented the absence of Jesus' body as a proof of His resurrection: ". . . He was raised up, he is not here. See! the place where they laid him" (NWT). If the body had nothing to do with Jesus' resurrection as the Witnesses teach, the absence of the body actually proved nothing! The angel either was deluded or presented false evidence. Luke 24:3 records: "And when they entered they did not find the body of the Lord Jesus" (NWT). Verse 7 records the words of the angels as they recall the words of Jesus, "'. . . and yet on the third day rise'" (NWT). Verse 8, "So they called his sayings to mind. . ."(NWT), speaks of the disciples of Christ. The sayings they called to mind are found in John 2:19-21. The disciples realized that Christ was speaking of the bodily resurrection when He spoke to the Jews.

The rejection of the bodily resurrection of Christ is actually a rejection of the doctrine of the resurrection. The resurrection of Christ carries with it the bodily resurrection of believers in Christ.

III. The Ransom and Salvation by Faith

Much of the verbiage the Witnesses produce on their doctrine of the ransom is camouflage for their autosoteric system. F. E. Mayer, a Lutheran theologian, went so far as to state:

> In reality Rutherford's system of work-righteousness has no need of Christ's death. But, claiming to be "Bible Students," they do not want to appear as though they ignored the fact of the Savior's death.[84]

> Jehovah's Witnesses do not want a savior. They want no mercy, no grace, no pardon. They want a chance to show how good they are. They want a theocracy in which law and order prevails and they can work out their own salvation.[85]

The Witnesses, while acknowledging inherited sin and guilt, do not have any real concept of sin's awfulness and penalty. It must be remembered that a false doctrine of redemption is a natural result of a wrong view on the Person of Christ.

The teaching of the Society on the ransom of Christ has been confused from the beginning, with C. T. Russell presenting three differing positions on this doctrine in the

---

[84] F. E. Mayer, *Jehovah's Witnesses* (revised 1957; St. Louis, Mo.: Concordia Publishing House, 1942), p. 32.

[85] *Ibid.*, p. 33.

publications of the Watch Tower Society.[86] The teaching on the subject since Russell's death has also been unsteady as to the extent and application of the ransom, first placing Adam under the ransom with a chance for life, and then removing him from this provision.

The Society editors reversed themselves on the fate of those destroyed in Sodom and Gomorrah by first excluding them as beneficiaries of the ransom, and then giving them the opportunity for a future acceptance of the ransom during the millennial period.[87]

The doctrine of the ransom as taught by the Witnesses is far short of what Scripture teaches concerning Christ and what He did. Their doctrine that Christ was a "corresponding ransom" is explained in the following quotation:

> It was the perfect man Adam that had sinned and so had lost for his offspring human perfection and its privileges. Jesus must likewise be humanly perfect, to correspond with the sinless Adam in Eden. In that way he could offer a ransom that *exactly* corresponded in value with what the sinner Adam lost for his descendents. This requirement of divine justice did not allow for Jesus to be more than a perfect man. That is why, in writing I Timothy 2:5, 6, the apostle Paul uses a special word in Greek, *antilytron,* to describe what Jesus offered in sacrifice to God.[88]

The *New World Translation* rendering of I Timothy 2:5, 6 reflects this understanding: ". . . Christ Jesus, who gave himself a corresponding ransom for all. . . ."

What is the origin of this unscriptural doctrine of a "corresponding ransom" in which Christ's sacrifice could be no more than the sacrifice of perfect man? This doctrine was first proposed in the *Watch Tower* issue of December, 1879, p. 8: "The ransom has relation to the thing bought as its *equivalent.*"[89] While the view was advanced by the associate editor of the *Watch Tower,* J. H. Paton, it was

---

[86] *Back to the Bible Way,* 5:412-15, January-February, 1956. The conflicting teachings are presented in three columns and documentation is given for each statement.

[87] See below, pp. 224, 225.

[88] *Things in Which It is Impossible for God to Lie* (Brooklyn: Watchtower Bible and Tract Society of New York, Inc., 1965), p. 232.

[89] *Watch Tower Reprints,* p. 62.

presented over the years by Russell[90] and as has been seen, the doctrine is still being taught.[91]

The "corresponding ransom" doctrine should be rejected on the following grounds: First, the Greek word *antilutron* occurs only once in the Bible (I Tim. 2:6) and the meaning need not be much different than *lutron* ("ransom").[92] After an examination of the words in the *lutron* group in the New Testament, Morris concludes that in meaning *antilutron*

> does not seem to differ greatly from the simple *lutron,* but the preposition emphasizes the thought of substitution; it is a "substitute-ransom" that is signified. Such a term well suits the context, for we read of Christ "who gave himself on behalf of all" (I Tim. ii. 6). The thought clearly resembles that of Mk. x. 45, i.e. that Jesus has died in the stead of those who deserved death. If the thought of substitution is there, we find it here to an even greater degree in view of the addition of the preposition which emphasizes substitution.[93]

It should be obvious to the reader that what the Watchtower writers convey with the words "corresponding ransom" and what is conveyed by the words "substitute ransom" as explained by Morris and the rest of Scripture are not remotely the same.

Second, Scripture is very clear that Jesus Christ was more than just a perfect man equivalent to Adam. The evi-

---

[90] *Studies in the Scriptures,* I, p. 133; Author's Foreword dated October 1, 1916, p. ii.

[91] *The Watchtower,* 74:205-07, April 1, 1953. The article is entitled, "The Corresponding Ransom."

[92] Arndt-Gingrich, *op. cit.,* p. 74; Grimm-Thayer, *op. cit.,* p. 50.

[93] Leon Morris, *The Apostolic Preaching of the Cross* (Grand Rapids: Wm. B. Eerdmans Publishing Company, 1956), p. 48. In support of the Witnesses' view *A Greek and English Lexicon of the New Testament* (1845 ed.) by John Parkhurst is cited. It is doubtful that the lexicon by "correspondent ransom" conveyed the same idea that the Witnesses have attributed to these words, and the listed definition is questionable from the standpoint of the meaning of the Greek word *antilutron.* If any emphasis beyond ransom is placed on the word, as Morris points out above, it should be "substitute." The present writer checked a number of translations, lexicons, and commentaries; none of them reflect the idea advanced by the Witnesses.

Dana and Mantey, *op. cit.,* p. 100, state that "there is conclusive proof now that the dominant meaning for *anti* in the first century was *instead of,*" which implies substitution.

dence which supports the deity of Christ adequately demonstrates this. In addition, several more scriptures may be cited to prove this point. (1) Jesus Christ was the Creator and is the sustainer of the universe (John 1:3; Col. 1:17; Heb. 1:3). Colossians 1:17 indicates that since the original creation, in Christ "all things consist" (*sunistemi* "continue, endure, exist,"[94] "to cohere, hold together"[95]). The universe, which was created by Christ, continues or is continuously sustained by Him. (2) Christ's claim in John 8:58, " 'Truly, truly, I say to you, before Abraham was born, I AM' ,"[96] indicated that He was more than a perfect man (cf. *The Septuagint,* Exod. 3:14 and Isa. 41:4). Scripture recognizes only one "I AM." (3) John 5:18 gives *John's* statement concerning Christ: ". . . The Jews began seeking all the more to kill him, because not only was he breaking the sabbath but he was also calling God his own Father, making himself equal to God" (NWT).

More Scriptural evidence which presents Jesus Christ as the God-man could be given, but the fact has already been established.

The Witnesses' doctrine of the ransom largely ignores the Biblical teaching on the subject, by claiming to accept the "ransom sacrifice" which was provided in the death of Christ not as a finished work, but only as a foundation from which man works to provide his own salvation. The Biblical doctrine of redemption and the salvation of man does not lay the burden upon man, but presents man with a finished work which has already been accomplished by God in man's behalf. The expression "once saved always saved," which the Witnesses so despise, is only dangerous if it is not balanced with the teaching of the Bible that man is saved unto good works (Eph. 2:8-10; Tit. 3:8).

Romans 5:10, 11 shows that the reconciliation of man by the death of Christ is complete; all men can do is to enter into it by faith. II Corinthians 5:20 teaches the same

---

[94] Arndt-Gingrich, *op. cit.,* p. 798.

[95] Grimm-Thayer, *op. cit.,* p. 605.

[96] *New American Standard Bible: New Testament* (La Habra Calif.: The Lockman Foundation, 1963), *loc. cit.* The Witnesses' translation of this verse which substituted "I have been" for "I AM," necessitated the use of a designation, "perfect indefinite," which is an invention of the Watchtower translators. Martin and Klann, *op. cit.,* p. 55. The footnote on this verse has been changed to read "perfect tense" in *The Kingdom Interlinear.*

thing. Hebrews 9:13-26 views the redemption as an accomplished and completed fact.

The acceptance of the ransom brings immediate results: (1) it satisfies God, (2) it removes guilt, (3) it redeems the sinner and gives a positive standing before God, and (4) it gives everlasting life. These results are through acceptance by faith of that which has already been done.

This writer would agree with the Witnesses that Christ's death did provide a ransom, but it also provided full satisfaction to God for sin to all who believe. When man believes, reconciliation takes place. There is a complete alteration and adjustment to God's required standard by the removal of the offense (Rom. 5:6-11). Although reconciliation was provided on Calvary, the believer enters into it when he places faith in Christ.

To illustrate the Witnesses' view of redemption, the insufficiency of Christ's sacrifice to save apart from the efforts of man, these headings from the book *Make Sure of All Things* are cited: "Salvation a Goal to Be Attained—Not 'Once Saved Always Saved' "[97]; "Growth to Salvation necessary"[98]; "Work Out Salvation With Fear and Trembling"[99]; "Study of Scriptures Necessary for Salvation"[100].

The Bible is clear concerning the means provided to receive salvation: (1) Salvation is a gift: "For the wages sin pays is death, but the gift God gives is everlasting life by Christ Jesus our Lord" (Rom. 6:23 NWT). (2) Salvation is by grace, received through faith; it is a gift, not a reward for work:

> By this undeserved kindness, indeed, YOU have been saved through faith; and this not owing to YOU, it is God's gift. No, it is not owing to works, in order that no man should have grounds for boasting [Eph. 2:8, 9 NWT].

Nothing can be more plain than this passage which shows salvation has already "been" received. The appropriating agency in salvation is "faith." Salvation is "not owing to

---

[97] *Make Sure of All Things, op. cit.*, p. 332.
[98] *Ibid.*
[99] *Ibid.*, p. 333.
[100] *Ibid.*

works." (3) Salvation cannot be earned. The *New World Translation* is a bit awkward as it reads:

> Owing to no activities in righteousness that we had performed, but according to his mercy he saved us through the bath that brought us to life and through the making of us new by holy spirit [Titus 3:5 NWT].

Two possible grounds of salvation are set forth; the ground of works, and the ground of God's grace and mercy. Salvation is not from (*ex*) works as the source, but on the contrary *(alla)* by the mercy and provision of God. Salvation is viewed as an already accomplished fact (*esosen,* aorist), accomplished before works of righteousness were evident. Man's new state of salvation does not rest on his merit. The remainder of the verse indicates the means by which the grace and mercy of God are realized in experience—in essence, a new birth by the Holy Spirit.

II Timothy 1:9 also shows salvation cannot be earned:

> He saved us and called us with a holy calling, not by reason of our works, but by reason of his own purpose and undeserved kindness. This was given us in connection with Christ Jesus before times long lasting [NWT].

Again salvation is viewed as a past event (*sosantos,* aorist), provided solely by God on the already completed sacrifice of Jesus Christ. God's calling and provision of salvation does not in any way depend on anything external or creaturely. (4) Salvation is received through faith: " 'For God loved the world so much that he gave his only-begotten Son, in order that everyone exercising faith in him might not be destroyed but have everlasting life' " (John 3:16 NWT). The NWT rendering of *pisteuon,* "exercising faith," in no way speaks of works for salvation. A better translation would be "everyone who believes." The identical participle is so translated in John 6:47. " '. . . He that believes has everlasting life' " (NWT). Salvation is a present possession (*echei,* "has," present indicative). "But these have been written down that YOU may believe that Jesus is the Christ the Son of God, and that, because of believing, YOU may have life by means of his name" (John 20:31 NWT). Romans 3:28 makes it clear that salvation is by faith: "For we reckon that a man is declared righteous by faith apart from works of law" (NWT). "Declared righteous" (*dikaioo*), means that a man is justified, guiltless, righteous and stands accepted. This declaring righteous, or justification, signifies the pronouncing of the sinner righteous before God. Justification is associated inseparably with the crucifixion of Christ, for sinners are "declared righteous now by his blood . . ." (Rom. 5:9 NWT). The declaring of the sinner righteous is viewed in this verse as an accomplished fact (aorist passive participle). Romans 4:5 emphasizes the basis of righteousness apart from works: "On the other hand, to the man that does not work but puts faith in him who declares the ungodly one righteous, his faith is counted as righteousness" (NWT).

Salvation's plan is built on three elements: (1) Man's need. "For all have sinned and fall short of the glory of God. . ." (Rom. 3:23 NWT). (2) God's provision (John 3:16). (3) Man's response. "However, as many as did receive him, to them he gave authority to become God's children, because they were exercising faith in his name" (John 1:12 NWT).

After accepting God's provision, a believer is viewed as having "everlasting life" and as having already "passed over from death to life" (John 5:24 NWT. See also I John 3:14). Romans 8:1 states: "Therefore those in union with [*en* "in"] Christ Jesus have no condemnation" (NWT). "No condemnation" means that all condemnatory judgment is past, because man has been "declared righteous." Salvation is a present possession.

Witnesses may claim that justification and a number of verses cited in this section have application only to the 144,000. According to the teaching of the Watch Tower Bible and Tract Society writers this may be true—but where is the authority for such a claim? The pronouncement of the Society, the same Society which through its writers, and especially through Judge Rutherford, promoted many time and doctrinal speculations.

The article, "Identifying the Present-Day Beneficiaries," in the February 15, 1966 issue of *The Watchtower,* presents the story of erroneous interpretations and speculations advanced by the Witnesses in the identification of the "Great Multitude" of Revelation 7. The mistakes which were published over the years are conveniently brushed aside with the claim that it was not "God's due time" for the correct understanding. Articles such as this are becoming important to the Watchtower writers because many Witnesses are aware that changes in doctrine have been made and Christians who know this are confronting the Witnesses with the evidence. The changes in doctrine are defended as the result of "progressive light," and most of the Witnesses will blindly be satisfied with this explanation. But, can the current interpretations be guaranteed to be any more accurate than any of the previous views?

The Great Multitude was viewed as a second-class heavenly group because Russell and Rutherford said that this was true. Presently the Society accepts the interpretation of the Great Multitude as an earthly class because Rutherford said this was the case. Why is the present interpretation correct? Because the Society says that it is. The previous interpretations were declared correct with the same degree of assurance and with the same claim of Scriptural authority.

The article cited above mentions volume three of *Vindication,* and the now erroneous view that the Great Multitude was a secondary spiritual class, but an important claim advanced in this book is not recorded. In the Introduction the reader is told:

> That vision of Ezekiel concerning the temple has been a mystery for ages and generations, but now is due to be understood. The Scriptures and the physical facts both show that this prophecy was not due to be understood by God's people on earth until the year 1932.[101]

If the reader accepted that claim he would read the book and on page 204 would find the following, which "now is due to be understood."

> Ever and anon someone advances the conclusion that the "great multitude" will not be a spiritual class. The prophecy of Ezekiel shows that such a conclusion is erroneous. The fact that their position is seven steps higher than the outside shows that they must be made spirit creatures. . . . They must be spirit creatures in

---

[101] J. F. Rutherford, *Vindication* (Brooklyn: Watchtower Bible and Tract Society, 1932), III, p. 5.

order to be in the outer court of the divine structure, described by Ezekiel.[102]

That which was claimed as God's revelation "due to be understood" was rejected in Rutherford's Convention speech on May 31, 1935, and that which was labeled as "erroneous" was accepted as God's revelation. The previous position, which had been advanced in *Zion's Watch Tower* and the other publications of the Society from the beginning, a period of over fifty years, was supposedly God's revelation, for as Rutherford pointed out in 1934:

> *The Watchtower* is not the teacher of God's people. *The Watchtower* merely brings to the attention of God's people that which *he has revealed* [emphasis mine], and it is the privilege of each and everyone of God's children to prove by the Word of God whether these things are from man or are from the Lord.[103]

This writer has taken Rutherford's advice and has concluded with millions of "born again" Christians around the world that the Witnesses' doctrinal position relative to salvation and the new birth is of man. He would rather take the Word of God as it stands and accept its message that man can have assurance of sins forgiven and eternal life as a present possession.

IV. The New Birth

The Witnesses believe in the new birth, but, as shown, the new birth is an experience to be expected only by Christ and his body members, the 144,000. By the "born again" experience this select group of individuals is spirit-begotten, receiving the holy spirit and position as a spiritual son of God with a heavenly hope. Thus the teaching of the Watchtower Society is that only 144,000 persons are to seek and receive the "born again" experience and the rest are actually to remain unregenerate, for theirs is an earthly hope. The Christian rejects this view of the new birth as wicked and unscriptural!

---

[102] *Ibid.*, p. 204.

[103] J. F. Rutherford, *Jehovah* (Brooklyn: Watch Tower Bible and Tract Society, 1934), p. 191.

The Bible knows nothing of a division among Christians of a "born again" group and an unregenerate group. In fact, up until 1935 the Witnesses themselves believed in the spiritual birth of all the Witnesses. The twofold division of "the little flock" and the "Great Company" was held before 1935, but it was taught that "the Scriptures show two degrees or kinds of Heavenly salvation. . . ."[104] There was also the teaching that there were two earthly groups, the "Ancient Worthies" Abraham, Issac, Jacob, etc., who were to be the earthly princes, and the world of unregenerate mankind, which would receive a second chance during the Millennial Kingdom.[105]

Most orthodox ministers seriously question whether any consistent Jehovah's Witness can be "born again," since his doctrine denies the means and Agent of the "new birth." It is possible that there are some Jehovah's Witnesses who may have been "born again" before their entrance into this movement.

When Rutherford received the "new light" on the spiritual class, it became the teaching that only the 144,000 needed to be "born again." As a result, all the other Witnesses, members of the "Great Multitude," are, according to the Scriptures, alienated from God. The Scriptures are very clear as they said: ". . . But if anyone does not have Christ's spirit, this one does not belong to him" (Rom. 8:9 NWT). Notice the all-inclusive "anyone," which would include all mankind. "Christ's spirit" is the Holy Spirit, designated in this way because it was Christ that promised the Spirit and sent Him: "When the helper arrives that I will send YOU from the Father, the spirit of the truth which proceeds from the Father, that one will bear witness about me" (John 15:26 NWT). See also Acts 2:33 and John 16:14.

On the day of Pentecost Peter declared that anyone who would believe and repent would receive the Holy Spirit:

> Peter said to them: "Repent, and let each one of YOU be baptized in the name of Jesus Christ for forgiveness of YOUR sins, and YOU will receive the free gift of the holy spirit. For the promise is to YOU and

---

[104] *The Finished Mystery, op. cit.*, p. 134.
[105] *Ibid.*

> to YOUR children and to all those afar off. . ." [Acts 2:38, 39 NWT].

Galatians 3:13, 14 states that the purpose of Christ's redemption was that those who believed could by faith receive the Holy Spirit: "Christ redeemed us . . . that we might receive the promise of the Spirit through faith" (ASV). This redemption includes more than the Witnesses' 144,000. John 7:38, 39 makes the coming spirit the possession of "those who put faith in him [Jesus]" (NWT). Everyone who truly believes in Jesus Christ should receive the new birth: "Everyone believing that Jesus is the Christ has been born from God, and everyone who loves the one that caused to be born loves him who has been born from that one" (I John 5:1 NWT).

First John 5:1 is clear for any who take it just as it stands. "Everyone" here is all inclusive. But, acceptance of what is stated in the verse places the average Jehovah's Witness in a dilemma: (1) As a member of the "Great Multitude," if he truly believes that "Jesus is the Christ," (and all that includes) he should claim to have been born from God, but this contradicts what the Society has said his experience could be. (2) If the Witness has not been born of God he certainly has not believed that "Jesus is the Christ," and therefore he is not a Christian. Whom should the Witness believe—the Society or the Scriptures? The Society must apply this verse and the verses in the marginal reference of the NWT (John 1:12; 3:3; I Peter 1:23 and I John 3:9) to the 144,000 alone.[106]

---

[106] The following explanation of the verse was sent to this writer by the Society in a letter dated December 21, 1962: "First John 5:1 applies to the anointed ones, the one hundred and forty-four thousand. The verse points out that if anyone wants to be born by God's spirit to a heavenly inheritance, he has to believe that Jesus is the Christ of God. Jehovah God is the one that caused even Jesus Christ to be born. We must love God who caused Jesus Christ to be born. First John 5:1 tells us that if we love God who caused Jesus Christ to be born, then we will also love Jesus Christ who is the one who has been born from God. In other words, we must love both Jehovah God and his son, Jesus Christ. We cannot love the one without loving the other if we want to be acceptable to God and gain salvation. Especially if we want to be born to become God's spiritual children with a heavenly inheritance is this true. This text, however, does not refer to those who will gain life on the earth. Yet, they do accept Christ. They acknowledge his posi-

A final passage should be examined, John 3:3-7, which mentions the born again experience several times. Verse 3 in the NWT reads in part, " 'Most truly I say to you, Unless anyone is born again, he cannot see the kingdom of God.' " The fifth verse would indicate that to "see" the kingdom of God means to enter into it. The Witnesses claim that only the heavenly class can make up or enter this kingdom.[107] The faithful men of old, such as Abel, Abraham, Isaac, and Jacob and the prophets, according to the Witnesses, are not in the kingdom of God but will be representatives of God on the earth and subjects under the kingdom.[108] This position is not in accord with what Scripture demands in Luke 13:28, 29:

> . . . When YOU see Abraham and Isaac and Jacob and all the prophets in the kingdom of God, but yourselves thrown outside. Furthermore, people will come from eastern parts and western, and from north and south, and will recline at the table in the kingdom of God [NWT].

Matthew 8:11, 12 is a parallel passage which substitutes "kingdom of the heavens" for "kingdom of God." Acceptance of these two passages refutes the Witnesses' understanding of who is to be *"in"* the kingdom of God. So when Jesus said " 'YOU people must be born again,' " (John 3:7 NWT) for entrance into the kingdom of God, it meant that *all* must be born again, without exception!

---

tion in God's arrangement of things. They know, for example, that he came to offer his soul or life as a ransom.—Matt. 20:28."

There are several interesting things in the statement: (1) An arbitrary application of the verse to the 144,000, without any proof or justification, except the Society's claim. (2) A wrong understanding of the last part of the verse, "loves him who has been born from that one." The RSV rendering makes the meaning clear: "Every one who believes that Jesus is the Christ is a child of God, and every one who loves the parent loves the child." Verse 2 follows this translation naturally and shows the Witness understanding wrong. (3) What distinguishes the way the Witnesses with an earthly hope accept Christ from the way Witnesses with a heavenly hope accept Him? Does a member of the 144,000 believe that Jesus is the Christ "more" than a member of the Great Multitude?

[107] *Let God Be True, op. cit.*, pp. 136-38

[108] *Ibid.*, p. 263.

V. Satan

Aside from wild speculations and knowledge concerning Satan's spiritual organization, and misrepresentations as to the beliefs of orthodoxy, the Witnesses' doctrine of Satan is reasonably sound except for the teaching that Satan's ultimate fate, and that of his followers, will be annihilation. This view is forced on the system by the rejection of eternal punishment.

That Satan's fate is not and cannot be annihilation is proven by several facts: (1) The Witnesses cannot give one word in either the Old or New Testament which states or implies that Satan will be annihilated. (2) Satan's everlasting, conscious punishment is clearly shown by Revelation 20:10:

> And the Devil who was misleading them was hurled into the lake of fire and sulphur, where both the wild beast and the false prophet already were; and they will be tormented day and night for ever and ever [NWT].

This verse establishes that after one thousand years in the lake of fire, the "beast" and the "false prophet" have still to face eternal punishment. Notice, "they will be tormented," not "he will be tormented." The future "they will" is an accurate translation of the future indicative passive. The beast and false prophet were already cast into the lake of fire a thousand years before, as stated in Revelation 19:20, and their punishment is still looked on as future. The expression "lake of fire," ("fiery lake" Rev. 19:20 NWT) therefore, could not symbolize annihilation. (3) Christ speaks of the fire which was "prepared for the Devil and his angels" (Matt. 25:41 NWT).

VI. The Nature of Man and His Destiny

In dealing with this subject much could be said, but in order to hold the discussion to manageable proportions the major arguments of the *Let God Be True* chapter, "What is Man?" (pp. 66-75) are examined and refuted. The book and chapter have been selected for the same reasons as the chapter "Is There a Trinity?" was chosen in the refutation of the Witnesses' position on that subject.[109]

---

[109] See above, p. 105.

The chapter begins with the important questions: "What is man? Has he an immortal soul? and, What is man's destiny?" (p. 66). In an attempt to misrepresent orthodoxy, the Witness writer states: "Religious leaders of this world answer the questions from the knowledge they got in divinity schools or theological seminaries" (p. 66). This statement conveys the idea that there is a dichotomy between the knowledge gained in theological seminaries and that which is found in the Scriptures. The average conservative theologian or theological treatise dealing with the subject above demonstrates a depth in the understanding and use of the Scriptures that makes the usual Witness publication look like the efforts of a novice.

On the same page the writer of the chapter says that scientists and surgeons "cannot find any evidence that indicates man has an immortal soul." This information is totally irrelevant, for the realm of spirit is outside the sphere of both these. From the standpoint of the theologian and theology, immortality is not a doctrine that requires scientific verification, but, belonging to the realm of faith, it is established by revelation.

The writer in *Let God Be True* next appeals to the Bible as the source of authority for answers to the questions proposed (p. 67). The present writer and all conservative Christians take the same position.

After quoting and commenting on several verses (Gen. 2:7; Gen. 1:20, 30; Num. 31:28) the Witness writer states:

> So we see that the claim of religionists that man has an immortal soul and therefore differs from the beast is not Scriptural. The Bible shows that both man and beast are souls, and that man's pre-eminence is due to the fact that he is a higher form of creature and was originally given dominion over the lower forms of animal life [p. 68].

The expression "living soul" or its equivalent is frequently used in Genesis (Gen. 1:20, 21, 24; 2:7, 19 etc.) to indicate that by His direct action God gave life to both man and animals as well. A comparison of the verses above indicates that the expression "living soul" refers to physical life.[110]

---

[110] But Genesis 2:7 reveals that man's creation differs from that of the rest of creation in that his life was directly inbreathed by God (Cf. Gen. 2:7; Job 32:8 with Gen. 1:20, 24, etc.).

Does this not prove that man is just what the above statement claims? Not at all, for this is only part of the information on man's creation, as Mickelson explains:

> By God's activity he became a living creature among other living creatures. He stands forth as a physical creature in God's creation. The phrase "living creature" shows man's identity with the rest of creation. The fact that man was made in the image and likeness of God (Gen. 1:26-27) shows man's distinctiveness in all of creation.[111]

Man's supremacy over the rest of creation is expressed in Genesis 1:26 and 27: "And God went on to say: 'Let us make man in our image' . . . And God proceeded to create the man in his image, in God's image he created him . . ." (NWT). What is included in the divine image? (1) It is an error to limit the divine image, as the Witnesses have (and the Socinians) in the statement above, to "dominion over the lower forms or animal life." This was contained in the idea, but only as a secondary element (cf. Gen. 1:26 and 9:6). (2) Oehler felt that

> the divine likeness is rather to be referred to the *whole dignity of man* . . . in virtue of which human nature is sharply distinguished from that of the beasts; *man as a free being is set over nature, and designed to hold communion with God, and to be his representative on earth.*[112]

(3) A summary of the significance of the divine image in man as created might include: spirituality, personality, holiness, love and dominion.[113] The image of God in man, although blurred by the fall, still exists.

On page 69 of *Let God Be True* the writer erects another "strawman" in supposed refutation of orthodoxy: "There is not one Bible text that states the human soul is immortal." The present writer would substantially agree with this statement and much of that which is stated on pp. 72-74. Scrip-

[111] A. Berkeley Mickelsen, *Interpreting the Bible* (Grand Rapids: Wm. B. Eerdmans Publishing Company, 1963), pp. 317, 318.

[112] Gustave Friedrich Oehler, *Theology of the Old Testament*, ed. George E. Day (Grand Rapids: Zondervan Publishing House, [n. d.]) p. 146.

[113] E. McChesney, "Image of God," *Unger's Bible Dictionary* (Chicago: Moody Press, 1957), p. 517.

turally, the attribute of "immortality" is not possessed by any human soul, because "immortality," when applied to man, relates to the *body* and will be received in the future when man's body is glorified (I Cor. 15:42, 50, 53, 54). Scripture states that only God has immortality (I Tim. 6:16). So "immortality," when translated from the Greek words *athanasia,* and *aphtharsia,* is not the present possession of man.

What Scripture does support is that man, once created, does possess a quality (soul or spirit) which can exist as a conscious entity apart from the body and which will continue in its existence through all eternity.

On page 69 the Witness writer admits that the Hebrew word *ruach* and the Greek word *psuche* are translatable by a number of English words such as "life, mind, heart, appetite, body, self, etc." Standard Greek and Hebrew lexicons also reflect this. Arndt-Gingrich, in commenting on *psuche,* say that "it is often impossible to draw hard and fast lines between the meanings of this many sided word."[113a] In one of its meanings it speaks of *"the soul as an essence which differs from the body and is not dissolved by death,"* illustrated by Matthew 10:28; and "the soul freed from the body, a disembodied soul" as is found in Acts 2:27, Revelation 6:9 and 20:4.[113b] Arndt-Gingrich are in substantial agreement, stating that "soul" is to be understood as existing after death in several instances: "The soul is delivered up to death . . . whereupon it leaves the realm of earth and lives on in Hades . . . or some other place outside the earth. . . ."[114] The New Testament verses listed by Arndt-Gingrich are the same ones used by Grimm-Thayer, except for Matthew 10:28, where "soul" is understood as the "seat and center of life that transcends the earthly," and specifically, "men cannot injure it, but God can hand it over to destruction" (Matt. 16:26; Mark 8:36).[115]

The *Let God Be True* writer ignores the word "spirit" (*pneuma*) in his discussion of the nature of man. The word can be translated by a number of different English words

---

[113a] Arndt-Gingrich, *op. cit.,* p. 901.
[113b] Grimm-Thayer, *op. cit.,* p. 677.
[114] Arndt-Gingrich, *op. cit.,* p. 901.
[115] *Ibid.,* p. 902.

as the treatment in Arndt-Gingrich demonstrates.[116] Although it has the meaning of wind and breath, etc., it also can denote an entity which survives man after death (Heb. 12:23; I Pet. 3:18).[117]

Several of the verses cited as presenting the existence of an entity apart from the body, if it be called a "soul" or "spirit," should be examined individually, for if such an entity exists the Witness concept of man as a mere combination of "the dust of the ground" and "the breath of life" and nothing more must be rejected. The verses to be examined are: Matthew 10:28; Revelation 6:9-11; 20:4; and Hebrews 12:23. I Peter 3:18 has already been dealt with.

Matthew 10:28. This is a very important verse whose meaning has been misinterpreted by the Witnesses. The verse reads: " 'And do not become fearful of those who kill the body but can not kill the soul; but rather be in fear of him that can destroy both soul and body in Gehenna' " (NWT). The *Let God Be True* writer explains:

> The gist of this text is that we should fear God, because he is able to destroy not only our present human body but the possibility of future life as well. The destruction in Gehenna here referred to means that death from which there is no resurrection to future life as a soul [p. 72].

It is evident that the Witnesses understand the word "destroy" (*apollumi*) to mean "annihilation," a meaning which the word does not have, as a study of the passages in which it appears shows.[118] In another Witness book the inability to kill the soul is interpreted as "their right and title to life in God's heavenly kingdom."[119] It is obvious that according to this verse the soul and the body are distinct entities, and a man can kill the body without killing the soul.

Revelation 6:9-11 and 20:4. In Revelation 20:4 it is recorded that John "saw the souls of those executed with the ax for the witness they bore to Jesus. . ." (NWT). "Souls"

---

[116] *Ibid.*, pp. 680-85.

[117] *Ibid.*, pp. 680, 681. Arndt-Gingrich explain *pneuma* in I Peter 3:18 as "that part of Christ which, in contrast to *sarx*, did not pass away in death, but survived as an individual entity after death. . . ."

[118] See below, p. 165.

[119] *Babylon the Great Has Fallen! God's Kingdom Rules!*, *op. cit.*, p. 636.

must be different from creatures or people because it says that John saw the "souls" of those who were martyred. Revelation 6: 9-11 is even clearer that souls exist apart from the body after death as conscious entities:

> . . . I saw underneath the altar the souls of those slaughtered because of the word of God and because of the witness work which they used to have. And they cried with a loud voice, saying "Until when, Sovereign Lord holy and true, are you refraining from judging and avenging our blood upon those who dwell on the earth?" And a white robe was given to each of them, and they were told to rest a little while longer until the number was filled also of their fellow slaves [NWT].

Verses 9 and 10 are understood by the Witnesses as occurring before their claimed resurrection of the 144,000 in 1918.[120] Rutherford attempted to avoid the difficulty of souls existing apart from their bodies before the resurrection by claiming that "souls"

> represents the value of their life-blood poured out which was pictured in the tabernacle service . . . As the blood of Abel cried out from the ground, so the blood of the faithful ones cries out against them that dwell on the earth as Satan's representatives.[121]

A reading of the passage shows Rutherford's explanation is impossible to support. The passage relates that the souls of the martyrs, not their blood, "cried with a loud voice" (cf. Gen. 4:10). "A white robe was given to each of them," indicates personal existence of those mentioned in verses 9 and 10. Since, according to the Witnesses' own interpretation, the resurrection of those mentioned in this passage did not occur until verse 11 (1918), how could those who did not exist (because man ceases to exist at death according to the Witnesses) be crying out between the time of their death and their resurrection? This could be true only if man's spirit or soul exists after death.

Hebrews 12:23. The mention in this verse of "spirits of just men made perfect" speaks of the redeemed who are not yet clothed with a resurrection body, but who are enjoying

---

[120] *The Kingdom Is at Hand* (Brooklyn: Watchtower Bible and Tract Society, Inc., 1944), pp. 336, 337; J. F. Rutherford, *Light* (Brooklyn: Watch Tower Bible and Tract Society, 1930), I, pp. 78-80.

[121] *Ibid.*, p. 79.

conscious fellowship with God in this state. It proves that there is some kind of existence between death and the resurrection. The NWT obscures this fact by translating *pneumasi* (the dative plural of *pneuma*) as "spiritual lives." This is a mistranslation of the Greek which should be literally translated, "(the) spirits," as the footnote in the NWT on this verse indicates. (The 1961 revision of the NWT retained the mistranslation.)

Several additional Scriptural proofs (Matt. 25:46; 27:50; Luke 23:46; Phil. 1:23, etc.) of the orthodox doctrine of the nature and destiny of man have been presented elsewhere in this book. The condition of the unrepentent as one of consciousness and eternal punishment is developed in the next section, "Eternal Punishment and the Future State."

In addition, the nature of death should be discussed. On page 74 of *Let God Be True* the Witness understanding of this doctrine is explained:

> Man being now a sinful mortal, his ultimate destiny is death. . . . God spoke very emphatically regarding the death sentence. He said: "Thou shalt surely die." There is nothing to indicate that God meant that sinner Adam would only appear to die but that his soul would live on forever.

In answer to this often repeated view the following can be stated: (1) It is true that because of disobedience man's destiny is death. But what is death? The answer to this question must follow the answer to the question, What is man? (2) It has been proven from the Bible that death of the body does not involve the death of the entire man, for man's soul or spirit does survive him. Thus, the Witness statement above is false. (3) Physical death is not the annihilation or ceasing to exist of the individual, as the use of the word *thanatos* in the New Testament proves. Death is primarily spiritual, i.e., the separation of the soul from God (Matt. 8:22; John 5:24, 25; 6:33; Eph. 2:1, 5; Col. 2:13). Those who are spiritually dead are physically alive. They are separated from God because of sin. Death of the body is only the physical reminder of that which has already happened in man's spiritual nature. When Adam disobeyed God he at that moment died because communion with God, which meant life, was broken. (4) If the first death of man is characterized by conscious existence, the same must also be true of the eternal state, "second death" (Rev. 2:11, 20:6, 14).

VII. Eternal Punishment and the Future State

In the early years of the present-day Jehovah's Witness movement, the rejection of eternal punishment was one of the leading attractions of Russellite theology. The subject of "hell" was one of Russell's favorite topics, and one of the most popular lectures which he delivered was titled "To Hell and Back." This lecture packed the meetings wherever it was presented, and is described by the Witnesses in the following words: "In this striking lecture he took his audience on a witty, humorous, imaginary trip to hell and back."[122] This description, as well as the sermon title, sounds like something the infidel Ingersol would present and shows the typical approach on many doctrines.

The Witnesses do a thorough job of misrepresenting the orthodox doctrine of eternal punishment. Several statements from Judge Rutherford's popular booklet, *Where are the Dead?*, are quoted as classic examples:

> When the war came the clergymen preached in favor of the war, urging young men to join the army, and telling them from their pulpits that those who died upon the battlefield would go straight to heaven. . . .[123]
>
> The substance of the Protestant preachers' conclusions was that if one dies who at the time of death is a member in good standing of some church, then he immediately goes to heaven, and there from that time forward enjoys endless bliss. . . .[124]

Another choice misrepresentation concerning hell is this statement: " '. . . Do not all the clergymen say that those who die outside of the church go to that terrible place?' "[125] Rutherford speaks ignorantly when he says: "Is it reasonable that God gives that creature an asbestos body so that he can be

---

[122] *Jehovah's Witnesses in the Divine Purpose* (Brooklyn: Watchtower Bible and Tract Society of New York, Inc., 1959), p. 43.

[123] J. F. Rutherford, *Where are the Dead?* (Brooklyn: Watch Tower Bible and Tract Society, 1932), p. 4.

[124] *Ibid.*, p. 5.

[125] *Ibid.*, pp. 7, 8.

burned forever?"[126] The following statement seems to be built upon the misrepresentation in Russell's "Photo-Drama":

> That [man being unconscious after death] is not very consistent with the theory of being in bliss or standing on his head in a vat of boiling oil or being otherwise tortured by fireproof devils wearing asbestos coats.[127]

Another typical misrepresentation is the one concerning Satan's present residence: "If hell is a place of eternal torment, and if the Devil is the chief fireman, who is going to keep up the fire when the Devil is destroyed?"[128] Misrepresentation is still in vogue, for the writer of *Let God Be True* states:

> But are not Satan the Devil and his demons down in hell keeping the fires and making it hard for those who are in it? This is what is taught by Christendom's clergy, but you will be surprised to know the Devil never was in such a place.[129]

If space permitted, more of these statements of deliberate misinformation could be quoted. It is obvious that the erroneous statements are intended to sway the minds of the untutored. One can conclude one of three things concerning the writers of these statements: (1) They were completely ignorant of the doctrines of orthodoxy, or (2) they were too dull to determine what they were, or (3) they were out to deliberately misrepresent, and thus deceive their readers.

The mistranslation of *sheol* and *hades* by the *King James* translators is the basis for much of the argumentation in the Witness rejection of the doctrine of eternal punishment. Actually, over half of the chapter dealing with hell in the book *Let God Be True*,[130] is built on the mistranslation of these two words and the misunderstanding of orthodoxy. The best way to clear up this problem, and most of the Witnesses' other arguments from Scripture, is to accept the readings of the *American Standard Version* which leave the words untranslated. To further clarify this subject and to see the

---

126 *Ibid.*, p. 15.
127 *Ibid.*, p. 17.
128 *Ibid.*, pp. 19-21.
129 *Let God Be True, op. cit.*, p. 93.
130 *Ibid.*, pp. 88-99.

term-switching of the Witnesses, it would be good at this point to define the meaning of several terms they misapply.

The Hebrew word *sheol* and the Greek word *hades, never* speak of eternal hell. These two words simply denote the place of the departed.

The eternal state of the wicked after the resurrection is designated in the Scriptures as "Gehenna" or "Lake of Fire." These terms designate the condition of eternal punishment or "hell."

"Tartarus," used only once (in II Pet. 2:4) is not "hell," although it is so translated in both the ASV and the KJV. This seems to be a separate place of detention for the fallen angels.

With these explanations in mind, examination of some of the main arguments and tactics of the Watchtower publications on this subject is in order.

In typical fashion, to place the discussion in the most unfair and nonrepresentative light, the Witnesses use "loaded words" such as "hell-fire screechers"[131] to describe orthodox theologians and others holding the doctrine of eternal punishment. They have also combined with this misrepresentations of orthodoxy which are repugnant to those who are being represented (the orthodox).

Again and again, from the false idea that orthodoxy teaches that *sheol* and *hades* are eternal hell, the Watchtower writers misrepresent orthodoxy. Concerning Jonah they write: "If hell were eternal, Jonah would not have gotten out."[132] The same argument is employed concerning Jesus. If hell is eternal, how did Jesus get out?[133] Again, the answer is that *sheol* and *hades* are not viewed by orthodoxy as eternal hell.

There are many other examples of misrepresentation. For example, on page 90 of *Let God Be True* the Witness writer has Joseph spending eternity in hell and Jacob going bodily into "hell" (*sheol*). Again, *sheol* is not hell, and man's soul or spirit, not his body, are conscious before the resurrection, a point that the Witness writer conveniently forgot to state on page 88 of the same book. More could

[131] *Ibid.*, p. 95.

[132] *The Watchtower*, 76:69, February 1, 1955.

[133] *Ibid.*, p. 70.

be said, but the reader is urged to get the doctrines of orthodoxy from those who know what they are.

The general argument from all Watchtower literature on the subject examined is that there is no hint of evidence in the Bible for life or activity after death.

Although the revelation is dim in the Old Testament, there are several passages which indicate that there is consciousness after death.

Ezekiel 32:21 gives such a testimony:

> The strong among the mighty shall speak to him out of the midst of Sheol with them that help him: they are gone down, they lie still, even the uncircumcised, slain by the sword.

Isaiah 14:4-17 is a similar example.

Some scholars find distinct mention of spirits living apart from the body in the spirit world. The word in Hebrew to designate them is *rapha* (*raphaim,* plural). The word is defined in *Gesenius Lexicon,*

> . . . *Flaccid, feeble, weak* . . . *manes,* shades living in Hades, according to the opinions of the ancient Hebrews, void of blood and animal life . . . but not devoid of powers of mind, such as memory. . . .[134]

The New Testament word *hades,* which appears ten times in the New Testament (Matt. 11:23; 16:18; Luke 10:15; 16:23; Acts 2:27, 31; Rev. 1:18; 6:8; 20:13, 14) also conveys evidence that the dead are conscious after death. The following quotation is an excellent summary of the orthodox view on *hades* and the condition of man after death:

> The notion of a soul-sleep is just as foreign to the NT as to Judaism; the image of the sleep is introduced (Mk. 5:39 and par.; I Th. 5:10; Jn. 11:11-12 etc. *koimao*) simply as an euphemistic description of death. The soul is certainly separated from the body at death, but it experiences temporary retribution in the time between death and the resurrection. When the NT refers to Hades, the reference is to the abode of souls loosed from their bodies (cf. Ac. 2:26 f., 31).

---

[134] Samuel Prideaux Tregelles (trans.), *Gesenius' Hebrew and Chaldee Lexicon to the Old Testament Scriptures* (Grand Rapids: Wm. B. Eerdmans Publishing Company, 1954), p. 776.

> . . . Finally, the NT agrees that the stay in Hades is limited, as may be seen from the sharp distinction between *hades* and *geenna.* Throughout the NT Hades serves only an interim purpose. It receives souls after death, and delivers them up again at the resurrection (Rev. 20:13). The resurrection constitutes its end (20:14), and it is replaced by *geenna* (19:20; 20:10, 14 f.: *limna tou puros*) as the final place of punishment.[135]
>
> . . . In virtue of the promise of Jesus His community knows that it is secure from the powers of Hades (Mt. 16:18) because by faith in Him it has access to the kingdom of God. . . . In particular it knows that its dead are not in Hades, but in the presence of Jesus. This certainty, first declared in the saying to the dying thief on the cross (Lk. 23:43: *met emou*), is most sharply expressed by Paul in the phrase *sun Christo einai* (Phil. 1:23).[136]

Witnesses claim that "Gehenna, or the Valley of Hinnom, became a symbol, not of eternal torment, but of eternal condemnation."[137] Eternal condemnation is explained as complete annihilation or destruction, a view which must be rejected on the following grounds.

1. The Witnesses cite Matthew 10:28 and interpret "destroy" as annihilation. "And do not become fearful of those who kill the body but can not kill the soul; but rather be in fear of him that can destroy both soul and body in Gehenna" (NWT). The word translated "destroy" (*apollumi*) cannot be construed to mean annihilation by any stretch of the imagination nor can such a meaning find support in any existing lexicon. The word occurs some eighty-five times in the New Testament and is rendered "lose," "destroy," and "perish." A study of this word in these contexts shows that it does not mean annihilation.[138] Grimm-Thayer define the word in the Matthew 10:28 context as

---

[135] Gerhard Kittel (ed.), *Theological Dictionary of the New Testament,* tran. and ed. Geoffrey W. Bromiley (Grand Rapids: Wm. B. Eerdmans Publishing Company, 1963), I, p. 148.

[136] *Ibid.,* p. 149.

[137] *Let God Be True, op. cit.,* p. 96.

[138] Robert Baker Gridlestone, *Synonyms of the Old Testament* (second edition; Grand Rapids: Wm. B. Eerdmans Publishing Company, 1953), pp. 275-77.

metaphorically used *"to devote or give over to eternal misery. . . ."*[139]

2. The Greek word *kolasis* in Matthew 25:46 is translated "cutting-off" by the *New World Translation,* and this meaning is claimed to be illustrative of the meaning of Gehenna. This study deals with this word at some length in the following chapter, and shows that there is not one scintilla of proof for this Watchtower translation of *kolasis.* The meaning of the word is "punishment," and it expresses pure retributive judgment. Let the words of Christ be man's warning: "And these shall go away into eternal punishment: but the righteous into eternal life" (Matt. 25:46).

3. Revelation 21:8 and other passages which mention the "lake of fire" are interpreted by the Witnesses as annihilation. That this is not the meaning can be demonstrated in several ways. (a) Revelation 19:20 records the casting of the Beast and the False Prophet into the lake of fire before the millennium. Revelation 20:10, referring to time one thousand years later, places the tormenting of them as still future. (b) On what grounds can an interpreter change the meaning of the phrase "tormented day and night for ever and ever" (NWT) to mean annihilation? If *basanizo* means "to torment" ("tormented," NWT) in Revelation 11:10, why does it change its meaning in Revelation 20:10? The passage in Revelation 11:10 becomes ridiculous if one would interpret it that the two prophets "annihilated" those dwelling on earth. (c) The Greek word *basanizo,* which Grimm-Thayer define as *"to vex with grievous pains* (of body or mind), *to torment,"*[140] in every case found in the New Testament speaks of pain and conscious suffering.[141]

4. The Appendix of the *New World Translation* (p. 767) gives this argument concerning Gehenna:

> No living animals or human creatures were pitched into Gehenna to be burned alive or tormented. Hence the place could never symbolize an invisible region where human souls are tormented in literal fire and attacked by undying immortal worms for ever and ever.

---

[139] Grimm-Thayer, *op. cit.,* p. 64.

[140] *Ibid.,* p. 96.

[141] Matthew 8:6, 29; Mark 5:7; Luke 8:28; II Peter 2:8; Revelations 9:5; 12:2, etc. See also Arndt-Gingrich, *op. cit.,* p. 134.

According to this statement, one could logically conclude that if living people were cast into Gehenna, it *could* symbolize a place of eternal torment. The Old Testament record gives the history of the Valley of Hinnom and shows that the practice of sacrificing the living was actually how the valley received its significance. The Valley of Hinnom became the technical designation of the place of eternal torment not because of its use as a dumping place but because of the worship of the idol Molech with living sacrifices (II Chron. 28:3; 33:6). The defilement of the Valley of Hinnom by Josiah (II Kings 23:10) became associated with prophecy as a picture of the judgment to be visited upon the people of Israel (Jer. 7:32). The further defilement of the valley by the dumping of rubbish and bodies into it may have contributed to the meaning of the term, but this is not the primary allusion. It was because of the living sacrifices to Molech — and the defilement of Josiah that the valley received its notoriety. The sin and suffering of this valley was well known by the Jews and this name was the most appropriate to describe the eternal conscious suffering of the unsaved. The *New World Translation* at Revelation 19:20 shows that the figure of being cast into Gehenna (identical in meaning with "lake of fire," "fiery lake" NWT) *alive* was still in use during the writing of the New Testament period: ". . . While still alive, they both were hurled into the fiery lake that burns with sulphur."

The Watchtower article, "Is Hell Hot?"[142] misses the point concerning belief in the place of eternal punishment. The question is not "Is Hell Hot?" but, "Is there a place where the unregenerate will be in separation from God throughout all eternity and where they will consciously experience punishment?" Dante's inferno certainly is not a Scriptural representation, nor does it represent the teaching of informed orthodoxy.

The Scriptural pronouncements on the future state of the unsaved need not be interpreted literally to teach the hopeless and conscious perdition of the unsaved. What is sure from the terminology of Scripture is that the state of the unsaved will be *even worse* than that which is so graphically presented by the terms "Gehenna," "lake of fire," "outer

[142] *The Watchtower*, 76:68-72, February 1, 1955.

darkness," "torment," "punishment," etc. The Lord uses the strongest language to warn man to avoid this punishment.

In *Let God Be True,* the Jehovah's Witnesses make this statement:

> The doctrine of a burning hell where the wicked are tortured eternally after death cannot be true, mainly for four reasons: (1) It is wholly unscriptural; (2) it is unreasonable; (3) it is contrary to God's love, and (4) it is repugnant to justice.[143]

Since the foregoing arguments are rather common and need an answer, the propositions presented by the Witnesses will be taken individually. First, "It is wholly unscriptural." This statement takes in quite a large territory, and only one verse would be sufficient to overthrow the view. One wonders if the writer of such a statement had at his disposal the same Bible orthodoxy possesses. Just the one scripture, Matthew 25:46, would be sufficient to answer this objection.[144] The doctrine of the eternal punishment of the wicked is not built on isolated passages, and to the honest student of the Word the teaching presents no problem.

Second, "It is unreasonable." In the first place, the question should be asked, "When does reason have precedence over the Word of God?" Must something be reasonable to be true? An argument of this type is founded upon human presupposition and sentimentality and not upon sound scholarship of the Word. Reason would dictate that man should be his own judge, and prescribe his own penalty. Sinful man cannot estimate sin's vileness. Only God knows and can declare the penalty that sin merits. Did reason determine that Adam's one act of disobedience committed in a moment should bring death and destruction to all his posterity? Or, by the same token, that men should receive everlasting life by trusting in Christ? No, reason is not the judge of truth in every case.

Third, "It is contrary to God's love." To punish men forever is said to be inconsistent with the character of God. Before going into this objection, it is necessary to know what God's character is. It is all too easy to make a one-

---

[143] *Let God Be True, op. cit.,* p. 99.

[144] See also: Isa. 66:24; Mark 9:43-48; Matt. 5:29, 30; 13:41, 42, 50; 18:8, 9; II Pet. 2:4-9, 17; Rev. 14:11; 20:10, 15.

sided presentation of God as "God is love." Such a presentation of God leaves an imperfect view of God's character. God is love, but He is more than just love. Man seems content to set forth one or two of the more tender attributes of God and point to the fragment and say: "This is God." But such is not the God of the Bible. How can man know what God is like? There are three sources: (1) ourselves; (2) nature; (3) and revelation.

Truly, when the evidence is examined, love and goodness are evident; yet how much more is seen a law in operation which works constantly and unchangingly not for human enjoyment, but which often involves the great suffering of creatures. Our God as a "consuming fire" (Hebrews 12:29) can scarcely signify that divine love is determined to spare rejectors of Him. Divine love is limited by the perverse freewill of man. All God's attributes may be summed up in one, holiness. God's justice is just the exercise and the outward expression of holiness. God's love lays upon Him the obligation to punish transgression, a fact seen throughout the Bible. God showed no love and mercy upon the sin of Noah's day; Noah and his family were spared, but the rest of the people perished. God spared Lot, but He had no mercy upon Sodom. God hates sin, and He must judge it.

Fourth, "It is repugnant to justice." If being justly punished for a crime is repugnant, the Witnesses are right. Only God can fully know the penalty of sin. Men are not punished eternally "merely because they had the misfortune to be born sinners."[145] The sinner is punished as a necessary consequence of his own sins. Is eternal punishment any more repugnant to justice than the view of annihilation which issues the same punishment to a Hitler and to a religious but unbelieving Jew? Justice which is true justice permits a man to reap just what he has sown. Man is permitted to live in that condition which he has chosen for himself. For example, if a man would live on this earth forever, he would live his life after his choice of either good or evil. Death can make no difference in the character of man, and if men may justly live here and reap as they have sown, why should it be deemed unjust in the world to come?

---

[145] *Let God Be True, op. cit.*, p. 99.

Thus, by showing the future conscious existence of eternal punishment, the best answer to the Witnesses' view of death as "annihilation" or "ceasing to exist" has also been established.

Does Scripture teach a second probation? The Witnesses teach that

> the "resurrection of judgment" is for those persons whose hearts may have been wanting to do right, but who died without ever having an opportunity to hear God's purposes or to learn what God expects of men. . . .
>
> These people will be brought back into the paradise earth. They will be taught the truth. They will be shown what is right. Then they will be judged according to what they do about it. If they obey God's commandments they will get life. If they do not obey God's commandments they will go into everlasting death. . . .[146]

To the Witnesses, then, the "resurrection of judgment" mentioned in John 5:29 is not a resurrection of those who already stand condemned before God, but one in which humans are afforded "an opportunity to live."[147] Hebrews 9:27 is interpreted in the same way.

In refutation of this unscriptural teaching, Jesus' words recorded in John 5:28, 29 should be examined. The *New World Translation* renders the passage as follows:

> "Do not marvel at this, because the hour is coming in which all those in the memorial tombs will hear his voice and come out, those who did good things to a resurrection of life, those who practiced vile things to a resurrection of judgment."

(1) To the unbiased reader it is evident that the destinies of those spoken of are already determined; one is a resurrection to life, the other to judgment. The past tense "did good things" and "practiced vile things" makes this clear. (2) Jesus' words recorded in John 3:18-21 show that a division among men has already taken place, for each man by choice has determined his own fate by acceptance or rejection of Christ. In verse 20 Jesus states: " 'For he that practices vile things hates the light and does not come to the light, in order that his works may not be reproved' " (NWT). These are the ones that according to John 3:16 are to be

---

[146] *From Paradise Lost to Paradise Regained* (Brooklyn: Watchtower Bible and Tract Society of New York, Inc., 1958), p. 229.

[147] *The Watchtower*, 86:448, July 15, 1965.

"destroyed" (NWT, "perish" ASV, KJV, RSV). The word rendered "vile things" (*phaulos*) is the same word found in John 5:29. The word translated "practices" (John 3:20) and "practiced" is the same Greek word (*prasso*) in different tenses appropriate to the statements. "Those who practiced vile things" certainly can not look forward to a future probation. (3) Arndt-Gingrich, commenting on the Greek word *krisis,* ("judgment") as used in this and other passages, state: "The word often means *judgment* that goes against a person, *condemnation,* and the *punishment* that follows. . . ."[148] Grimm-Thayer comment on *krisis* as used in John 5:29: "The last judgment, the damnation of the wicked: *anastasis kriseos* followed by condemnation. . . .[149] (5) In conclusion, the Witnesses' attempt to pervert the clear teaching of the Bible cannot stand the investigation of the Scriptures. The same result is true in their understanding of Hebrews 9:27: "And inasmuch as it is appointed unto men once to die, and after this cometh judgment" (ASV. The RSV renders, "and after that comes judgment."). The NWT rendering insinuates the Witnesses' heresy into the Bible: "And as it is reserved for men to die once for all time, but after this a judgment." Grimm-Thayer define "judgment" in this verse as *"sentence of condemnation, damnatory judgment, condemnation and punishment. . . ."*[150]

Certainly, if salvation is possible beyond physical death it is God that must reveal this to man. It is the Bible that must make this clear, not men who reason from emotion or who deal in speculation. It is the contention of this writer that, if language has any meaning, the Bible makes man responsible in this life for where he will spend eternity; his fate cannot be changed after death.

The Witnesses' position says in effect that a person is not truly lost or in danger of a final judgment until he has heard of God's provisions for salvation. Logically then,

---

[148] Arndt-Gingrich, *op. cit.*, p. 453. Is there any hint that "judgment" holds out any hope for avoidance of punishment? See how the word "judgment" is used in the following verses: Revelation 18:10 (Babylon's judgment); Hebrews 10:27 (the judgment of one who rejects the truth with full understanding); Matthew 23:33 (the judgment of Gehenna), and John 5:24 (the judgment of those who do not accept Christ).

[149] Grimm-Thayer, *op. cit.*, p. 362.

[150] *Ibid.*, p. 361.

Christians should rejoice that the heathen have never heard of Christ, and the frustration of the outreach of the Gospel should be a matter of thanks, for conditions during the millennium should place man in a more favorable position to gain eternal life.

Scripture is clear that men of all ages and locations are guilty in God's sight and "inexcusable" before God (Rom. 1:18-23; 3:23). They are lost and already dead (Luke 19:10; Eph. 2:1-5). Those who have not had the advantages of others will be judged in the light of what they know, for as Romans 2:12 states: "For instance, all those who sinned without law will also perish without law; but all those who sinned under law will be judged by law" (NWT). According to this verse, those "without law" who choose sin will perish.

No, Scripture does not hold out the hope of a second probation, but it does say: "He that believeth on him is not judged: he that believeth not hath been judged already, because he hath not believed on the name of the only begotten Son of God" (John 3:18).

VIII. THE "SECOND PRESENCE" (SECOND COMING) OF CHRIST [150a]

Two very important questions are considered at this point: (1) Did Jesus Christ return in 1914? (2) Is the "second presence" to be secret or invisible? If it can be shown that Christ did not return invisibly in 1914 the Watchtower edifice is completely undermined. If He did not return, most of the Witnesses' prophetic interpretation is wrong, the Kingdom was not established, Christ was not enthroned in the heavens, the Society is not God's visible representative on earth, etc.

Did Christ return in 1914? This writer maintains that it is impossible to objectively, historically, and Scripturally arrive at 1914 as the year of the Lord's return. How have the Watchtower writers arrived at this date?

In Luke 21:24 it is recorded that "Jerusalem will be trampled on by the nations, until the appointed times of the nations are fulfilled" (NWT).

> The "appointed times of the nations" indicated a period in which there would be no representative government of Jehovah on earth, such as the kingdom of Israel was; but the Gentile nations would dominate the earth.[151]

[150a] For a thorough treatment see the author's book: *The Jehovah's Witnesses and Prophetic Speculation.*

[151] *Let God Be True, op. cit.*, p. 250.

Israel lost her independence and the "appointed times of the nations" began in 607 B. C. with the overthrow of Zedekiah the last king of Israel.[152] When will this period end? The background for the answer is found in the fourth chapter of Daniel in the prophetic dream of Nebuchadnezzar:

> The prophetic dream disclosed a great tree which grew from the earth and reached to heaven and furnished food and shelter to all creatures. Suddenly a holy one from heaven commanded: "Hew down the tree, . . . nevertheless leave the stump of his roots in the earth, even with a band of iron and brass, . . . and let seven times pass over him."[153]

Then it is explained:

> "Seven times" meant seven literal years in the case of Nebuchadnezzar, deprived of his throne. The seven years were equal to 84 months, or Scripturally allowing 30 days for each month, 2,520 days. At Revelation 12:6, 14, there are 1,260 days mentioned and described as a "time, and times, and half a time," or 3½ times. Seven times would be twice 1,260 days or 2,520 days. By his faithful prophet Ezekiel Jehovah said: "I have appointed thee each day for a year." (Ezekiel 4:6) By applying this divine rule the 2,520 days mean 2,520 years. Therefore, since God's typical kingdom with its capital at Jerusalem ceased to exist in the autumn of 607 B. C., then, by counting the appointed times from that date, the 2,520 years extend to the autumn of A. D. 1914.[154]

Objections to this elaborate *theory,* which forms such an important part of the Witnesses' theology, include the following:

1. The starting point of 607 B.C., when it is claimed that the "king of Babylon took Zedekiah, the last king of Israel, off 'Jehovah's throne' "[155] is not supported by historical evidence. Scholars both Biblical and secular indicate the fall of Jerusalem was in 587 or 586 B. C. and not in 607 B. C. as the Witnesses' theory demands. In fact, Zedekiah

---

[152] *Ibid.*, p. 251; *From Paradise Lost to Paradise Regained, op. cit.*, pp. 171, 172.

[153] *Let God Be True, op. cit.*, p. 251.

[154] *Ibid.*, pp. 251, 252.

[155] *From Paradise Lost to Paradise Regained, op. cit.*, p. 172.

was not installed as king by Nebuchadnezzar until 598 or 597 B. C.![156]

2. What proof is there that the "times of the nations" have ended. The Gentile nations still dominate this earth and only wishful thinking can change the present situation.

3. How valid is the "year-day theory" advanced in the Witnesses' time calculations? If the theory is correct it obviously is a very important key to the understanding of prophecy. Its validity must certainly be based upon a Scriptural foundation. There are several lines of argument which can be urged against the theory: (a) Numbers 14:34 and Ezekiel 4:6 are interpreted to mean that "with God each day counts for a year."[157] Numbers 14:33, 34 simply states that because of sin Israel was to suffer " 'by the number of the days that YOU spied out the land, forty days, a day for a year . . .' " (NWT). Terry concludes:

> Here then is certainly no ground on which to base the universal proposition that, in prophetic designations of time, a day means a year. The passage is exceptional and explicit, and the words are used in a strictly literal sense; the days evidently mean days, and the years mean years.[158]

The same is true of Ezekiel 4:5, 6:

> The days of his prostration were literal days, and they were typical of years, as is explicitly stated. But to derive from this symbolic-typical action of Ezekiel a hermeneutical principle or law of universal application, namely, that days in prophecy mean years, would be a most unwarrantable procedure.[159]

---

[156] J. C. Waite, "Zedekiah," *The New Bible Dictionary* (Grand Rapids: Wm. B. Eerdmans Publishing Company, 1962), p. 1357. Raymond Albert Bowman, *et al.*, "Zedekiah," *Encyclopaedia Britannica* (1964 ed.), XXIII, 939; Jack Finegan, *Light From the Ancient Past* (Princeton: Princeton University Press, 1946), pp. 160-62. Waite points out that "both Jeremiah and Ezekiel seem to regard Jehoiachin as the last legitimate king of Judah" (*loc. cit.*). He was appointed king c. 598 and after a short reign was deposed and succeeded by Zedekiah. It is interesting to note that for the period under discussion the latest Witness books still contain their unique but unhistorical chronology.

[157] *From Paradise Lost to Paradise Regained, op. cit.*, p. 173.

[158] Milton S. Terry, *Biblical Hermeneutics* (second edition; Grand Rapids: Zondervan Publishing House, [n. d.]), p. 387.

[159] *Ibid.*

(b) If the two passages mentioned did in fact represent an universal law it is only reasonable that this law could be easily verified by examples of fulfilled prophecy. Terry cites a number of examples which are overwhelmingly against the year-day theory. In Genesis 7:4 God told Noah that " 'in just seven days more I am making it rain upon the earth forty days and forty nights. . .' " (NWT). Would it be proper to understand these days as years? In Genesis 15:13 God told Abram that his seed was to be a resident in a foreign land and would be afflicted for four hundred years. Are these years to be multiplied by 360 to get the proper understanding? The same point can be made on the sixty-five years of Isaiah 7:8 the three years of Isaiah 16:14, and the seventy years of Jeremiah 25:12 (cf. Dan. 9:2). Should Jonah's prophecy, which announced the judgment of Ninevah in forty days, be interpreted as symbolizing forty years? The year-day theory cannot be supported by the only possible understanding of other prophecies, that which Terry calls, "the analogy of prophetic scriptures."[160]

(c) One of the strongest arguments against the year-day theory is that all who have utilized the theory and predicted the coming of Christ, etc., have failed in their predictions.

> We have lived to see his [William Miller's] theories thoroughly exploded, and yet there have not been wanting others who have adopted his hermeneutical principles, and named A. D. 1866 and A. D. 1870 as "the time of the end." A theory which is so destitute of scriptural analogy and support as we have seen above, and presumes to rest on such a slender showing of divine authority, is on these grounds alone to be suspected; but when it has again and again proved to be false and misleading in its application, we may safely reject it, as furnishing no valid principle or rule in a true science of hermeneutics.[161]

That failure to realize what was predicted found no exception in Russell's calculations has been proven elsewhere in this book.[162] A number of former Jehovah's Witnesses have seen

---

[160] *Ibid.*, pp. 387, 388.

[161] *Ibid.*, pp. 389, 390.

[162] See below, pp. 225, 232, 233.

the light on this point.[163] Ezekiel 13:3 seems appropriate in application to the Watchtower prophets: "Thus saith the Lord Jehovah, Woe unto the foolish prophets, that follow their own spirit, and have seen nothing!"

4. Jesus Christ could not have come into His "second presence" in 1914 because the living saints were not glorified in 1918. As the reader will remember, the Witnesses teach that a partial rapture occurred in 1918 in which all of the 144,000 who had died up to that time were raised to join Christ, with the remainder of the body members raptured individually at death. I Thessalonians 4:16, 17 and I Corinthians 15: 51, 52 when correctly interpreted make such a view impossible. The NWT renders the passages as follows:

> Because the Lord himself will descend from heaven with a commanding call, with an archangel's voice and with God's trumpet, and those who are dead in union with Christ will rise first. Afterward we the living who are surviving will together ["at the same time," footnote] with them be caught away in clouds to meet the Lord in the air; and thus we shall always be with the Lord.
>
> Look! I tell YOU a sacred secret: We shall not all fall asleep in death, but we shall all be changed, in a moment, in the twinkling of an eye, during the last trumpet. For the trumpet will sound, and the dead will be raised up incorruptible, and we shall be changed.

(a) According to the grammar of the Thessalonians passage the "dead in union with Christ" and the "living" will experience the "catching" or "snatching away" at the same time. Lightfoot makes this clear:

> [*Hama*] is not to be taken apart from *sun autois* in the sense "at the same time, together with them"; for the combination *hama sun* is too common to allow of the separation of the two words....[164]

What Lightfoot said is that there can be no separation of the two groups (the dead and the living) in the rapture. Ellicott commenting on *hama sun autois* explains the word *epeita* ("Afterward" NWT, "Then" ASV) as following im-

---

[163] *Bible Student Examiner,* 6:1-5, May, 1965; *Back to the Bible Way,* 12:138, May-June, 1963.

[164] J. B. Lightfoot, *Notes on the Epistles of Saint Paul* (1895 edition; Grand Rapids: Zondervan Publishing House, 1957), p. 68.

mediately after the resurrection of the dead in Christ, and that the presence of *epeita* and *hama* "specifies not only continuity but the proximity of the two events. . . ."[165] (b) The purpose of being "caught away" (*harpagesometha*) is to "meet the Lord"; *eis aera* designates the place of meeting as "in the air"; the result, "we shall always be with the Lord." (c) It is obvious that I Corinthians 15:51, 52 and I Thessalonians 4:16, 17 deal with the same events. Verse 17 of I Thessalonians is parallel to "and we shall be changed" of I Corinthians 15:52. But the Jehovah's Witnesses do not, nor can they, understand verse 17 of I Thessalonians literally! Their view of a partial rapture is destroyed by such an acceptance of what the Bible actually says. In one case they interpret both verses 16 and 17 allegorically:

> At the marked time in 1919 Michael, the reigning Jesus Christ, delivered his people, spiritual Israel, for he was their great Prince. With an "archangel's voice" he issued a "commanding call" to them to awake from their sleep in that abased, captive condition. (I Thessalonians 4:16, 17)[166]

In another case verse 16 is taken literally and verse 17 is taken literally in the sense that there are those who remain after the "dead in union with Christ" had been raptured. But verse 17 is not viewed as dealing with a literal rapture of the "remnant." Scriptural evidence for this is found in the I Corinthians 15:51-53 passage.[167] (d) In a letter to this writer dated December 21, 1962 the Watchtower Society explains its impossible view:

> Verse 16 does refer to the resurrection of the spiritual class that took place in 1918 when Christ came to the temple. However, verse 17 does not have reference to the later, instantaneous resurrection on the part of those who are of the anointed class. To what does

[165] Charles John Ellicott, *Commentary on the Epistles of St. Paul to the Thessalonians* (second edition; Grand Rapids: Zondervan Publishing House, 1957), p. 65.

The *Emphatic Diaglott* also translates *hama sun* with "at the same time with them."

[166] *Your will Be Done on Earth* (Brooklyn: Watchtower Bible and Tract Society of New York, Inc., 1958), p. 326.

[167] *From Paradise Lost to Paradise Regained, op. cit.*, pp. 231, 232.

> 17 apply? Those of the anointed class who are in union with Christ, although still in the flesh, have been caught away from this world's system of things. They have been united with him in the service and worship of Almighty God. . . . As far as the literal resurrection of faithful anointed ones in our day is concerned, Paul shows that it will be instantaneous in the apostle's comments at I Corinthians 15:51-53.

Such an explanation is impossible. First, because it violates the context which discusses the resurrection of the dead as well as the living. Secondly, it violates the grammar which views the two groups as one joint host that meets the Lord. Third, how is is possible for those who remain to "always be with the Lord" in the same sense as those who had been raised from the dead? Many of the "anointed" after 1918 no longer followed the Watchtower Society and certainly would not be viewed by it as being united with Christ "in the service and worship of Almighty God." Fourth, there is no legitimate reason to understand a literal resurrection in one passage and not in the other. In fact, I Corinthians 15:51 in the NWT is cross referenced to I Thessalonians 4:17.

5. In 1907 Charles T. Russell, writing in the *Watch Tower,* made a statement that should be seriously considered by all who look to the Witnesses' chronology as the truth.

> But let us suppose a case far from our expectations: Suppose that A. D. 1915 should pass with the world's affairs all serene and with evidence that the "very elect" had not all been "changed" and without the restoration of natural Israel to favor under the New Covenant. (Rom. 11:12, 15) What then? Would not that prove our chronology wrong? Yes, surely! And would not that prove a keen disappointment? Indeed it would! It would work irreparable wreck to the parallel dispensations and Israel's double, and to the Jubilee calculations, and to the prophecy of the 2300 days of Daniel, and to the epoch called "Gentile times," and to the 1260, 1290 and 1335 days . . . None of these would be available longer. What a blow that would be! One of the strings of our "harp" would be quite broken![168]

---

[168] *The Watch Tower,* October 1, 1907 (republished December 15, 1913), reprinted in *Watch Tower Reprints,* p. 5368.

It does not matter if the present Watchtower organization has discarded some of the teachings mentioned above. Russell's conclusion (that if these predictions failed the chronology was wrong) still stands. Of course, when the time came, Russell, like so many other false prophets, tried to salvage the wreck and that which was no longer available is still being paraded as fact.

6. The setting of dates for the second coming of Christ is in clear contradiction to the words of the Saviour.

> "Concerning that day and hour nobody knows, neither the angels of the heavens nor the Son, but only the Father. . . . Keep on the watch, therefore, because YOU do not know on what day YOUR Master is coming. . . . At an hour that YOU do not think to be it, the Son of man is coming. . . .
>
> Keep on the watch, therefore, because YOU know neither the day nor the hour" [NWT, Matt. 24:36, 42, 44; 25:13].

The Witnesses' claims that the "invisible secret presence" began and the Kingdom was established on about October 1, 1914 are in direct contradiction to our Lord's statements.

Is Christ's "second presence" (second coming) to be secret or invisible? An acceptance of the bodily resurrection of Christ would require one to answer this question in the negative. Since Russell denied the bodily resurrection and believed that Christ rose as a spirit creature he naturally concluded that His second coming would be invisible. What was the source of the "secret presence" idea? The theory that Christ was already "present" in 1874 came from the *Herald of the Morning*, edited by N. H. Barbour. Concerning this new "light" Russell wrote:

> . . . The editor believed the prophecies to indicate that the Lord was already *present* in the world (unseen and invisible), and that the harvest work of gathering the wheat was already due,—and that this view was warranted by the time—prophecies which but a few months before he supposed had failed.
>
> Here was a new thought: Could it be that the *time prophecies* which I had so long despised, because of their misuse by the Adventists, were really meant to indicate when the Lord would be *invisibly present* to set up his kingdom—a thing which I clearly saw could be known in no other way?[169]

[169] *Watch Tower Reprints*, p. 3822.

This writer feels that the "secret presence" theory originated as a result of the failure of dates which were set for visible phenomena in connection with the second coming of Christ. Instead of rejecting the attempts to set dates for this event, the dates were retained and the expectations for them revised. A brief recounting of several such examples should illustrate this point: (1) The followers of William Miller *finally* set the date October 22, 1844 for the visible, bodily return of Christ to earth to rapture the Church and to bring judgment. When Christ did not return on that date, Hiram Edson came up with the idea that the date had been right but instead of the return being to earth as expected, Christ actually had entered into the second compartment of the heavenly sanctuary. O. R. L. Crosier, Edson's friend, presented this new view in 1846 and it has been accepted by the Seventh-day Adventists to this day.[170] Notice the sequence: a date was set for certain definite events to occur, the date came and the events did not, and the reinterpretation salvaged the date. (2) The editor of the Second Adventist journal, *Herald of the Morning,* N. H. Barbour, and his associate J. H. Paton, had predicted that the autumn of 1874 would mark Christ's visible return. When the period passed they were, as Russell records,

> dumbfounded. They had examined the time-prophecies that had seemingly passed unfulfilled, and had been unable to find any flaw, and had begun to wonder whether the *time* was right and their *expectations* wrong. [171]

The translation of *parousia* as "presence" in Matthew 24:27, 37, and 39 was the clue that led them to believe that Christ was invisibily present. This interpretation (and the date of 1874) was accepted by C. T. Russell, and his followers, and many still accept it. Notice the sequence here: a date was set for certain definite events to occur; the date came and the events did not, and the reinterpretation salvaged the date. (3) C. T. Russell predicted that the invisible Christ would come to rapture the living saints and to bring judgment to the earth in the autumn of 1914. The Kingdom

---

[170] Norman F. Douty, *Another Look at Seventh-day Adventism* (Grand Rapids: Baker Book House, 1962), pp. 105, 106.

[171] *Watch Tower Reprints, loc. cit.*

was to be fully established in the earth at that time. When that prediction failed, a reinterpretation of what was to be expected took place. It was said that the Kingdom actually was established, but in heaven and not on the earth. Christ's invisible "second presence" eventually was reexplained as beginning in 1914 instead of 1874. The Witnesses currently hold this position. Note again the repetition of the pattern presented before: a date was set, failure followed and a new explanation was made to salvage the date. (4) These failures and those of other predictions and dates, such as 1925, would lead any objective student of the Word to conclude that the dates were wrong and that the invisible "second presence" is an unscriptural idea needed to support a defunct theory.[172]

Before concluding this discussion, several key passages used by the Witnesses in support of the invisible "second presence" should be examined and refuted.

1. John 14:19 is interpreted to teach that Christ's return would be invisible and that he would not be seen by the world again:[173] " 'A little longer and the world will behold me no more, but YOU will behold me, because I live and YOU will live' " (NWT). To understand the true meaning of this verse the reader should turn to John 16:16 where Jesus, speaking to his disciples, said: " 'In a little while YOU will behold me no longer, and, further, in a little while YOU will see me.' " Neither verse has application to the second coming of Christ. In each case the words "no longer" are translated from the same Greek word *ouketi*. "No longer" cannot be understood absolutely, but must be taken in a limited sense. Christ was looking forward to His death and resurrection and in this context the verses are easily understood. " 'In a little while [a short time until the crucifixon] YOU will behold me no longer [during the period between His death and resurrection], and, further, in a little while YOU will see me' " [during His post-resurrection ministry until the ascension He appeared to His own]. He did not appear to the world because His public ministry was finished. After the resurrection His appearances were to

---

[172] For documentation on many of the changes mentioned at this point see below, pp. 225, 226, 231-34.

[173] *Make Sure of All Things*, *op. cit.*, p. 321

His chosen witnesses (Acts 10:40, 41), but at the time of His second coming it will be different: " 'For I say to YOU, YOU will by no means see me from henceforth until YOU say, "Blessed is he that comes in Jehovah's name!" ' " (Matt. 23:39 NWT). This verse does *not* say that Christ would not be seen again; to the contrary, the word "until" indicates that He will. When will He be seen? At the second coming, when the Jews will recognize Him as their Messiah. Zechariah 12:10 presents this coming scene:

> And I will pour out on the house of David and the inhabitants of Jerusalem a spirit of compassion and supplication, so that, when they look on him whom they have pierced, they shall mourn for him, as one mourns for an only child, and weep bitterly over him, as one weeps over a first-born [RSV].

Revelation 1:7 is a composite of the thought of Zechariah 12:10, 12, 14, and Daniel 7:13. It is a reflection of the Witnesses' theology to omit a marginal reference to these Zechariah verses (at least Zech. 12:10) under Revelation 1:7 in the *New World Translation.* The relationship between Zechariah 12:10 and Revelation 1:7, which requires a visible appearance of Christ at His second coming, is seen clearly in all three of the Greek texts in this writer's library,[174] as well as by C. T. Russell.[175] The Witnesses presently try to avoid the implications of Zechariah 12:10 by making it a prophecy which relates exclusively to Christ's first advent (cf. John 19:37).[176] Because Zechariah 12:10 and Revelation 1:7 have been united by John, a future fulfillment is demanded as well as a literal appearance of Christ, as Revelation 1:7 states:

> Look! he is coming with the clouds, and every eye will see him, and those who pierced him; and all the tribes of the earth will beat themselves in grief because of him. Yes, Amen [NWT].

---

[174] As one example see: *The Greek New Testament, op. cit.*, pp. 837, 918.

[175] *The Finished Mystery, op. cit.*, p. 15.

[176] *All Scripture Is Inspired of God and Beneficial* (Brooklyn: Watchtower Bible and Tract Society of New York, Inc., 1963), pp. 169, 171, 197.

2. I Timothy 6:14-16 is taken as a reference to Christ in support of the invisible "second presence" theory.[177] Stress is placed on the clause in verse 16, "whom not one of men has seen or can see" (NWT). The truth is, verses 15 and 16 are not to be understood of Christ, but are a doxology to the greatness and glory of God. A check of more than ten sources by this writer revealed this same understanding, with none to the contrary. Included in these sources were five books published by the Society, written by C. T. Russell and J. F. Rutherford![178] In addition, both Grimm-Thayer and Arndt-Gingrich also understand the verses to refer to God.[179] Therefore (other reasons could be given), there is no reason to apply the passage to Christ.

3. Acts 1:11 is also interpreted in such a way as to support the Witnesses theory of an invisible return: ". . . This Jesus who was received up from YOU into heaven will come thus in the same manner as YOU have beheld him going into heaven" (NWT). If, as has been shown, Christ experienced a bodily resurrection, the expression "in the same manner" would certainly convey the idea of the visible, glorious return.

In conclusion, this quotation from Grimm-Thayer commenting on the word *parousia* seems appropriate:

> In the N. T. esp. of *the advent,* i.e. the future, visible *return* from heaven of Jesus, the Messiah, to raise the dead, hold the last judgment, and set up formally and gloriously the kingdom of God. . . .[180]

IX. Blood Transfusion

The Witnesses' official doctrine on blood transfusion, which teaches that receiving a transfusion or permitting one to be given endangers one's chances of eternal life, first appeared in an article entitled, "Sanctity of Blood," in *The*

---

[177] *Things in Which it is Impossible for God to Lie, op. cit.,* p. 330.

[178] *Studies in the Scriptures,* II, 132; *The Harp of God,* p. 44; *Deliverance,* p. 12; *Reconciliation,* p. 79; *Creation,* p. 252.

[179] Grimm-Thayer, *op. cit.,* p. 12; Arndt-Gingrich, *op.* cit., p. 207 (see under *dunastes*).

[180] Grimm-Thayer, *op. cit.,* p. 490. It should be pointed out that *parousia* is only one of the Greek words used in the New Testament in reference to the second coming of Christ.

Watchtower issue of July 1, 1945. Since that time this view has gained much publicity, being frequently mentioned in the press, and on T. V. and radio, especially in cases where small children were faced with death without a transfusion. Several years ago a "Dr. Kildare" television presentation, which specifically named the Jehovah's Witnesses, dealt with their position. That the subject is an important one to the Witnesses is made clear by the frequent mention of the subject in the publications of the Society. There are many more entries in the *Watch Tower Publication Index* under "Blood Transfusion" than under "Salvation." The subject is even more important because of the claim that "blood transfusion violates the law of God,"[181] and disobedience to it can mean the loss of everlasting life.[182] Rejection of transfusion has led to the loss of physical life for many Witnesses.

The problem, as this writer sees it, is not whether transfusions are necessary or unnecesary, whether they involve risk or not, whether they save lives, etc.—but, are transfusions a violation of God's law? Does the violation of this law result in the loss of everlasting life? It is significant that, as far as this writer knows, all the Russellite splinter groups strongly oppose the Watchtower Society on the blood transfusion doctrine.[183]

The following treatment, quoted almost completely, is that of the Dawn Bible Students Association:

---

[181] *Blood, Medicine and the Law of God* (Brooklyn: Watchtower Bible and Tract Society of New York, Inc., 1961), p. 3.

[182] *Ibid.*, pp. 54, 55.

[183] Three examples of attacks on the Witnesses' position are: (1) Roy D. Goodrich, BTTBW publications, 276, 273; (2) Dawn Bible Students Association, *The Grace of Jehovah* (third edition; East Rutherford, N. J.: Dawn Bible Student Association, 1961), pp. 60-64; (3) Raymond G. Jolly, (ed.), *The Teachings of "Jehovah's Witnesses" Examined in the Light of the Scriptures* (Philadelphia: Laymen's Home Missionary Movement, [n. d.]), pp. 19-25.

ARE BLOOD TRANSFUSIONS FORBIDDEN BY GOD?

"But flesh with the life thereof, which is the blood thereof, shall ye not eat."—Genesis 9:4

This and other similar texts of Scripture are being used by some in an effort to prove that donating blood to save another's life, or receiving a transfusion of blood, are forbidden by God, and a sin so gross as to result in eternal death. Are we justified in placing such an interpretation upon the divine injunction against eating or drinking the blood of lower animals?

The science of transferring blood from one human being to another in order to save life was not known in ancient times. Obviously, then, there is no direct reference to it in the Word of God; so our conclusions as to whether or not it can properly be placed in the same category, from God's standpoint, as the assimilation of the blood of beasts through the digestive organs must be based wholly upon the principles involved rather than from direct statements of the Bible.

What common factors are involved in drinking the blood of lower animals and the medical science of blood transfusion? So far as we are able to see there is only one, which is the word blood. Apart from this, the two practices have nothing in common whatsoever.

God forbade his ancient people to drink the blood of lower animals. It is human blood that is used in the science of blood transfusion.

Drinking blood of lower animals necessitates their death. Blood transfusions do not require the death of those who donate their blood.

The life-sustaining vitamins derived from drinking blood reach the system through the digestive organs, the remaining element being eliminated from the body as waste; thus the blood, as such, is destroyed. In transfusions the blood of the donor is channeled directly into the bloodstream of the patient.

Thus we see that there is no similarity at all between the ancient custom of drinking blood, which was forbidden by the Lord, and the modern science of blood transfusion. Therefore, only by definitely misapplying the Scriptures can they be construed to forbid deriving benefit from this very humane application of medical science. No one should permit such a flagrant misapplication of God's commands to deter him from receiving the benefits of blood transfusion through fear of disobeying God and of being sentenced to the "second death."

The Blood of Atonement

In Leviticus 17:10, 11 we read, "And whatsoever man there be of the house of Israel, or of the strangers that sojourn among you, that eateth any manner of blood; I will even set my face against that soul that eateth blood, and will cut him off from among his people. For the life of the flesh is in the blood: and I have given it to you upon the altar to make an atonement for your souls: for it is the blood that maketh an atonement for the soul." The expression, "any manner of blood," cannot be construed to include human blood, for human blood was not offered on altars by Israel.

The "atonement" made by the blood of animals was of a typical nature only, and pointed forward to the atonement . . . by Jesus' blood.

The "blood of bulls and goats" did not actually take away the sins of the Israelites, but God used those sacrificed to point forward to the shedding of Jesus' blood; so he attached a great sacredness to animal blood, and for this reason did not want the Israelites to consider it common, or as ordinary food. . . .
Since Jehovah wants his people to consider the blood of Jesus as sacred and holy, it is understandable why he limited the use of animal blood to picture the real blood of atonement. With the Israelites it was a part of a school of experience designed to lead them to Christ. But this could not be construed in the remotest sense to be related to the modern medical science of blood transfusion. . . .

Heathen Customs Banned

A problem was presented to Jewish Christians in the Early Church when Gentile converts began to associate with them. These Gentiles were sincere in their acceptance of Christ, but seemingly in many cases their Chrisian faith was merely super-imposed upon their forms of heathen worship, many of which were repugnant to Jewish believers, and some even licentious. Certain Jewish teachers in the church thought to discipline their Gentile brethren by insisting that they obey the ordinaces of the Law, such as circumcision.

The apostles, and others more mature in the faith, met in conference at Jerusalem to decide what should be done about this problem. In view of the circumstances, they agreed on a minimum requirement of Gentile converts—they were to "abstain from meats offered to idols, and from blood, and from things strangled, and from fornication." (Acts 15:29). Fornication is unequivocally condemned in the Scriptures.

The idolatrous worship of the heathen of that day included feasting on the meats which had been offered to idols, and fornication. Partaking of blood could easily have been associated with these revelries. The immature Gentile Christian would see no wrong in these things, but to bring them into the church would have been disastrous; so the apostles wisely insisted that they abstain from them. However, these instructions to Gentile believers in the Early Church have no bearing whatever on the present-day medical science of blood transfusion.

The Watchtower of July 1, 1951 endeavors to prove that the divine injunction against drinking blood includes human blood. They cite the case of David, who refused to drink the water secured for him by three men at the risk of their lives. David said, "My God forbid it me, that I should do this thing: shall I drink the blood of these men that have put their lives in jeopardy? for with the jeopardy of their lives they brought it."—I Chron. 11:17-19.

Here David is speaking symbolically [metaphorically]. Instead of drinking the water secured at the risk of life, he poured it "out to the Lord." As David reasoned it, the water represented the blood of his benefactors, and this, he thought, should be offered to the Lord rather than to accept the sacrifice on his own behalf. There is no relationship here whatever to God's command not to drink the blood of lower animals, and certainly it is wholly unrelated to blood transfusion.

If you have an opportunity to donate your blood to save the life of a relative or friend, or a brother in Christ, do not hesitate thus to serve. Or if your doctor says that a blood transfusion will save your life, or the life of your child, by all means avail yourself of this modern blessing.[184]

The foregoing brief article presents an adequate refutation of the Witnesses' doctrine. In addition, let the reader consider the following:

1. The Witnesses cannot find one verse of Scripture in the New Testament that teaches that partaking of blood will result in eternal death.

2. If the Old Testament position on blood was still binding and so clear, and the penalty so severe, why didn't Jesus warn against the breaking of this commandment and why was the decision of the council at Jerusalem in Acts 15 necessary?

---

[184] *The Grace of Jehovah, loc. cit.*

3. In the New Testament, about the only passage that possibly could be misunderstood to support the Witnesses' doctrine is Acts 15, especially verses 19-21 and 28, 29. The decision of the council is repeated in Acts 21:25. James' words to the council are recorded in verses 19 and 20:

> "Hence my decision is not to trouble those from the nations who are turning to God, but to write them to keep themselves free from things polluted by idols and from fornication and from what is killed without draining its blood and from blood" [NWT].

The letter from the council to the brothers in Antioch, Syria and Cilicia is recorded in verses 28 and 29:

> "For the holy spirit and we ourselves have favored adding no further burden to YOU, except these necessary things, to keep yourselves free from things sacrificed to idols and from blood and from things killed without draining their blood and from fornication. If YOU carefully keep yourselves from these things, YOU will prosper. Good health to YOU!" [NWT].

(a) In reading the entire chapter of Acts 15 the subject of loss of eternal life is never hinted at or mentioned. (b) Salvation, according to the passage, is clearly by faith (15:9-11). Salvation by any other means or loss of salvation by any action is never mentioned. (c) The reason for the decision is explained in verse 21: " 'For from ancient times Moses has had in city after city those who preach him, because he is read aloud in the synagogues on every sabbath.' " The Gentiles were to abstain from practices offensive to the Jews. The abstinence from blood was a matter of fellowship between Jewish and Gentile Christians.

> This decree was issued to the Gentile churches not as a means of salvation but as a basis for fellowship, in the spirit of Paul's exhortation that those who were strong in faith should be willing to restrict their liberty in such matters rather than offend the weaker brother (Rom. 14:1 ff.; I Cor. 8:1 ff.).[185]

Most who claim to be Christians today do respect the rulings of the Old and New Testaments governing the eating of

---

[185] George Ladd, "The Acts of the Apostles," *The Wycliffe Bible Commentary*, C. F. Pfeiffer and E. F. Harrison editors (Chicago: Moody Press, 1962), p. 1152.

blood. (d) In the decision that was passed down there was no appeal to Old Testament law. It was not issued as a command. What was passed down was a strong statement of opinion which conveyed moral authority.

4. A little reflection on the Old Testament sacrifices and the work of Christ completed on Calvary will show how wrong the Witnesses are. Before the death of Christ the blood sacrifices were the only acceptable way of atonement for sin; thus animal blood was an important symbol of obedience to God. Since the death of Christ, the only blood with this significance is His blood, and the sin which has no forgiveness is committed by the one who rejects the blood of Christ and the work of the Spirit (Hebrews 10:29). Since animal sacrifices are no longer being offered in behalf of the sinner for an atonement, it is evident that Old Testament injunctions against the partaking of blood no longer have any force today.

5. The study by A. M. Stibbs, dealing with the meaning of the word "blood" in the Bible, also shows the Witnesses are wrong. Contrary to the emphasis of the Witnesses that the significance of the blood is life, Stibbs concludes that it is death.

> To sum up thus far, the general witness of the Old Testament is, therefore, that "blood" stands not for life released, but first for the fact, and then for the significance, of life laid down or taken in death.[186]

In the conclusion of the study Stibbs makes a significant observation: ". . . There is nothing in the ideas of the Bible about 'blood' which is at all comparable to the modern practice of blood transfusion."[187] Blood in the Bible speaks of death; blood transfusion could not possibly be the same, for no one dies to give a transfusion, and life is given through the process. Again it should be remembered that the only blood with significance as far as salvation is concerned is the blood of Christ, which testifies of His death for the sins of mankind (Rom. 5:9; Eph. 1:7; I Pet. 1:18, 19).

---

[186] A. M. Stibbs, *The Meaning of the Word "Blood" in Scripture* (third edition, 1962; London: The Tyndale Press, 1948), pp. 15, 16.

[187] *Ibid.*, p. 29.

X. Conclusion

Although the doctrinal study in this chapter has been far from complete, the seeker for the truth can see that the doctrines upon which the Watchtower edifice has been built form a faulty foundation which causes the entire structure to topple. The study has revealed, among other things, that the doctrines of the Jehovah's Witnesses have been based upon and defended by misrepresentation, false logic, unscriptural claims, a faulty understanding of church history, a faulty exegesis of the original Bible languages, and an ignoring of the clear declarations of Scripture. The examination of the doctrines of this group in the light of the Word of God and the other findings of sound scholarship yields only one conclusion: the doctrines of this group find their source in the Watchtower Society and not in the Bible.

CHAPTER X

THE TRANSLATIONS AND BIBLES OF THE WATCH TOWER BIBLE AND TRACT SOCIETY

From the time of the founding of the Watch Tower Bible and Tract Society, more than seventy translations in English and other languages have been used by the Society. These various translations had been used eclectically in setting forth the teachings of the group.

I. SOME BIBLES USED AND PRINTED BY THE WATCH TOWER BIBLE AND TRACT SOCIETY

Although other Bibles were printed for the Watch Tower Society[1], *The Emphatic Diaglott* was the first Bible portion published on the Watch Tower presses. This interlinear New Testament was published in 1926.[2] Since that time (up until 1963) 202,147 copies have been printed.[3] The plates for the *King James Version* were purchased and printing of the version was begun in 1942. Some 1,436,949 copies have been printed up to 1963.[4] In 1944 the use of the plates for

[1] In 1896 Rotherham's New Testament, the ***Emphasized New Testament*** was printed for the Watch Tower, bearing its imprint. In 1901 the ***Holman Linear Bible*** with references to the publications of the Society in the margins was ordered printed. Additional details on the subject are found in ***Jehovah's Witnesses in the Divine Purpose*** (pp. 255, 256) and ***All Scripture Is Inspired of God and Beneficial*** (pp. 320-23).

[2] The plates for ***The Emphatic Diaglott*** came into the possession of the Society in 1902, although it was previously used by the Bible Students.

[3] ***All Scripture Is Inspired of God and Beneficial*** (Brooklyn: Watchtower Bible and Tract Society of New York, Inc., 1963), p. 322.

[4] *Ibid.*, p. 323.

the *American Standard Version* was purchased, and printing began in the same year. Some 884,944 copies were printed up to 1963.[5]

Both the *King James Version* and the *American Standard Version* produced by the Society have special appendix material. The most important section of the four-section Appendix in the *King James Version* is the "Concordance of Bible Words and Expressions." This is not a standard concordance, but in the words of *Theocratic Aid to Kingdom Publishers,* "This is a 'new world' Theocratic concordance."[6] The special feature is the presence of such "theocratic terms" as "Theocracy" and "vindication," as well as other Biblical phrases much used by the Witnesses.

The *American Standard Version* Appendix is more complete than that of the *King James*, the concordance cantaining more than 3,000 entries. This concordance is also "Theocratic" in orientation.[7]

The *American Standard Version* is spoken of as "an excellent Bible translation."[8] But its most commendable feature to the Jehovah's Witnesses is the inclusion of the name "Jehovah." In the book, *Jehovah's Witnesses in the Divine Purpose,* an overall view of other translations is presented with the conclusion stated that although the Witnesses have used many versions they "have found them defective."[9] The book (quoting *The Watchtower*) goes on to say that the other versions

> are inconsistent or unsatisfactory, infected with religious traditions or worldly philosophy and hence not in harmony with the sacred truths which Jehovah God has restored to his devoted people. . . More and more the need has been felt for a translation in modern speech, in harmony with revealed truth. . . .[10]

In 1972 the Society published *The Bible in Living English* by the late Steven Byington.

---

[5] *Ibid.*

[6] *Theocratic Aid to Kingdom Publishers* (Brooklyn: Watchtower Bible and Tract Society, Inc., 1945), p. 242.

[7] For a more detailed analysis of these appendices see *ibid.*, pp. 242-49.

[8] *Jehovah's Witnesses in the Divine Purpose* (Watchtower Bible and Tract Society of New York, Inc., 1959), p. 256.

[9] *Ibid.*, p. 257.

[10] *Ibid.*

In short, then, while acknowledging some indebtedness to other translations, they find none satisfactory, for none agree with the "revealed truth" of the Jehovah's Witnesses. Translations which agree with their theology are commended where they agree. To give authority to some doctrine or rendering, the Witnesses often cite as authority a translation by a liberal or one who has no respect for the Bible as the inspired Word of God.[11]

II. The Emphatic Diaglott

Bruce M. Metzger, in his article, "The Jehovah's Witnesses and Jesus Christ," mentions *The Emphatic Diaglott* in a footnote and writes that in several particulars it "is an ancestor of the New World Translation."[12]

That this is the case can be clearly seen by a comparison of such passages as: Matthew 21: 42; 22:37, 44; 23:39; 24:3, 27, 37, 39; 25:46; Mark 11:9; Luke 23:46; John 1:1; 14:17; Philippians 2:6 and Hebrews 1:8. The translation of *parousia* by "presence" uniformly in the *New World Translation* and *The Emphatic Diaglott,* except at I Thessalonians 3: 13, also shows the relationship. It would be surprising, to say the least, to find agreement on such crucial passages were it not for a common theology.

---

[11] An example of the latter is the Watchtower's use of the translation of John 1:1 by Leo Tolstoy in his *Four Gospels Harmonized and Translated* (Included in *"The Word"—Who is He? According to John,* p. 53). It is recorded that Tolstoy "renounced the Church, and out of his own reading of the Gospels gradually evolved a new Christianity, from which all the metaphysical and non-ethical elements were eliminated." (p. 279). His teachings were that "God is not personal . . . Jesus was a great man, whose teaching is true not because he was the Son of God, but because it coincides with the light of human conscience. The Buddha and other men were as great, and Jesus holds no monopoly of the truth.... His religion is purely anthropocentic." Dimitri Mirsky, "Tolstoy, Leo (Lyev) Nikolyevich," *Encyclopaedia Britannica* (1964 ed.), XXII, 279. It is evident that the Watchtower Society is not concerned with the unbelief of the author if a translation agrees with their theology.

[12] Bruce M. Metzger, "The Jehovah's Witnesses and Jesus Christ," *Theology Today,* 10:67, April 1953.

In *All Scripture Is Inspired of God and Beneficial, op. cit.,* p. 309, the *Diaglott* is included as one of the sources of the *New World Translation of the Christian Greek Scriptures.*

The Watch Tower makes much of the fact that the author of *The Emphatic Diaglott,* Wilson, "was never associated with the Watch Tower Bible and Tract Society."[13]

Since the Jehovah's Witnesses regarded *The Emphatic Diaglott* so highly and based much on its authority, it would be well to look further into this work. It was published in 1864 by Benjamin Wilson, a newspaper editor of Geneva, Illinois. An important fact concerning this man is that he was a Christadelphian, which would explain why he would agree on critical passages with the Witnesses. The Christadelphians also reject the Trinity, the personality of the Holy Spirit, eternal punishment, and the full atonement, and they are strong millennialists. Wilson published a monthly magazine, *The Gospel Banner and Millennial Advocate.*[14]

---

[13] *Jehovah's Witnesses in the Divine Purpose, op. cit.,* p. 256.

[14] *The Restitution Herald* of Oregon, Illinois, a publication of the Church of God General Conference, published a series of articles on Benjamin Wilson and the *Emphatic Diaglott* which were condensed and published by the Associated Bible Students in their journal, *The Herald of Christ's Kingdom,* July-August, September-October, November-December, 1964 issues. The writer of the articles establishes Wilson's contacts with the founder of the Christadelphians: "There is strong evidence that Benjamin Wilson was aided in the study of the Scriptures by Dr. John Thomas . . . in the years preceding his undertaking of the translation of the Greek New Testament into the English tongue. For a short while Dr. Thomas had a farm in the vicinity of Geneva, but his main interest was in preaching and publishing religious material. . . . Thomas and Wilson were cordial friends . . . . It was expressed by both John Thomas and Benjamin Wilson that Alexander Campbell stopped short of true enlightenment. . . ." "Benjamin F. Wilson and The Emphatic Diaglott," *The Herald of Christ's Kingdom,* 47:72, 73, September-October, 1964.

As to Wilson's doctrinal position the following is included in his obituary, printed in the *Evening Bee* of Sacramento, May 9, 1900: "'Among the doctrines and teachings of modern theology that he could not harmonize with what he believed to be the teachings of the early church were the following: infant damnation, infant baptism, foreordination, doctrine of eternal torment, inherent immortality of the soul, and the doctrine of the Trinity. . . .'" "Benjamin F. Wilson and the Emphatic Diaglott," *The Herald of Christ's Kingdom,* 47:63, July-August, 1964. From the foregoing it is clear that Wilson's theology and Russell's were very close, and from the facts pointed out here and in chapter 2, it appears probable that both Russell and Wilson drew from a common source, Dr. John Thomas.

What about his scholarship? Wilson was self-educated; his work shows that he certainly was not a scholar. Neither did he have the respect of those who were scholars. Obviously, his purpose was not to translate, but to justify his theological views. In a review of *The Emphatic Diaglott,* Isaac Hall writes:

> This is the notorious "Emphatic Diaglott" now regularly published by the "phrenological" firm, S. R. Wells & Co., of New York. It is an astonishing edition. . . . No remarks need be made upon the style of editing, or upon either of the translations: unless it be to say that the only respectable portion of the prefactory matter is the "History of the Greek Text"; and that is not faultless.[15]

It should be also noticed that Hall's work was published in 1883, years before *The Diaglott* was in general use or printed by the Watch Tower Society. It may be concluded, then, that *The Emphatic Diaglott* was adopted because of its Christadelphian bias which agreed almost perfectly with the new Russellite group which was forming. The Russellites accepted the renderings of Wilson, for they did not have the linguistic ability either to evaluate or to determine their correctness, nor did they wish to question that which so perfectly supported their theories. As has already been stated, the scholarship of Wilson is questionable, and his renderings do not indicate any authority should be attached to his work. Contemporary scholars did not respect the work; among them, Hall branded the work "notorious," "astonishing," and most of the prefatory matter not worthy of respect. The translation is based on the poor, dated recension of J. J. Griesbach

---

The late Wesley J. Ladwig, who edited *The Roundtable of the Scriptures* (a universal restitutionist journal), gave this information concerning the Church of God and Benjamin Wilson: "These people were brought together through the efforts of Dr. Wilson, the translator of the Diaglott. Some of these churches are scattered throughout Illinois, Iowa and other midwestern states. . . . The teachings of the Church of God are much in line with what Pastor Russell taught." *The Roundtable of the Scriptures,* July-August 1951, pp. 7, 8.

[15] Isaac H. Hall, *A Critical Bibliography of the Greek New Testament as Published in America* (Philadelphia: Pickwick and Co., 1883), pp. 31, 32.

(1806) which does not command the respect of present-day scholarship.

Wilson's *Emphatic Diaglott* makes claims very much like the claims made by the translators of the *New World Translation.* On page 3 of the Preface it reads:

> Scrupulous fidelity has been maintained throughout this version in giving the true rendering of the original text into English; no regard whatever being paid to the prevailing doctrines or prejudices of sects, or the peculiar tenets of theologians.

What Wilson failed to state was that his own personal, unbiased, unsectarian, non-theological readings did get into the work. As far as authority and scholarship is concerned, then, *The Emphatic Diaglott* is found wanting in both departments. (In the summer of 1969 the Witnesses released a new Interlinear, *The Kingdom Interlinear Translation of the Greek Scriptures.* A cursory examination reveals the bias of the Translation Committee. This work combines the Wescott and Hort Greek text with an English translation and an improved text of the 1961 *New World Translation.*

III. The New World Translation of the Holy Scriptures

The *New World Translation* of the entire Bible was completed and published in 1961. The following examination of this work deals with the volumes as they appeared: (1) The *New World Translation of the Christian Greek Scriptures* (includes the entire New Testament), (2) the *New World Translation of the Hebrew Scriptures* (includes the entire Old Testament), and (3) the *New World Translation of the Holy Scriptures* (the entire Bible).[16]

---

[16] In *All Scripture Is Inspired of God and Beneficial,* (*op. cit.*, p. 11), the Witnesses claim that "it is a mistake of tradition to divide God's written Word into two sections, calling the first section, from Genesis to Malachi, 'The Old Testament,' and the second section, from Matthew to Revelation, 'The New Testament.'" This explains the use of the designations "Christian Greek Scriptures" and "Hebrew Scriptures."

THE NEW WORLD TRANSLATION OF THE CHRISTIAN GREEK SCRIPTURES[17]

The *New World Translation of the Christian Greek Scriptures* was first released on August 2, 1950 at the Jehovah's Witnesses' international assembly held in Yankee Stadium, New York. The first edition was 480,000 copies. A second edition, with minor additions and revisions in the marginal references and the concluding notes, was published May 1, 1951. In less than ten years over 1,400,000 volumes had been printed.

Since Watchtower representatives claim the work was done by competent scholars and approved by the same—and since this translation is acclaimed as the only unbiased, unprejudiced, consistent, literal, etc., version—it behooves the Christian to see if these claims are valid. Space forces one to choose some of the outstanding errors of the work to show the caliber of the translation. If all the errors of this work would be followed through, it would be a book-length treatment.

Claims Made in the Foreword

On page 6 of the Foreword the purpose of the translation is stated: "The endeavor of the New World Bible Translation Committee has been to avoid this snare of religious traditionalism" (which they claim for all translations other than their own). On the same page, one reads of other translations:

> Much good has been accomplished by them and will yet be. But honesty compels us to remark that, while each of them has its points of merit, they have fallen victim to the power of human traditionalism in varying degrees. Consequently, religious traditions, hoary with age, have been taken for granted and gone unchallenged and uninvestigated. These have been interwoven into the translations to color the thought. In support of a preferred religious view, an inconsistency and unreason-

---

[17] The 1951 revised second edition of the *New World Translation of the Christian Greek Scriptures* is used in this section because of the marginal references and notes. Revisions found in the 1961 edition of the *New World Translation of the Holy Scriptures* are noted.

ableness have been insinuated into the teachings of the inspired writings.

With this arrogant statement the Watchtower Committee waves aside hundreds of the greatest linguists of all time and substitutes the Committee of seven, headed by N. H. Knorr and F. W. Franz,[18] a Committee composed of unknowns who hold comparatively little in the way of degrees or scholarly recognition. Could this be the reason why the Committee members wish to "remain anonymous even after their death?"[19] A further stated purpose appears on page 9 of the Foreword: "We offer no paraphrase of the Scriptures. Our endeavor all through has been to give as literal a translation as possible . . . " with the purpose of "getting, as nearly as possible, word for word, the exact statement of the original."

The Foreword devotes some fifteen pages in word and photographic illustration to the justification of the insertion of the Tetragrammaton (JHVH, translated "Jehovah") 237 times into the text, and 72 times in the margin of the translation. The following "evidence" is adduced:

> The evidence is, therefore, that the original text of the Christian Greek Scriptures has been tampered with the same as the text of the LXX has been. And, at least from the 3d century A. D. onward, the divine name in tetragrammaton form has been eliminated from the text by copyists who did not understand or appreciate the divine name or who developed an aversion to it, possibly under the influence of anti-Semitism. In place of it they substituted the words *kyrios* (usually translated "the Lord") and *theos,* meaning "God" [p. 18].

The "evidence" referred to is a papyrus roll dated in the first or second century B. C. of the latter part of the book of Deuteronomy. In this fragment of the LXX the Tetragrammaton appears. The conclusion is drawn: "It proves that the original LXX did contain the divine name wherever it occurred in the Hebrew original" (p. 12).

What this actually shows is that, of all the existing copies of the Septuagint, only *one* had the divine name in Hebrew and that *one* copyist felt that it should appear. In

[18] See above, p. 32.

[19] *Jehovah's Witnesses in the Divine Purpose, op. cit.*, p. 258.

the quest for the proper text, weight must go to the majority and not to one instance. Actually, upon close observation of the fragments shown upon pages 13 and 14, the Tetragrammaton looks as though it was not part of the original writing at all, but inserted by a later hand. The Hebrew letters are much smaller than the surrounding Greek letters and are quite cramped. On some of the fragments the ink of the Tetragrammaton seems of a different color than the surrounding Greek letters. One would conclude, then that the available evidence shows conclusively that the original LXX used *kurios* and *theos,* and that the "proof" offered by the *New World Translation* only confirms this fact.

The appearance of the Tetragrammaton in Aquila's Greek version about 128 A. D. and in Origen's Hexapla about 245 A. D., along with Jerome mentioning its presence in certain Greek texts in his day, are also cited as proofs of its existence in the New Testament. What does this demonstrate? It shows only that the divine name was sometimes used in copies of the Septuagint, but the general rule is that the Septuagint uses *kurios* or *theos* in place of the divine name. Mayer writes concerning Aquila's version:

> True, in one out of nearly 7,000 instances this version uses the Hebrew form of JHWH. It must, however, be observed that Aquila's version was written more than 2-300 years after the original Septuagint; that Aquila uses the Hebrew form JHWH only once; that he uses archaic Hebrew letters.[20]

In the New Testament, of the thousands of manuscripts available, *not one* has been produced which contains even the slightest indication of either the use of the Tetragrammaton in the original, or the "tampered with" text upon which the Witnesses base their claim to insert the Tetragrammaton.

The other "evidence" (various versions) for the insertion of the divine name, listed as J^1 through J^{19}, the earliest of which is dated 1385, offers no evidence for the insertion of the divine name. These sources are merely Greek translated into Hebrew. The originals from which these Hebrew versions were translated originally all contained the Greek *kurios* and *theos.*

---

[20] F. E. Mayer, *The Religious Bodies of America* (fourth edition; St. Louis, Missouri: Concordia Publishing House, 1956), p. 468.

In his review of the translation, Bruce Metzger includes the insertion of "Jehovah" among the renderings which "are simply indefensible" and states:

> The introduction of the word "Jehovah" into the New Testament text, in spite of much ingenuity in an argument filled with a considerable amount of irrelevant material (pp. 10-25), is a plain piece of special pleading. It is entirely without critical significance to be told that modern translations of the New Testament into Hebrew render the word "Lord" by the tetragrammaton, nor does the fact that it is possible to name thirty-eight translations into languages other than Hebrew and Greek which use a vernacular form of "Jehovah" bear upon the question in the slightest.[21]

After inserting the divine name in the text so many times, why did the Committee neglect to insert the divine name in Romans 14:9-11 and Philippians 2:10, 11? Both of these passages are based on Isaiah 45:22-25 which speaks of Jehovah.

One purpose of the translators is to destroy the impact of the substitution found in the New Testament of the equivalent term "Lord," applied to Christ and carrying with it all the Old Testament meaning of "Jehovah." As has already been shown, after the resurrection, in the outlook of the early church, Christ was actually designated "Jehovah" whenever He was termed "Lord."

Thus the many "proofs" that are devoted to a justification of the insertion of the divine name in the New Testament, fall upon adequate investigation.

Criticisms of the Translation

Of the many objections that could be given to demonstrate the definite bias and untrustworthiness of this translation the following are cited.

1. *The use of paraphrasing in contradiction to the stated purpose.* Although the translators stated, "We offer no paraphrase of the Scriptures. Our endeavor all through has been to give as literal a translation as possible" (p. 9), this is not carried out in the work. The glorious fact of the believer being "in Christ" is paraphrased repeatedly by the transla-

[21] Bruce M. Metzger, Book Review: *"New World Translation of the Christian Greek Scriptures," The Bible Translator*, 15: 152, July, 1964.

tors. This phrase or its cognate such as "in Him" and "in the Lord" is used 164 times in the Pauline Epistles. Although union with Christ is a clear teaching of the Bible, the *New World Translation* and the teaching of the Witnesses cannot include it, for as Metzger points out: "It cannot do so because its teaching is directly and fundamentally anti-Trinitarian. It is only because Jesus Christ is God that we can be in him."[22] An example of paraphrasing when dealing with the union of the believer with Christ is found in John 15:1-11. In order to destroy the truth of Christ's personal presence with the believer, the Greek word *en* is inconsistently translated "in" part of the time, and "in union with" the remainder of the time. The translation "in union with" is a paraphrase. Why is this so serious? Because this union is explained as the "unity of the believers in serving God and proclaiming his word. . . ."[23] The personal presence of Christ in every believer becomes a unity of idea and purpose.

A similar attempt to destroy the Biblical teaching of the personal presence of Christ in the believer is found in John 17:23 and 26. In these two verses *en* is rendered "in union with" three times. Again the inconsistency is manifest when in verse 26 *en autois* is correctly translated "in them" when it applies to love, but when immediately afterward it applies to Christ, the translation of *en* goes back to "in union with." For more examples of such paraphrasing, see: John 14: 20; Colossians 1: 27, 28; and Galatians 1: 16.

With the *same* Greek word being translated properly in every case except when it refers to the believer's personal relationship with Christ, it must be concluded that the translator's paraphrasing is nothing less than interpretation. One loses confidence in a translation which professes to be literal when it is replete with biased paraphrases.

2. *The unwarranted insertion of words not found in the Greek.* The translators, in their attempts to remove the import of Christological passages, found it necessary to alter the translations and to read in words that are not in the text.

---

[22] Bruce M. Metzger, "The Jehovah's Witnesses and Jesus Christ," *op. cit.*, p. 68.

[23] *This Means Everlasting Life* (Brooklyn: Watchtower Bible and Tract Society, Inc., 1950), p. 18.

A pioneer Witness who came to the door one day was shocked by the passage in Colossians 1:16, 17 when he found, after looking at the Greek, that the *New World Translation of the Christian Greek Scriptures* had included the word "other" four times, although the Greek neither has the word nor implies it! The 1961 revised edition of the *New World Translation* has the word "other" in brackets, indicating that the word was added by the translators. This change would make the rendering more honest, although just as biased. But what is a reader to think when he uses the other publications of the Jehovah's Witnesses, which indicate that they are quoting from the 1961 revised edition, and finds that the word "other" is not bracketed in them?[24] The passage cited in order to justify this insertion, Luke 13:2, 4 is not at all parallel, because it has "other" clearly implied. The Witnesses' attempt is to make Christ a created being, to make the Creator a creation, through which all other things are created. The inconsistency of the translation of Colossians 1: 16, 17 is evident when compared with John 1:3: "All things came into existence through him, and apart from him not even one thing came into existence" (NWT).

In Matthew 24:6, 14; I Peter 4:7; and II Corinthians 11:15, the same Greek expression is translated "the accomplished end," "the complete end," and "their end." The added words "accomplished" and "complete" are actually interpretation and not called for in a literal translation.[25] Hebrews 9:27 adds "time," Philippians 1:23 adds "but," and Revelation 19:20 adds "still." The adding of a word, however small,

---

[24]For examples see: *Awake!* 44:27, January 8, 1963; *1963 Yearbook*, 9/10/64; *Make Sure of All Things; Hold Fast to What is Fine*, p. 132. It might also be mentioned that the one-volume *New World Translation*, which contains all the notes of the previous volumes of the Old and New Testaments, which was prepared in 1963, has left the text as it stood in the *New World Translation of the Christian Greek Scriptures*. So, in conclusion, for all practical purposes the insertion of "other," a clear *addition* to the Word of God, stands unchanged.

[25] The 1961 revision changed Matthew 24:6, 14 and I Peter 4:7 to read uniformly, "the end." Again, the revision is in keeping with the demands of the passages, but the rendering is vitiated because of lengthy points made on the basis of the wrong translations in such books as *From Paradise Lost to Paradise Regained*, pp. 178, 179. This book was published before the 1961 revision, but it is currently being circulated.

at times can completely change the meaning of a passage. The insertion of words in Colossians 1:16, 17, Hebrews 9:27, and Philippians 1: 23 are good examples.

Heydt points out from examples in John 13:18; 17:12; 19:24 and 19:36 that the identical Greek expression has (for no good reason) been translated four different ways.[26] After a study of the translation's minor insertions, Heydt concludes:

> *If such liberty is taken in a case where no particular doctrine is at stake, how can we trust the translators to be accurate with those Scriptures involving controversial issues?*[27]

The treatment of passages cited seriously questions the literality of this version. Again Heydt writes, "*We are driven to conclude that the translators either did not know their Greek or else had no concept of what the responsibilities of a literal translator are.*"[28]

3. *Erroneous rendering of Greek words.* Again the Witnesses show their attempts to make the Scriptures conform to a preconceived theology. On the crucial passage in Matthew 25:46 which, if properly translated, would clearly teach eternal punishment, the NWT translates: "And these will depart into everlasting cutting-off, but the righteous ones into everlasting life." A footnote on "cutting-off" states, "Literally, 'pruning' ; hence a curtailing, a holding in check."

The word translated "cutting off," (in the footnote "pruning"), is the Greek word *kolasis (kolasin)*. This word is used four times in the New Testament; also the noun and verb occur six times in the Septuagint, and eighteen times in the Apocrypha. In each instance the idea conveyed by this word is *punishment,* although the word *kolasis* is used in the classics three hundred years before as "pruning" and "holding in check." But whatever its meaning was in the classics, it is clear that all writers at the time of Christ used it to express pure retributive punishment.[29]

---

[26] Henry J. Heydt, *Jehovah's Witnesses: Their Translation* (New York: American Board of Missions to the Jews, Inc., [n. d.]), p. 9. John 13:18 has been revised in the 1961 edition.

[27] *Ibid.,* pp. 9, 10.

[28] *Ibid.,* p. 10.

[29] James Fyfe, *The Hereafter: Sheol, Hades and Hell, the World To Come, and the Scripture Doctrine of Retribution According to Law* (Edinburgh: T. & T. Clark, 1890), pp. 181-83.

J. R. Mantey, co-author of *A Manual Grammar of the Greek New Testament,* writes in his comment on *kolasis* as translated in the *New World Translation of the Christian Greek Scriptures*:

> In Jehovah's Witnesses' *New World Translation* (Matt. 25:46) the Greek word *kolasin* which is regularly defined *punishment* in Greek lexicons is translated "cutting off," in spite of the fact that not one shred of lexical evidence exists anywhere for such a translation. We have found this word in first century Greek writings in 107 different contexts and in every one of them it has the meaning of *punishment, and never "cutting off."*[30]

This word has been dealt with at some length for one reason, to show to what lengths a biased translator will go to justify a translation which bolsters a preconceived theology.

Another such example is found in Colossians 2:9 which the *New World Translation* renders, "because it is in him that all the fullness of the divine quality dwells for the body [dwells bodily, 1961 ed.]." The word *theotes* is here translated "divine quality," which is not a literal or correct rendering. Grimm-Thayer give as the meaning of this word, "*deity* i.e. the state of being God, *Godhead*: Col. ii. 9."[31] The word for "divinity" or "divine character" is found in Romans 1:20 and is *theiotes* which is rendered by Grimm-Thayer as "*divinity, divine nature,*"[32] Cremer gives "the Godhead" as the meaning of *theotes* and then says that the two words are to be distinguished: "*theotes=that which God is, theiotes* =that which is of God."[33] In the discussion of these two words Trench writes concerning Colossians 2:9:

> . . . St. Paul is declaring that in the Son there dwells all the fulness of absolute Godhead: they were no mere rays of divine glory which gilded Him, lighting up his

---

[30] J. R. Mantey, "Is Death the Only Punishment for Unbelievers?" *Bibliotheca Sacra,* 112: 341, October, 1955.

[31] Joseph Henry Thayer (ed. and trans.), *A Greek-English Lexicon of the New Testament Being Grimm's Wilke's Clavis Novi Testamenti* (fourth edition; Edinburgh: T. & T. Clark [n. d.]), p. 288. Hereafter this work will be designated Grimm-Thayer.

[32] *Ibid.,* p. 285.

[33] Hermann Cremer, *Biblico-Theological Lexicon of New Testament Greek,* trans. William Urwick (fourth English edition; Edinburgh: T. & T. Clark, 1895), p. 281.

person for a season and with a splendour not his own; but He was, and is, absolute and perfect God. . . . [34]

In Philippians 3:11 the Greek word *exanastasis,* which occurs only once in the New Testament, is rendered "earlier resurrection" though there is no lexical evidence for such a translation. It is explained in *The Watchtower* that "basically, in Greek *exanastasis* means a getting up early in the morning, so it suggests earliness and therefore an earlier rising from the dead."[35] The writers do not give any source of authority for this claim or for the translation.

As one further example of many that could be discussed, the Witnesses translate Matthew 27:50: "Again Jesus cried out with a loud voice, and ceased to breathe." A footnote renders: "Yielded up his breath [used in the text in the 1961 ed.]." The parallel passage in Luke 23:46 reads "And Jesus called with a loud voice and said: 'Father, into your hands I entrust my spirit.' When he had said this, he expired."

The account in Matthew 27:50 has the Greek word *pneuma* rendered "breath." In the parallel passage of the same scene, the same word is translated correctly "spirit." The rendering in Matthew is not possible in the light of the Biblical usage of the term and in the light of this parallel passage. Luke 23:46 would become ridiculous if one would translate according to the Witnesses' understanding: "Father into your hands I entrust my breath." The very fact that Christ committed His spirit is ample proof that there is more to man than breath and body. Man is not a soul—man possesses a soul, or more properly, a spirit. This fact caused the translators to try to avoid the meaning in Matthew 27:50 since their theology would not allow such a rendering.

This discussion of several of many wrongly translated words should adequately demonstrate the intention of the translators to disregard the truth in defense of a man-centered theology.

---

[34] Richard Chenevix Trench, *Synonyms of the New Testament* (ninth edition of 1880; Grand Rapids: Wm. B. Eerdmans Publishing Company, 1953), p. 8. The reader is urged to read the discussion in Trench as he discusses the two words *theotes* and *theiotes* (pp. 7-10).

[35] *The Watchtower,* 83:736, December 1, 1962.

4. *Deceptive and misleading footnotes and Appendix.* It has been the favorite trick of the cultists to quote passages in defense of their doctrine, but out of context. The Witnesses have used this method also. It is not strange, then, that in the footnotes of the *New World Translation* wrong information on parallel passages and on other renderings is also given. The footnotes are often deceptive in not only what they say, but also in what they omit. Such a case has already been seen when Colossians 1:16, 17 was footnoted to Luke 13: 2,4, which was not a parallel case at all.

John 10: 30 is translated "I and the Father are one," but a footnote reads: "Or, 'are at unity.'" This footnote explains the verse in typical Socinian fashion. This rendering is so lacking in justification that the translators could not introduce it into the text (the 1961 ed. retains the reading in the text). The use of the neuter *hen* shows Christ was claiming oneness of essence. This understanding is seen in the response of the Jews found in John 10:31, 33, and Christ's statement in verse 38.

The important Christological passage in Hebrew 1:8 is translated: "But with reference to the Son: 'God is your throne forever, and the scepter of your kingdom is the scepter of straight principles [uprightness, 1961 ed.].'" This verse is quoted from Psalm 45:6 which the translation gives in the marginal reference. But the omission of an alternate reading is evident here. The far more preferable translation, "Thy throne, O God," is not so much as noted. This alternative is found in the text in such versions as the ASV, RSV and KJV. The translators could not introduce the reading "Thy throne, O God," for besides calling Christ "God" it also shows that the first Christians without hesitation applied to Christ what the Old Testament applied only to Jehovah!

In another crucial passage, Philippians 1:21-23, the *New World Translation* combines a false translation with a misleading explanation. The footnote to this passage directs the reader to the Appendix (pp. 780, 781), where a discussion on Philippians 1:23 is found. Correctly translated, the passage teaches that the believer will be with Christ immediately after death. Since the Witness theology cannot have this in Scripture, for they teach that this could not be until after 1918, they twist the words of the translation. The key verse reads: "I am under pressure from these two things; but what I do desire is the releasing and the being with Christ, for this, to be sure, is far better." Although Paul only mentions two alternatives the Witnesses introduce a third one. This third alternative interprets "releasing" as taking place at the return of Christ. The word "but" is not found in the Greek. The explanation given in the Appendix is not supported by the text. Concerning the Appendix at this point, Stedman writes:

> To anyone acquainted with the Greek language, the argument of this footnote is so ludicrous that it makes one wonder if the translators knew anything about the Greek at all.[36]

The Greek word, *analuo,* (translated "releasing" NWT) as used by Paul is a euphemism for "to die."[37] Grimm-Thayer give the meaning, *to depart from life:* Phil. i. 23."[38] The writers of the Appendix on Philippians 1:23 (p. 781) admit that *analusis* is a related noun and translate the verse where it appears in II Timothy 4:6 ". . . and the due time for my releasing is imminent." From the context it is obvious that Paul was using the same metaphor as found in Philippians 1:23 to refer to his approaching death. Arndt-Gingrich give the meaning of this word as "fig., of departure from life, *death.*"[39] A similar figure speaking of death is found in II Peter 1:15 (Peter's death) and Luke 9:31 (Christ's death) where the word used is *exodos.*

In the key verse in John 1:1, which the Witnesses render: "Originally the [In the beginning, 1961 ed.]Word was, and the Word was with God, and the Word was a god," the translators have not only introduced four footnotes but a lengthly Appendix as well. Footnote (d) makes their "a god" rendering supposedly in contrast with "the God." This

---

[36] Ray C. Stedman, "The New World Translation of the Christian Greek Scriptures," *Our Hope,* 50:34, July, 1953.

[37] Walter Bauer, *A Greek-English Lexicon of the New Testament and Other Early Christian Literature,* ed. and trans. William F. Arndt and F. Wilbur Gingrich (Chicago: The University of Chicago Press, 1957), p. 57. Hereafter this work will be designated Arndt-Gingrich.

[38] Grimm-Thayer, *op. cit.,* p. 40.

[39] Arndt-Gingrich, *loc. cit.*

is totally out of harmony with the context, for the Greek construction, *pros ton theon* is certainly not contrast but fellowship. Metzger points out the flaw of such a rendering: "It must be stated quite frankly that, if the Jehovah's Witnesses take this translation seriously, they are polytheists."[40] Readers of the John 1:1 passage are then directed to the Appendix which actually forms the strongest defense against the Witnesses' rendering. This verse has been discussed at length in the preceding chapter.

In Matthew 10:38, and wherever else the Greek word *stauros* ("cross") appears in the New Testament, the *New World Translation* has "torture stake." A lengthy Appendix (pp. 768-71) in justification and explanation of the reading has been included. On page 771 of the Appendix the reader is informed that "the evidence is, therefore, completely lacking that Jesus Christ was crucified on two pieces of timber placed at a right angle."

In an answer to this claim Steven Byington in his review of the translation directly contradicts what is said:

> An appendix says very positively that Jesus was fastened to a simple upright pole, not to a pole with a crosspiece. This agrees with Fulda's book *Das Kreuz*, but is against the weight of evidence, though the appendix says there is no evidence at all for the crosspiece.[41]

In conclusion, then, there are many such faulty footnotes in the *New World Translation*, which either footnote to nonparallel passages or introduce alternate translations which are not at all justified in the Greek. In some cases alternate readings are actually better than the reading given, and some footnotes and notes give erroneous information.

5. *Arbitrary use and non-use of capitals when dealing with the divine name.* The place where this is especially

---

[40] Metzger, *op. cit.*, p. 75.

[41] Steven T. Byington, "Review of the *New World Translation*," *The Christian Century*, 67:1295, November 1, 1950. In the first edition of the *New World Translation* on pages 770 and 771 a quotation from the *Encyclopedia Britannica* is employed in typical fashion, i. e. only those words are quoted which seem to support the position of the Witnesses. Actually, the entire article, which is only quoted in part, destroys the position taken by them, and shows how they many times abuse the sources they quote. The second edition of the *New World Translation* dropped the reference from the *Britannica*. *The Epistle of Barnabus* (10:8), *Irenaeus Against Heresies* (II, 24, 4) and *Newsweek* (January 18, 1971, pp. 52, 53) present evidence against the Witnesses' position.

evident is John 1:1 where the *New World Translation* translates "the Word was a god." According to the Witnesses' argument "god" appears here without the article. If this is the rule that the Witnesses themselves establish, why are they not consistent? In John 1: 18, which is a parallel passage, why have they not translated it: "No man has seen a god," as there is no definite article before "God"? The same might be asked concerning Romans 8:8; Philippians 2:6; and Philippians 2:11. It also causes one to wonder, if Christ is "god" with a little "g," how, when Thomas in John 20:28 gives his great declaration of faith to Christ's deity, does the NWT have "My Master and my God." It can be seen that the *theos* in John 20:28 is with the definite article, but how can the translators apply both "god" and "God" to Christ in the same book?

Other reviewers' comments on the New World Translation of the Christian Greek Scriptures. What do qualified men say concerning this Watch Tower translation? What is the purpose of the translation?

Ray C. Stedman writes:

> . . . A close examination, which gets beneath the outward veneer of scholarship, reveals a veritable shambles of bigotry, ignorance, prejudice, and bias which violates every rule of biblical criticism and every standard of scholarly integrity.[42]

Henry J. Heydt draws his conclusion: "We consider the New World Translation a gross miscarriage of what a translation should be, and a biased travesty of God's Holy Word."[43]

Martin and Klann conclude their chapter on the *New World Translation* with the following comments:

> Once it is perceived that Jehovah's Witnesses are only interested in what they can make the Scriptures say, and not in what the Holy Spirit has already perfectly revealed, then the careful student will reject entirely Jehovah's Witnesses and their Watchtower translations.[44]

---

[42] Stedman, *op. cit.*, p. 30.

[43] Heydt, *op. cit.*, p. 19.

[44] Walter R. Martin and Norman H. Klann, *Jehovah of the Watchtower* (sixth revised edition, 1963; Grand Rapids: Zondervan Publishing House, 1953), p. 161.

F. E. Mayer shows the purpose of the translation as he writes:

> The *New World Translation* sets forth other distinctive views which are essential to the entire doctrinal structure of the witnesses' message. It is a version that lends support to the denial of doctrines which the Christian churches consider basic, such as the co-equality of Jesus Christ with the Father, the personhood of the Holy Spirit, and the survival of the human person after physical death. It teaches the annihilation of the wicked, the non-existence of hell, and the purely animal nature of man's soul.[45]

Lewis W. Spitz, writing in the Introduction to Mayer's booklet, *Jehovah's Witnesses* says:

> The purpose of this translation is to support the basic tenets of the cult with the use of its own sectarian terminology. Theological discussions with the Witnesses will in the future prove more futile, for they will insist on using this translation as their authority.[46]

In his appraisal of the entire translation Anthony Hoekema says that

> their *New World Translation* of the Bible is by no means an objective rendering of the sacred text into modern English, but is *a biased translation in which manyof the peculiar teachings of the Watchtower Society are smuggled into the text of the Bible itself.*[47]

In a balanced statement dealing with the *New World Translation* F. F. Bruce states that

> some of its distinctive renderings reflect the biblical interpretations which we have come to associate with Jehovah's Witnesses (e.g. ""the Word was a god" in John 1:1). . . . Some of the renderings which are free from a theological tendency strike one as quite good. . . .[48]

Bruce M. Metzger in his article "The Jehovah's Witnesses and Jesus Christ," clearly shows the errors of many

[45] Mayer, *op. cit.*, p. 469.

[46] F. E. Mayer, *Jehovah's Witnesses* (revised 1957; St. Louis, Missouri: Concordia Publishing House, 1942), p. 4.

[47] Anthony A. Hoekema, *The Four Major Cults* (Grand Rapids: Wm. B. Eerdmans Publishing Company, 1963), pp. 238, 239.

[48] F. F. Bruce, *The English Bible: A History of Translations* (London: Lutterworth Press, 1961), p. 184.

Christological passages found in the *New World Translation.* For the reader who either agrees or disagrees with this reviewer's comments, this writer urges a study into the evidence presented by Metzger and the articles of the other reviewers cited.

Conclusion. After just this cursory look at the *New World Translation of the Christian Greek Scriptures* the honest mind can only conclude that this work, although outwardly scholarly, is plainly in many places, just the opposite. Its purpose is to bring the errors of the Witnesses into the Word of God. This translation carries no authority except to its originators and their faithful followers, and should be rejected as a perversion of the Word of God.

THE NEW WORLD TRANSLATION OF THE HEBREW SCRIPTURES

After the translation of the *New World Translation of the Christian Greek Scriptures,* the translation Committee set to work on the Old Testament, a project which witnessed its first results several years after the New Testament volume appeared.

The Plan of the Work

The first volume of the *New World Translation of the Hebrew Scriptures* appeared in 1953, the original plan being a three-volume set of the Old Testament—Volume I covering Genesis to Ruth; Volume II, I Samuel through the Song of Solomon; Volume III, completing the Old Testament, Isaiah through Malachi. In actual production, however, the volumes went to five and they were distributed and appeared as follows: Volume I, Genesis through Ruth, 1953; Volume II, I Samuel through Esther, 1955; Volume III, Job through the Song of Solomon, 1957; Volume IV, Isaiah, Jeremiah and Lamentations, 1958; Volume V, Ezekiel through Malachi, 1960. Thus the New World Translation Committee has now finished the entire Bible.

The first Old Testament volume contains a lengthy foreword, explaining the purpose, method, and plan of the work. Volume I states, under method: "It has been our endeavor to make this translation as literal as possible to the point of understandableness."[49] An Appendix dealing with the terms "souls," "'Sheol," and "Gehenna" is included, as well as a table of the seventy families after the flood. Volume V contains a ninety-page Appendix.

An Evaluation of the Translation

With all this effort, is the new translation as superior as the Committee would have one believe? For review purposes, only the first two volumes will be commented on.

The foreword of Volume I contains a lengthy discussion on Hebrew tenses, and the views of the translators, of course, are carried over into the translation.

The eminent British Old Testament scholar, H. H. Rowley, reviewed two volumes, and with his findings this writer most heartily agrees. Concerning the Committees' translation of tenses, Rowley writes:

> The translators have their own views on Hebrew tenses, but prefer to offer them to uninstructed readers before submitting their justification of them to the scrutiny of scholars. This is probably wise. They profess to offer a rendering into modern English which is as faithful as possible. In fact, the jargon which they use is often scarcely English at all. . . .[50]

Neither is the claim for an understandable literalness carried out. Rowley comments:

> The translation is marked by a wooden literalism which will only exasperate any intelligent reader — if such it finds—and instead of showing reverence for the Bible which the translators profess, it is an insult to the Word of God.[51]

The reader should check such passages as Genesis 4:13; 6:3; 10:9; 15:5; and 18:20. Commenting again on the English renderings, Rowley writes:

> Even readers who know only English will wonder whether writers who are so poorly equipped to write

---

[49] *New World Translation of the Hebrew Scriptures* (Brooklyn: Watchtower Bible and Tract Society, Inc., 1953), p. 9.

[50] H. H. Rowley, "How Not To Translate the Bible," *The Expository Times*, 65: 41, November, 1953.

[51] *Ibid.*, p. 42.

their own language can really be authorities on Hebrew tenses![52]

After a review[53] of the translation Rowley concludes:

> From beginning to end this volume is a shining example of how the Bible should not be translated, and a reminder that the Bible is great literature, which deserves to be translated by those who have a feeling for style and who both understand the original and know how to express its meanings with elegance.[54]

In his review of Volume II, Rowley writes, ". . . The second volume shows the same faults as the first."[55]

The *New World Translation of the Hebrew Scriptures* has but one real purpose—the same as is found in the translation of the New Testament. The Old Testament translation and material is written to support the Witnesses' denials of the Trinity, the personality of the Holy Spirit, existence of eternal punishment, and man's possession of a soul (spirit).

The New World Translation of the Holy Scriptures

The comments on the completed *New World Translation of the Holy Scriptures* need not be lengthy. The six individual volumes, one New Testament and five Old Testament, were reduced to one volume with all the marginal references and notes dropped in the 1961 edition. In 1963 the entire Bible, with all the original references and notes, was published in one volume.

The reader is informed in the Foreword of the 1961 edition that the translators felt a responsibility toward God "to transmit his thoughts and declarations as accurately as possible" (p. 5). It is obvious from much that has already been presented that by objective standards the translators did not live up to their declared responsibility, but rather insinuated into the Bible their thoughts and theology. Reviewers of the translation, especially the New Testament volume, have

[52] *Ibid.*

[53] For two other reviews the reader is referred to *The Christian Century*, Vol. 72:1145, 1146, October 5, 1955; and Vol. 70:1133, 1134, October 7, 1953.

[54] *Ibid.*

[55] H. H. Rowley, "Jehovah's Witnesses' Translation of the Bible," *The Expository Times*, 67:107, January, 1956.

made many strong remarks questioning the accuracy of many of the translations and the objectivity of the translators.

In a lengthy presentation of the *New World Translation,* in the book *All Scripture Is Inspired of God and Beneficial,* only one reviewer is cited, although many reviews were written. Alexander Thomson, the late editor of *The Differentiator,* is quoted twice. Investigation shows that Thomson was a universal restitutionist and the circulation of the bi-monthly magazine mentioned was very small.[56]

Revisions in the 1961 edition are explained as an attempt to "attain to closer conformity to the literal reading in the original language" (p. 6). Some improvements have been effected.

The distribution of the 1961 edition of the *New World Translation* has been very successful. Some Witnesses report the placement of as many as sixty Bibles in less than a month.[57] (This edition was revised again in 1970 and 1971.)

IV. Summary

The examination of the Watchtower publications, *The Emphatic Diaglott* and the *New World Translation,* has revealed that these works are biased propaganda tools. These publications, which are highly praised by the Watchtower Society and all faithful Jehovah's Witnesses, do not commend themselves to the informed Christian scholar. The Christian who is confronted with the renderings or evidence from these translations which is contradictory to orthodox Christianity should be aware of their utter lack of authority and dishonesty in the handling of many portions of the Word of God.

---

[56] Alexander Thomson made the following statement in another issue of his journal: "Although on three occasions I have given in the Differentiator brief reviews on parts of the New World Version of the Bible, it must not be inferred that I agree with the teachings of 'Jehovah's Witnesses,' so called. On the whole the Version was quite a good one, even though it was padded with many English words which had no equivalent in the Greek or Hebrew." *The Differentiator,* 21:98, June, 1959. Thomson's mention of the addition of words not in the Greek or Hebrew again questions the translators' claimed literality.

[57] *The Watchtower,* 83:350, June 1, 1962.

CHAPTER XI

THE JEHOVAH'S WITNESSES AND BIBLICAL INTERPRETATION

The popular notion, often expressed by the uninformed, is that the Bible can be made to teach anything. This would be true if there were no principles or laws of Biblical interpretation. The fault of most conflicting interpretations does not lie in the ambiguity of the Bible—there is very little—but in the interpreter's method.[1] The endeavor of this chapter is to determine what rules or methods of interpretation have been employed by the writers of the Watchtower publications, and to see from the result, in the passages under consideration, if the methods and rules employed demonstrate their validity. If it can be shown from such an examination that they are invalid, the entire doctrinal structure of the Watchtower Society and its claim to being God's visible channel of communication is called into question.

I. INTERPRETATION FOR THE INDIVIDUAL WITNESS

Since the Watch Tower Bible and Tract Society is the producer of the Jehovah's Witness material, and it supposedly supplies God's light on the Bible, very little instruction is given the individual Witness to come to Biblical truth for

[1] The Witnesses make the same observation: "Reasonably, then, his Book, the Bible, could not be all mixed up and allowing any interpretation to be made of it. The mix-up lies with its would-be interpreters. . . ." *Let God Be True*, (revised ed.), p. 8. All subsequent quotations will be from the revised edition.

All entries, unless otherwise noted, will refer to Watchtower publications. The footnote entries will also be abbreviated.

himself. A few statements can be gleaned from Witnesses' material in connection with the interpretation of Scripture, but in final analysis, the individual member of the group interprets every passage in the light of the pronouncements passed down by the Society. Not only does the Witness not need rules of interpretation, but his future in the movement is dependent upon his unswerving acceptance of the material provided.

Each Witness is brainwashed so that he develops a way of thinking which is utterly incapable of understanding the Bible apart from Watchtower explanations.[2] Bible reading is channeled by means of *The Watchtower* and *Awake!* magazines, the books which appear at a rate of about one a year, and the many other "Bible helps." If an individual would check subjects on his own he would probably use the "Theocratic" concordance in the rear of Witness works or the *Watch Tower Publications Index*. If he wished to look up his own passages he would rely on the *New World Translation of the Holy Scriptures* and its translation of a passage, which in many cases is more an interpretation than a translation. In conclusion, the individual member of this movement needs no rules of interpretation—just good eyes, the ability to read, and a little time.

In keeping with the methods of the Society which began with Russell, the Witnesses are instructed to gather scriptures in the following manner:

> His servants must "run to and fro" through its pages to draw together topically outlined discussions on doctrine, that such may be presented clearly and forcibly to those blinded by religion.[3]

---

[2] This writer has had many Witnesses in his presence who have argued a Watchtower interpretation in contradiction to the clear statements of the Bible, even the readings of the *New World Translation* and *The Emphatic Diaglott!* The Witness has been conditioned to accept the Watchtower interpretation and it is claimed for *The Watchtower*: "By means of his singular channel of reliable spiritual guidance all sincere, honest persons who love righteousness are being directed toward the 'perfect day' in the post-Armageddon new world." *The Watchtower*, 76:316, May 15, 1955.

[3] *Theocratic Aid to Kingdom Publishers*, p. 132.

II. The Interpretive Methods of the Jehovah's Witnesses as Viewed by Those Outside the Society

Many strong words have been employed by those who oppose the Jehovah's Witnesses' interpretations of the Bible. It would be appropriate at this point to review some of these criticisms to see if they have any real foundation, a matter which will be demonstrated or not demonstrated as this point is developed.

E. L. Eaton, who engaged Russell in public debate in 1903, had much experience with Russellite theology and interpretation. In his book *The Millennial Dawn Heresy* he describes the methods of the Russellites of his time used in the interpretation of the Bible and in support of their doctrines:

> It finds here and there a single passage of Scripture, takes it out of its natural setting, disjoints it from the context, wrests and tortures it out of all recognition, and by that means manages to make show of Scriptural support for its doctrinal fictions and vagaries.[4]

Eaton's charges were serious, and if shown to be true could clearly invalidate the Watchtower's findings in doctrine.

F. E. Mayer wrote the following description of the Jehovah's Witnesses' interpretive methods and their results as they were under Russell and Rutherford:

> They tear passages completely out of their context to prove a preconceived notion. . . . Both Russell and Rutherford ignore every principle of Scriptural interpretation and allegorize to their heart's content. . . . Their arbitrary interpretation becomes evident particularly in their time-setting, especially as it affects their present work. The absurd, unscientific, and groundless interpretations ofttimes beggar all description.[5]

In an excellent treatment of the Witnesses' interpretive methods at present, Anthony Hoekema concludes:

> . . . They do not really subject themselves to the authority of the Bible alone, apart from human traditions, as

---

[4] E. L. Eaton, *The Millennial Dawn Heresy* (Cincinatti: Jennings and Graham, 1911), pp. 12, 13.

[5] F. E. Mayer, *Jehovah's Witnesses* (revised 1957; Saint Louis: Concordia Publishing House, 1942), p. 11.

they claim they do. Rather, as we now see more clearly, their very method of interpreting the Scriptures makes it impossible for them really to listen to God's Word. Given the methods described above, one can draw from the Bible virtually any doctrine his imagination can concoct. These doctrines may be interesting, novel, appealing—but they suffer one fatal defect: they do not rest upon the authority of God's Word, but upon the fabrications of man's mind![6]

III. The Watch Tower Bible and Tract Society as "The Channel"

How long has God used the Society as his instrument of revelation and the correct understanding of the Bible?

> The WATCH TOWER BIBLE AND TRACT SOCIETY is the greatest corporation in the world, because from the time of its organization until now the Lord has used it as His channel through which to make known the Glad Tidings.[7]

The Watchtower magazine is viewed as an instrument which will bring life or destruction according to how it is received:

> . . . Jehovah had chosen the publication we now call *The Watchtower* to be used as a channel through which to bring to the world of mankind a revelation of the divine will and, through the words revealed in its columns, to bring a division of the world's population into those who would do the divine will and those who would not.[8]

---

[6] Anthony A. Hoekema, *The Four Major Cults* (Grand Rapids: Wm. B. Eerdman's Publishing Company, 1963), p. 225. Hoekema criticizes the Witnesses' interpretive methods and shows how they are characterized by: (1) Absurd literalism, (2) absurd typology, (3) "knight-jump exegesis," which is "the way Witnesses jump from one part of the Bible to another, with utter disregard of context, to 'prove' their points" (p. 251), and (4) a "rear-view method" of interpreting prophecy. This method finds some event in the past and searches out passages which can be made to apply, and then this is termed fulfilled prophecy. For these foregoing points and examples of the method, the reader should see pages 249-55 of Hoekema's book.

[7] *Zion's Watch Tower*, 1917, p. 22, quoted in *Studies in the Scriptures*, VII, p. 144. *The Watchtower*, 81:439, July 15, 1960 issue identifies the Society as God's "sole collective channel for the flow of Biblical truth to men on earth," especially since 1919.

[8] *Jehovah's Witnesses in the Divine Purpose*, p. 22.

The claim is made that the Bible cannot be understood accurately without God's spirit and that His spirit is not received until one recognizes the Watchtower Society as God's visible organization.

> He does not impart his holy spirit and an understanding and appreciation of his Word apart from his visible organization. . . .
>
> Should we expect the same today? Yes, for Jesus prophesied that he would have a visible agency upon earth at the time of the end of this system of things where we now are. . . .
>
> . . . However, for God to answer our prayers for his spirit we must meet his conditions, among which is that we recognize the visible channel he is using for that very purpose.[9]

How does God communicate his messages to his sole channel of communication? The answer is found in testimony given by F. W. Franz, Society vice-president who testified before the Court of Session, Edinburgh, November 23, 1954. The account in the *Scottish Daily Express* reports the following:

> Asked by Sir John to explain how translations and interpretations of the Bible were made, Mr. Franz said that these emanated from God.
>
> "They are passed to the Holy Spirit who invisibly, communicates with Jehovah's Witnesses — and the publicity department," he said.
>
> Mr. Franz said that the Witnesses believed in angels "of different ranks who controlled Witnesses;" . . .[10]

The foregoing quotations have established the following claims and points of information: (1) The Watchtower Bible and Tract Society is God's sole channel of communication for the interpretation of the Bible. (2) The Society has been the channel from its founding. (3) *The Watchtower* magazine reveals God's will and those who reject what it contains cannot know God's will. (4) God's holy spirit and an understanding of the Bible is not communicated apart

---

[9] *The Watchtower*, 86:391, July 1, 1965.

[10] BTTBW publication 321, which includes a reproduction of the article from the *Scottish Daily Express*, November 24, 1954. Jehovah's Witnesses would not accept the capitalized "Holy Spirit" and "Witnesses" in the above quotation.

from his visible organization. (5) Bible interpretations are communicated by God to his channel by the holy spirit.

Surely these claims can be established or shown to be false by the record of the Society which has been established on the pages of Watchtower publications.

IV. The Witnesses' Interpretive System in Operation

Rationalism

It would be quite accurate to say that in one respect the method of interpretation followed by the Witnesses is identical to that of the Socinians who advanced no hermeneutical principle, but, as Berkhof states:

> . . . All their exposition proceeded on the assumption *that the Bible must be interpreted in a rational way, or —perhaps better—in harmony with reason.* As the Word of God could not contain anything that was in contradistinction to reason, that is, . . . *nothing that could not be rationally apprehended.*[11]

Van Baalen's observation that "Russell's professed championship of the Scriptures hides a thorough-going rationalism,"[12] is confirmed by the Pastor's own words in the first volume of *Studies in the Scriptures*:

> We have endeavored to uncover enough of the foundation upon which all faith should be built—the Word of God—to give confidence and assurance in its testimony, even to the unbeliever. And we have endeavored to do this in a manner that will appeal to and can be accepted by reason as a foundation. Then we have endeavored to build upon that foundation the teachings of Scripture, in such a manner that, so far as possible, pure human judgment may try its squares and angles by the most exacting rules of justice which it can command.[13]

This quotation establishes that the interpretation of the Bible is based on a foundation of reason, and not the Holy Spirit as a guide. It is the attempt to make the Bible acceptable to even the unbeliever. In the same volume, Russell

---

[11] Louis Berkhof, *Principles of Biblical Interpretation* (second edition; Baker Book House, 1950), p. 29.

[12] J. K. van Baalen, *The Chaos of Cults* (fourteenth edition; Grand Rapids: Wm. B. Eerdmans Publishing Company, 1951), p. 224.

[13] *Studies in the Scriptures*, I, pp. 10, 11.

again writes reason into the approach to the Bible: ". . . Let us examine the character of the writings claimed as inspired, to see whether their teachings correspond with the character we have *reasonably* imputed to God. . . ."[14]

The natural outgrowth of such an approach is the rejection of all that is beyond reason's comprehension. In place of sound principles of interpretation based upon the Bible, Russell substituted a preconceived theology based on reason. Russell's credo, as well as that of the Witnesses of today, is based on a wrong understanding of Isaiah 1:18, and consists of, "come and reason with me."

As fruits of a rational approach to the Bible, the Witnesses have rejected such doctrines as eternal punishment, predestination, and the Trinity. To illustrate that Russell's credo ("Come now, and let us reason together") is still the approach of Witnesses today, this statement on the Trinity is cited:

> Those holding the trinity doctrine admit that it is "impenetrable to reason," that it is an unfathomable mystery. But God through his Word says: "Come now, and let us reason together," (Isaiah 1:18) . . . . How can we reason together on a teaching impenetrable to reason? . . . God gave us reasoning faculties and he does not fly in the face of those gifts by asking us to believe something incompatible with reason.[15]

In rejecting the doctrine of eternal punishment the Witnesses argue that "it is unreasonable."[16] Since the Trinity and eternal punishment are viewed as "unreasonable" every scripture that seems to teach these doctrines must be explained away or retranslated. True Christians reject this rationalistic approach to Biblical interpretation on the following grounds: (1) Reason is not the ultimate yardstick in determining the validity of doctrine. How can finite man through reason fully know and comprehend the infinite? Scripture places a limit on man's understanding (Job 11:7; Rom. 11:33, 34). This writer does not maintain that reason and logic are to be abandoned in one's inquiry into doctrine, but he does maintain that man must realize his limitations.

---

[14] *Ibid.*, p. 41.

[15] *Awake!* 33:25, 26, June 22, 1952.

[16] *Let God Be True*, p. 99.

(2) The Witnesses' appeal to Isaiah 1:18, to enthrone reason as final judge, is to read into the verse that which it was never intended to convey. The verse is an invitation for sinful man to realize his need to accept God's pardon and provision. (3) The doctrine of the Trinity is not "incompatible with reason," but *beyond* reason. The possibility of the Trinity cannot be denied except by assuming that depraved human reason is in all respects the measure of the divine. (4) Lastly, the elevation of reason as man's guide in religious affairs when fully carried out renders God's special revelation unnecessary.

If the reader would take the time, he would find that many doctrines once held, but since rejected, were presented with the statement that they were "reasonable"!

Progressive Revelation

Another principle which enters very strongly into Watchtower interpretation, especially in the exposition of prophecy, is that of progressive revelation, or light which makes truth clearer with the advance of time. To a certain extent this is true of prophecy, but the Witnesses apply this progression of light to doctrine and by its process have produced an entire book or evolved a new doctrine and then repudiated these as error. An actual case, already mentioned, was the book *Life* written by Rutherford in 1929.[17]

The favorite passage used to reinforce this principle is Proverbs 4:18, quoted in this excerpt:

> As the witnesses kept on expanding their preaching work, God gave them a clearer understanding of the Bible. This was in fulfillment of the Bible promise: "The path of the righteous ones is like the bright light that is getting lighter and lighter until the day is firmly established."[18]

Following progressive light, the Watchtower publications have advanced new doctrines over the years on the *same* passages of Scripture.

The following illustration of "progressive revelation" would be humorous if it were not so serious. Paul Johnson

[17] Evangelical Christians believe in progressive revelation, explained as advancing clarity in the unfolding of God's revelation and purpose to man; but never the changing of error to truth and truth into error.

[18] *From Paradise Lost to Paradise Regained*, p. 192.

recorded the following incident which transpired between two elders:

> In that drawer I keep Bro. Russell's writing locked up as out of date and full of error, while I keep the recent Towers and Society's recent books in the open as meat in due season. I keep Tabernacle Shadows, the Six Volumes and the Berean Bible in the back part of the drawer as most out of date and erroneous, and the Tower reprints in front of them as not quite so out of date and erroneous, but all of them so out of date and erroneous as to be unfit for use any longer, while I feed on the truth now due and coming through the channel.[19]

Hundreds of illustrations of the results of "progressive light" could be given, but the few examples cited should convince the reader that the claimed progressive revelation is extremely difficult for the thinking person to accept.

The resurrection of Adam. Russell, in the Russell-White debate of 1908 said:

> So, then, in Adam's case it may be plainly seen that he not only will be awakened in the condition in which he died, but he will be granted the opportunity of standing up again, of resurrection, of full recovery from his fall into sin and imperfection.[20]

Rutherford agreed with Russell in the first books that he wrote. The book *Reconciliation,* published in 1928, tells the reader that "just when Adam will be awakened, only the Lord knows."[21] *Salvation,* which was published in 1939, rejects the former conclusion:

> There is no promise found in the Scriptures that Adam's redemption and resurrection and salvation will take place at any time. Adam had a fair trial for life and completely failed.[22]

---

[19] Paul S. L. Johnson, *Merariism* (Vol. VI of *Epiphany Studies in the Scriptures.* 17 vols.; Philadelphia: Paul S. L. Johnson, 1938), pp. 392, 393. The *Watch Tower Publications Index 1930-1960* cautions its user: ". . . Of course, he will want to use discretion in his selection of material, being guided by the more recent references cited, since there has been much advancement over the years in the understanding of many Bible truths" (p. 5).

[20] John Allen Hudson (ed.), *Russell-White Debate* (second edition; Cincinnati: F. L. Rowe, 1912), p. 97.

[21] *Reconciliation,* p. 323.

[22] *Salvation,* p. 43.

In recent books, Adam and Eve are viewed as incorrigible sinners who "proved that they were not worthy of life, and they will not be resurrected."[23]

The "superior authorities" of Romans 13:1-7. Pastor Russell and the Society taught until 1929 that the "superior authorities" (NWT) or, "higher powers" of Romans 13 were earthly rulers to whom the Christian should pay taxes, etc.[24] From 1929 to 1962 identification of the "superior authorities" was changed. In the chapter entitled "Subjection to the Superior Authorities" in the book, *This Means Everlasting Life,* it is explained that the "Superior Authorities" "are the Most High God Jehovah and his exalted Son Jesus Christ."[25]

In late 1962 the interpretation of the passage reverted back to that held in the beginning:

> In spite of the end of the Gentile Times in 1914, God permitted the political authorities of this world to continue as the "higher powers" or the "powers that be," which are "ordained of God."[26]

Sodom and Gomorrah. Pastor Russell taught that the Sodomites would have another opportunity to gain life:

> And why should not the Sodomites have an opportunity to reach perfection and everylasting life as well as Israel, or as any of us? . . .
>
> Thus our Lord teaches that the Sodomites did not have a full opportunity; and he guarantees them such opportunity. . . .[27]

In 1954 just the opposite was taught through God's channel *The Watchtower*:

> He was pinpointing the utter impossibility of ransom for unbelievers or those willfully wicked, because Sodom and Gomorrah were irrevocably condemned and destroyed, beyond any possible recovery.[28]

---

[23] *From Paradise Lost to Paradise Regained,* p. 236.

[24] *Studies in the Scriptures, I,* p. 266.

[25] *This Means Everlasting Life,* p. 197.

[26] *Babylon the Great Has Fallen! God's Kingdom Rules!,* p. 548. See *The Watchtower* issues for November 1, 15, and December 1, 1962. Compare p. 362 of *Make Sure of All Things; Hold Fast to What Is Fine* with *Make Sure of All Things,* p. 369.

[27] *Studies in the Scriptures,* I, p. 110.

[28] *The Watchtower,* 75:85, February 1, 1954.

Through the same channel a reversal of doctrine was evident in 1965. In the article, "Who Will Be Resurrected From the Dead," a direct contradiction is presented: "As in the case of Tyre and Sidon, Jesus showed that Sodom, bad as it was, had not got to the state of being unable to repent."[29]

Procreation mandate. Before 1938 the procreation mandate or divine mandate to Adam to "be fruitful and multiply" was never questioned. "The truth concerning the divine mandate was revealed in 1938." The new revelation was that the "great multitude" will marry and have children during the millennium.[30] What about those who die before Armageddon?

> Will these have a part in the carrying out of the divine mandate in the new world?
> It suggests itself as reasonable that, God having held this hope before them, and they having died faithful and blameless to him, he would not deny them the privilege of the divine mandate.[31]

The current "light" on the subject states that only those who survive Armageddon "will enjoy also the grand privilege of fulfilling a divine mandate to procreate."[32]

The princes. Russell taught that the "ancient worthies" or "princes," Abraham, Isaac, Jacob, etc. would be resurrected "after the Gospel Church has been glorified. . . ."[33] In the same volume the time for glorification of the Church and the resurrection of the princes is given as 1914.[34]

Rutherford, writing in 1920, changed the date to 1925:

> . . . Scriptures definitely fix the fact that there will be a resurrection of Abraham, Isaac, Jacob and other faithful ones of old, and that these will have the first

[29] *The Watchtower,* 86:139, March 1, 1965. See *The Watchtower,* 86:479, August 1, 1965.

[30] *The Truth Shall Make You Free,* p. 362.

[31] *Ibid.,* pp. 362, 363.

[32] *Let God Be True,* p. 268. See also *The Watchtower,* 82: 703, 704, November 15, 1961; 76:763, December 15, 1955.

[33] *Studies in the Scriptures,* III, p. 265.

[34] *Ibid.,* p. 94.

> favor, we may expect 1925 to witness the return of these faithful men of Israel. . . .[35]

The return did not materialize as expected, and thus a new "revelation" came to the "channel" and Rutherford wrote in 1928 that "it may be reasonably concluded that the 'ancient worthies' will be back on earth as perfect men within a comparatively short time."[36]

In 1929, to give sagging hopes for the princes' return a boost, Rutherford had "Beth Sarim" ("House of the Princes") built in San Diego. The house was built to provide a place for the princes to stay when they returned. In 1939 Rutherford stated:

> . . . The purpose of acquiring that property and building the house was that there might be some tangible proof that there are those on earth today who fully believe God and Jesus Christ and in His kingdom, and who believe that the faithful men of old will soon be resurrected by the Lord, be back on earth, and take charge of the visible affairs of earth. . . . The house has served as a testimony to many persons throughout the earth, and while the unbelievers have mocked concerning it and spoken contemptuously of it, yet it stands there as a testimony to Jehovah's name. . . .[37]

"Beth-Sarim," a symbol of faith, was sold shortly after Rutherford's death!

In 1950 the Watchtower's new view concerning the princes was presented. The book *Jehovah's Witnesses in the Divine Purpose* explains:

> For many years it had been the view of *The Watchtower* that the faithful men of old who served God faithfully before Jesus' time would be raised from the dead even before Armageddon to join in organizing Jehovah's modern-day people and to share in shouldering the remnant's responsibility of representing the Lord Jesus Christ in the capacity of overseers of the flock of God on earth.[38]

---

[35] *Millions Now Living Will Never Die!*, p. 88.

[36] *Government*, p. 276.

[37] *Salvation*, p. 311.

[38] *Jehovah's Witnesses in the Divine Purpose*. p. 252.

The presentation goes on to explain that outstanding Jehovah's Witnesses of today can also become princes.[39] In subsequent development of this new view the princes of old would experience a resurrection early during the millennium.[40]

This writer agrees with Rutherford's statement made in 1929, relative to the interpretation of prophecy, but with a wider application: "Jehovah never makes any mistakes. Where the student relies on man, he is certain to be led into difficulties."[41] If the Watchtower writers would only learn this lesson from past mistakes!

Allegorizing and Spiritualizing

Progressive revelation, treated above, many times overlaps allegorizing, for progressive light has often indicated an allegorical interpretation of a passage in place of a former literal interpretation. A. B. Mickelsen's explanation on the nature of allegorizing is helpful:

> Allegory, a very legitimate way of teaching truth, should not be confused with allegorizing, which takes a narrative that was not meant to teach truth by identification. By a point by point comparison, allegorizing makes the narrative convey ideas different from those intended by the original author. Thus allegorizing is an arbitrary way of handling any narrative.[42]

Although allegory is relatively rare in the Scriptures, the Jehovah's Witnesses find the Bible literally filled with passages in both the Old and New Testaments which can only be understood in the light of allegorical interpretation. Simple stories of the Old Testament have become prophetic dramas in which present-day events are depicted with the main actors being the Jehovah's Witnesses and their enemies. The allegorical method was not as prominent under Russell as it later became under Rutherford's administration and under the leadership of Knorr. Especially from 1930 on,

[39] *Ibid.* A comparision of *Let God Be True,* first and second editions (pp. 263, 265) also shows the addition of this new doctrine.

[40] *From Paradise Lost to Paradise Regained,* p. 232.

[41] *Prophecy,* pp. 67, 68.

[42] A. Berkeley Mickelson, *Interpreting the Bible* (Grand Rapids: *Wm. B. Eerdmans Publishing Company,* 1963), p. 231.

allegorizing of the Old Testament was practiced frequently. In part, the explanation for this is that Rutherford found it necessary in order to advance new doctrines and to shift the years of prophetic importance from Russell's emphasis on 1874 to 1914, to the period from 1914 or 1918 on. Under the allegorical interpreter the Bible becomes like putty in his hands and a premium is put on subjective understanding. With the abandonment of historical sense, there is actually no sound principle to govern the exposition of the Bible.

The rich man and Lazarus. This passage, which has been embarrassing to all who deny the conscious existence and punishment of the wicked after death, has been subjected to some rather interesting and varying interpretations which certainly prove the subjective nature of allegorizing. Russell interpreted the passage and explained:

> The interpretation must be looked for along the lines of a parable. The fulfilment came when the Jews of this country, in a general petition, requested the president of the United States to cooperate with other Christian nations and intercede on behalf of their members in Russia that they might have more liberty and less persecution, that their torments might be cooled.[43]

In the Russell-White debate in 1908 Russell explained the characters of this passage in the following way: (1) "The rich man was the Jewish nation" (2) "Lazarus represented the Gentiles, all those who were outside of the pale of Jewish influence. . . . He represents you and me, and all who by nature are Gentiles—not Jews." (3) Abraham pictured God.[44]

In Rutherford's book *Reconciliation,* published in 1928, the interpretation of the characters were still the same, but Russell's fulfillment was not mentioned, and a new emphasis was placed on the "Lazarus class."[45]

The book *The New World,* the first book published after Rutherford's death, presented a new teaching on the passage. This marked the first appearance of the view generally held

---

[43] *People's Pulpit,* I, number 4, p. 2, quoted in Charles C. Cook, *All About One Russell* (Philadelphia: Philadelphia School of the Bible, [n. d.]), pp. 9, 10.

[44] Hudson, *op. cit.,* pp. 92-94.

[45] *Reconciliation,* pp. 175, 176.

by the Witnesses today: The rich man became a "rich man class," made up of all who oppose the "Theocracy." "Since the temple judgment began in 1918 this 'rich man' class have had a change of condition and are dead in hell as to Jehovah's Theocracy and its service." Lazarus also became a class, representing the Jehovah's Witnesses who experienced a change of position after 1918. Abraham was still viewed as God.[46] The first edition of *Let God Be True* gave this interpretation:

> By this parable Jesus uttered a prophecy which undergoes fulfillment in its modern setting since A. D. 1918. It has its application to two classes existing on earth today. The rich man represents the ultraselfish class of the clergy of "Christendom," who are now alienated from God and dead to his favor and tormented by the truth proclaimed. Lazarus depicts the remnant of the "body of Christ" and also that class of persons who are of good-will. These, on abandoning religion, receive God's favor and comfort through his Word.[47]

In the 1952 revision of this text the interpretation is changed again. The 1918 became 1919. Lazarus no longer pictured "the remnant of the 'body of Christ' " and the "persons who are of good-will," but instead "Lazarus depicts the faithful remnant of the 'body of Christ' " alone.[48] In the exposition of the passage in *What Has Religion Done for Mankind?* the Lazarus class is explained as "that Jewish Remnant who hungered and thirsted for truth and righteousness. . . ."[49]

In summary, what method demonstrates its validity by two or three fulfillments? How valid is a method of interpretation which makes Lazarus represent: (1) the Gentiles and all believers, (2) the remnant and the persons of good-will, (3) the remnant alone, and (4) the faithful Jewish remnant?

Examples of allegorizing or spiritualizing in the Old Testament. (1) Job 28:35, in which Jehovah says, "Canst thou send forth lightenings, that they may go, And say unto

---

[46] *The New World,* pp. 360, 361.
[47] *Let God Be True,* (first ed.), p. 79.
[48] *Let God Be True,* p. 98.
[49] *What Has Religion Done for Mankind?,* p. 249.

thee, Here we are?" is interpreted by Rutherford: ". . . God tells that the radio is a manifestation of His power, and not man's, and that *He* is presenting the message of truth by the carrier wave of the radio."[50] (2) The "locusts" of Joel's prophecy are the Jehovah's Witnesses: "Jehovah's witnesses, that is, his army of 'locusts', are without fear of creatures because they know that they are backed up by the almighty power of God."[51] (3) The book *Preservation* (1932) is a "commentary" on the books of Esther and Ruth. In the Preface of the book Rutherford describes the prophetic importance of them. Of Esther, he writes:

> The book of Esther is a record of a prophetic drama directed by Jehovah to show his faithful witnesses at the end of the world his provision made for their protection and complete preservation, and is therefore comfort to all such.[52]

Of the book of Ruth, Rutherford declares:

> . . . Ruth is also a record of a wonderful prophetic drama directed by Jehovah God. . . . The players in that drama did not understand its purpose at the time, and no man since then could possibly understand the meaning thereof until God's due time for it to be understood.[53]

In the interpretation of the two books literal interpretation and application is replaced by allegorical interpretation with such claims as "Esther, the Jewish maiden who became queen, pictured God's remnant now on earth" and Ahasuerus in a triple role "pictured Satan the rebel God, and then again he pictured the Lord Jesus Christ who is earth's rightful King, and sometimes he pictured Jehovah."[54] (Ahasuerus was quite versatile, to say the least!) (4) A final example of transition from literal to spiritual interpretation relates to the place of Israel during the millennial kingdom. Russell strongly affirmed:

> That the re-establishment of Israel in the land of Palestine is one of the events to be expected in this Day of the Lord, we are fully assured by the above expres-

[50] *Life*, p. 303.
[51] *Religion*, p. 186.
[52] *Preservation*, p. 5.
[53] *Ibid.*, pp. 5, 6.
[54] *Ibid.*, p. 17.

> sion of the Prophet [commenting on Amos 9:11, 14, 15]. Notice, particularly, that *the prophecy cannot be interpreted in any symbolic sense* [Emphasis added].[55]

Writing in 1925, Rutherford said that many prophecies

> give assurance that Israel will be regathered to Palestine and never again be plucked up. . . . The promise, time and again repeated, that the Lord would regather them and bless them. . . .[56]

The modern Jehovah's Witnesses have now become spiritual Israel.

> Nothing in the modern return of the Jews to Palestine and the setting up of the Israeli republic corresponds with the Bible prophecies concerning the restoration of Jehovah's name-people to his favor and organization. . . . The remnant of spiritual Israelites, as Jehovah's Witnesses, have proclaimed world-wide the establishment of God's kingdom in 1914.[57]

A study of the most recent books reveals that allegorizing or spiritualizing is still a dominant method of Biblical interpretation. For further examples, the interested reader is referred to many of the texts published under the present administration.[58]

Speculation

Much of the Witnesses' Biblical exposition and theology has been and is still very speculative. One area which has been marked by speculation is the area of Bible chronology as it relates to eschatology. The charge of speculation is proved by the results and the rejection or revision of dates which supposedly marked certain Biblical developments.

---

[55] *Studies in the Scriptures,* III, p. 244.

[56] *Comfort For the Jews,* p. 55.

[57] *Let God Be True,* pp. 217, 218.

[58] Allegorical interpretation in its extreme form will be found in many of the expositions of the late Paul S. L. Johnson, the founder of L.H.M.M.

Roy D. Goodrich, in BTTBW publication 96, gives several additional examples of change in Watchtower position: "In the Cities of Refuge type, Satan used to be the 'avenger of blood.' Now Christ Jesus is such avenger." In the New Testament "the prodigal son used to be the scribes and pharisees; but now he blossoms out to be the *present day earthly sons of Christ.*"

When did the "time of the end" begin? Russell stated: "The 'Time of the End,' a period of one hundred and fifteen (115) years, from A. D. 1799 to A. D. 1914, is particularly marked in the Scriptures."[59] Rutherford, writing in 1921, said that the evidence was "sufficient to convince any reasonable mind that we have been in the 'time of the end' since 1799."[60] Rutherford later abandoned this date as having any prophetic significance.[61] The present explanation, one held for many years, is that "the 'time of the end' began in 1914; it ends when the Devil's world is destroyed at the 'accomplished end.' "[62]

When did the "second presence," or second advent of Christ occur? Russell was confident as he wrote:

> . . . The time-prophecies thus point to and harmonize with 1874 as the date of our Lord's second presence, assuring us of the fact with mathematical precision, we find ourselves overwhelmed with evidence of another character. . . .[63]

In *The Harp of God* (1921), Rutherford agreed with Russell's date: "The time of the Lord's second presence dates from 1874. . . ."[64] In the *Watch Tower Publications Index 1930 - 1960*, under "DATES OF PROPHETIC SIGNIFICANCE," the year 1874 does not appear.[65] The position that has been accepted for years is that the "return of Christ began in the year 1914."[66]

What was prophesied to occur in 1914? Note the switching of what was actually predicted by Russell with what the Watchtower Society says was predicted. Russell's predictions were very clear.

> . . . We consider it an established truth that the final end of the kingdoms of this world, and the full establishment of the Kingdom of God, will be accomplished by the end of A. D. 1914.[67]

---

[59] *Studies in the Scriptures*, III, p. 23.
[60] *The Harp of God*, p. 239.
[61] *Watch Tower Publications Index 1930-1960*, pp. 77, 78.
[62] *From Paradise Lost to Paradise Regained*, p. 178.
[63] *Studies in the Scriptures*, III, p. 129.
[64] *The Harp of God*, p. 236; *Creation*, p. 298.
[65] *Watch Tower Publications Index 1930-1960*, pp. 77, 78.
[66] *Make Sure of All Things*, p. 319.
[67] *Studies in the Scriptures*, II, p. 99.

The same volume, in a later edition, changes the last part of the quotation to read, "will be accomplished near the end of A. D. 1915."[68] In the same volume the reader is told that "the 'Gentile Times' prove that the present governments must all be overthrown about the close of A. D. 1914,"[69] with the later edition changing the statement to "about the close of A. D. 1915. . . ."[70] The kingdom prophesied for establishment was not just a heavenly kingdom, but 1914 was to mark the "full establishment of the Kingdom of God in the earth. . . ."[71] Note what is stated in this book published in 1958: "Of all people, only the witnesses pointed to 1914 as the year for God's kingdom to be fully set up in heaven."[72]

When did the "first resurrection" occur? According to Russell,

> 1878, A. D., marked the date at which the "dead in Christ" should rise "first." It is in full harmony with the Scriptures, therefore, that we believe that the Apostles and faithful saints of the entire age, down to our day, are already glorified. . . .[73]

It is currently being taught that it was in the "year of 1918, that the heavenly resurrection of faithful dead Christians happened unseen to us, and these members of the spiritual nation began living with Christ."[74]

The Church Glorified — When? Russell originally believed that the Church would be glorified in 1878.[75] When this prediction failed the date was advanced to 1914.[76] Russell had written in *Thy Kingdom Come* (1891): "That the deliverance of the saints must take place some time before 1914 is manifest. . . ."[77] The 1924 edition of the same book was changed to read: "That the deliverance of the saints

---

[68] *Ibid.*, (1915 ed.).
[69] *Ibid.*, p. 242.
[70] *Ibid.*, (1915 ed.).
[71] *Studies in the Scriptures*, III, p. 126.
[72] *From Paradise Lost to Paradise Regained*, p. 170.
[73] *Studies in the Scriptures*, VI, p. 663.
[74] *From Paradise Lost to Paradise Regained*, p. 213.
[75] *Jehovah's Witnesses in the Divine Purpose*, p. 19.
[76] *Ibid.*, p. 23.
[77] *Studies in the Scriptures*, III, p. 228.

must take place very soon after 1914 is manifest. . . ."[78] Next the date for the rapture of the living saints was set for 1918.[79] When this date was not marked by the glorification of the Church, Judge Rutherford predicted a new one, 1925.[80] Other masked predictions for the time of glorification were subsequently made, but the glorification of the Church at a point of time is no longer a problem because according to present teaching some members of this body will actually live through Armageddon and will only be added to the Church at their death during the millennium.[81]

The days of creation and the termination of the six thousand years. From the early days of Pastor Russell until the change in 1943, all Watchtower pronouncements agreed with Russell's statement that the "six thousand years from the creation of Adam were complete with A. D. 1872; and hence, that, since 1872 A. D., we are chronologically entered upon the seventh thousand. . . ."[82] With the appearance of *The Truth Shall Make You Free* in 1943, a new chronology was presented which made that year only 5,971 years after Adam's creation. This meant that the year 1972 marked the end of the 6,000 years, a date exactly 100 years later than that formerly held. [83] That the more recent chronology was a revision of a previously held position was never mentioned or explained. This writer's position is that both positions are untenable. (See the Author's Note on page 239.)

Summary. The speculations which have been presented are only a small example of what can be found in a limited area. It should be remembered that this speculation was presented with definiteness, as reasonable and as Scriptural.

---

[78] *Ibid.*, (1924 ed.).

[79] *Studies in the Scriptures*, VII, p. 64; *Studies in the Scriptures*, III, (1924 ed.), author's forward dated October 1, 1916, p. ii. Russell predicted "that before a very long time—perhaps a year or two or three—the full number of the Elect will be completed, and all will have gone beyond the Veil and the door will be shut."

[80] See above, pp. 25, 26.

[81] *Babylon the Great Has Fallen! God's Kingdom Rules!*, p. 637.

[82] *Studies in the Scriptures*, II, p. 33.

[83] *The Truth Shall Make You Free*, p. 152. The Book, *Life Everlasting in Freedom of the Sons of God*, published in 1966, shows the 6,000 years to terminate in the autumn of 1975 (pp. 28, 29, 35).

Arbitrary Classes

As a result of the twofold division in the Jehovah's Witnesses, there is an arbitrary dividing of the contents of the Bible. Certain passages are applicable only to the 144,000 who are the Watchtower "body of Christ"; other scriptures refer only to the "Great Multitude."

Scriptures ordinarily accepted by orthodox Christians which relate to such doctrines as consecration, sanctification, immortality, resurrection, the new birth, the Kingdom of God, the Church and heaven, have no relevance to the vast majority of Jehovah's Witnesses who have only an earthly hope. In effect, such a position robs the average Witness of much of the Bible.

Nowhere is arbitrary application of the Word of God better illustrated than in the book, *Make Sure of All Things,* with its topical listing of scriptures.[84]

One example of how this arbitrary division works should suffice. On pages 48-50 of *Make Sure of All Things* there is a compilation of scripture verses under the heading, "Born Again." Such verses as John 1:12, 13; 3:3, 5, 6; Romans 8:16, 17; I Corinthians 15: 50, 53; I Peter 1:23, and I John 3:2, 9, supposedly relate to the 144,000 alone.

This Witness-originated approach to the Bible makes for chaos and certainly cannot be accepted as "handling the word of truth aright" (II Tim. 2:15 NWT).

Context

Watchtower interpreters do not hesitate to ignore context when such will further their end. Context becomes important only when it benefits their interpretation. Many doctrines advanced by the Witnesses are built upon out-of-context verses. To handle the Bible in such a way is to teach error for truth. As Mickelson points out, "Neglect of context is a common cause of erroneous interpretation and irrelevant application."[85]

---

[84] According to *Make Sure of All Things,* the following have application only to the 144,000. (1) Consecration (p. 91), (2) sanctification (p. 91), (3) Kingdom of God (p. 226), (4) immortality (p. 243), (5) first resurrection (p. 315), (6) born again (p. 48), (7) Church (p. 70), and (8) heaven (p. 196).

[85] Mickelsen, *op. cit.,* p. 99.

Several examples of how context is violated serve to illustrate the point. (1) Isaiah 43:9-12 is used to prove that the Jehovah's Witnesses have received their name from Jehovah as his witnesses. Reading the entire chapter identifies the subject of the passage as literal Israel and her relationship with Jehovah. (2) Jeremiah 10:3, 4 has been used to teach against the erection of Christmas trees. Properly understood and in context, the passage has nothing to do with Christmas trees, but rather deals with the fashioning of idols from wood, the impotence of idols and the folly of idolatry. (3) Galatians 4:8-11 is interpreted as an injunction against Christians keeping holidays. What Paul is condemning is scrupulous observance of the Jewish sacred days as a means of salvation. Paul urged the Galatians to abandon legalism and to enjoy the liberty they had in Christ (Gal. 3:12). (4) There are many examples in Watchtower publications of the destruction of the context by use of only a portion of a verse, often without the indication of this because ellipses are not included. One such example is the quotation of Luke 22:28-30 in *Let God Be True.*[86] Verse 30 is quoted, "that you may eat and drink at my table in my kingdom, and sit on thrones." Why was the last part of this verse, "to judge the twelve tribes of Israel," not included? The answer seems evident. The passage was applied to the 144,000 who, according to the Witnesses' interpretation of Revelation chapters 7 and 14, have taken the place of the twelve tribes of Israel. How then, can these 144,000 "judge the twelve tribes of Israel" when the 144,000 have taken their place and these tribes no longer exist?

Grammatical Interpretation

Complexities of thought must be conveyed by sentences. Grammar sets forth the principles by which words are arranged into meaningful sentences. A sound interpretation

---

[86] *Let God Be True,* p. 137. Many examples of abridged verses and verses isolated from context can be examined in *Make Sure of All Things.* For an enlightening study of a number of examples of out-of-context verses restored to their context see: William J. Schnell, *Into the Light of Christianity* (Grand Rapids: Baker Book House, 1959), *passim.*

of any passage requires a careful grammatical exegesis. Watchtower publications repeatedly present doctrines and interpretations of the Scriptures which completely misunderstand or ignore grammar.

Before the Society entered into the field of translation, there were many verses which gave them trouble because of their direct contradiction of the Witnesses' doctrines. With the appearance of the *New World Translation* the difficult passages in many cases were weakened or eliminated by a translation that violated or ignored the rules of grammar.

Such verses as John 1:1, Titus 2:13 and Revelation 3:14, examined elsewhere in this work, are all examples of ungrammatical attempts to defend the preconceived doctrines of the group.

The Meaning of Words

All proper interpretation of the Bible is based on the meaning of the words in the passage under consideration. On numerous occasions the Watchtower writers have supported their unscriptural doctrines by violating the meaning of a particular word. Ramm warns against reading "our own theological meanings into words rather than investigating the meanings of these words during Old and New Testament times."[87] Numerous examples of that which Ramm warned against have characterized the Witnesses' efforts. Several examples of words whose meanings have been altered by translation or interpretation have been considered in the course of this study. For example: (1) The Greek word *kolasis* was translated "cutting-off" and interpreted as annihilation (the true meaning is "punishment"). (2) *Theotes* was translated as "divine quality" (the true meaning is "Godhead," or "fullness of diety"). (3) The Greek word *prototokos* was interpreted to mean that Christ was created (the true meaning it conveys is that Christ is prior to and sovereign over all creation). (4) The Greek word *monogenes* was also interpreted to mean that Christ was created (the true meaning need not be more than Christ is "unique").

---

[87] Bernard Ramm, *Protestant Biblical Interpretation* (revised edition; Boston: W. A. Wilde Company, 1956), p. 132.

The Witnesses have been able to construct an entirely new theology just on the basis of giving new meanings to words.

The Tenor of Scripture

Although Watchtower publications often connect and compare scripture with scripture, those connected many times are not related, which results in what Hoekema termed "knight-jump exegesis." A good example of this is the Witnesses' attempted connection between the "one" of Christ's statement, "I and the Father are one" (John 10:30 , a oneness of being) with the "one" of John 17:11ff. (a oneness of unity).

A humanly constructed system cannot stand the test of correctly comparing one scripture with another. A typical example of ignoring the tenor of Scripture is found in the way the Witnesses deal with the Person of Christ. The texts emphasized are those which deal with his humanity. They cite, for example, John 14:28 (" . . . The Father is greater than I am" NWT) as if it were the only verse that had any bearing on the status of Jesus while upon the earth. They totally ignore the rest of the scriptures which relate to our Lord's earthly ministry and preexistence.

V. Conclusion

Although the pronouncements of the Jehovah's Witnesses on the inspiration and trustworthiness of the Scriptures are to be commended, one certainly cannot commend what they have done with the Bible. With the methods employed by the Society in interpreting the Scriptures, it really would not matter if the Witnesses held the doctrine of inspiration or not, for the Word of God is twisted so that the infallible (at the time of the doctrinal pronouncement at least) interpreter is more inspired than the Bible.

By holding the doctrine of an infallible Bible, the Watchtower Society puts itself in the strongest of positions, for it has its own unique translation and it is the channel through which Bible understanding proceeds!

The opening words of this chapter, "The popular notion often expressed by the uninformed is that the Bible can be made to teach anything," would be proved by what has been seen in this chapter. The Bible has been subordinated to the subjective outlook of the interpreter.

This writer would agree with the general presentation in this statement from *The Watchtower*:

> Why all this lack of understanding of the Bible? One of the chief reasons for it is the failure to appreciate the importance of God's holy spirit. It is needed to understand the Bible, even as in the first place God used it to inspire men to write down his thoughts.[88]

This writer feels that this statement touches upon the problem of the Watchtower Society: "Why all this lack of understanding of the Bible?" Those who claim to be the visible representatives of God on earth obviously do not have the Holy Spirit's guidance which the Lord Jesus promised to his own in John 16:13, 14:

> Howbeit when he, the Spirit of truth is come, he shall guide you into all the truth: for he shall not speak from himself; but what things soever he shall hear, these shall he speak and he shall declare unto you things that are to come. He shall glorify me: for he shall take of mine, and shall declare it unto you.

A Spirit-directed ministry is one that magnifies the Person and work of Jesus Christ.

---

[88] *The Watchtower*, 86:389, July 1, 1965.

Author's Note

An extensive treatment on the Witnesses' 6,000-year-chronology, which in 1966 was calculated to terminate in the autumn of 1975, is found in the author's book, *The Jehovah's Witnesses and Prophetic Speculation*.

Chapter XII

SOME TOOLS AND METHODS OF THE NEW WORLD SOCIETY

I. Literature

Under the administration of N. H. Knorr, the Watchtower presses have turned out on an average more than one book each year. *The Watchtower* and *Awake!* have a monthly circulation of over thirty-seven million. Millions of pieces of other literature, such as tracts and booklets have also been printed.

The printed page is the leading tool of the Jehovah's Witness organization.[1] The magazines usually make the opening into the home of the prospective convert. At times a booklet, tract, or book makes the contact in the home. A most effective tool is the magazine *Awake!*, which carries on its front cover some of the subjects to be dealt with on the inside. The subjects are usually of some current interest or of a controversial nature to arouse interest in the reader. Once a person begins to read the magazine he becomes slowly indoctrinated. In addition to the Watchtower slant in all the secular articles, there is always a section (many times the main article) fully devoted to an exposition of Witness theology or the tearing down of orthodox beliefs.[2] *The Watchtower*

---

[1] *"Their total output exceeds that of all Catholic publishers in the United States combined."* Albert Muller, "Jehovah Witnesses Call," *Homiletic and Pastoral Review*, (Reprint) 679, May 1963.

[2] *Awake!* and *The Watchtower* can be likened to bait and a hook. The *Awake!* magazine is written primarily for those who have not as yet been sold on the teachings of the Jehovah's Witnesses. It contains many articles of real interest, a point that is easy to demonstrate from a random sampling of issues. The "Special issues" are the clinchers.

magazine could be termed the cult's religious journal. It is studied as God's "meat in due season." "None can afford to miss his weekly spiritual meal at the *Watchtower* study."[3]

With an average of at least one new book coming off the Watchtower presses each year, the Witnesses always have something new to put into the hands of the people. Except for the *New World Translation* volumes, the minimum printing for an edition has been 1,000,000 copies, with some running as high as 5,000,000. This last figure represents the first edition of *The Truth That Leads to Eternal Life* (1968). The book, *From Paradise Lost to Paradise Regained,* which appeared in 1958, had a first printing of 3,500,000. This was the first book under the Knorr administration with a new format, and is filled with illustrations. Other features are its simple language and large easy-to-read print. This is an ideal tool to reach children, the uneducated, and the elderly. Even the cover of the book arouses interest in the contents inside. This writer was told by a Jehovah's Witness minister, from whom the book was received, that it was unsectar-

---

Several examples follow: (1) *Awake!*, October 8, 1965 issue, "World Conditions Explained—By the Bible in Your Home." "It is the keen desire of Jehovah's Witnesses to help you to gain faith in the Bible as God's Word and the benefit from its wise guidance in these critical times. They will be pleased to conduct a regular Bible study with you in your own home free of charge" (p. 28). (2) *Awake!*, April 22, 1965 issue, "Movements Toward Religious Unity— What They Mean to You!" "Appreciate that you are being separated either for life in God's new system of things, or for destruction with opposers of God. . . . Jehovah's witnesses desire to help you to acquire the knowledge necessary to make this right decision. They will be pleased to conduct a Bible study with you in your home on regular basis and free of charge. You are also welcome to attend meetings at their Kingdom Hall in your locality" (p. 29). (3) *Awake!*, April 22, 1966 issue, "Your Life and Bible Prophecy." "The facts show that Jehovah's witnesses conform to this description of people who have God's approval. You can too if you take action now to bring your life into harmony with the things set out in God's prophetic Word" (p. 28). Once the bait (*Awake!*) has been swallowed the hook (*The Watchtower* and other publications) is in order.

Many *Awake!* articles have an appeal to a certain occupational group. In the June 8, 1962 issue (p. 19) responses to such are included (firemen, policemen, teachers, printers and doctors).

[3] *Theocratic Aid to Kingdom Publishers* (Brooklyn: Watchtower Bible and Tract Society, Inc., 1945), p. 182.

ian and contained "just" the Bible. After examination it was found to be filled with the "New World" theology.[4]

Another book which has been a real tool for the Witnesses is *Let God Be True,* first appearing in 1946 and revised in 1952. With a publication figure of over 19,000,000 reported by 1965 this has been one of the most popular books the Watchtower Society has ever produced. This book is literally fabrications and misrepresentations almost from beginning to end.[5] It could be called the Witnesses' systematic theology, for the Witnesses say that "its twenty-six chapters set out the basic doctrines of the Bible, God's Word."[6] In 1965, *Things in Which It Is Impossible for God to Lie* was published. With a distribution of over 8,000,000 early in 1968, this book appears to be a replacement for *Let God Be True.* (See the Author's Note on page 249.)

A book which the Witness often carried in his street-corner or door-to-door preaching assignment is the little book *Make Sure of All Things.* This publication is advertised as "the Bible handbook for every Christian minister who wants handy proof from the Bible for all he believes and preaches."[7] The last part of this quotation reveals just what this book is, a combining of "proof-texts" for everything that the Witness "believes and preaches." The claim is made:

> *"Make Sure of All Things"* sets forth seventy principle themes and gives you a balanced picture or rounded-out coverage by answering the outstanding questions and objections on each of these themes just by using scriptures from the Bible.[8]

---

[4] The May 8, 1962 issue of *Awake!* (p. 32) reported that the *Paradise* book "is rapidly becoming one of the most popular Bible-study aids yet published. . . . Already over 7 million copies have been printed in 31 languages." The popularity of the book may be explained in the statement in *The Watchtower,* September 15, 1958 issue: "Not only is its size different, but it is filled with large illustrations, and it is written in a manner that even poorly educated people can understand" (p. 576).

[5] See the examination of *Let God Be True* in chapter 9.

[6] *Jehovah's Witnesses in the Divine Purpose* (Brooklyn: Watchtower Bible and Tract Society of New York, Inc., 1959), p. 295.

[7] *You May Survive Armageddon into God's New World* (Brooklyn: Watchtower Bible and Tract Society, Inc., 1955), advertisement in rear of text.

[8] *Make Sure of All Things* (Brooklyn: Watchtower Bible and Tract Society, Inc., 1953), pp. 7, 8.

The text actually furnishes the methods for wrongly dividing the Word of God. The best way to find the errors of such a work as this, is to study the contexts from which the verses are taken. The book discusses seventy major subjects. Each subject is introduced by an overall statement which forms a wrong background and starting point for the subject under discussion. The Scriptures cited are then oriented under this false definition.

Another book, very much like *Make Sure of All Things,* is the one entitled, *Make Sure of All Things*: *Hold Fast To What Is Fine.* This text contains a compilation of scriptures under one hundred and twenty-three headings. There are no definitions introducing each subject as in the previous book. Another difference between these volumes is the incorporation of the *New World Translation of the Holy Scriptures* into the references almost to the exclusion of the other versions. There are also quotations from non-Witness texts dealing with selected subjects, such as archeology and science.

An important addition to the Watchtower arsenal has been the book dealing with the history of the Witnesses, *Jehovah's Witnesses in the Divine Purpose.* Its shortcomings have already been discussed in a previous chapter.

The six volumes of the *New World Translation* and the complete Bible have already proven to be effective tools in the Witnesses' propaganda program. The intent of the work and the reasons for its rejection have been dealt with in the chapter on "The Translations and Bibles of the Watch Tower Bible and Tract Society."

The Witnesses also have effective propaganda tools in the tracts which they use, and in the leaflets which advertise their usual Sunday afternoon meetings.[9]

---

[9] The tracts examined were all six pages in length, with the front containing the title and a few remarks, and the last page carrying approximately one-half page of advertising for a Watchtower text or the *Awake!* or *Watchtower* magazines. The titles are listed in Appendix C.

II. Meetings

The Jehovah's Witnesses schedule five hours of regular meetings each week. In addition to these congregational meetings every Witness is urged to conduct one or more "Home Bible Studies" (more accurately, "book studies") in the homes of those who show interest in the teachings of the group. The study may be with one "person of good will," or with others of the household or neighborhood.

Watchtower Study. This meeting, which generally follows the Sunday public talk, is viewed as the most important meeting of the week. It is important because it is believed that *The Watchtower* is the channel through which God gives increased light on His Word. This congregational study is conducted by the "Study Conductor." The members are expected to study the magazine before coming, and this meeting further implants the teachings of the group through channeled open discussion.

Congregation Book Study. The territory of each congregation is divided into areas, with studies held in each by direct congregational supervision. These meetings in neighborhood homes are very effective in that the groups are smaller and the opportunity for participation is greater. Many interested in the Witnesses are more easily induced to attend these meetings. The home selected for the study is also designated a "Service Center," because it acts as a meeting place for witnessing in the area. The coming activities and plans of the local congregation are announced at the Congregation Book Study.

Service Meeting. One night each week (in the congregations this writer attended the night was Wednesday or Thursday) the Witnesses are trained for Watchtower service. The meeting is much like what a sales meeting would be to the business world. Better methods and means of presentation of the message and literature of the group are discussed. There is a service theme for the month and special offers for each month.[10] The order of this service is

[10] For example, the *Kingdom Ministry*, May, 1958 issue, lists the offer for May as "two books and two booklets on a contribution of $1," and the theme for the month as "Keeping Filled with the Spirit of God.—Ephesians 5:18."

outlined in the monthly publication, *Kingdom Ministry.* The congregation also studies its efforts in relation to its own quota and the national quota.

Theocratic Ministry School. This meeting is generally held following the Service Meeting. The training received in this school is an advanced study of "Theocratic" truth. It is in this course that the "ministers" are also thoroughly trained in message preparation, public speaking, refutation and argumentation. Such books as *Theocratic Aid to Kingdom Publishers, Equipped for Every Good Work, Qualified to be Ministers,* and *All Scripture Is Inspired of God and Beneficial,* have been used in this training program.[11]

Public Talks. The Witnesses have public talks on selected Sunday afternoons. These one-hour talks are usually heavily advertised by house-to-house canvasing and handbills. The Society provides new topics and outlines for these talks each year. The speakers are drawn from the mature male Witnesses of the local congregation or they are visiting representatives of the Society.

III. Conventions or Assemblies

In order of size, from the smaller to the larger, the Witnesses have used Circuit Assemblies, District Assemblies, and National and International Conventions in furthering their work.

The "Divine Will International Assembly of Jehovah's Witnesses" which met July 17 to August 3, 1958, had an attendance of 253,922 persons on the final day. Such conventions give the movement much publicity and serve to unite the work. Albert Muller observes:

> Not only do these conventions receive much space in the local press and free publicity on the radio and television, but they also give an ostentatious display of their unanimity, discipline, and organizational drive. Calculated to stimulate the members so that they will increase their efforts, these conventions and the resultant augmented activity will bring in more members.[12]

---

[11] A more detailed presentation of the Theocratic Ministry School is included in *The Watchtower,* 86:188-91, March 15, 1965.

[12] Muller, *op. cit.*, p. 680.

The conventions are planned for another definite purpose. Strategic cities are picked out for conventions and assemblies, and the cities are prepared for a Witness invasion of every home. The Witnesses come to witness and to get new converts. During the convention period they room in thousands of homes around the assembly center, make contacts in them and leave literature.[13] Reports on these contacts are turned in to the local "Congregation Servant," so that the placements can be followed-up. The tremendous success of this method is attested by Schnell, who writes concerning the 1958 convention in New York:

> Now, one and one-half years later, the Watchtower Society has a glowing report. They report that Jehovah's Witnesses had increased from the summer of 1958 to the winter, or until January 1960, in the greater New York area, from 75 to 91 units. I am not here talking of individuals, I am here speaking of congregations.[14]

The convention idea has been a key factor in the growth of the Witness movement. It has unified the work, given stimulus to the members, produced great publicity, caused great growth, and added many otherwise unreachable converts.

IV. Films

Under the leadership of Pastor Russell, "The Photo-Drama of Creation" was produced and shown as a propaganda device beginning in 1914. Realizing the potential of films, the Watchtower Society produced several motion pictures for the same purpose.

"The New World Society in Action," an hour and twenty minute film was released in 1954. In 1956 the one-hour "Happiness of the New World Society" was shown, followed

---

[13] It was this writer's personal experience to see how effective contacts were. If a homeowner had opened his home to the Witnesses and provided a room for the duration of the convention, at a small cost, it generally was assured that there was no strong prejudice against the group. With the Witness in the home the contact between the householder and the Witness and the placing of literature was automatically assured. Many such contacts resulted in the winning of the person to the Witness fold.

[14] William J. Schnell, *Witnessing to Jehovah's Witnesses* (Youngstown, Ohio: The Converted Jehovah's Witness Expositor, 1960), p. 8.

by the full-color film "Divine Will International Assembly of Jehovah's Witnesses" (1959) and "Proclaiming 'Everlasting Good News' Around the World." The last is a two-hour color production released in 1964. Other films are titled "God Cannot Lie" and "Heritage."

These films have been widely shown in Witness assemblies, and many reports from the mission fields indicate that the showings have been very successful in selling the Witnesses' doctrinal and organizational message. In each case the attendance at the film presentation was larger than that usual for the local congregation, and in some meetings the entire village or town was present.

In conclusion, it is interesting to note that the Dawn Bible Students Association has also utilized motion pictures in the outreach of its ministry. Very good results were obtained in public showings, on television ("The Bible Answers"), and through film loan services. Many denominational churches have used films produced by the Dawn organization.

V. Jehovah's Witness Seven-Step Program

All movements have a program of some kind to bring in converts. This writer believes that of the many plans in existence, that used by the Jehovah's Witnesses is equaled by none. This plan has been described by others as a "brainwashing" program, for such it is. The writer can speak from experience, for he has been in it and has observed others who have been in the same program. Once it has run its seven-step course, it is truly a miracle if its victim gets free.[15]

1. The first step in making Jehovah's Witness converts is getting literature (books preferably, but any literature will do) into the people's hands.

2. After a book is finally placed, the second step is a "back-call." This is a visit to encourage the individual's interest in the book to the point that a "home book study" can be started.

---

[15] The plan which is outlined can be found in far more detail in the book, *Thirty Years a Watchtower Slave*, pp. 131-41. See also: Ted Dencher, *The Watchtower Heresy versus the Bible* (Chicago: Moody Press, 1961), pp. 118-23.

3. The "book study" is started and the publisher or minister of the Watchtower Society presses the new "person of good will" to subscribe to *The Watchtower* and *Awake!* as part of his study. The "book studies," of which many Witnesses have one or more, have a double effect. They indoctrinate the "person of good will" and also continually "brainwash" the conductor of the study. In fact the routine of the "book study" is so fixed that even a child can conduct it. The Watchtower Society advises:

> Even youths and children can conduct effective studies. No special training is required to conduct these studies, as the method is easy to follow and all the questions and scriptures are supplied for the study.[16]

4. From the study in the home, the "person of good will" is introduced to the area book study. The congregation's territory is divided into areas. Here the interested individual is actually going to a Kingdom Hall away from the central building. The "person of goodwill" is brought to the position where he must cut old ties and form new ones. In the area study there is encouragement to participate and to look up out-of-context verses. The "person of good will" feels that he is studying the Bible.

5. From this stage, the new candidate is invited to the "Watchtower Study," usually at the Kingdom Hall. Here the individual is made welcome and impressed with the "light" which he is receiving. "The Watchtower Study" is a channeled study of the Bible, isolating "proof-texts" to prove the Watchtower point. *The Watchtower* and the other publications of the Society make it clear that salvation is only gained within the "New World Society," and as the quoted statements already examined elsewhere have shown, the new converts too must be preachers in the world for salvation.

6. To do this preaching effectively and in harmony with the plan of God, the candidate must unite with the Jehovah's Witnesses as they plan their preaching work. This is done in the "Service Meeting" where instructions are given.

7. The final step is to make the attendance of the "person of good will" consistent at the meetings, and then to

---

[16] *Theocratic Aid to Kingdom Publishers, op. cit.,* p. 187.

convince this one that he must dedicate himself to God's service through water baptism. Baptism officially inducts the candidate into the organization of Jehovah's Witnesses as a "Kingdom publisher" or "minister."

VI. Conclusion

The foregoing survey of the tools and methods of the New World Society has shown that the Witnesses have a well-planned program for the gaining of new converts and the training of those in the group. The literature of the movement acts as a powerful and constant propaganda weapon which reaches around the world. Its meetings not only indoctrinate the new converts, but thoroughly train the members of the group in doctrine and in presentation of the cult's message. Its conventions or assemblies and films have been seen to be leading factors in unifying the group and in propagating its doctrines. And lastly, the seven-step program of the Witnesses is an exceedingly successful method, as is attested by the growth of this group. The survey in this chapter shows why the Jehovah's Witnesses organization has been one of the world's fastest growing religious movements.

Author's Note

The January 8, 1975 *Awake!* reported that the book *The Truth That Leads to Eternal Life,* which was first published in 1968, has had a printing of "74 million copies in 91 languages, about three times as many as the next all-time best-selling book in the Western world, aside from the Bible" (p. 13).

CHAPTER XIII

DEALING WITH JEHOVAH'S WITNESSES

I. M. Haldeman, who opposed Russellism in his day, wrote: "From beginning to end it is one of the most terrific religious perils that ever came forth in the name of Christ, or sought to authorize itself with a 'thus saith the Lord.' "[1] Many other strong warnings and words have been used to describe this peril which is leading many astray, breaking up families, ruining much Christian work, and growing at such an alarming rate.

How can these messengers who are carrying "another gospel," a message of denial, be stopped? How can they be reached with the Gospel? The following brief treatment supplies helpful information for the Christian as it sets forth some methods of dealing with the Witnesses both in public encounter and in private study of the literature of the cult. [2]

---

[1] I. M. Haldeman, *Millennial Dawnism: The Blasphemous Religion Which Teaches the Annihilation of Jesus Christ* (Los Angeles: Bible Institute of Los Angeles, [n. d.]), p. 4.

[2] As the contents of this chapter are necessarily limited the reader is referred to these additional books which contain suggestions on dealing with the Witnesses. Some of the presentations deal with the cults in general but have specific information on the approach to the Witnesses: *Christians Awake!*, by W. J. Schnell; *The Kingdom of the Cults,* by Walter Martin, chapter 18; *The Four Major Cults,* by Anthony Hoekema chapter 7; *The Chaos of Cults* (fourth revised edition) by Jan van Baalen, chapter 17; *Masters of Deception,* by F. W. Thomas; *Confronting the Cults,* by Gordon R. Lewis, Part 2. Dr. Walter R. Martin has produced a set of four cassette tapes, "How to Witness to Jehovah's Witnesses" (One Way Library).

I. Previous Preparation

1. *Christian experience.* The first prerequisite for any Christian work is a personal and vital knowledge of Jesus Christ as one's personal Saviour. First, a man must realize and accept that he is a sinner (Rom. 3:23); secondly, he must recognize that as a sinner he is helpless to save himself and that he is spiritually dead (Eph. 2:1); thirdly, he must accept the fact that the death and resurrection of Christ provides the means by which he might be reconciled to God (Rom. 5:10, 11; Col. 1:21, 22); and finally he must realize his responsibility to repent of sin (Acts 17:30) and to believe in Christ, receiving Him as Saviour (John 1:12).

2. *Knowledge of the Bible.* Most persons are inadequate in this qualification, which is the reason why cults thrive and draw largely from Christian ranks. The average Christian does not know his Bible well enough to detect and refute the errors of half-truths. The cult cannot stand before the truth and light of the Word of God. If nothing else, a Christian should read the Bible each day, several chapters a day. When confronted by a Jehovah's Witness, the Christian should always use the Bible and read the passage which the Witness claims confirms his teaching.

3. *Devotional life.* Any worker for God must realize that without prayer and a deep spiritual life defeat is almost assured. It is God's will that the Christian should radiate the spirit and zeal of the early church. The early church had such a testimony for Christ in the midst of opposition, and its message was so clear to those without, that the ones outside the church named them "Christians" (Acts 11:26).

4. *Attitude for service.* Enter the task with humility and a sympathetic spirit. The Christian should realize that he is not out to represent a church or denomination, but to represent Christ. Just as He hated error, so each believer also should hate error, yet love the one who is in need. Most Witnesses blindly follow the teachings of the Society with little thinking of their own.

5. *Know the Witnesses' doctrinal system.* In order to achieve success in refuting the doctrines of this group one must be thoroughly familiar with what the Witnesses believe.

This knowledge should be gained as much as possible from primary sources (i.e., recent Watch Tower publications).[3]

It should not be necessary to repeat that the Christian must also know his own doctrinal position, but Walter Martin is right when he says that

> many Christians have taken for granted the great doctrines of the Bible which they learned and accepted at their conversion and have not "studied, to show themselves approved by God, workmen who do not need to be ashamed, rightly dividing the word of truth."[4]

Most Witnesses are not prepared to deal with one who thoroughly knows their doctrinal system as well as his own.

II. The Encounter

All of the following suggestions cannot be used in each contact with the Witnesses (which will vary from the call at the door, discussion on the street-corner or in the home, etc.), but all should be kept in mind and used as the occasion demands. (See the Author's Note on page 257.)

1. *Lead in prayer.* In most cases it is possible to lead in prayer before any discussion takes place. This is not standard procedure for the Witnesses and therefore they are off guard.[5]

---

[3] Two easy to understand publications of the Witnesses which could be used for study of their doctrinal views are: *Let God Be True* and *From Paradise Lost To Paradise Regained.* For materials presenting and refuting their views see Appendix D.

[4] Walter R. Martin, *The Kingdom of the Cults* (Grand Rapids: Zondervan Publishing House, 1965), p. 343.

[5] It has been this writer's experience that most Jehovah's Witnesses will not enter into your prayer, but the Christian should take the initiative and lead in prayer anyway. Prayer should be addressed to "Jehovah-God." The power and presence of the Holy Spirit can accomplish more than lengthy discussion. The period of prayer has been used by some Christians as a very effective period of evangelism. Martin relates his approach: "During my opening and closing prayers I would totally preach the Gospel, emphasizing the Deity of Christ, His death for our sins, the certainty of knowing that we have eternal life *now,* by faith in Him, and that salvation comes by grace alone, independent of human works. I would profusely quote the Scriptures, and in actuality be preaching a three-minute sermonette, subliminally implanting the true Gospel of Jesus Christ and, I might add, blissfully uninterrupted." *Ibid,* p. 349.

2. *Do not argue.* Many have learned from experience that argument with a Jehovah's Witness or any other cultist is a waste of time. In fact the best thing that can be done after listening to a typical Jehovah's Witness presentation or sermonette is to ignore what has been said. Discount his entire argument as though he never said anything, for the average Witness is prepared to counter what the Christian says. This tactic leaves the Witness dangling. At this point it would be excellent to give a personal testimony. This is beyond argument, for it is the Christian's own experience.

3. *Do not get sidetracked.* The main purpose of discussing doctrine with the Witness is not to give him arguments on why he should salute the flag, or to refute the errors of Russell. The main issue to discuss is the individual's personal relationship with Christ. To avoid getting sidetracked the Christian should hold discussion to one or two issues of importance. If one gets sidetracked into argumentation, he will have gotten on a Watchtower merry-go-round with no place to get off, and the time will have been totally wasted.

4. *Deal only with fundamental errors.* The discussions with the Witnesses should center around the Person of Christ, the atonement, and the plan of salvation. If progress is being made on these issues, then other errors can be discussed. Select beforehand one or two points, rather than just what may happen to come up.

5. *Stress the strongest Scriptural arguments.* When a weakness is found, thrust in the "Sword" again and again. Hold the Witness rigidly to the point being discussed and press insistently the strongest Scriptural arguments. When you see that you have struck home, again assert the Word of God. If at all possible get him to acknowledge that your point has a solid Scriptural basis, and that it undercuts the very foundation of his Watchtower system.

6. *Present Christ and His claims.* The claims of Christ are numerous: They attest to His deity, His pre-existence, His incarnation, His earthly work, and His unique position in the world as man's only hope of salvation. The book of John is excellent to present the Person, work and claims of Christ.

7. *Give a positive witness for the truth.* In the spirit of love, be as dogmatic in the defense of the historic Christian truth as he is in defense of error. A Christian does not have to be apologetic for what he believes if it is the truth supported by the Bible. The Watchtower representative is one of the most dogmatic persons, yet without Scriptural support. To be dogmatic one must also know what to be dogmatic about. To break down the statements of the Witness, ask to see what he preaches in the Bible, and then check the context and read it aloud. Ask him why he is using this verse as he is, since it does not have any bearing on the doctrine he is discussing. (This will usually be the case.)

8. *Use Gospel tracts.* Many persons who know Christ as their personal Savior and are living for Him use Gospel tracts. But many Christians pass by the opportunity to give a Gospel tract to a cultist. The Jehovah's Witness has been won to the cult by literature: by the same method use literature to win him to Christ. The Jehovah's Witness is just as lost as anyone else who rejects Christ. Therefore, tracts, booklets, and books prepared to reach him for Christ should be distributed. But, tracts and other good material should *never* be used as a substitute for one's personal verbal testimony.

9. *Give your own personal testimony.* Even the youngest babe in Christ can give a personal testimony of what Christ has done in his own life.[6]

10. *Remind the Witness that sincerity and zeal can be misplaced.* An outstanding example of this is Saul of Tarsus. Concerning misplaced zeal, Matthew 23:15 is effective: " . . . For ye compass sea and land to make one proselyte;

[6] A former Jehovah's Witness reported that she encountered three types of responses in her work for the cult: (1) Those who slammed the door in her face. These made her feel good because she felt that she was being persecuted for her faith. (2) Those who argued with her. These made her stronger in her convictions because she had stock answers for them. (3) "A third group gave her a personal testimony of their faith in Christ. These, so she said, made the most lasting impression on her; when she went to bed at night, she would think about these people and reflect on what they had said. Surely every true believer ought to be able to give this kind of testimony." Anthony A. Hoekema, *The Four Major Cults* (Grand Rapids: Wm. B. Eerdmans Publishing Company, 1963), pp. 406, 407.

and when he is become so, ye make him twofold more a son of hell than yourselves."

III. Dealing with Watch Tower Publications in Private Study

1. *What do the scriptures actually say?* Check the context and completeness of each scripture cited, and which translation is used. As has been noted, the favorite device of the Witnesses is to snatch verses from context to bolster their position. Moreover, the matter of the translation cited is becoming increasingly important as the *New World Translation* is being used more frequently as authority for doctrine.

2. *Has the source quoted been accurately represented?* Check the original source of any authority cited. This writer has found that in many cases the Watchtower publications have either misrepresented or misunderstood the sources they have utilized. Of many examples given, this book has shown the Witnesses' misuse of Hislop's, *The Two Babylons.*

3. *Does the evidence support the contention?* Check to see what proof is offered to substantiate their claim. As has already been shown, the Watchtower Society does not need any evidence at all to say that "Satan is the originator" of a doctrine. It has also been seen, for example, in the insertion of the Tetragrammaton into the text of the New Testament how such little evidence could be magnified so far out of proportion. It has also been observed that in the Witnesses' use of the original languages the lack of evidence for a translation or an addition to the text did not hamper the Watchtower translators at all.

4. *Who is the authority?* Check the authorities cited. It has been found that often the authority cited has been a Watchtower publication; or, at times, a liberal is considered an authority. Whenever conservative scholars appear to prove anything the Witnesses say, do not fail to check the original sources.

5. *Is the presentation historically or linguistically sound?* See if the linguistic finding or historical point presented is accepted by the best of scholarship. For example, what do the accepted authorities say concerning the use of the word *kolasis* found in Matthew 25:46, the issue under dis-

cussion and the events of the Council of Nicea, or the date of the capture of Zedekiah and the fall of Jerusalem?

6. *Is the conclusion logical?* Check to see if the Witnesses' conclusion and argument is based on sound logic. Is the argument based on a false major premise or on a faulty minor one? The book *Let God Be True* gives numerous examples of faulty logic.

7. *Diligent study is needed.* At times the error of the Watchtower publication will not at once be seen; therefore, the question remains unanswered. It will be found that a more detailed study of the matter will always supply the answer. The greatest handicap is lack of information, not the strength of the Witness' argument. Christians should be willing to spend time in a study of what they believe.

8. *Progressive revelation and changing doctrine.* Be aware of inconsistencies in the Witnesses' doctrinal explanations. Over the years the Watchtower has changed interpretations on some passages and prophecies several times. In fact, when the Witnesses changed from literal to allegorical interpretation on the prophecy and promises concerning Israel, entire Old Testament books and thousands of verses had new meanings. There have been many changes in the interpretation of the New Testament also. Chapter 11 has adequately illustrated results of progressive revelation. Study the current literature.

9. *Be aware of the use of "strawmen."* An excellent example of a "strawman" (the attributing of a position or doctrine to one's opponent which he does not hold and which can be easily refuted) is found in *Let God Be True* (p. 102), where the Witnesses claim to give the leading arguments for belief in the Trinity and then cite four references, two of which the informed theologian would never use.

10. *Access to reference volumes.* The Christian should have several good books which deal with the Jehovah's Witnesses for reference purposes. A Christian home should not be without sound Bible commentaries and theologies. Christian college, seminary or church libraries should be employed.

11. *Biblical hermeneutics.* Know and apply the rules of sound Biblical interpretation. Space permits only a few general rules: (1) Interpret grammatically, (2) Interpret according to context. (3) Interpret according to the scope

of the book. (4) Compare Scripture with Scripture. This matter will not be pursued further, but the reader is urged to get a good text dealing with Biblical hermeneutics or interpretation for both study and reference.[7]

The Jehovah's Witnesses are a real challenge to orthodox Christianity, and only as Christians prepare themselves through Bible study, prayer, acquaintance with the group's doctrinal system, and diligent work, can there be victory.

---

[7] Any of the following books would be helpful: *Principles of Biblical Interpretation,* by L. Berkhof; *The Science of Biblical Hermeneutics,* by R. T. Chafer; *Interpreting the Bible,* by A. B. Mickelsen; *Protestant Biblical Interpretation,* by B. Ramm; *Biblical Hermeneutics,* by M. S. Terry.

Author's Note

It has been the experience of this writer and other Christian workers that Witnesses and those studying with them were often difficult to reach initially with a doctrinal approach. It was first necessary to undermine their confidence in the Watchtower Society before any headway could be made. It must be remembered that the Jehovah's Witness views this organization as representing or speaking for God. The July 1, 1973 *Watchtower* (pp. 401-407) is a good orientation on the significance of the organization.

Areas effectively used in undermining confidence in the organization include: false prophecies, scholastic dishonesty, doctrinal changes, dishonest handling of history and faulty renderings in the *New World Translation.*

CHAPTER XIV

CONCLUSION

I. A SUMMARY OF THE STUDY

The primary purpose of this book has been to examine the history, doctrines and claims of the Jehovah's Witnesses, and to determine whether the title "Apostles of Denial" has been justly given to this organization. While it has been impossible to examine every detail of these three categories, from the main points discussed the weak foundations on which the Watchtower movement has been built were clearly seen.

From the examination of the background of the Jehovah's Witnesses one can see the present-day building and enlarging of a system on the condemned remains of former heresies. The study of Watchtower history and recent publications has shown the history of a man-made organization and theology. The history has also revealed an evolution of a rational and progressive theology and a strong central Society. The theology and the central Society were both elevated by means of misapplied Scripture.

The transition of this group from an insignificant organization to the huge propaganda machine of today has been traced and the reasons for its growth explained.

The examination of the Watchtower doctrines has clearly demonstrated the faulty, illogical, unscriptural and unhistorical basis of the Witnesses' theology. The doctrines of this group have shown themselves to be those of outright denial of almost everything orthodox Christianity stands upon. In establishing these doctrines the Watchtower method shows that anything which can be used to dupe the uninformed is legitimate. The study has revealed changes in history, changes in the Bible, the overriding of the Biblical languages to justify a preconceived theory, the changing and misrepresentation of facts, and the blatant rejection of clear statements of scripture.

The *New World Translation* has shown itself to be one of the cleverest propaganda tools the Witnesses have ever produced — the "Word of man" is now called the "Word of God."

The interpretive methods employed by the Society were examined and found to yield differing interpretations of the Scriptures at different times. Subjected to these methods the Bible could be made to say anything. It is evident that the leadership of the Witnesses is not really interested in what the Bible says, but what they can make it say.

The tools and methods of the Watchtower Society have been revealed as efficient implements in bringing in converts to one of the cleverest and most effective "brainwashing" schemes this world has ever seen.

This writer believes that the reader, after a careful examination and consideration of the facts herein presented, must admit that the proposition that the Jehovah's Witnesses represent a system of denial is an accurate and fair appraisal.

II. The Problem and How It Must Be Met

The problem. The Jehovah's Witnesses cult is a definite menace to every Christian pastor and missionary in the world today. Going forward with a rationalistic message and a weak doctrine of sin, after having abolished hell as a place of true retribution, the Witnesses will reach millions of people with their Christless message. According to the present rate of growth many thousands each year will close the door to salvation in a process of Jehovah's Witness indoctrination. The lax spiritual condition, and the spirit of procrastination on the part of many church members will permit this menace to continue without opposition. Indeed, the key cause of this and other contemporary cults' great growth, has been the utter neglect of God's children to do anything in the way of consistent personal evangelism. The average Christian does not have a firm grasp on what he believes, and if he does, it is likely that he cannot defend his belief Scripturally.

What can be done to meet this problem? First, the average church needs to affirm strongly the deity of Jesus Christ as well as His work wrought on the cross in behalf of man. Second, our Bible schools and seminaries need to offer a strong course, or courses, in cult apologetics. Many schools do not offer such specialized courses. Third, the average Christian needs to take Christianity seriously, to study the Bible and pray as never before. A dedicated life is needed. A spiritual, consecrated life is a life which has a telling effect upon the Watchtower representatives. Fourth, ministers and laymen need to arm themselves with the facts on the Witnesses so as to deal effectively with the members of this group. Many such facts have been set forth in this study.

III. Testimonies of Former Jehovah's Witnesses

In February of 1964 this writer gave a series of messages one Sunday on the "History, Doctrines and Claims of the Jehovah's Witnesses." The meeting was public and at least six Jehovah's Witnesses attended the meeting. In the course of presenting the message it was stated that the Jehovah's Witnesses were "brainwashed" by the organization which they followed. After the meeting, the Congregational Servant of the local Kingdom Hall, who was in the audience, objected to some of the statements made and denied that brainwashing occurred. At other times Witnesses have denied that they were slaves to a system. In answer to these objections the following letters and statements are cited, with the hope that Witnesses might see in the experiences of others their own condition and that there is no real life, freedom, peace or joy in such a system. It should be evident to the reader that the following statements were not solicited, but were written by those who had to tell their stories. Many who have left the Jehovah's Witnesses never have made the next step to find their all-sufficiency in Christ — but their experience in the Jehovah's Witnesses is still valuable.

Brainwashing. Ted Dencher, who served in the Jehovah's Witnesses ten years before he found salvation in Christ alone, gives an insight into how the brainwashing process operates:

> Convincing themselves by constant repetition of their teachings, the Witnesses constantly talk themselves deeper into their beliefs. Individual thought is discouraged in order to give full authority to *Organizational Mindedness.* That is why it is so difficult for followers to break away from the organization.[1]

In the October 18, 1964 issue of *Power For Living,* Mr. James M. Aiken gave his testimony of his experiences as a follower of the Witnesses. His article is entitled, "I Was Brainwashed by the Jehovah's Witnesses."[2] He too found peace and security in acceptance of Jesus Christ.

A mature college student relates his experience:

> I was drawn into the W. T. organization in the fall of 1958, and was soon brainwashed to the extent of undergoing J. W. baptism in 1960 . . . But I did not long remain in W. T. truth, for by 1961 I was entertaining serious doubts concerning the movement. The first doubts, curiously enough, came from reading the Watch Tower's own literature. . . . Since all my efforts at trying to obtain old literature from the society were frustrated . . . I turned to second hand book stores. . . .
>
> Of course after doing a bit of background reading I began to see the utter temporal relativism of W. T. truth. Conflicting doctrines were held at various times, all with the infallible authority of Jehovah behind them. This led to serious doubts in my mind. I now know that the society has taken steps to avoid losing precious publishers by this means. You see, I was told at the second hand stores that the big wigs from . . . Bethel come there periodically themselves to buy all (! ! !) the W. T. out of print books which turn up, and supplanting them with current literature. The faithful and discreet slave is certainly doing its best to be the only source of information for deluded J. W.'s.[3]

---

[1] Ted Dencher, *The Watchtower Heresy versus the Bible* (Chicago: Moody Press, 1961), p. 129.

[2] This testimony and testimonies of those who left other cults have been combined in a booklet, *We Found Our Way Out,* published by Baker Book House. The Aiken testimony is on pp. 12-15.

[3] Letter to this writer dated December 5, 1964.

A number of former Jehovah's Witnesses have never come to an acceptance of orthodoxy and many are still searching for the satisfaction that only Christ can give. These too tell their story of brainwashing. The following were gleaned from various issues of *Back to the Bible Way.*

> I've been a JW since 1934; but was never allowed to think for myself. But when I got enough nerve to read something else beside the Watchtower, then I started to see that I would have to think for myself.[4]

> It is amazing how many people can be so completely brainwashed by the extravagent claims of the Watchtower in New York.[5]

> That Society is certainly a very efficient source of brain-washing, even better than the communists.[6]

William C. Stevenson tells his experience after leaving the Witnesses:

> One has been brainwashed so thoroughly that one has to take a definite stand against the "Big Brother" complex which one has developed. . . . But I have been so thoroughly brainwashed into thinking that all religion, apart from the Witnesses, originates with the Devil, that as yet I have been unable to bring myself to attend a church service.[7]

The Society identified as a dictatorial organization of fear, domination and hate.

> ". . . We were once 'J. W.'s', and are so relieved and glad to be free of their fear-dominated Society. It certainly caused us to lose a lot of happiness and freedom the 14 years we were prisoners in it."[8]

> "I and my family have been JW's for about 13 years and I do pity some of the brethren who have been caught in the WT web; they preach freedom, but they do not

---

[4] *Back to the Bible Way,* 12:144, May-June, 1963.

[5] *Back to the Bible Way,* 13:242, May-June, 1964.

[6] *Back to the Bible Way,* 14:348, May-June, 1965.

[7] William C. Stevenson, *The Inside Story of Jehovah's Witnesses* (New York: Hart Publishing Company, Inc., 1967), p. 203. See p. 35 where Stevenson concludes that Witness "study methods are in fact a subtle form of indoctrination or brain-washing."

[8] *Back to the Bible Way,* 14:348, May-June, 1965.

> know what real freedom is until they have broken the dictatorial chain the WT has woven around them."[9]
>
> "I spent the most of my life in an organization of HATE, until now I feel like a bird out of a cage. Keep a bird in a cage for twenty-five years, then turn it out it is slow learning to fly again. . . . I have been taught the Watchtower language so long I feel very weak in learning the language of love. . . . "[10]

Many hundreds of similar testimonies could be recorded, but space does not permit. This writer has recently talked with a former Jehovah's Witness who admits that he finds himself in the same position as those quoted above.[11]

IV. The Challenge

The study in this book has served to bring a twofold challenge. First, a challenge is issued to the member or follower of the Witnesses' movement to set aside the teachings of deceived men, and to come, not to a church or a religion, but to Jesus Christ as Savior.[12] The second challenge is to the Christian. The zealous work of the Jehovah's Witnesses should challenge every Christian to a new dedication to Jesus Christ. Only a dedicated Christian Church will bring the glorious gospel of Jesus Christ to lost humanity and bring defeat to the "Apostles of Denial."

---

[9] *Back to the Bible Way,* 9:331, May-June, 1960.

[10] *Back to the Bible Way,* 12:111, January-February, 1963.

[11] For testimonies of born again ex-Witnesses see the author's book, *We Left Jehovah's Witnesses* (Presbyterian and Reformed, 1974; Baker, 1975).

[12] The writer wishes to mention that the Witnesses he has had contact with were evidently sincere and sacrificially zealous in the propagation of their beliefs. But being sincere and zealous does not guarantee the correctness of one's message or religion.

Appendix A

OTHER RUSSELLITE GROUPS

Over the years since the first edition of *Zion's Watch Tower and Herald of Christ's Presence* in 1879, there have been many splits from the parent Watch Tower organization. The Witnesses often point out and emphasize the many divisions of Christendom, yet when one looks at the schisms from this movement one wonders if such criticism is not even more appropriate in reference to this group. The history of the Watch Tower movement has been one of difficulties, disputes, and secession of both individuals and groups from the Society.

I. Reasons for Secession

During the early years of the movement, many left because of doctrinal disagreements. Others left because Russell was regarding his writings, so they felt, as of equal value to the Bible. Still others left when Russell's divorce proceedings created a scandal. When the hopes for 1914 did not materialize it caused much disillusionment, and many left the fold.

After Russell's death in 1916, there was a fight for power in which Rutherford came out the victor. More groups and individuals left. The period between 1921 and 1931 was marked by many other defections from the Society as the elective elders in the local ecclesiae were pushed out and the Watch Tower organization tried to replace the democratic practices of the individual groups with authoritative rule from on top. The Watch Tower Society at this time welcomed the withdrawal of many of its adherents, for the ones remaining were of the type which needed and submitted to the leadership of the Society. Schnell writes:

> In the decade from 1921 to 1931 almost three-fourths of the Bible Students originally associated with the Society in a loose fashion left the Society's supervision behind. That is precisely what the new Watch Tower Society wanted and what they had hoped to accomplish.[1]

It was in 1931 that the new name, Jehovah's Witnesses, was taken to distinguish the parent body from the numerous bodies of Bible Students.[2]

Since 1931 there have been many other splits, as can be seen from the splinter sects treated in this chapter. The reason for the separation in each case is not known, but the iron hand of the Watch Tower hierarchy can be cited as a primary cause. When an individual or a group stood in the way, the ax of excommunication fell. Very few of these individuals or groups ever got into orthodox churches, so the tendency was to form another group and to wage a battle against the parent organization, and in many cases with one another. Many who were not excommunicated left the Society because they could not agree with the policies and doctrinal changes of that organization.

The handling of those who leave and oppose the Society is clearly illustrated by the experience of eight pioneers, led by Roy D. Goodrich, who appeared at the Cleveland Convention (Aug. 4-11, 1946) to distribute handbills. The account of their experience sounds much like what the Witnesses had experienced at the hands of the "Satanic world." Excerpts from the published account of their attempts to distribute their material outside the Convention Stadium follow:

> Again and again these jeering, accusing, mocking multitudes would collect in angry mobs about the worker entirely isolating and cutting him or her off from the passing stream of conventioners. They snatched and destroyed our papers; they howled every imaginable evil cognomen, epithet and threat, like packs of howling wolves or hyenas. They snatched and pulled at our bags. They shouted, "Evil servant stuff, DON'T READ IT!" "Working for the Hierarchy!" . . . "Devils!" . . .
>
> Both Lawrence and Merwyn were threatened repeatedly by mobs, and each of them had a magazine bag

---

[1] William J. Schnell, *Thirty Years a Watch Tower Slave* (Grand Rapids: Baker Book House, 1956), p. 41.

[2] The resolution is included in the *1932 Year Book*, pp. 20-24.

> cut off them with a knife. . . . sandwich signs were moored to our persons with steel chains; and about this they let out various grumblings and complaints that they could not cut these off from us as they would have liked to do. . . . Those who did not carry knives, finally thought of the defacing power of lip-stick. A few hours before the convention was over, they began using that on our sandwich signs.
>
> . . . One husky claiming to be an usher . . . carried on like possessed, snatching papers from the sister and destroying them before her. He also snatched them from those who received them, tearing them to shreds and encouraging others to do the same.
>
> . . . one did say to me: "I'll get the rope to hang you!" Later the same man or another, came by growling,—"A rope for Judas!!"[3]

From this account, and from others that are similar,[4] the Jehovah's Witnesses are seen to be practicing the same intolerance and methods they have so dramatically condemned others for using!

II. Secession Groups

It is very difficult to establish exactly how many new groups have been formed by separation from the Society, but the number has been large. Milton S. Czatt, writing in 1933, records: "The secretary of the Society has given the information that at least seventeen smaller sects . . . have separated from the International Bible Students Association."[5] That this tendency for division is still the case is evidenced

---

[3] "Kingdom Issue vs. Mob Action," December, 1946. This is a BTTBW publication, published under the name Jehovah's Witnesses, 517 N. E. Second Street, Fort Lauderdale, Florida.

Although the article by Bill Davidson ("Jehovah's Traveling Salesman," *Colliers*, November 2, 1946) is very inaccurate as it deals with this episode, according to Goodrich (correspondence with this writer dated December 9, 1964), the *Colliers* article does record the mob action: "The rebels were immediately surrounded by 200 Witnesses who deliberately cut the canvas bags of Watchtowers [sic] from the insurgents' shoulders. . ." (p. 75).

[4] Roy D. Goodrich has published several accounts of similar efforts at Jehovah's Witness conventions. Some of the reports record physical violence against those attempting to reach the Witnesses with literature.

[5] Milton Stacy Czatt, *The International Bible Students: Jehovah's Witnesses* (Scottdale, Pennsylvania: Mennonite Press, 1933), pp. 22, 23.

by the presence (according to Schnell) of at least eleven Russellite sects.[6] Roy D. Goodrich lists twelve active groups (including the "Watch Tower Witnesses") and in a subsequent edition of *Back to the Bible Way* adds another.[7] Several of these sects number over 10,000 followers, and possibly more will eventually fall into this category.

The two largest and most progressive groups in the United States are the *Laymen's Home Missionary Movement,* with headquarters in Philadelphia, Pennsylvania,* and *The Dawn Bible Students Association,* with headquarters in East Rutherford, New Jersey. (*Presently, Chester Springs, Pa.)

III. The Laymen's Home Missionary Movement

Under the leadership of Paul S. L. Johnson, the Laymen's Home Missionary Movement of Philadelphia, Pennsylvania, gradually separated from the parent body after Russell's death in 1916, a final break being made in 1918. Although minimized by the Jehovah's Witnesses, this group is growing. According to the information given to this writer by Raymond G. Jolly, the editor and present director of the movement, this group numbers some 50,000 members throughout the world, although no official record of numbers is kept.[8]

This movement views Charles Taze Russell as "that Faithful and Wise Servant." While attending lectures given by Raymond Jolly, this writer heard such statements as, "Our dear brother Russell . . . that Faithful and Wise Servant," etc. Russell was quoted as authority in doctrine. In

---

[6] William J. Schnell, *Into the Light of Christianity* (Grand Rapids: Baker Book House, 1959), p. 27. These groups are discussed in "Sects of Russellism," *The Converted Jehovah's Witness Expositor,* 7:1-6, Issue 1, 1964.

[7] *Back to the Bible Way,* 14:393, November-December, 1965; 15:446, May-August, 1966. Goodrich stated that years before he had read that after Russell's death there had been created some sixty "Truth Movements." Although he could not remember where he had read this, nor verify the accuracy, it probably was based upon the statements of Paul S. L. Johnson, *The Epiphany Messenger* (Vol. X of *Epiphany Studies in the Scriptures,* 17 vols.; Philadelphia: Paul S. L. Johnson, 1941), pp. 212-15; v, vi.

[8] Schnell, in correspondence with this writer (1960), gave a more conservative, and possibly more accurate figure, of 10,000 members.

answering doctrinal questions, Jolly said: "So I am not speaking without authority; brother Russell put that in print."

Until his death in 1950, Paul S. L. Johnson was the director of the cult, this position being filled since then by Mr. Jolly. Paul Johnson viewed himself, and was viewed, as the "Epiphany Messenger" (the Pastor's successor) and his successor, Raymond Jolly is viewed as the "Epiphany Scribe."[9]

Under Johnson's administration the series entitled *Epiphany Studies in the Scriptures* was published with fifteen volumes appearing before the author's death and two after. The volumes follow the format of Russell's *Studies in the Scriptures* exactly and average about 600 pages each.

A monthly magazine of eight pages is published by this group: *The Bible Standard and Herald of Christ's Kingdom* (formerly *The Herald of the Epiphany* through 1951).* The six volumes of *Studies in the Scriptures,* written by Pastor Russell were reprinted and are still advertised by the group

---

[9] Series 10 in the *Epiphany Studies in the Scriptures,* entitled *The Epiphany Messenger,* "contains an exposition of some of the main prophecies and types that point out the Epiphany messenger in his experiences and works as the Divinely chosen teacher and executive, under the Lord Jesus as Head, as to Epiphany conditions and matters. Having been written by himself, it is autobiographical of him in his office work and experience" p. iv).

Two entire volumes in this same series entitled *The Parousia Messenger* present pastor Russell in types and prophecies: "Apart from our Lord Jesus, no servant of God in the large application of types and prophecies is referred to so much as our Pastor. . . . Whole books and large parts of others in type treat of him. . . except the work of our Lord Jesus, the greatest work ever done on earth in advancing God's cause was that of the Parousia Messenger, hence its detailed description in type and prophecy." Paul S. L. Johnson, *The Parousia Messenger* (Vol. IX of *Epiphany Studies in the Scriptures,* 17 vols.; Philadelphia: Paul S. L. Johnson, 1938), pp. iii, iv.

As to the word "Epiphany," it is explained that "Jesus' Second Advent progresses through three stages, indicated by the Greek words Parousia, Epiphaneia, or Apocalypsis, and Basileia. . . About two years before that Servant's death, we passed out of the Parousia (presence) stage into the Epiphaneia (manifestation) or Apocalypsis (revelation) stage. . . ." Paul S. L. Johnson, *The Epiphany's Elect* (Vol. IV of *Epiphany Studies in the Scriptures,* 17 vols.; Philadelphia: Paul S. L. Johnson, 1938), p. iii.

* A bi-monthly, *The Present Truth and Herald of Christ's Epiphany,* is also published.

as basic texts.[10] Some of his other works have also been edited and reprinted. Among new literature propagated are a number of free tracts on such subjects as, "Where are the Dead?," "Life and Immortality," "What is the Soul?" etc.

The group follows the pattern established by Russell, with visiting speakers to serve the ecclesiae upon request and numerous conventions to encourage and unify the followers.

Of interest is the fact that Johnson adopted the Biblical Numerics of Ivan Panin, and this system is still in vogue in the group today. After Johnson bought up the last 300 copies of one edition of Panin's *Numeric Greek Testament* he offered to guarantee to buy an additional 5,000 of a new edition at five dollars a copy.[11]

In all fairness to this cult, the writer found its adherents friendly, and sincere in their beliefs. Sincere, yet wrong! In visiting their meetings, one had the feeling that Pastor Russell had left for a moment and would shortly return. The songs that were sung and the conduct of the meetings attended seemed a throwback of some sixty years.

The movement strongly opposes the Jehovah's Witnesses where Russell's teachings have been changed. The Laymen's Home Missionary Movement opposes the Jehovah's Witnesses' refusal to salute the flag, the refusal of blood transfusion, the setting aside of the promises to Israel, and the dogmatic sectarianism of the parent organization, to list some of the points of conflict.[12] Although there is clearly some disagreement, these two groups do not in final analysis differ radically on most major fundamental doctrinal issues.

What are the dangers of this group called the Laymen's Home Missionary Movement? First, this writer would cite its *anti-Biblical teachings.* Following as it does in the footsteps of Russell, the movement might also be well designated

---

[10] Volume seven of the *Studies in the Scriptures,* entitled *The Finished Mystery* is repudiated by the group. The same position is taken by the Dawn Bible Students Association and many other Russellite groups.

[11] A. B. King, *et al., Ivan Panin's Scientific Demonstration of the Inspiration of the Scriptures* (revised edition; Toronto, Canada: [no publisher], 1924), pp. 29-35.

[12] See *The Teachings of "Jehovah's Witnesses" Examined in the Light of the Scriptures* and *Merarism* for additional points of conflict.

a system of denial. Although their writings are liberally sprinkled with "proof texts" from the Bible, this cult denies the deity of Christ, and with this the Trinity. The existence of an eternal hell and eternal punishment for the wicked is also denied. The bodily resurrection of Christ is denied, and so is His personal, visible return. The cult denies the atonement and offers no assurance of a present salvation. They deny that a man's fate is necessarily sealed at death. Many men who have lived and died in the past are viewed as never having had a full chance or trial for life and they will receive such a chance during the millennium.

The cult also follows in the footsteps of Russell's method of Biblical exposition which results in interpretations and applications of the Scriptures which often beggar all description.

Secondly, there is a danger in the very *name of this cult.* Under the attractive and harmless sounding name, The Laymen's Home Missionary Movement, is concealed a very real form of Russellite heresy. Undetected, this group has access to many unsuspecting churches. Indeed this boast was made to this writer by Jolly and several of his followers. In their monthly publication, *The Bible Standard and Herald of Christ's Kingdom,* November 1958 issue (p. 88), this announcement is found:

> We have available a program of professional quality Bible films in sound and color and Bible filmstrips in beautiful natural color, including speakers, for use in many localities, in churches, young people's groups, Y. M. and Y.W.C.A.'s, Bible Study classes, etc. Due to a special fund supplied by voluntary contributions, there is no charge.

Many unsuspecting groups and churches have called upon this sect to put on programs. Another effective method of propagating their teachings is a special form letter sent to those who have lost loved ones. These letters are sent out with an appropriate tract containing the views of the cult slanted to this particular crisis, [13] which often makes a strong contact with the recipient. The effectiveness of this

[13] These letters are accompanied by the booklet, *Where are the Dead?*

method is attested by the correspondence received from those who received the form letters. Many such responses are often found in the cult's monthly periodical.

This group also makes many contacts through its literature placed in tract racks in stores and other public places, which can be easily found by the unwary and unsuspecting. The author came into contact with this cult in just such a way. Free *Bible Standard* subscriptions are supplied to public places, such as hospitals, schools, public libraries, etc. "Our magazine is being displayed in over 1,000 public places. . . ."[14]

In reading through *The Bible Standard* it was noticed that at times those in charge of church tract racks have requested tracts from this cult. In some cases even Sunday School teachers or ministers, who from their statements seem to be orthodox in belief, request tracts.[15] The tract ministry is world-wide in its outreach.

Even the Jehovah's Witnesses have felt the impact of this sister cult, which may account for the detailed and slanted account of the schism of these two groups found in *Jehovah's Witnesses in the Divine Purpose.* The movement has successfully made proselytes of both Jehovah's Witnesses and members of the Dawn Bible Students Association.

A lesson in semantics. In dealing with any cult it is important that terms be defined, for as Walter Martin warns, it is possible for a cultist

> to utilize the terminology of Biblical Christianity with absolute freedom, having already redesigned these terms in a theological framework of his own making and to

[14] *The Bible Standard and Herald of Christ's Kingdom,* 47:8, January, 1966.

[15] This writer has verified this by his own experience when among tracts on display dealing with Creation, the Bible and science, he found a quantity of the tract "The Bible vs. Evolution" published by the L.H.M.M. The orthodox minister who was handling the display was not aware of the doctrines of the group, some of which were included in the tract itself! Here was an example of how a Russellite sect can make contacts through the efforts of orthodox Christians. One must be careful!

his own liking, but almost always at direct variance with the historically accepted meaning of the terms.[16]

This writer had written a brief article on the Laymen's Home Missionary Movement which stated the following:

> Although their writings are liberally sprinkled with "proof texts" from the Bible, this cult denies the deity of Christ and with this the Trinity. The existence of an eternal hell and eternal punishment for the wicked is also denied. The bodily resurrection of Christ is denied, and so is His personal, visible return. The cult denies the atonement and offers no present salvation to its followers.[17]

The article, and especially this section, resulted in a three-page letter in which director of the movement, R. G. Jolly, argues that the article

> states falsely that the Laymen's Home Missionary Movement denies [2] "the deity of Christ," [3] "an eternal hell," [4] "eternal punishment for the wicked," [5] "the bodily resurrection of Christ," [6] "his personal," [7] "visible return," [8] "the atonement," and that we [9] "offer no assurance of a present salvation, but [10] only an opportunity for salvation in the future."

Was this writer of the article so totally uninformed as to make these blunders? The answer lies in the area of semantics. Martin's statement above is perfectly illustrated. To the orthodox audience to which the article was aimed the teachings of the Laymen's Home Missionary Movement *did* deny all the doctrines mentioned, as a perusal of the publications of this cult will show.

IV. The Dawn Bible Students Association

The Dawn Bible Students Association is a group which is made up of members who are true followers of Charles

---

[16] Walter R. Martin, *The Kingdom of the Cults* (Grand Rapids: Zondervan Publishing House, 1965), p. 18. It would be enlightening for the reader to read the entire chapter from which this quotation is taken.

[17] Edmond Gruss, "Beware of the 'Laymen's Home Missionary Movement,'" *The Baptist Bulletin*, 27:13, April 1962.

Taze Russell.[18] As Judge Rutherford exerted his control more and brought about new changes of doctrine, pushing Pastor Russell's writings and views into the background, many dedicated Bible Students left the Watch Tower Society. In the late 1920's "in Pittsburgh, Pennsylvania, a sufficient number left at one time to form an ecclesia. Soon thereafter (in October 1929), this ecclesia arranged to hold a convention. . . ."[19] Another convention, held the next year, decided that possibilities for some way to help the Bible Students in their ministry should be investigated. A short time later the Brooklyn Ecclesia joined the effort and a radio ministry was started. The depression curtailed the radio ministry after only a few months, but not before the ministry had rallied a number of Bible Students around this effort. Literature to follow up the radio contacts was published, but when this ministry was ended the publishing continued.[20]

The four-page weekly tract, "The Radio Echo," published in conjunction with the radio ministry, was eventually enlarged into the current sixty-four-page monthly magazine, *The Dawn,* which appeared for the first time in October, 1932. Although this writer has never seen a published statement of the circulation of this periodical, a prominent brother at one of the Dawn conventions said it was around 30,000 per month. Subscriptions to *The Dawn* are not necessarily a tally of the membership of the group, but they do indicate a sizeable following. Martin points out that the group shows

---

[18] "Did The Dawn come into being as a medium for the dissemination of new light? Were the friends stirred to action because something had been found and was being proclaimed through The Dawn? No! The Lord's consecrated people throughout the world are, as a whole, well satisfied with the truth as it was brought to them through the ministry of Brother Russell. The brethren directly responsible for what appears in The Dawn are well satisfied with that truth. . . . They see no need for instructions along doctrinal or devotional lines which are contrary to those which we have in the *Studies in the Scriptures.*" *When Pastor Russell Died* (third edition; East Rutherford, N. J.: Dawn Bible Students Association, 1957), pp. 29, 30.

[19] *Ibid.,* p. 26.

[20] *Ibid.,* pp. 26, 27.

a growth of almost 1,000 members each year, which shows that it is not to be ignored as unimportant.[21]

Recent attempts at advertising in secular magazines have shown the drawing power of the group. An advertisement inserted in *Look* magazine (October 11, 1960 issue) offering the cult's booklet, *Life After Death,* in a short time yielded 1,000 responses.[22] The report for 1965 indicated that more than 90,000 free booklets were distributed, most in response to requests from those contacted through the public media.[23] More than 60,000 names were received through a Dawn display at the New York World's Fair.[24] This group has also found a fruitful field in literature to the bereaved.

The work of the Association is carried on by an annually elected board of twelve trustees. They in turn elect the officers of the Association, who cannot serve in the same office for more than two years.

The headquarters and the publishing plant of this group is located in East Rutherford, New Jersey. The Dawn movement is quite active in publishing literature, and distribution points are located in a number of countries. Dawn addresses are listed in New Zealand, Australia, France, Greece, Denmark, Germany and Italy, with materials available in a number of additional languages. In like manner as the Laymen's Home Missionary Movement, the Dawn Bible Students have republished the six volumes by Russell and some of his other works in new Dawn editions. Numerous tracts and booklets have also been published.

The radio ministry which was dropped in 1932 was started again in 1940. The Dawn Bible Students Association

---

[21] Walter R. Martin, *The Rise of the Cults* (revised and enlarged, 1957; Grand Rapids: Zondervan Publishing House, 1955), p. 22.

[22] *The Dawn,* 28:55, November, 1960. A number of announcements were placed in various magazines during 1964 and the response was very good: "Many thousands of truth booklets were requested as a result of these announcements, and already an encouraging number of those who wrote for literature have become subscribers to The Dawn. . . ." *The Dawn,* 33:55, January, 1965. An announcement in *Parade* magazine on February 7, 1965 "brought a response of well over four thousand." *The Dawn,* 33:60, May, 1965.

[23] *The Dawn,* 34:60, January, 1966.

[24] *Ibid.,* p. 54.

sponsors the coast-to-coast radio program, "Frank and Ernest," which has proved to be an effective propaganda outreach. At one time this program was heard on over 300 stations each Sunday. Now it is reported that more than a hundred stations carry this message.[25] With the advent of television the radio ministry declined, but the Dawn organization has been successful in getting free television time, with more than fifty stations showing its films in 1965. It is reported that "The Bible Answers" television series had been or was shown by more than one hundred and fifty stations.[26] The recently completed films were produced in color. The film "The Unknown God," has been shown to "approximately thirty-five hundred churches, clubs, and schools, with a total attendance of more than one hundred and fifty thousand."[27] To round out the ministry of the group there is a Recorded Lecture Service, where taped messages are made available, and a Pilgrim Department which supplies speakers on request.

The foregoing facts and figures were presented in order to underscore the point that this cult has an outreach which has had good success and one which represents a potential and a danger that cannot be ignored.

Although the Dawn Bible Students are sure that their message is right and that they have the truth, there is no hatred for other religions as is found in the Witnesses. This writer heard it stated that differences of opinion on doctrine were to be tolerated among brethren unless they were published and began appearing in the mails. The Jehovah's Witnesses are viewed as perverters of the truth, but the publications of the Dawn do not name them, although the doctrines they propagate are strongly attacked. All the doctrines of denial of Russell are held as basic truth.

There is definite evidence that the Dawn Bible Students Association is being successful in bringing a number of Jehovah's Witnesses into its camp.

---

[25] *Ibid.*, p. 53.

[26] *Ibid.*, pp. 51, 52.

[27] *The Dawn*, 33:53, January, 1965. The use of the radio, television, films for public distribution and showing, and magazine advertising, distinguish the outreach of this group from the Jehovah's Witnesses.

V. The Associated Bible Students and the Pastoral Bible Institute

The Pastoral Bible Institute, chartered in 1918, is the association or agency through which the Associated Bible Students work. After the death of Pastor Russell the control of the International Bible Students was taken over by Rutherford. With this change of administration, it is explained, came a dismissal of many brethren who had occupied positions of prominence and responsibility under Pastor Russell. Other issues of vital importance came up at this time and out of this period of crisis the Pastoral Bible Institute came into being. The form of church government under Russell was congregational, where each ecclesia acted as an independent, self-governing body. "It was the infringement of this principle after Mr. Russell's death which first led to the withdrawal of support of the corporate organization by these congregations."[28]

The classes of Bible Students that separated from the parent body "'quite generally assumed the name *Associated Bible Students,* and in some instances, *Berean Bible Students.*"[29]

The Pastoral Bible Institute maintained its headquarters in Brooklyn until 1960, at which time it moved to St. Louis, Missouri. Correspondants are also listed in England and Australia (Berean Bible Institute). The purpose of the Institute is explained:

> . . . This association of the Institute is not in any sense a religious organization nor does it represent the formation of a Church or Ecclesia, but acts merely as a means or agency by which a religious work can be carried on by brethren of various Ecclesias or Churches and by which they might co-operate and act together "decently and in order."[30]

The work of the Institute is handled by seven Directors, elected annually, who in turn annually appoint five Editors

---

[28] "History, Organization, and Doctrine of Associated Bible Students," *The Herald of Christ's Kingdom,* 44:87, June, 1961.

[29] *Ibid.,* p. 86.

[30] *Herald Supplement,* "Our Association Together in the Ministry Methods and Forms of Edifying the Body of Christ," p. 2.

to the Editorial Committee of the Journal. The principal features of the Institute ministry are: (1) To publish *The Herald,* (2) to publish and/or distribute the Divine Message in printed form through books, booklets, tracts, etc. (3) to assist brethren "to travel from place to place and minister the word of grace to larger and smaller groups of friends who desire and request such service."[31] The July-August 1966 edition of *The Herald of Christ's Kingdom* lists fourteen speakers and their itineraries. Conventions are also announced.

The Herald of Christ's Kingdom magazine is a sixteen-page bimonthly (formerly monthly). Subscription figures to this journal have shown a significant rise, more than doubling in four years, growing from 3,035 in April in 1962, to 7,181 in April of 1966. While totals are small, subscriptions came from about thirty countries. Although these numbers do not look impressive when compared to those of larger groups, the work has been steadily progressing. The association has also published, and distributes free, twenty booklets and several tracts. Russell's six volumes have been republished and are viewed as basic to Bible understanding.

The doctrinal position of the Associated Bible Students is best explained by themselves:

> The corporate organization [The Watch Tower Bible and Tract Society] has departed in many respects from the understanding of doctrines as presented in "*Studies in the Scriptures,*" and has ceased to distribute Mr. Russell's writings, which has led to the loss of many of its former supporters, while Associated Bible Students Classes as a whole still adhere quite closely to the views presented in his writings.[32]

As a further clarification, it is explained that although they feel that Russell's works are to be given first place as Bible "helps,"

> We were not recommending these works "as being the whole truth." . . . However, we did not, nor do we now, recommend them *instead* of the Bible, but as *helps to its study.*[33]

---

[31] *Ibid.*, p. 4.

[32] *The Herald of Christ's Kingdom,* 44:86, 87, June, 1961.

[33] *The Herald of Christ's Kingdom,* 45:92, November-December, 1962.

VI. Back to the Bible Way

The *Back to the Bible Way* journal and other publications which number several hundred, are essentially the work of one man, Roy D. Goodrich who is remarkably active for an octogenarian. He is assisted by his wife, Maud, who is also the same age, and what little additional help they can afford. The Goodriches were pioneers before the 1920's up until their excommunication from the Jehovah's Witnesses in 1944 and 1945.[34]

Back to the Bible Way,[35] currently a sixteen-page bi-monthly, was first published on January 1, 1952. The regular mailing list for the journal for early 1966 was over 3,000.[36] The other publications of the Bible Way Publications, Inc., range from one-page mimeographed items to printed booklets. Many of the publications deal with the errors of the Jehovah's Witnesses and Pastor Russell's interpretations.

Putting action behind his attacks upon the Watchtower Society, Goodrich and his wife, with others who joined them, made many tract distribution forays to the large assemblies of the Jehovah's Witnesses "from Los Angeles to Providence, and from Chicago to Miami. . . ."[37] These distribution campaigns resulted in very harsh treatment by the Witnesses. There is evidence that a number of disillusioned and disfellowshiped Jehovah's Witnesses have taken an interest in Goodrich's work.

The convention pattern was begun by this movement in 1957. "Memorial Assemblies" in April of each year are now held in Fort Lauderdale.

---

[34] In a letter to this writer dated December 9, 1964, Goodrich stated: "I had been excommunicated by them without cause, evidence, facts, or opportunity of hearing or defense in the summer and fall of 1944." Mrs. Goodrich was excommunicated after more than thirty-one years of full time service for standing with her husband. BTTBW publication 41.

[35] "Way" was added to the journal title under pressure of the Lincoln, Nebraska, "Back to the Bible" broadcasts because of the possible confusion of these two organizations.

[36] *Back to the Bible Way,* 15:412, January-February, 1966. Looking through some back issues yielded letters from ten countries besides the U.S.A.

[37] Letter to this writer dated December 9, 1964.

Goodrich holds most of the "fundamentals" advocated by Pastor Russell (no Trinity, no immortal soul, no hell, Jesus was not a God-man, Christendom is apostate, etc.). But he disagrees very strongly with Russell's invisible "second coming" of Christ teaching for the year 1914. Concerning Russell's predictions relative to that year he states: "His multiplied predictions of things to happen in or before 1914, *had failed completely and by* 100%."[38] He also rejects (among other views) Russell's claim of being the "Faithful and Wise Servant," his view of the ransom as merely a "corresponding price," and his teaching on the Harvest of the Gospel Age.[39]

His strongest denunciations are reserved for the "Watch Tower Hierarchy" with its claim to being the exclusive "channel" for Biblical truth, and the doctrines and actions which have resulted from that assumed position.[40]

The Watchtower Society and the many splinter groups are viewed as "reason shaken sects," and "heretical" and "apostate" are terms attached to many (all?) of them.[41]

What the fate of this extensive one-man movement will be only time will tell.

VII. Other Sects and Publications in America

Through the years a number of other Russellite sects and publications have come and gone. Development of this section presents (1) those movements which are still functioning and journals which are currently being distributed, and (2) the movements and publications which have become defunct.

The *Christian Believers* (formerly New Covenant Believers) originally were one of the early schisms from Watch Tower leadership. In an "Open Letter" dated October 24, 1909 they set forth the reasons why they were forced to remove themselves from under Pastor Russell's teaching. Among the listed reasons for separation were his new teachings on

[38] *Back to the Bible Way,* 12:138, May-June, 1963.

[39] BTTBW publication 419.

[40] *Ibid.*

[41] *Back to the Bible Way,* 14:390, 393, November-December, 1965. BTTBW publication 203 (a letter to the Dawn) has hand-written in red, "Another Heretical Russellite Sect."

the atonement, his claim of being "that servant" of Matthew 24: 45-47, and his position on Bible study. A statement from the "Open Letter" on this last point is very interesting:

> Pastor Russell has, through the Watch Tower and in answer to questions at meetings of the Tabernacle congregation, expressed his disapproval of meetings held for BIBLE study, unless such study was in connection with those works of which he is the author or editor, and has stated that "he doubted whether much good had ever been derived from all the independent Bible study undertaken in the past."[42]

This group has held an annual conference since 1910. The official journal of the Christian Believers is *The Kingdom Scribe,* which is published under a Publications Committee.

The New Creation Bible Students Association is a small group of Bible Students who sponsor *The New Creation,* a monthly magazine which has been published continuously for more than thirty years. A letter to this writer dated July 6, 1966 explained that

> the New Creation magazine is not controlled by any organization, but is really free in the Lord. Its editorial committee selects the articles to be published every month, and a good 90% of these are contributed by the readers themselves.
>
> . . . The Editor of the New Creation magazine is also the Editor of the L'Aurora Millenniale Magazine published in the Italian language every other month.

The New Creation is published in Hartford, Connecticut.

The *Bible Student Examiner* is the name of a monthly journal published in Baltimore, Maryland. The editor, Henry Wallace, had years before helped Olin Moyle start the publication of the *Bible Student Inquirer* in Wisconsin.

> At the end of 1959 he folded up publication of *Bible Student Inquirer* in favor of Brother Henry Wallace of Baltimore, who has since carried on under the name, *Bible Student Examiner.*[43]

---

[42] *Back to the Bible Way,* 4:399, September-October, 1955.

[43] Letter to this writer from Roy D. Goodrich dated June 9, 1966.

To this writer's knowledge the following groups and publications are now defunct, but they give an interesting story of developments among the Bible Students.

One of the most unusual groups of Russellite background was the *Servants of Yah* led by C. H. Zook until his death.[44] The mailing address of this group was a G. P. O. Box in Brooklyn, New York. Whalen included a brief treatment of the Yahites in his book on the Jehovah's Witnesses and stated that the group was established in 1943. Then he presented some of their weird views:

> They decided that Jehovah was actually the name of the devil. The name of God is Yah. Clearly then the Witnesses were servants of Satan.
>
> . . . According to the Servants of Yah only 144,000 people were ever destined to discover the hidden meaning of the Scriptures. . . .
>
> The Servants of Yah see the Bible as nothing but prophecy, all of which relates to the present day. . . . The Servants deny Armageddon, the Genesis flood, the existence of Satan, and the value of water baptism.[45]

Some of Zook's other denials are included in this writing entitled, "Jesus Christ—Mythical Legend":

> "The Servants of Yah have long discarded the doctrine of the ransom sacrifice. Learning that it has no Scriptural basis, that since man had not been sentenced to death, there existed no necessity for a purchase price to be given for man's recovery, thus Jesus was eliminated at that time, in that connection. Now we learn that our heavenly Father does not need him at all, and since the Bible does not teach his existence, we can gladly renounce any belief in him, even though at first we are shocked to learn the truth of it."[46]

Paul S. L. Johnson records some interesting history in his account of the schism and organization of *The Standfast Movement*:

---

[44] In BTTBW publication 166, C. H. Zook is identified as "a former 'pilgrim' and worker at the Watch Tower headquarters, some thirty years ago [written 1949] . . . ."

[45] William J. Whalen, *Armageddon Around the Corner* (New York: The John Day Company, 1962), p. 212.

[46] "Jesus Christ—Mythical Legend," quoted in BTTBW publication 166.

> ALL OF US recall how the Society leaders repudiated their stand on liberty bonds and non-combative service, *after their arrest.* The publication of their reversal of front in several Towers during the Spring of 1918 provoked resentment among not a few brethren the world over, especially in Oregon, Washington and British Columbia. Out of this opposition was born a movement which its adherents called the Standfast Movement, in allusion to their determination to stand fast on the war principles that our dear Pastor announced . . . This movement at a Convention held in Portland, Ore., Dec. 1, 1918, adopted a platform of principles and appointed a Committee of seven brothers . . . to manage what they considered the work of the General Church.[47]

The seventh volume of *Studies in the Scriptures,* which was rejected by the Laymen's Home Missionary Movement and the Dawn Bible Students, was accepted by The Standfasters

> as the very book which Pastor Russell intended to write, but didn't. They believed that it was the posthumous work of Brother Russell. So, when those who published the Seventh Volume repudiated it, they stood fast in its support; and some of these brethren still do.[48]

At first the efforts of the movement were quite successful in organizing classes of former adherents of the Society who did not accept the compromises on the war.

Johnson mentions an interesting episode which he designates the "'Westward Movement." All Standfasters not on the West Coast were prevailed upon to move to the West if possible. An added inducement was the prediction that the rapture for the Standfasters would take place in 1920, "but to make it certain that one was of the select company, he had to go West, where as a group the Lord would take all of them in a company away at the Passover."[49]

---

[47] Paul S. L. Johnson, *Merariism* (Vol. VI of *Epiphany Studies in the Scriptures,* 17 vols; Philadelphia: Paul S. L. Johnson, 1938), p. 731.

[48] *When Pastor Russell Died, op. cit.,* p. 14. Concerning the Seventh Volume it is explained: "It is well nigh impossible to believe, yet true, that whereas when this book was first published those who did not accept it were condemned and disfellowshiped, within a few years those who did accept it were disfellowshiped." *Ibid.,* p. 7.

[49] Johnson, *Merariism, op. cit.,* p. 736.

In 1923 C. E. Heard and I. C. Edwards, led a movement which involved about 300 Standfasters "that in the course of less than two years degenerated into communism."[50] This experiment at communal living known as the "Sooke movement" (after the location at Sooke Harbor, B. C.) ended in failure.

Another separation came about because some objected to the activities of the Committee which had been organized to manage the affairs of the group. This body Johnson calls the "No-committeeites."[51]

The small (less than 300) Elijah Voice Society which broke from the Standfasters in 1923 felt that the time had come to regather scattered believers of the "Little Flock." Along with other efforts they published tracts and a periodical, *The Elijah Voice Monthly*.[52] They also felt that they had been called to "smite Babylon." The group's extreme pacifism and "fanaticism is seen in their claiming that to contribute to the Red Cross, to buy Liberty Bonds and to salute the flag were parts of the mark of the beast."[53] The "fanaticism" of the Elijah Voice Society became the "will of God" to the Jehovah's Witnesses. Jehovah's Witnesses cannot claim to be first on the flag salute issue. The stand on this issue was first taken by some Mennonites in 1918 and by followers of the Elijah Voice Society in 1925. [54]

The Standfast movement which started quite strong numerically, with between 2,000 and 3,000 adherents, was short-lived as a united effort.

Two additional publications should be mentioned before concluding this section: (1) *The Watchers of the Morning,* published and edited by I. F. Hoskins until his death several years ago, and (2) *The Roundtable of the Scriptures,* edited and published by Wesley J. Ladwig for ten years until his death in 1952. Ladwig subscribed to universal restitutionism (i.e., all would eventually be saved).

---

[50] *Ibid.*, p. 738.
[51] *Ibid.*, p. 740, 741.
[52] *Ibid.*, p. 742.
[53] *Ibid.*, p. 743.
[54] David R. Manwaring, *Render Unto Caesar* (Chicago: University of Chicago Press, 1962), pp. 11-14.

VIII. Other Sects and Publications in Europe

Much could be said about the Bible Students currently active in Europe, but space does not permit a detailed presentation.

Britain. There are many free Bible Students in Britain. These do not have a national headquarters, but fellowship within their own ecclesiae, with each other, and with their brethren in America and elsewhere.

A magazine which finds its source in Britain and is circulated among free Bible Students is the *Bible Study Monthly.* This twenty-four page bimonthly was founded in 1924. It is edited by A. O. Hudson and published by the Bible Fellowship Union. A brief explanation of the magazine included in each issue states:

> This Journal is published for the promotion of Bible knowledge and the furtherance of the Gospel of the Kingdom, its circulation being largely among independent Bible fellowships and study circles which share in varying degree the viewpoint of the Divine Plan herein set forth.

The publication was quite interesting to this writer because in the issues examined the name C. T. Russell never appeared, nor was there any mention of *Studies in the Scriptures.* But Russell's doctrinal system was very evident.

The annual August London Convention, which has been held for more than a generation, is the most widely attended assembly of the British free Bible Students.

Another journal which is published in Britain is *Maran-atha,* a magazine of anonymous editorship. There is a week-long Maran-atha Conference each year.

Both the London and Maran-atha assemblies are announced each year in *The Herald of Christ's Kingdom,* the publication of the Associated Bible Students in America.

Jesse Hemery, who was a veteran of 56 years service for the Watch Tower Society, the manager of the British Branch in London for forty-six years, and the vice-president of the International Bible Students until 1947, was disfellowshiped and afterward started another group which was called the Goshen Fellowship. Hemery came to the realization that the invisible "second coming" of Christ was a dogma without foundation. Before his death he wrote two small books (possibly more), *Revelation Unfolded* and *Christ's Great Prophecy*.[55]

The Continent. There are many free Bible Students in many of the countries of the Continent. The situation there is much like that of the Bible Students in Britain.

The German publication, *Christliche Warte* (*Christian Watch Tower*), edited and published by Emil and Otto Sadlack, has been circulated for many years. The movement of these free Bible Students is identified by one of their adherents as the "Frie Bibelgemeinde" (Free Bible Community).[56]

As it has already been stated, *The New Creation's* affiliate is *L'Aurora Milleniale,* which serves some of the Bible Students in Italy.

The *Church of the Kingdom of God,* or the *Freytag Bewegung* (Movement),[57] was started in Geneva, Switzerland by F. L. Alexander Freytag in 1917. He became an International Bible Student in 1898 and later he took charge of the Watch Tower Bible and Tract Society Bureau in Geneva.

After Russell's death he began to attack the position set forth in *The Divine Plan of the Ages.* Freytag set forth the attack upon the Society and his new doctrinal position in the books *Message of Laodicea* (1920), *The Divine Revelation* (1922), *Message to Mankind* (1922), and *Eternal Life* (1933).

The heart of Freytag's theology is universal law and the idea that God's universal law of love was broken by Satan's and man's selfish disobedience which resulted in suffering, death and disharmony. God's will is that universal harmony be restored and this will be accomplished eventually when all are saved.

---

[55] *Back To The Bible,* 1:26, April, 1952. Roy Goodrich later stated that Hemery still retained a limited version of the "secret presence heresy" and that he was preparing the way for the recognition of himself as the "Faithful and Wise Servant." *Back to the Bible,* 4:336, May-June, 1955.

[56] *Back to the Bible Way,* 9:335, May-June, 1960.

[57] All the information on the Church of the Kingdom of God has been taken from, "The Sects of Russellism," *The Converted Jehovah's Witness Expositor,* 7:4-7 Issue 1, 1964.

Schnell concludes that Rutherford's new emphasis on the vindication of God's sovereignty was demanded by Freytag's theology because he

> came close to inheriting Russell's position in Europe. Rutherford saw Freytag's flaw and stepped in. First, he transliterated the universal-law breach with subsequent results of sufferings and death, and brought Jehovah into the picture by saying, "God lost His good name in the fall," and His "universal sovereignty was thus challenged by Satan. Restitution can come only by the vindication of Jehovah's name at Armageddon."
>
> Are you beginning to see from whence present-day Jehovah's Witness propaganda emanates? It has arisen not from the Bible, but from a rational reaction to Freytag's bid to establish his succession to Russell [pp. 6, 7].

Although the Church of the Kingdom of God is not known in the United States, its work has spread over much of Europe, South America and the English speaking world. According to Schnell, the membership in Germany alone is 75,000.

IX. The International Bible Students and the Concordant Publishing Concern, a Non-Russellite Organization

This chapter would not be complete without a brief mention of the Bible Students that left the Society, especially during the 1920's and became followers of the views of A. E. Knoch and the *Concordant Version.*

The Concordant Publishing Concern became known to the Bible Students with the inclusion of an announcement and high recommendation for "THE CONCORDANT NEW TESTAMENT" in *The Watch Tower.* The announcement covers all of page 191 and a good portion of page 190 of the June 15, 1920 issue. The Version was to be published and sold as the parts were ready and the Watch Tower was to act as the forwarder of the orders. In time 2,000 parts were ordered. Later another announcement appeared which cancelled the previous one.[58]

---

[58] The Society had ordered 10,000 copies of each part of the Version and with 2,000 parts of the first section sold it left 8,000 specially printed parts in the hands of the publisher when the order was cancelled. The second part of 10,000 copies had also been published. When this story was told in *Unsearchable Riches* (18:327, November, 1927) a

In an interview with Ernest O. Knoch, son of the founder of the Concordant Publishing Concern, this writer was told that several thousand International Bible Students became interested in this group. Among these were several prominent men: F. H. Robison, who was a member of *The Watch Tower* Editorial Committee; Menta Sturgeon, who had accompanied Pastor Russell as his secretary and who was with him when he died; Walter H. Bundy, Watch Tower "Pilgrim," and W. F. Salter of Canada.

In his effort to win more of the Bible Students to the new views, Bundy wrote an 158-page booklet entitled *Studies in the Scriptures*: *Investigating Bible Statements Analytically.* The publication was addressed "to Those Interested In the Work and Publications of the International Bible Students Association."

In the November, 1927 issue of *Unsearchable Riches* (p. 324) A. E. Knoch wrote:

> The Lord has graciously enabled us to help many who once believed the International Bible Students Association philosophy, and the indications are that He will use us to bless very many more.

What was the drawing power of Knoch's movement? Many of the Concordant beliefs as developed by A. E. Knoch would immediately appeal to the Bible Students, such as rejection of: the Trinity, the deity of Christ, the personality of the Holy Spirit, and eternal punishment. Knoch even went one better than Russell; he advocated the universal reconciliation of all, even the Devil himself. As has been mentioned before, the core of Russell's theology was a rejection of eternal punishment and a modified universalism. Knoch also appealed to Scripture, which would attract the members of I. B. S. A. Many Bible Students were undoubtedly drawn

---

letter in answer was sent by Judge Rutherford (dated November 25, 1927) in which he claims that "the notice was inserted in the WATCH TOWER by one who had no authority. The order was given by one who had no authority to order them." Could it be that Rutherford had cancelled the taking of orders for the Concordant Version because his organization was losing too many members to this movement, among them one of the most capable members of the Watch Tower Editorial Committee?

toward the Concordant work by those who had already made the move.

X. Conclusion

Although Charles T. Russell is dead, the organization which he founded and the theology which he propagated are still very much alive.

There are still thousands today, fifty-nine years after his death who refer to him as "Our Pastor," and defend his theology fully or to some degree.

Russell's *Studies in the Scriptures* and other writings are still being published and presented by many as the key to the understanding of the Bible. His *Divine Plan of the Ages* is available in hard cover for as little as fifty cents. The Chicago Bible Students have organized a Book Republishing Committee which has recently republished *The Watch Tower* issues of 1879 to 1916 with an index. His articles are still being published in many of the journals of the Bible Students.

The results of his hermeneutical principles and theological system have come to fruition for all to assess. What is found? (1) Russell's claim to being the "Faithful and Wise Servant" sowed the seeds for the "sole channel" claims of the Watch Tower Bible and Tract Society with control of the interpretation of the Scriptures; presenting "truth" which becomes error, and error which becomes "truth" and disfellowshiping those who do not agree at each stage. (2) Russell's subjective and speculative exposition of the Bible produced on the one hand, a Paul S. L. Johnson who saw himself in the Bible and wrote an entire book on the subject; and on the other hand, a C. H. Zook who concluded that Jehovah was the Devil and Jesus Christ was a myth. (3) Russell's modified universal restitutionism, with most of humanity getting a trial for life during the millennium, produced many Bible Students that eagerly accepted the universal restitutionism (with salvation for even Satan himself) of A. E. Knoch and others. (4) His views on the second coming of Christ and time speculations brought a great crop of erroneous conclusions within the Watch Tower Society itself, illustrated by Rutherford's "Millions Now Living Will

Never Die" campaign, with predictions for 1925, and illustrated outside the parent body by the Standfasters "'Western Rapture" predicted for 1920. (5) Fanatism of position, such as the communal living of the "Sooke movement," the extreme pacifism of the Elijah Voice Society, and the death before blood transfusion of the Jehovah's Witnesses, also illustrates the results of the seeds planted by Russell. (6) Many schisms and great discord have been seen among those that claim to have the truth. The sects view the parent organization as apostate and the Jehovah's Witnesses view these former brethren, now outside their organization, as the "evil slave class." What "unity" of the brethren Russellism has wrought! Surely a scene of Psalm 133:1 in reverse!

The standard of judgment for any movement or supposed Christian system should not be the claims of those who founded it, or those who follow, but rather the Word of God. Matthew 7:17, 18, 20 could be taken as a standard by which to judge what has been presented thus far:

> Even so every good tree bringeth forth good fruit; but the corrupt tree bringeth forth evil fruit. A good tree cannot bring forth evil fruit, neither can a corrupt tree bring forth good fruit. . . . Therefore by their fruits ye shall know them.

Author's Note

Since this Appendix was written the author has located a number of additional splinter groups and their publications. Probably the most extensive listing of the movements and materials which stem from C. T. Russell and the Watchtower is that prepared by J. Gordon Melton, Research Director of The Institute for the Study of American Religion, P. O. Box 1311, Evanston, Illinois 60201.

Appendix B

OLIN MOYLE'S ORIGINAL LETTERS

Olin Moyle had been in the Watchtower movement for more than twenty years when the first of the following letters was written. He had served as legal advisor to the organization, without pay, for four years. He was deposed from his position in 1939 and excommunicated from the Milwaukee Congregation of the Jehovah's Witnesses in March 1940. In August, 1941, a Resolution discrediting Moyle was read and unanimously adopted by an "Aye" vote of the crowd of 65,000 Witnesses assembled in convention in St. Louis, Missouri. Having been falsely attacked in *The Watchtower,* Moyle brought a libel suit against Rutherford and the Board of Directors of the Society which he won, receiving a settlement of $15,000 in 1944.[1]

The following letters, reproduced in full, present what Moyle saw from firsthand experience and they reveal what kind of a leader Judge Rutherford was.

As to the authenticity of these letters, Roy D. Goodrich stated: "'Hundreds of these have been reproduced by me and sent out, and neither Brother Moyle or the Society has ever called in question their authenticity."[2]

---

[1] David Manwaring, *Render Unto Caesar* (Chicago: The University of Chicago Press, 1962), pp. 222, 306, note 71.

[2] BTTBW publication 141, p. 2. The letters are in mimeographed form and are BTTBW publication 79.

Sept. 25, 1940

To: Jehovah's Witnesses,
Milwaukee, Wisconsin.

Dear Brethren:

On March 21st of this year I was excommunicated from the Milwaukee Company of Jehovah's Witnesses under orders from the Society's president. Many of you brethren are still in ignorance of this fact, and some have inquired as to why Sister Moyle and I do not now attend meetings. Others have wondered about the controversy between Judge Rutherford and myself. During the year you have heard and read just one side of the controversy — the Society's side — and strenuous efforts have been made to keep you from knowing any facts I might present. Any consideration of my side of the case is branded by the Society as an act of treason against the "Theocracy" and a stirring up of dissension.

In order that you may know some of the FACTS, I am attaching to this letter copies of two letters to Judge Rutherford, to-wit: First: my letter of July 21, 1939, tendering my resignation as the Society's counselor. Second: Copy of letter of May 18, 1940, reviewing Judge Rutherford's subsequent actions in the matter. These letters contain FACTS of which the Society's president is desperately trying to keep you and all of Jehovah's witnesses in ignorance.

Many have wondered why the Judge has waged such a malicious and vindictive campaign against me. There is just one answer: FEAR. The whole story was not told in my letter of protest. There are many additional FACTS about this self-styled administrator of "The Theocracy," which if generally known would cause him to be looked upon with abhorrence and disgust. FEAR of exposure impelled him to embark on a smearing campaign against my good name and reputation with the purpose of thoroughly discrediting me in the eyes of his supporters. FEAR is the motive which causes him to blacken others rather than have his own misdeeds brought to light. FEAR of the truth has brought to birth many a religious inquisition and Judge Rutherford follows in that well-beaten path. Whether the whole story of his monumental deception of God's people shall be published is a matter of time and the Lord's leadings to determine.

For more than twenty years Sister Moyle and I gave our best efforts and service to the work directed by the Society. We did this as unto the Lord and it has been heart-rending for us to believe that the organization has departed from the faith. BUT WE CANNOT DENY FACTS. The Society's intolerant attitude and practices cannot be reconciled with Christianity. Real Bible study has been gagged and suppressed by the organization. The comforting doctrines of

Restitution, Resurrection and the Kingdom have been set aside and are replaced with the wondrous delusion that the Jonadab babies will fill the earth. God's people among Jehovah's witnesses are being ensnared into bondage to a Rutherford Hierarchy which is of the same order and just as intolerant as the Papal machine. Truly the message, "Come out of her my people, that ye be not partakers of her sins," applies as fully to the Watch Tower organization as to any other false religious organization.

It is my hope and prayer that this letter and its accompanying enclosures will help some to break these chains of restraint and come forth into the liberty wherewith Christ has made us free.

Your brother in His service,
Olin R. Moyle

July 21, 1939

Judge J. F. Rutherford,
Brooklyn, N. Y.

Dear Brother Rutherford:

This letter is to give you notice of our intention to leave Bethel on September 1st next. The reasons for leaving are stated herein and we ask that you give them careful and thoughtful consideration.

Conditions at Bethel are a matter of concern to all of the Lord's people. Nowhere among imperfect men can there be perfect freedom from oppression, discrimination and unfair treatment, but at the Lord's headquarters on earth conditions should be such that injustice would be reduced to the minimum. That is not the case here at Bethel and a protest should be made against it. I am in a good position to make such a protest because your treatment of me has been generally kind, considerate and fair. I can make this protest in the interests of the Bethel family and of the Kingdom work without any personal interest entering into the matter.

Ill Treatment of the Bethel Family

Shortly after coming to Bethel we were shocked to witness the spectacle of our brethren receiving what is designated as a "trimming" from you. The first, if memory serves me correctly, was a tongue-lashing given to C. J. Woodworth. Woodworth, in a personal letter to you, stated something to the effect that it would be serving the devil to continue using our present day calendar. For that he was humiliated, called a jackass, and given a public lambasting. Others have been similarly treated. MacAulay, McCormick, Knorr, Prosser, Price, Van Sipma, Ness and others, have been similarly scolded. They have been publicly called to account, condemned, and reprimanded without any previous notice.

This summer some of the most unfair public reproaches have been given. J. Y. MacAulay asked a question which carried with it a criticism of the present method of Watch Tower study. For that he was severely reprimanded. Your action constituted a violation of the principle for which we are fighting, to wit, freedom of speech. It was the action of a boss and not that of a fellow servant. Securing an efficient mode of study with imperfect study leaders is no easy task, and no method yet produced has proved to be one hundred percent perfect. You stated that no complaints had come to you concerning this method of study. If that be the case you have not had all the facts presented to you. There is complaint in various places that the Watch Tower studies have degenerated into mere reading lessons. It may be that the present method is the best that can be used, but in view of known limitations honest criticism should not be censored nor honest critics punished.

Brother Worsley received a public denunciation from you because he prepared and handed to the brethren a list of helpful Scripture citations on fundamental topics. How can we consistently condemn religionists for being intolerant when you exercise intolerance against those who work with you? Doesn't this prove that the only freedom permitted at Bethel is freedom to do and say that which you wish to be said and done? The Lord certainly never authorized you to exercise such high-handed authority over your fellow servants.

Since the Madison Square Garden meeting there has been a distressing condition of restraint and suspicion at Bethel. The ushers were placed in a tough spot, but did an excellent piece of work. They exercised care and diligence in watching arrivals at the Garden, and preventing a number of suspicious characters from entering. They were on the job immediately when the disturbance started and quelled a disturbance which would have otherwise reached serious proportions. But for two weeks following the convention, there has been constant criticism and condemnation from you. They have been charged with dereliction of duty and labeled as "sissies." To see some of these boys break down and cry because of your unkind remarks is, to say the least, saddening.

The brethren at Bethel have thoroughly demonstrated their loyalty and devotion to the Lord, and do not need to be berated for wrong doing. A suggestion or a kindly admonition from you would be more than sufficient and induce greater happiness and comfort for the whole family. You have stated many times that there are no bosses in the Lord's organization, but the undeniable fact cannot be evaded that your actions in scolding and upbraiding these boys are the actions of a boss. It makes one sick at heart, and disgusted, to listen to them. If you will cease smiting your fellow servants Bethel will be a happier place and the Kingdom work will prosper accordingly.

Discrimination

We publish to the world that all in the Lord's organization are treated alike and receive the same as far as this world's goods are concerned. You know that is not the case. The facts cannot be denied. Take for instance the difference between the accommodations furnished to you and your personal attendants, compared with those furnished to some of the brethren. You have many homes, to wit, Bethel, Staten Island, California, etc. I am informed that even at Kingdom Farm one house is kept for your sole use during the short periods you spend there. And what do the Brethren at the farm receive? Small rooms, unheated through the bitter cold winter weather. They live in their trunks like campers. That may be all right, IF NECESSARY, but there are many houses on the farm standing idle, or used for other purposes, which could be used to give some comfort to those who work so long and so hard.

You work in a nice air-conditioned room. You and your attendants spend a portion of each week in the quiet of country surroundings. The boys at the factory diligently work without such helps, or any effort made to give them. That is discrimination which should receive your thoughtful consideration.

Marriage

Here again is shown unequal or discriminatory treatment. One brother left Bethel some time ago for the purpose of getting married and, so I am informed, was refused the privilege of pioneering in New York, apparently as an action of official disapproval of his leaving Bethel. On the other hand when Bonnie Boyd got married she didn't leave Bethel. She was permitted to bring her husband into Bethel in spite of the printed rule providing that both parties should have lived there five years. Harsh treatment of one and favored treatment of another is discrimination, and should not have a place in the Lord's organization.

Filthy and Vulgar Language

The Biblical injunctions against unclean, filthy speaking and jesting have never been abrogated. It is shocking and nauseating to hear vulgar speaking and smut at Bethel. It was stated by a sister that that was one of the things you had to get used to at Bethel. The loudest laughter at the table comes when a filthy or near filthy joke goes through, and your skirts are not clear.

Liquor

Under your tutelage there has grown up a glorification of alcohol and condemnation of total abstinence which is unseemly. Whether a servant of Jehovah drinks alcoholic liquor is none of my business, except in giving a helping hand to a brother who is stumbled thereby. Whether I am a total abstainer is nobody's business but my own. But not so at Bethel. There appears to be a definite policy of breaking in newcomers into the use of liquor and resentment is shown against those who do not join them. The claim is made, "One can't be a real Bethelite without drinking beer." Shortly after we arrived it was arrogantly stated, "We can't do much with Moyle, but we'll make a man out of Peter." A New York brother intimated that I was out of harmony with the truth and with the Society because I didn't drink liquor. A New York sister stated that she had never used liquor or served it until some of the Bethel boys insisted upon it. A brother who used to drink liquor to excess became a total abstainer after getting the truth. He knew that a single drink would start him off to his former drinking habits, but in spite of that, brethren from Bethel insisted upon his imbibing liquor and inferred that he was out of harmony with the organization through refusing. Total abstainers are looked upon with scorn as weaklings. You have publicly labeled total abstainers as prudes and therefore must assume your share of the responsibility for the Bacchus-like attitude exhibited by members of the family.

These are a few of the things which should have no place in the Lord's Organization. There are other more grievous injustices but I have had no personal contact with them and therefore do not discuss them.

It hasn't been an easy or pleasant task to write these things to you, and it is still harder to make this protest effective by leaving Bethel. We sold our home and business when we came to Bethel and fully intended to spend the rest of our lives at this place in the Lord's service. We leave in order to register most emphatically our disagreement with the unjust conditions related in this letter. We are not leaving the Lord's service but will continue to serve Him and His organization as fully as strength and means will allow.

Neither am I running away from battling the devil's crowd in the courts. I expect to return to the private practice of law, probably in Milwaukee, Wisconsin, and hope to be in the fight in every way possible. With this letter I am enclosing a statement of the major cases now pending in which I am actively participating. It would be unreasonable and unfair to drop these matters into your lap without further assistance or consideration. I am ready and willing to press these issues in the courts just as vigorously and carefully as though I remained at Bethel, and will do so if that is your desire.

We have considered this action for some time, but this letter is delivered to you, just as we are leaving on a vacation trip for very specific reasons. First: It is desirable that you take time for thought and consideration of the matters herein set forth before taking any action. Hasty and ill-considered action might be regrettable. Second: Frankly I have no desire for verbal argument with you over these matters. I have had plenty of occasion to observe that a controversial matter does not receive a calm and reasoned discussion of the facts. Too often it turns into a denunciation of some person by you. I am not interested in that kind of a wordy battle. These statements are the reasons presented by Sister Moyle and myself for leaving Bethel. If we speak erroneously or wrongfully we are responsible before the Lord for so speaking. If we speak truthfully and we stoutly contend that everything here related is the truth, then there is immediate responsibility on your part to remedy the conditions necessitating this protest. May the Lord direct and guide you into fair and kindly treatment of your fellow servants is my wish and prayer.

Your Brother in the King's service,
Olin R. Moyle.

May 18, 1940

Judge J. F. Rutherford,
124 Columbia Heights
Brooklyn, New York

Dear Brother Rutherford:

Recently the Milwaukee Company Servant, in accordance with your directions, handed me a letter excommunicating me from the Milwaukee Company, at the same time stating, "I am sorry to do this, Olin. I like you as a man, but you are in bad with the Society." He well knew that my course of action in Milwaukee had always been in harmony with the Truth, but nevertheless felt obligated to put on the ban of excommunication because you desired it. Some others of the Company took a similar stand. They realize that I am loyal to the Lord and to the Truth, but for fear of incurring your displeasure they comply with the interdict.

This raises an issue of great importance. Which is Supreme: An edict from you, or the principles of righteousness? Must Jehovah's witnesses condone and support that which is evil solely because you request it? Do your commands as president of the Society supersede and set aside the laws of Almighty God?

Abstractly stated, there is no doubt but what you will agree that the laws of God and the principles of truth and justice set forth in God's Word are superior to any demands, requests, or directions issued by you or the Society. But in the discord and division you are stirring up about me there has been a very definite disregard of this fundamental principle of Supremacy. This should cause you to seriously consider your course, and for your own welfare I am again reviewing the matter.

During the past few months you have used the Society's facilities to discredit and degrade my name and reputation regardless of facts, truth or justice. You have hurled forth false accusations and circulated lies promiscuously in manner similar to those who propagate false religion. I cite a few instances:

FIRST: The September 1st Watch Tower contained a notice that my services as Counselor were terminated because of "unfaithfulness to the Kingdom interests and the brethren." This was wholly untrue. The work I did speaks for itself. And up to within a short time of my leaving you often commended my zeal and earnestness in fighting our cases. The truth is that I resigned my position and gave you thirty days notice thereof. You speeded my exit because I told you the truth about your own wrongful acts.

SECOND: You caused to be published in the October 15th Tower a statement alleging that every paragraph, except the first of my letter of July 21st to you was false. This was a whopper. Your record of scoldings, petulant outbursts of temper, and discrimination against the Bethel brethren is too well known to be successfully denied. C. J. Woodworth admitted the truth in his letter to me on August 15th. Then under your direction he reversed himself and signed a letter or statement alleging my letter to be totally false. Thus under coercion from you the Lord's people are required to speak lies and bring false accusations. Others even among the Board of Directors have privately deplored your tirades against your brethren, but they still retain your favor by keeping quiet. Fear of you and the desire for your favor more than the favor of God could be the only motive for the Directors to sign such a slanderous statement.

THIRD: Early in September you sent M. A. Howlett to spread and enlarge your campaign of defamation. It is now clearly evident that his job was to spread the idea that

I am busy circulating falsehoods and stirring up strife and division in the Companies. He made no investigation to determine FACTS but did a very successful job of building up a case of opprobrium upon nothing.

May I remind you that the circulation of TRUTH does not constitute the stirring up of strife and division. If I had circulated the letter of July 21st among the brethren I would be doing no more than giving them information to which they are entitled. I have actually shown it to about a dozen of my friends, but no more. The brethren of Milwaukee who ex-communicated me under orders from you, are still ignorant of the contents of that letter. But Howlett had to "make a case" and thereupon arranged for a bunch of letters and declarations referring to "malicious letters of Moyle" and Moyle's "attempts to cause division among the brethren." Chicago, Rockford, Aurora, Kankakee, Waukegan, and other places arose to the occasion and turned in such declarations. The striking facts is THAT I HAVEN'T BEEN NEAR ANY OF THOSE TOWNS OR CIRCULATED ANYTHING IN THEM. Nevertheless, you continue publishing the statements in order to cause brethren throughout the country to believe a lie.

We are told that a "false witness that speaketh lies" is an abomination unto the Lord. How can you reconcile your tactics with this plain declaration from Jehovah?

FOURTH: By the use of falsehood and compulsion you secured my excommunication from the Milwaukee Company of Jehovah's witnesses. The brethren here know that I am loyal to the Lord. But you wrote that I had "committed an assault upon the Society" (which is another lie out of whole cloth) and that I should be gagged and not tolerated. The brethren through fear then complied with your autocratic demand.

NOW MARK THIS: There wasn't the slightest sign of division or strife in the Milwaukee Company until you and Howlett sowed the seeds of discord. Now there is dissatisfaction and unrest. Why? Because you stirred up a false issue and caused confusion among the brethren. On account of the falsehoods of a henpecked sycophant of Racine you kicked Harry Fink, Zone Servant, out of office. And because he would not join in your interdict against me he has been treated like a leprous person by the brethren of the Company. The fact that Harvey Fink is thoroughly loyal to the Lord and active in Kingdom work has been disregarded by you. Obedience to your demands thus comes ahead of loyalty to Almighty God. Many are sick at heart over such unrighteous acts, and others follow your example of spreading false accusations and poison. That is the kind of discord you have brought to birth in the Milwaukee Company.

This isn't the whole story. One evil begets another and the perverse course you started on August 8th, has spread until it has reached voluminous proportions. No individual has heretofore received the extensive calumnies accorded to me in the Watch Tower. The conclusion is inescapable that while pouring out much condemnation on religion, you are guilty of indulging in the worst kind of religious practice, to wit, that of persecuting a brother who had the temerity to tell you the truth. And it is FEAR that has led you into this trap. You were afraid that I would broadcast to all brethren the facts concerning your unbridled use of the tongue, and you thereby determined to smear me so badly that no one would believe me. You have had some measure of success. BUT AT WHAT COST. "Wherefore hast thou despised the commandment of the Lord, to do evil in His sight?" Truly you have placed yourself and your reputation ahead of the laws of God. That is of much greater consequence to you than the degradation of reputation is to me.

You claim that I had no right to send you that letter even though its statements be true. In other words, your position is so lofty as to give you immunity from criticism or protest even though you commit the most wrongful of acts. This is further evidence that in your unrighteous course you have exalted and placed yourself and your commands above the laws of God. You have through coercion required Jehovah's witnesses to condone and support your wrongful course. You have punished those who would not, and have thereby engendered a woeful spirit of fear and restraint among the brethren. That is a vicious use of God-given facilities and a trampling upon the rights of your brethren.

My standing with Jehovah God has not suffered in the slightest by reason of your onslaught. I still love the Lord and still engage regularly in the witness work. I shall continue to do so regardless of your embargo. But through malice and fear you have been ensnared into Satan's trap, and you have violated so many of the plain decrees of Almighty God that a continuance therein must surely merit His stern disapproval. For your own welfare then may I urge you to carefully, honestly and prayerfully review this whole matter, and do that which is right before God and man.

Yours in Kingdom service,

Olin R. Moyle
(Johnson Creek, Wis.)

APPENDIX C

A CHRONOLOGICAL LISTING OF SOME OF THE MOST IMPORTANT WATCH TOWER PUBLICATIONS

I. BOOKS BY CHARLES TAZE RUSSELL

Studies in the Scriptures (originally named *Millennial Dawn* until the end of 1904).[1]

The names of the individual volumes:

Volume I: *The Plan of the Ages* (later named *The Divine Plan of the Ages,* 1886).
Volume II: *The Time is at Hand* (1889).
Volume III: *Thy Kingdom Come* (1891).
Volume IV: *The Battle of Armageddon* (originally called *The Day of Vengeance,* 1897).
Volume V: *The At-one-ment Between God and Man* (1899).
Volume VI: *The New Creation* (1904).
Volume VII: *The Finished Mystery* (A posthumus work prepared by Clayton J. Woodworth and George H. Fisher under the direction of the Watch Tower Bible and Tract Society, 1917.).
Tabernacle Shadows of the "Better Sacrifices" (1881).
The Photo-Drama of Creation (1914).

II. BOOKS BY JOSEPH FRANKLIN RUTHERFORD

The Harp of God (1921).
Comfort for the Jews (1925).

---

[1] The edition or publishing date is important on some of the volumes as the books have been revised in selected places. This is true of volumes II, III, IV, VII.

Deliverance (1926).
Creation (1927).
Government (1928).
Reconciliation (1928).
Life (1929).
Prophecy (1929).
Light I and *II* (1930).
Vindication I, II, and *III* (1931, 1932).
Preservation (1932).
Preparation (1933).
Jehovah (1934).
Riches (1936).
Enemies (1937).
Salvation (1939).
Religion (1940).
Children (1941).

In addition to these books, each (with one exception) numbering more than 345 pages, Rutherford wrote scores of booklets. The interested reader is referred to page 306 of *the Watch Tower Publications Index of Subjects Discussed and Scripture Explained 1930-1960* for titles and years of publication.

III. Anonymous Books Published by the Watch Tower Bible and Tract Society

The New World (1942).
The Truth Shall Make You Free (1943).
The Kingdom Is at Hand (1944).
Theocratic Aid to Kingdom Publishers (1945).
Let God Be True (1946, revised in 1952).
Equipped for Every Good Work (1946).
This Means Everlasting Life (1950).
What Has Religion Done for Mankind? (1951).
New Heavens and a New Earth (1953).
Make Sure of All Things (1953, revised 1957).
You May Survive Armageddon into God's New World (1955).
Qualified to Be Ministers (1955, revised 1967).
From Paradise Lost to Paradise Regained (1958).
Your Will Be Done on Earth (1958).
Jehovah's Witnesses in the Divine Purpose (1959).

Let Your Name Be Sanctified (1961).
All Scripture Is Inspired of God and Beneficial (1963).
Babylon the Great Has Fallen! God's Kingdom Rules! (1963).
Make Sure of All Things; Hold Fast to What Is Fine (1965).
Things in Which It Is Impossible for God to Lie (1965).
Life Everlasting in Freedom of the Sons of God (1966).
Did Man Get Here By Evolution or By Creation? (1967).
Your Word Is a Lamp to My Feet (1967).
The Truth That Leads to Eternal Life (1968).
Aid to Bible Understanding (1969, completed 1971).
Is the Bible Really the Word of God? (1969).
Then is Finished the Mystery of God (1969). (See page 304.)

In addition to these books, many booklets have been published. For titles and years of publication the reader is referred to the *Watch Tower Publication Index (1930-1960), (1961-1965)*. Some of the more important titles are:

**Counsel on Theocratic Organization for Jehovah's Witnesses* (1949).
**Defending and Legally Establishing the Good News* (1950).
**Preaching Together in Unity* (1955).
What Do the Scriptures Say About "Survival After Death"? (1955).
Blood, Medicine and the Law of God (1961).
"The Word"—Who is He? According to John (1962).

IV. Bibles and Translations Printed by the Watch Tower Bible and Tract Society with Date of First Issue

The Emphatic Diaglott (1926).
King James Version (1942).
American Standard Version (1944).
New World Translation of the Christian Greek Scriptures (1950, revised in 1951).
New World Translation of the Hebrew Scriptures (in five volumes, 1953-60).

The volumes appeared and are divided as follows:
Volume I: Genesis through Ruth (1953).
Volume II: I Samuel through Esther (1955).
Volume III: Job through the Song of Solomon (1957).

---

*These are not for public distribution but are handbooks of instruction and counsel for the Jehovah's Witnesses.

Volume IV: Isaiah, Jeremiah, Lamentations (1958).
Volume V: Ezekiel through Malachi (1960).
New World Translation of the Holy Scriptures (1961, is the entire *New World Translation,* revised and without the notes of the volumes appearing progressively from 1950-60). (Revised 1970, 1971).
New World Translation of the Holy Scriptures (1963, is the entire *New World Translation* with all the notes of the volumes appearing progressively from 1950-60).
The Kingdom Interlinear Translation of the Greek Scriptures (1969).
The Bible In Living English (1972).

V. Periodicals Appearing Semi-Monthly

The Watchtower Announcing Jehovah's Kingdom (*The Watchtower*).

This title has been used since early 1939. The first issue under the title *Zion's Watch Tower and Herald of Christ's Presence* appeared July 1, 1879 and was published monthly until January 1892, at which time it became semi-monthly. In 1909 the name was changed to *The Watch Tower and Herald of Christ's Presence.* In 1931 the name became *The Watchtower and Herald of Christ's Presence.* On January 1, 1939, the name became *The Watchtower and Herald of Christ's Kingdom,* after which, in March of the same year, it was changed to its present title.

Awake! Originally this magazine was *The Golden Age* which first appeared in October, 1919. In October, 1937, the name became *Consolation* which was changed to *Awake!* in 1946.

VI. Yearbook

Yearbook (A Yearbook has appeared every year since 1927.)

The *Yearbook* gives a world-wide report of the Witnesses' activities throughout the world for the previous year of its publication. In addition there is a Scripture text and comment (taken from *The Watchtower* of the previous year) for each day of the new year.

VII. Watch Tower Publications Index

Watch Tower Publications Index of Subjects Discussed and Scriptures Explained (1930-1960) (1961).

Watch Tower Publications Index of Subjects Discussed and Scriptures Explained (1961-1965) (1966).

An *Index* is published each year.

VIII. Tracts

"What Do Jehovah's Witnesses Believe?" (1951).

"Hell-Fire—Bible Truth or Pagan Scare?" (1951).

"Jehovah's Witnesses, Communists or Christians?" (1951).

" 'Awake From Sleep!' " (1951).

"Hope For the Dead" (1952).

"The Trinity—Divine Mystery or Pagan Myth?" (1952).

"How Valuable Is the Bible?" (1952).

"Life in a New World" (1952).

"The Sign of Christ's Presence" (1953).

"Man's Only Hope for Peace" (1953).

"Which Is the Right Religion?" (1953).

"Do You Believe in Evolution or the Bible?" (1953).

"How Has Christendom Failed All Mankind?" (1958).

The Society has recently published a number of mass-distribution "Kingdom News" tracts.

Books Published Since 1969

Listening to the Great Teacher (1971).

The Nations Shall Know that I Am Jehovah—How? (1971).

Theocratic Ministry School Guidebook (1971).

Organization for Kingdom-Preaching and Disciple-Making (1972).

Paradise Restored to Mankind by Theocracy! (1972).

God's Kingdom of a Thousand Years Has Approached (1973).

Comprehensive Concordance of the New World Translation of the Holy Scriptures (1973).

True Peace and Security—From What Source? (1973).

God's Eternal Purpose Now Triumphing For Man's Good (1974).

Is This Life All There Is? (1974).

Man's Salvation Out of World Distress at Hand! (1975).

Appendix D

AN ANNOTATED SELECTIVE BIBLIOGRAPHY OF MATERIALS FOR THE CHRISTIAN WORKER

Much good material has been published to help in the understanding and combating of the doctrines of Jehovah's Witnesses. This same material can also be helpful to the cult member who desires to read other publications dealing with the movement. The items listed in this Bibliography are not the only good ones available, but they are, in this writer's opinion, the ones which should prove the most helpful.

I. Books

Dencher, Ted. *Why I Left Jehovah's Witnesses.* Toronto, Canada: Evangelical Publishers, 1966. 222 pp.

Mr. Dencher was a Jehovah's Witness for ten years before he left the movement. His testimony of his years as a member and why he left are very helpful. Beyond his testimony, Dencher presents a Scriptural refutation of several key Watchtower heresies. He takes up such important doctrines as the deity of Christ, life after death and the "born again" experience. This book is a good one to lend to those who are beginning to study with the Witnesses.

Gruss, Edmond C. *The Jehovah's Witnesses and Prophetic Speculation.* Nutley, N. J.: Presbyterian and Reformed Publishing Company, 1972. 127 pp.

Presents an examination and refutation of the Witnesses' position on the second "coming" of Christ in 1914, Armageddon, and the "end of the world."

————. *We Left Jehovah's Witnesses—A Non Prophet Organization.* Nutley, N. J.: Presbyterian and Reformed Publishing Company, 1974. 169 pp.

Features the personal accounts of six couples who after association with the Jehovah's Witnesses, concluded that this organization was not God's "prophet" or His sole channel of biblical truth as it claims. The writers have all accepted Jesus Christ as their personal Savior and are practicing Christians.

Hoekema, Anthony A. *The Four Major Cults.* Grand Rapids: Wm. B. Eerdmans Publishing Company, 1963. (pp. 223-371).

A scholarly treatment of the Witnesses' doctrines, based on primary sources. The book includes a refutation of the Witneses' denial of the deity of Christ and eternal punishment in two Appendices. The section on the Witnesses is also published as a separate book titled *Jehovah's Witnesses.* (Eerdmans, 1972). 147 pp.

Martin, Walter R., and Norman H. Klann. *Jehovah of the Watch Tower.* Sixth revised edition, 1963. Grand Rapids: Zondervan Publishing House, 1953. 221 pp.

This book is a must for every library. It is one of the most comprehensive books on the subject and has gone through a number of revisions, with its present content doubling the original material. Revised and reprinted by Moody Press, 1974. 192 pp.

Schnell, William J. *Thirty Years a Watch Tower Slave.* Grand Rapids: Baker Book House, 1956. 207 pp.

This book contains the writer's experience of thirty years in the movement. It reveals the inner workings of the Watch Tower and has been effective in freeing thousands of Witnesses from the group.

———. *Into the Light of Christianity.* Grand Rapids: Baker Book House, 1959. 211 pp.

Deals with the Witnesses' doctrines in the light of the Scriptures. The reader will not always agree with his interpretations, but it is a must book for those who are trying to help the Jehovah's Witnesses.

Thomas, F. W. *Masters of Deception.* Vancouver, B. C.: F. W. Thomas, 1970. xiv+162 pp. Baker Book House, 1972.

The author of this book has had numerous dealings with Jehovah's Witnesses and his treatment is very helpful as he examines and refutes their major doctrinal errors.

Whalen, William J. *Armageddon Around the Corner.* New York: The John Day Company, 1962. 249 pp.

This fairly comprehensive book by a Catholic layman deals with the history, doctrines, organization and schisms of the group. He leaves the refutations of doctrine to other writers. Interesting and informative.

II. Booklets

Barnett, Maurice. *Jehovah's Witnesses* (Vols. 1 & 2). Phoenix, Arizona: Church of Christ (1606 W. Indian School Road, Phoenix 85015).

These spiral-bound publications contain much helpful and well-organized material. Volume 1 deals with the history, organization and doctrines of the Jehovah's Witnesses and contains a further section on the deity of Christ. Volume 2 deals with the nature of man, death, resurrection, the J. W.'s dual classes, eternal punishment, etc.

Bruce, F. F. and W. J. Martin. *The Deity of Christ.* Manchester: North of England Evangelical Trust, 1964. 24 pp.

This booklet on the deity of Christ, written by two Bible scholars, is one of the best brief presentations on the subject. A number of favorite Arian texts are refuted in a note at the rear, pp. 21-24.

Martin, Walter R. *Jehovah's Witnesses.* Grand Rapids: Zondervan Publishing House, 1957. 64 pp.

This booklet contains much of the material in *Jehovah of the Watch Tower.* It is a good booklet for the Christain to become oriented in a study of the Witnesses.

Metzger, Bruce M. *The Jehovah's Witnesses and Jesus Christ.* 22 pp. Reprinted in pamphlet form from the April 1953, issue of *Theology Today.* This pamphlet is excellent as it deals with the Witnesses' doctrine of Christ on their own grounds and from their own *New World Translation.* Available from The Theological Book Agency, Princeton, New Jersey.

Wallis, Arthur. *Jesus of Nazareth—Who is He?* Fort Washington, Pa.: Christian Literature Crusade, 1959.

A clear and forceful answer to the question asked in the title.

III. Tracts and Sources of Material

The following Christian individuals and organizations are sources of tracts, booklets, books and tapes. Since these materials are subject to revision and new ones are often added, no attempt has been made to list individual items available from each source.

1. Rodney Bias, P. O. Box 1641, Scottsdale, Ariz. 85252.
2. CARIS, P. O. Box 1783, Santa Ana, Calif. 92702. Michael Van Buskirk, Director. Literature address: CARIS, P. O. Box 265, Whittier, Calif. 90608.
3. Ted Dencher, P. O. Box 199, Sharon, Pa. 16146.
4. Department of Apologetics, Los Angeles Baptist College, Newhall, Calif. 91321. Edmond Gruss, Chairman.
5. Homer Duncan, Missionary Crusader, 4606 Avenue H, Lubbock, Tex. 79404.
6. Kenneth Guindon, Pastoral Care Center, 14800 Sherman Way, Van Nuys, Calif. 91405.
7. HELP JESUS, P. O. Box 28, Canterbury, Kent CT1 1AA, England. Paul Alcuri, Director. (HELP JESUS materials are distributed by CARIS in the USA.)
8. Religion Analysis Service, 2708 E. Lake St., Suite 231, Minneapolis, Minn. 55406. John Dahlin, Director.
9. F. W. Thomas, P. O. Box 2784, Vancouver, B. C., Canada.

IV. Department of Apologetics Los Angeles Baptist College

The author of this book welcomes letters from readers. Tracts, booklets and books on the Jehovah's Witnesses and other cults are available. The book *Cults and The Occult in the Age of Aquarius* ($1.25 retail) has brief chapters on a number of contemporary cults and movements. For information and material address: Department of Apologetics, Los Angeles Baptist College, Newhall, California 91321.

Appendix E

THE WRITER'S PERSONAL TESTIMONY[1]

Although my testimony can not be such as the testimony of *Thirty Years A Watch Tower Slave,* I praise God that the truth of the Gospel of Jesus Christ reached me before I became a lifetime member and slave in the Watchtower system. The following brief account of my experiences is intended to show the background of many young children who are raised in a Jehovah's Witness home. I also wish to show the great struggle and vacuum that a freed Witness finds himself in after being saved—free because of salvation (John 8:32, 36; 14:6)—but still ensnared by a way of thinking and a way of Bible study that takes years to change through the study of the Word.

We lived in Palms, California and one day in 1940 a woman came to our door with the familiar phonograph and records by Judge Rutherford. Since my mother's arrival from Germany in the early 1920's, she had not attended church and the message of the Witness woman interested her, so the woman was invited back. The message that was brought into our home, which was slanted against other religions and the current state of political affairs, was just the message that struck home (on the political angle, my mother had campaigned for Upton Sinclair, who had been defeated). A few months of study in our home brought obvious changes. I still remember the Christmas decorations being thrown out

[1] A brief account of the writer's conversion testimony, "I Was a Teen-Age Jehovah's Witness," is in the June 13, 1965 issue of *Teen Power.*

in the trash. Birthdays were no longer observed, as such celebrations were of pagan origin.[2]

A short time after the first visit in our home, my mother and I departed for St. Louis, Missouri, where the national convention was held in 1941. It was there that I saw Judge Rutherford, and where I received my copy of the book *Children.* After our return to California, we started attending the company "Watchtower Studies" and the "Service Meetings."

During this "religious awakening" in our home, my father had not been infected by the Witnesses' theology. He took the entire thing rather passively, a pattern found in many of the Witness homes. The mother and the children go into the Witness group and the husband remains on the outside. I have frequently seen the woman of the house with two or more children neglect them and her home to attend meetings, to call house-to-house, and to stand on street-corners. Often the presence of a Jehovah's Witness wife or husband in the home causes so much agitation and discord that a divorce is the result.[3]

After a short time our home knew almost nothing except the writings of Judge Rutherford. In the book *Children,* which we received in St. Louis, we were led to believe that the end of the world was just around the corner. The story of *Children* is about John (twenty) and Eunice (eighteen) who came to the place where, although they were in love, they decided to wait until the ushering in of the new world. The reasoning in back of this decision is as follows:

---

[2] It is interesting to note that in the earlier years of the movement, the Society published devotional books with a birthday record! The book, entitled *Daily Manna* (1907) has the following on the title page: "Interleaved for Autographs A Birthday Record." "Some use them [the book] as birthday presents and holiday gifts. . . ." "In this edition we have added the Autograph and Birthday record feature. . .To see the autographs of our friends daily is a pleasure and to be reminded of their birthday is a great convenience." G. W. Siebert (comp.), *Daily Heavenly Manna for the Household of Faith* (Allegheny, Pennsylvania: Watch Tower Bible and Tract Society, 1907).

[3] It has been my personal experience to counsel with husbands and wives, individually and together, to try to save their marriage after one of the partners had become a Jehovah's Witness. In most cases the Witness became almost impossible to live with.

> Our hope is that within a few years our marriage may be consummated and, by the Lord's grace, we shall have sweet children that will be an honor to the Lord. We can well defer our marriage until lasting peace comes to the earth. Now we must add nothing to our burdens, but be free and equipped to serve the Lord. When THE THEOCRACY is in full sway it will not be burdensome to have a family.[4]

Rutherford, who wrote the book, in this way made another masked prediction that this old "system of things" was near the Battle of Armageddon. It has been thirty-four years since the book *Children* was printed, and John and Eunice, middle-aged now, are still waiting to get married!

During this time I had become my mother's "phonograph bearer." I can still remember trudging from house to house with the record player and the Judge's records. I could not understand why some people welcomed us and others almost threw us out. In the days during the war the Witnesses were hated because of their pacifism, or (as they like to term it) their neutrality.

In the period just before the Second World War, the Witnesses either met in homes or rented halls for their meetings. In our contact with the Witnesses we were associated with companies in Venice, Culver City, Encinitas and Carlsbad, all in California. The congregations were mostly small, but all were steadily growing.

I was baptized at about the age of ten and although I cannot remember the exact time, I do remember the immersion. It signified my dedication to service for Jehovah. (Afterward I was to learn the true significance of baptism and union with Christ, in his death, burial and resurrection —Rom. 6:5-11.) At about the same time I enrolled in the Theocratic Ministry School and thus began to get experience in the delivery of six-minute talks on various subjects outlined by the Society, and specifically assigned by the "School Servant."

When I was twelve, we moved to Encinitas, California. The pattern which began in the Los Angeles area was carried on. There were meetings, conventions, street-corner

[4] J. F. Rutherford, *Children* (Brooklyn: Watchtower Bible and Tract Society, Inc., 1941), p. 366.

and house-to-house work. I worked in the kitchens in several conventions in the Los Angeles area. All was doing and going, but there was no peace of mind and no Gospel being proclaimed.

I cannot claim that I was a perfect Jehovah's Witness—few are—but I do know that I was thoroughly convinced of the system in which I was reared, for I knew nothing else. I cannot remember ever having attended a church service until I was seventeen.

While in High School I invited boy and girl friends over to our home to take part in our "book studies." Some of my friends began to get interested in the Witness movement.

At the age of seventeen, in my last year of high school, I was invited by one of my boy friends, who had recently accepted Christ as his personal Saviour, to the home of his minister—a fundamental and soul-loving Baptist. The pastor presented Christ to me and then got down on his knees and prayed for me. I left his home that night a bit shaken, but amused that he should try to change that which I believed. I had "the truth." It was a short time later that I learned that "The Truth" was Jesus Christ (John 14:6).

My friends continued to witness to me. At first I rebelled, but one night in the privacy of my own room I accepted Christ as my own personal Saviour. I knew from that time onward that a change came into my life. I do not remember the verse that brought conviction, but I do know that I realized my need and saw that Christ could meet that need. I was like the Philippian jailor as he asked, "What must I do to be saved?" The answer came, "Believe on the Lord Jesus, and thou shalt be saved" (Acts 16: 31). I believed and was saved. I realized later that this was something that could never be lost, for Christ Himself said, "He that believeth hath eternal life" (John 6:47). And in John 5:24 Christ said: "Verily, verily, I say unto you, He that heareth my word, and believeth him that sent me, hath eternal life, and cometh not into judgment, but hath passed out of death into life." The simple word of Jesus Christ received by faith had accomplished everything. It had given life, and delivered from judgment!

At this time I stopped going to the Kingdom Hall, and quit reading the Watchtower literature, but I found that I still had many doubts. Two years later I still had problems concerning most of the doctrines of orthodoxy. I found that as I read the Bible, old interpretations and patterns of thinking were still with me. A short time after my conversion, when I told my mother that I would not go to the Kingdom Hall meetings, for I had been saved, she grew very angry and said that I was a child of the Devil. I was almost disowned!

I feel now that the reason I could make such a clean break with the Witnesses was that I did not continue reading any of their literature after accepting Christ, and I was not contacted by them concerning my new faith. I had a chance to grow and associate with other born again people in a friendly fundamental church. This contact with other Christians is a necessity for converts from the Jehovah's Witnesses. The new convert needs help desperately. He has to see for himself that the lies about other churches progagated by the Witnesses are not true. He has questions and many doubts. I found that these doubts left as I studied what I had believed and been taught in the light of the Bible. Only the Word of God can wash out the error.

In 1951, with salvation a reality in my life, but many doubts and questions remaining, I felt led of the Lord to attend a Christian College. By my fourth year in college all my doubts and questions had been answered, and I thought seriously about writing something that would help other Christians and Jehovah's Witnesses to see the Watchtower religion for what it is. Three years of seminary followed. I still had the desire to write concerning the Jehovah's Witnesses but nothing had been written. I had felt that this writing was important and something that was needed, but it seemed there had been satanic opposition all the way. In order to make sure that this work should be written, I attended Talbot Theological Seminary and wrote a thesis as a partial requirement for the Master of Theology degree. The thesis written in 1961 has been revised and expanded into this book.

The new life which I gained when I accepted Christ is something that all the money in the world could not buy. I never have regretted that decision. I never will cease to thank God that He delivered me from the "Apostles of Denial."

> Everyone believing that Jesus is the Christ has been born from God.... And this is the witness given, that God gave us everlasting life, and this life is in his Son. He that has the Son has this life; he that does not have the Son of God does not have this life. I write YOU these things that YOU may know that YOU have life everlasting, YOU who turn YOUR faith to the name of the Son of God [I John 5:1, 11-13 NWT].[5]

---

[5] The Watchtower Society only allows the "remnant," the 144,000, to accept the experience of I John 5:1 ff. I and millions of other Christians the world over have had the experience of being "born from God" (being born again).

Author's Note

During the Spring of 1971, after almost twenty-one years as a Christian, and as a teacher at a Christian college for eleven, I was visited by a three-man committee from the local Kingdom Hall and charged with "apostasy." I subsequently found out that my name had been brought up in the Kingdom Hall and that I had been "disfellowshiped"! How they concluded that I was still a Jehovah's Witness after my lapse of over twenty years is difficult to determine.

I wish to praise God that my mother accepted Christ as her personal Savior. My father, although not a Witness, also accepted Christ. God is certainly gracious and good to us (Eph. 3:20, 21).

BIBLIOGRAPHY

A. PRIMARY SOURCES: PUBLICATIONS OR MATERIALS ORIGINATING FROM THE WATCH TOWER SOCIETY[1]

1. Books and Booklets

Russell, Charles Taze. *Studies in the Scriptures* (7 Vols., 1886-1917).

______________. *Pastor Russell's Sermons* (1917).

______________. *Scenario of the Photo-Drama of Creation* (1914).

Rutherford, Joseph Franklin. The following books are all by Rutherford:

Children (1941).

Comfort for the Jews (1925).

Creation (1927).

Deliverance (1926).

Enemies (1937).

Government (1928).

Jehovah (1934).

Life (1929).

Light (2 vols., 1930).

Millions Now Living Will Never Die! (1920).

Preparation (1933).

Preservation (1932).

Prophecy (1929).

Reconciliation (1928).

Religion (1940).

Riches (1936).

Salvation (1939).

The Harp of God (1921).

Vindication (3 vols., 1931, 1932).

Where are the Dead? (1932).

Anonymous publications:

All Scripture Is Inspired of God and Beneficial (1963).

Babylon the Great Has Fallen! God's Kingdom Rules! (1963).

Blood, Medicine and the Law of God (1961).

Did Man Get Here By Evolution or By Creation? (1967).

Equipped for Every Good Work (1946).

From Paradise Lost to Paradise Regained (1958).

Jehovah's Witnesses in the Divine Purpose (1959).

Let God Be True (1946, revised 1952).

Let Your Name Be Sanctified (1961).

Life Everlasting in Freedom of the Sons of God (1966).

Make Sure of All Things (1953, revised 1957).

Make Sure of All Things; Hold Fast to What Is Fine (1965).

New Heavens and a New Earth (1953).

[1] These have been published under several imprints.

Preaching Together in Unity (1955).
Qualified to Be Ministers (1955).
Sermon Outlines (n. d.).
The Kingdom Is at Hand (1944).
The New World (1942).
Theocratic Aid to Kingdom Publishers (1945).
The Truth Shall Make You Free (1943).
The Truth That Leads to Eternal Life (1968).
Things in Which It Is Impossible for God to Lie (1965).
This Means Everlasting Life (1950).
You May Survive Armageddon into God's New World (1955).
Your Will Be Done on Earth (1958).
Watch Tower Publications Index 1930-1960 (1961).
Watch Tower Publications Index 1961-1965 (1966).
What Do the Scriptures Say About "Survival After Death"? (1955).
What Has Religion Done for Mankind? (1951).
Yearbook (various editions, 1927-69).
Siebert, G. (comp.). *Daily Heavenly Manna for the Household of Faith* (1907).

2. Bibles and Translations

The Holy Bible . . . Authorized or King James Version (n. d.).
The Holy Bible . . . Newly Edited by the American Revision Committee A. D. 1901 (n. d.).
New World Translation of the Christian Greek Scriptures (1950, revised 1951).
New World Translation of the Hebrew Scriptures (5 vols., 1953-60).
New World Translation of the Holy Scriptures (1961).
New World Translation of the Holy Scriptures (1963).

3. Periodicals

Awake! (various issues).
Kingdom Ministry (various issues).
The Watchtower (various issues). The entry designated *Watch Tower Reprints* is a 7-volume set and Index of this publication from its first issue of July, 1879, through June, 1919.

4. Unpublished Materials

Letters from the Watchtower Bible and Tract Society to this writer dated November 30, 1960, December 21, 1962, and November 5, 1964.
Letter to the Concordant Publishing Concern from the Watch Tower Bible and Tract Society dated November 25, 1927.

B. PRIMARY SOURCES: MATERIALS NOT PUBLISHED BY THE WATCHTOWER SOCIETY

1. Books

Cole, Marley. *Jehovah's Witnesses: The New World Society*. New York: Vantage Press, 1955.
______________. *Triumphant Kingdom*. New York: Criterion Books, 1957.

Knorr, Nathan Homer. "Jehovah's Witnesses of Modern Times," *Religion in the Twentieth Century*, Vergilius Ferm, editor. New York: The Philosophical Library, 1948. pp. 381-92.

Macmillan, A. H. *Faith on the March.* Englewood Cliffs, New Jersey: Prentice-Hall, 1957.

2. Periodicals

Stewart, E. D. "Life of Pastor Russell," *Overland Monthly*, 69:126-32, February, 1917.

3. Unpublished Materials

Letter to W. J. Schnell Company from Marley Cole dated April 1, 1954.

C. PRIMARY SOURCES: MATERIALS OF RUSSELLITE SPLINTER SECTS AND BIBLE STUDENTS

1. Book and Booklets

Hollister, Robert. *Meet Our British Brethren.* (No imprint, but distributed by the Associated Bible Students.)

Johnson, Paul S. L. *Epiphany Studies in the Scriptures.* 17 vols. Philadelphia: Paul S. L. Johnson, 1938-1956.

Jolly, Raymond G. (ed.). *The Teachings of "Jehovah's Witnesses" Examined in the Light of the Scriptures.* Philadelphia: Laymen's Home Missionary Movement, [n. d.]

The Grace of Jehovah. Third edition. East Rutherford, N. J.: Dawn Bible Students Association, 1961.

When Pastor Russell Died. Third edition. East Rutherford, N. J.: Dawn Bible Students Association, 1957.

2. Periodicals

Back to the Bible Way (various issues).

Bible Student Examiner (various issues).

Bible Study Monthly (various issues).

The Bible Standard and Herald of Christ's Kingdom (various issues).

The Dawn (various issues).

The Herald of Christ's Kingdom (various issues).

The Kingdom Scribe (various issues).

The New Creation (various issues).

The Roundtable of the Scriptures (various issues).

3. Unpublished Materials

Back to the Bible Way Publications (mimeographed), 41, 79, 96, 141, 166, 203, 273, 276, 306, 321, 419, etc.

Letters from Roy D. Goodrich of Back to the Bible Way to this writer dated December 9, 1964, January 4, 1965, May 6, 1966 and June 9, 1966.

Letter from *The New Creation* magazine editor dated July 6, 1966.

D. SECONDARY SOURCES

1. Books and Booklets

Adair, James R. and Ted Miller. *We Found Our Way Out.* Grand Rapids: Baker Book House, 1964.

Berkhof, Louis. *Principles of Biblical Interpretation.* Second edition. Grand Rapids: Baker Book House, 1950.

_____________. *The History of Christian Doctrines.* Grand Rapids: Wm. B. Eerdmans Publishing Company, 1937.

Braden, Charles S. *These Also Believe.* New York: The Macmillan Company, 1949.

Brown, John Elward. *"In The Cult Kingdom" Mormonism, Eddyism and Russellism.* Siloam Springs, Arkansas: International Federation Publishing Company, [n. d.].

Bruce, F. and W. J. Martin. *The Deity of Christ.* Manchester: North of England Evangelical Truth, 1964.

Bruce, F. F. *The English Bible: A History of Translations.* London: Lutterworth Press, 1961.

Bundy, Walter H. (comp.). *Studies in the Scriptures Investigating Bible Statements Analytically.* Los Angeles: Concordant Publishing Concern, [n. d.].

Chafer, Rollin Thomas. *The Science of Biblical Hermeneutics.* Dallas, Texas: Hicks Printing Company, 1939.

Cook, Charles C. *All About One Russell.* Philadelphia: Philadelphia School of the Bible, [n. d.].

Cullmann, Oscar. *The Christology of the New Testament,* trans. S. C. Guthrie and Charles A. M. Hall. Philadelphia: The Westminster Press, 1959.

Czatt, Milton Stacey. *The International Bible Students: Jehovah's Witnesses.* Scottdale, Pa.: Mennonite Press, 1933.

Davies Horton. *The Challenge of the Sects.* Philadelphia: The Westminster Press, 1961.

Dencher, Ted. *The Watchtower Heresy versus the Bible.* Chicago: Moody Press, 1961.

_____________. *Why I Left Jehovah's Witnesses.* Toronto, Canada: Evangelical Publishers, 1966.

Douty, Norman F. *Another Look At Seventh-day Adventism.* Grand Rapids: Baker Book House, 1962.

Eaton, E. L. *The Millennial Dawn Heresy.* Cincinnati: Jennings and Graham, 1911.

Ellicott, Charles John. *Commentary on the Epistles of St. Paul to the Thessalonians.* Second edition. Grand Rapids: Zondervan Publishing House, 1957.

Elliott, Philip. *"Jehovah's Witnesses" in the First and Twentieth Centuries.* Second edition revised. Stirling, Scotland: Drummond Tract Depot, [n. d.].

Ferguson, Charles W. *The Confusion of Tongues.* Garden City, New York: Doubleday, Doran and Co., 1929.

Finegan, Jack. *Light From the Ancient Past.* Princeton: University Press, 1946.

Fyfe, James. *The Hereafter: Sheol, Hades and Hell, the World to Come, and the Scripture Doctrine of Retribution According to Law.* Edinburgh: T. & T. Clark, 1890.

Gerstner, John H. *The Theology of the Major Sects.* Grand Rapids: Baker Book House, 1960.

Haldeman. I. M. *Millennial Dawnism: The Blasphemous Religion Which Teaches the Annihilation of Jesus Christ.* Los Angeles: Bible Institute of Los Angeles, [n. d.].

Hall, Isaac H. *A Critical Bibliography of the Greek New Testament as Published in America.* Philadelphia: Pickwick and Co., 1883.

Hewitt, P. E. *Russellism Exposed.* Second edition. Grand Rapids: Zondervan Publishing House, 1941.

Heydt, Henry J. *Jehovah's Witnesses: Their Translation.* New York American Board of Missions to the Jews, Inc., [n. d.].

Hislop, Alexander. *The Two Babylons.* First American edition. New York: Loizeaux Brothers, 1916.

Hodgson, Leonard. *The Doctrine of the Trinity--Croall Lectures 1942-1943.* London: Nisbet and Co., Ltd., 1943.

Hoekema, Anthony A. *The Four Major Cults.* Grand Rapids: Wm. B. Eerdmans Publishing Co., 1963.

Hudson John Allen. (ed.). *Russell-White Debate.* Second edition. Cincinnati, Ohio: F. L. Rowe. 1912.

Kelly, J. N. D. *Early Christian Creeds.* New York: Longmans, Green and Co., Inc., 1950.

____________. *Early Christian Doctrines.* New York: Harper and Brothers, Publishers, 1958.

King, A. B. *et al. Ivan Panin's Scientific Demonstration of the Inspiration of the Scriptures.* Revised edition. Toronto, Canada: [No publisher], 1924.

Kneedler, William H. *Christian Answers to Jehovah's Witnesses.* Chicago: Moody Press, 1953.

Knight, G. A. *A Biblical Approach to the Doctrine of the Trinity.* Scottish Journal of Theology Occasional Papers No. 1. Edinburgh: Oliver and Boyd Ltd., 1953.

Ladd, George. "The Acts of the Apostles," *The Wycliffe Bible Commentary.* C. F. Pfeiffer and E. F. Harrison editors. Chicago: Moody Press, 1962.

Lewis, C. S. *Beyond Personality: The Christian Idea of God.* New York: The Macmillan Co., 1945.

Lewis, Gordon R. *Confronting the Cults.* Philadelphia: Presbyterian and Reformed Publishing Company, 1966.

Lightfoot, J. B. *Notes on the Epistles of Saint Paul.* 1895 edition. Grand Rapids: Zondervan Publishing House, 1957.

____________. *Saint Paul's Epistles to the Colossians and to Philemon.* Revised text. Grand Rapids: Zondervan Publishing House, [n. d.].

____________. *Saint Paul's Epistle to the Philippians.* Revised text. London: Macmillan and Company, 1913.

____________. *The Apostolic Fathers.* (ed.). J. R. Harmer. 1891 edition. Grand Rapids: Baker Book House, 1962.

Manwaring, David R. *Render Unto Caesar.* Chicago: The University of Chicago Press, 1962.

Martin, Walter R. *Jehovah's Witnesses.* Grand Rapids: Zondervan Publishing House, 1957.

Martin, Walter R. and Norman H. Klann. *Jehovah of the Watchtower.* Sixth Revised edition, 1963. Grand Rapids: Zondervan Publishing House, 1953.

Martin, Walter R. *The Kingdom of the Cults.* Grand Rapids: Zondervan Publishing House, 1965.

_____________. *The Rise of the Cults.* Revised and enlarged, 1957. Grand Rapids: Zondervan Publishing House, 1955.

Mayer, F. E. *Jehovah's Witnesses.* Revised 1957. St. Louis, Mo.: Concoria Publishing House, 1942.

_____________.*The Religious Bodies of America.* Fourth edition. St. Louis, Missouri: Concordia Publishing House, 1956.

McKinney, George D. *The Theology of Jehovah's Witnesses.* Grand Rapids: Zondervan Publishing House, 1962.

Mickelsen, A. Berkeley. *Interpreting The Bible.* Grand Rapids: Wm. B. Eerdmans Publishing Company, 1963.

Morris, Leon. *The Apostolic Preaching of the Cross.* Grand Rapids: Wm. B. Erdmans Publishing Company, 1956.

Muller, Albert. *Meet Jehovah's Witnesses: Their Confusion, Doubts and Contradictions.* Pulaski, Wisconsin: Franciscan Publishers, 1964.

Oehler, Gustave Friedrich. *Theology of the Old Testament.* Edited by George E. Day. Grand Rapids: Zondervan Publishing House, [n. d.].

Orr, James. *The Christian View of God and the World.* Wm. B. Eerdmans Publishing Company, 1954.

Pike, Royston. *Jehovah's Witnesses: Who They Are, What They Teach, What They Do.* New York: Philosophical Library, 1954.

Quidam, Roger D. *The Doctrine of Jehovah's Witnesses, A Criticism.* New York: Philosophical Library, 1959.

Rackham, Richard Belward. *The Acts of the Apostles.* Fourteenth edition. London: Methuen and Co. Ltd., 1901.

Ramm, Bernard. *Protestant Biblical Interpretation.* Revised edition. Boston: W. A. Wilde Company, 1956.

Robertson, A. T. *Word Pictures in the New Testament.* 5 vols. New York: Harper and Brothers, 1933.

Ross, J. J. *Some Facts and More Facts About the Self-Styled "Pastor" Charles T. Russell.* Philadelphia: Philadelphia School of the Bible, [n. d.].

Rowell, J. B. *The Deity of Jesus Christ Our Lord.* Canada: Hebden Printing Co. Ltd., [n. d.].

Sanday, William and Arthur C. Headlam. *A Critical and Exegetical Commentary on the Epistle to the Romans.* Fifth edition. New York: Charles Scribner's Sons, 1915.

Schep, J. A. *The Nature of the Resurrection Body.* Grand Rapids: Wm. B. Eerdmans Publishing Company, 1964.

Schnell, William J. *Another Gospel.* Second edition. Seattle, Washington: The Life Messengers [n. d.].

____________. *Christians: Awake!* Grand Rapids: Baker Book House, 1962. Reissued 1965, *How to Witness to Jehovah's Witnesses.*

____________. *Into the Light of Christianity.* Grand Rapids: Baker Book House, 1959.

____________. *Thirty Years A Watch Tower Slave.* Grand Rapids: Baker Book House, 1956.

____________. *Witnessing to Jehovah's Witnesses.* Youngstown, Ohio: The Converted Jehovah's Witness Expositor, 1960.

Shadduck, B. H. *The Seven Thunders of Millennial Dawn.* Third edition. Ashtabula, Ohio: Homo Publishing Co., 1928.

Stevenson, William C. *The Inside Story of Jehovah's Witnesses.* New York: Hart Publishing Company, Inc., 1967.

Stibbs, A. M. *The Meaning of the Word "Blood" in Scripture.* Third edition, 1962; London: The Tyndale Press, 1948.

Stilson, Max. *How to Deal with Jehovah's Witnesses.* Grand Rapids: Zondervan Publishing House, 1962.

Strauss, Lehman. *An Examination of the Doctrine of "Jehovah's Witnesses."* New York: Loizeaux Brothers, 1942.

Stroup, Herbert Hewitt. *The Jehovah's Witnesses.* New York: Columbia University Press, 1945.

Tanis, Edward J. *What the Sects Teach.* Grand Rapids: Baker Book House, 1958.

Terry, Milton S. *Biblical Hermeneutics.* Second edition. Grand Rapids: Zondervan Publishing House, [n. d.].

Thomas, Stan. *Jehovah's Witnesses and What They Believe.* Grand Rapids: Zondervan Publishing House, 1967.

Van Baalen, Jan Karel. *The Chaos of Cults.* Fourteenth edition. Wm. B. Eerdmans Publishing Company, 1951.

____________. *The Chaos of Cults.* Fourth Revised and Enlarged edition. Grand Rapids: Wm. B. Eerdmans Publishing Company, 1962.

Warfield, Benjamin B. *Biblical and Theological Studies.* Philadelphia, Pennsylvania: The Presbyterian and Reformed Publishing Company, 1952.

Whalen, William J. *Armageddon Around the Corner.* New York: The John Day Company, 1962.

Williams, J. Paul. *What Americans Believe and How They Worship.* Revised edition. New York: Harper & Row, Publishers, 1962.

Wilson, Bryan R. *Sects and Society: A Sociological Study of the Elim Tabernacle, Christian Science, and Christadelphians.* Los Angeles: University of California Press, 1961.

2. Periodicals

"A Peculiar Investigation of Missions," *The Missionary Review of the World,* 25 New series :538, July, 1912.

Bach, Marcus. "The Startling Witnesses," *Christian Century,* 74:197-99, February 13, 1957.

Beatty, Jerome. "Peddlers of Paradise," *American Magazine,* 130:52-54, 61-67, 69-71, November, 1940.

Byington, Steven T. "Review of the *New World Translation*," *The Christian Century*, 67:1295, 1296, November 1, 1950.

Christianity Today, 9:305, December 18, 1964.

Cohn, Werner. "Jehovah's Witnesses and Racial Prejudice," *The Crisis*, 63:5-9, January, 1956.

_____________. "Jehovah's Witnesses as a Proletarian Movement," *The American Scholar*, 24:281-98, Summer, 1955.

_____________. "Letters to the Editor," *The Christian Century*, 75:1055, September 17, 1958.

Colwell, E. C. "A Definite Rule for the Use of the Article in the Greek New Testament," *Journal of Biblical Literature*, 52:12-21, January, 1933.

Countess. Robert H. "The Translation of *Theos* in the *New World Translation*," *Bulletin of the Evangelical Theological Society*, 10:153-60, Summer, 1967.

Davidson, Bill. "Jehovah's Traveling Salesman," *Colliers*, 118:12, 13 72, 75, 77, November 2, 1946.

Eckman, Edward W. "The Identification of Christ with *Yahweh* by New Testament Writers," *The Gordon Review*. 6:145-53, Summer, 1964.

Ellis, William T. "Investigating An Investigator," *The Continent*. (microfilm), September 26, 1912.

_____________. "Investigating An Investigator," *The Continent*. (Microfilm), October 10, 1912.

Gruss, Edmond. "Beware of the 'Laymen's Home Missionary Movement,'" *The Baptist Bulletin*, 27:13, 31, April, 1962.

_____________. (as told to Jeanette W. Lockerbie), "I Was A Teen-age Jehovah's Witness," *Teen Power*. 23:1, 2, 6, 7, June 13, 1965.

High, Stanley. "Armageddon, Inc.," *Saturday Evening Post*, 213:18, 19, 50, 52-54, 58, September 14, 1940.

Mantey, J. R. "Is Death the Only Punishment for Unbelievers?" *Bibliotheca Sacra*, 112:340-43, October, 1955.

Martin, Pete. "Pete Martin Visits a Family of Jehovah's Witnesses," *Christian Herald*, 89:23-25, 42-49, 76-79, April, 1966.

Metzger, Bruce M. Book Review: "*New World Translation of the Christian Greek Scriptures*," *The Bible Translator*, 15:150-52, July, 1964.

_____________. "On the Translation of John I. 1," *The Expository Times*, 63:125, 126, January, 1952.

_____________. "The Jehovah's Witnesses and Jesus Christ," *Theology Today*, 10:65-85, April, 1953.

Muller, Albert. "Jehovah's Witnesses Call," *Homiletic and Pastoral Review*. Reprint: 676-83, May 1963.

O'Brian, John A. "Jehovah's Witnesses: A Visit to Headquarters," *Catholic Digest*, 27:61-63, December, 1962.

Ostling, Dick. "The Mormon Surge," *Christianity Today*, 8: 1072, 1073, August 28, 1964.

Parker, Everett C. "News of the Christian World," *The Christian Century*, 75:953, 954, August 20, 1958.

Perry, Victor. "Jehovah's Witnesses and the Deity of Christ," *The Evangelical Quarterly*, 35:15-22, January-March, 1963.

Rowley, H. H. "How Not To Translate the Bible," *The Expository Times*, 65:41, 42, November, 1953.

______________. "Jehovah's Witnesses' Translation of the Bible," *The Expository Times*, 76:107, 108, January, 1956.

Stedman, Ray C. "The New World Translation of the Christian Greek Scriptures," *Our Hope*, 50:29-39, July, 1953.

Stuermann, Walter E. "The Bible and Modern Religions: III. Jehovah's Witnesses," *Interpretation*, 10:323-46, July, 1956.

The Christian Century, 70:1133, 1134, October 7, 1953.

The Christian Century, 72:1145, 1146, October 5, 1955.

The Converted Jehovah's Witness Expositor (various issues).

The Differentiator (various issues).

Unsearchable Riches (various issues).

3. Reference Works, Translations, etc.

Bauer, Walter. *A Greek-English Lexicon of the New Testament and Other Early Christian Literature.* Ed. and trans. William F. Arndt and F. Wilbur Gingrich. Chicago: The University of Chicago Press, 1957.

Blunt, John Henry. (ed.). "Christadelphians," *Dictionary of Sects, Heresies, Ecclesiastical Parties, and Schools of Religious Thought*, p. 106. London: Rivingtons, 1874.

Bowman, Raymond Albert. *et al.* "Zedekiah," *Encyclopaedia Britannica* (14th ed.), XXIII, 939.

Cremer, Hermann. *Biblio-Theological Lexicon of New Testament Greek.* Trans. William Urwick. Fourth English edition. Edinburgh: T. & T. Clark, 1895.

Dana, H. E. and Julius R. Mantey. *A Manual Grammar of the Greek New Testament.* New York: The Macmillan Company, 1955.

Girdlestone, Robert Baker. *Synonyms of the Old Testament.* Second edition. Grand Rapids: Wm. B. Eerdmans Publishing Company, 1953.

Kittel, Gerhard (ed.). *Theological Dictionary of the New Testament.* 8 vols. (when complete). Trans. and ed. Geoffrey W. Bromiley. Grand Rapids: Wm. B. Eerdmans Publishing Company, 1963.

Kittel, R. (ed.). *Biblia Hebraica.* Stuttgart: Wurttemberggische Bibelanstalt, [n. d.].

McChesney, E. "Image of God," *Unger's Bible Dictionary.* Edited by Merrill F. Unger. Chicago: Moody Press, 1957, pp. 516-517.

McClintock, John and James Strong, "Trinity," *Cyclopaedia of Biblical, Theological, and Ecclesiastical Literature.* New York: Harper & Brothers, Publishers, 1881, X, 551-56.

Mirsky, Dimitri. "Tolstoy, Leo (Lyev) Nikolyevich," *Encyclopedia Britannica*, (1964 ed.) XXII, 278-81.

New American Standard Bible: New Testament. La Habra, Calif.: The Lockman Foundation, 1963.

Phillips, J. B. *Letters to Young Churches.* New York: The Macmillan Company, 1948.

Revised Standard Version of the Bible. New York: Thomas Nelson and Sons, 1952.

Robertson, A. T. and W. Hersey Davis. *A New Short Grammar of the Greek Testament.* New York: Harper and Brothers Publishers, 1933.

Robertson, A. T. *A Grammar of the Greek New Testament in the Light of Historical Research.* Fourth edition. New York: George H. Doran Company, 1923.

Scofield, C. I. (ed.). *The Scofield Reference Bible.* New and improved edition. New York: Oxford University Press, 1945.

Thayer, Joseph Henry. (ed. and trans.). *A Greek-English Lexicon of the New Testament Being Grimm's Wilke's Clavis Novi Testamenti.* Fourth edition. Edinburgh: T. & T. Clark, 1901.

The Greek New Testament. Edited by Kurt Aland, Matthew Black, *et al.* New York: American Bible Society, 1966.

Tregelles, Samuel Prideaux, (trans.). *Gesenius' Hebrew and Chaldee Lexicon to the Old Testament Scriptures.* Grand Rapids: Wm. B. Eerdmans Publishing Co., 1954.

Trench, Richard Chenevix. *Synonyms of the New Testament.* Ninth edition of 1880. Grand Rapids: Wm. B. Eerdmans Publishing Company, 1953.

Verkuyl, Gerrit. (ed.). *The Berkeley Version in Modern English.* Grand Rapids: Zondervan Publishing House, 1959.

Waite, J. C. J. "Zedekiah," *The New Bible Dictionary.* Grand Rapids: Wm. B. Eerdmans Publishing Company, 1962, p. 1357.

Way, Arthur S. *The Letters of St. Paul.* London: Marshall, Morgan & Scott, Ltd., 1950.

Webster's New Collegiate Dictionary. Second edition. Springfield, Mass.: G. C. Merriam Company, 1951.

Weymouth, Richard Francis. Ed. and Rev. by Ernest Hampden-Cook. *The New Testament in Modern Speech.* Boston: Pilgrim Press, n. d.

4. Unpublished Materials

Cumberland, William H. "A History of Jehovah's Witnesses," Unpublished Doctor's thesis, The State University of Iowa, Iowa City, Iowa, 1958. 309 pp.

Muller, Albert. Letter from Albert Muller to this writer dated July 19, 1966.

Schnell, William J. Letters from William J. Schnell to this writer dated October 20, 1960, November 3, 1960 and May 12, 1966. In addition, several mass-distribution letters were used.

Tuura, Stephen. Letter from Stephen Tuura to this writer dated December 5, 1964.

5. Newspapers

Los Angeles Tribune, April 22-26, 1915.

New York Times. September 21, 28; October 12, 19, 26; November 2, 9, 29; December 7, 14, 1914. October 17, 1967.

BX
8525.7
G892
8854
Gruss
Apostles of denial